In Search of the Global Labor Market

Studies in Critical Social Sciences

Series Editor
David Fasenfest (*Wayne State University*)

Editorial Board
Eduardo Bonilla-Silva (*Duke University*)
Chris Chase-Dunn (*University of California–Riverside*)
William Carroll (*University of Victoria*)
Raewyn Connell (*University of Sydney*)
Kimberlé W. Crenshaw (*University of California, Los Angeles/
Columbia University*)
Raju Das (*York University*)
Heidi Gottfried (*Wayne State University*)
Karin Gottschall (*University of Bremen*)
Alfredo Saad-Filho (*King's College London*)
Chizuko Ueno (*University of Tokyo*)
Sylvia Walby (*Lancaster University*)

VOLUME 219

The titles published in this series are listed at *brill.com/scss*

In Search of the Global Labor Market

Edited by

Ursula Mense-Petermann
Thomas Welskopp
Anna Zaharieva

BRILL

LEIDEN | BOSTON

Cover illustration: Designed for the Center for Interdisciplinary Research/Zentrum für Interdisziplinäre Forschung (ZiF), Universität Bielefeld, Germany, by Stefan Adamick, Hamburg, Germany, 2018.

The Library of Congress Cataloging-in-Publication Data is available online at https://catalog.loc.gov
LC record available at https://lccn.loc.gov/2022007676

Typeface for the Latin, Greek, and Cyrillic scripts: "Brill". See and download: brill.com/brill-typeface.

ISSN 1573-4234
ISBN 978-90-04-51452-2 (hardback)
ISBN 978-90-04-51453-9 (e-book)

Copyright 2022 by Koninklijke Brill NV, Leiden, The Netherlands.
Koninklijke Brill NV incorporates the imprints Brill, Brill Nijhoff, Brill Hotei, Brill Schöningh, Brill Fink, Brill mentis, Vandenhoeck & Ruprecht, Böhlau and V&R unipress.
Koninklijke Brill NV reserves the right to protect this publication against unauthorized use. Requests for re-use and/or translations must be addressed to Koninklijke Brill NV via brill.com or copyright.com.

This book is printed on acid-free paper and produced in a sustainable manner.

In memory of our dear colleague, friend, and co-editor, Thomas Welskopp

Contents

Preface XI
List of Figures and Tables XIII
Notes on Contributors XIV

Introduction
In Search of the Global Labor Market: Conceptual Meanings, Empirical Evidence and Open Questions 1
   Ursula Mense-Petermann, Thomas Welskopp and Anna Zaharieva

PART 1
What Is Meant by Labor Exchanged in Labor Markets?

Introduction to Part 1
What Is Meant by Labor Exchanged in Labor Markets? 15
   Richard Hyman and Thomas Welskopp

1   Labor Markets in History
     A Global View 18
       Marcel van der Linden

2   Free Wage Labor as the Most System-Relevant Mode for Allocating Work under Capitalism 50
       Thomas Welskopp

3   Reflections on Violence
     Some Contradictions of "Free Labor" 64
       Richard Hyman

4   The Role of Gender in the Making of Global Labor Markets 87
       Alexandra Scheele

PART 2
The Market Concept and Its Heuristic Potential

Introduction to Part 2
The Market Concept and Its Heuristic Potential 103
   Peter-Paul Bänziger and Ursula Mense-Petermann

5   What Is Unique about Labor Markets?   106
    Patrik Aspers

6   The Contributions and Limits of Market Theory for the Study of Labor Markets   119
    Karen Shire

7   An Object of Analysis Rather Than a Research Tool
    The Coproduction of Labor Markets and Nation States in the Decades around 1900   132
    Peter-Paul Bänziger

8   Analytical Capacities and "Blind Spots" of the Market Concept in Analyzing Cross-Border Labor Migration   145
    Ursula Mense-Petermann and Helen Schwenken

PART 3
What Enables Labor to Cross Borders?

Introduction to Part 3
What Enables Labor to Cross Borders?   165
   Sven Kesselring and Karen Shire

9   The Role of Social Networks for Job Search in National and Transnational Labor Markets   169
    Anna Zaharieva

10 Transnational Labor Markets and the Role of Market Makers—The Case of Eastern European Service Contract Workers in the German Meat Industry   183
    Ursula Mense-Petermann

11 Emergence and Demise of Labor Market Institutions
    A Transnational Perspective   198
    Sigrid Quack

PART 4
What Is the Global in Labor Markets?

Introduction to Part 4
What Is the Global in Labor Markets? 219
  Rebecca Gumbrell-McCormick and Eleonore Kofman

12 Scales and Spaces of Global Labor Markets 225
  Eleonore Kofman

13 Global Institutions and Governance 239
  Rebecca Gumbrell-McCormick

14 What Is Global about Global Markets?
  A Historical Sociological Approach 260
  Martin Bühler and Tobias Werron

  Concluding Remarks and Avenues for Future Research 281
  Ursula Mense-Petermann, Thomas Welskopp and Anna Zaharieva

  Index 291

Preface

This volume presents the results of the international interdisciplinary research group "In Search of the Global Labour Market" that convened during the academic year 2017/18 at the ZiF (*Zentrum für Interdisziplinäre Forschung*[1] at the University of Bielefeld). In a series of workshops, fellows and guest lecturers discussed theoretical and methodological problems that arise in the process of conceiving and scrutinizing border-crossing labor markets from the perspectives of economics, history, international business and management studies, migration studies, political economy, social policy, and sociology.

At the very moment that the manuscript of this volume was completed, we were confronted with the sad news that our colleague and friend, the co-editor of this volume Thomas Welskopp, had passed away at the age of 59. Thomas was part of the project to set up a ZiF research group on border-crossing labor markets from the beginning, and the eventual shape taken on by the whole project goes back to his ideas and proposals. He was a brilliant historian: he held an important place in German Social History studies and always brought historical depth to our discussions. His passionate interest in the role of wage labor in capitalism, together with his constructive interventions, made him highly esteemed as a discussion partner by all the other fellows. Both the ZiF research group and the present volume owe much to Thomas' intellectual inspiration and contributions, and it is hard to express how sad all of us are that he did not live to see the volume published. In him we lost not only an admired co-worker, but a friend whose modest and respectful manner and subtle sense of humor will be sadly missed.

We know how much Thomas enjoyed his year in residence at ZiF and his collaboration with the participants in the research group. It is on his behalf, therefore, as well as our own, that we wish to thank the contributors for their engaging and productive discussions and their contributions to the research group and the present volume alike. We very much enjoyed our workshop discussions as well as our informal gatherings at the ZiF and are sure that the readers of this volume will be able to perceive, between the lines of the chapters, something of the immensely inspiring and invigorating atmosphere that characterized our collaboration in the research group.

We are also very grateful to the ZiF and its whole team—particularly Britta Padberg, the executive manager during our research, and our research group

---

[1] Center for Interdisciplinary Research.

assistant, Annika Andresen—for their commitment and dedicated support. The ZiF offered us a tremendously productive research environment, in terms of both its workstations, meeting rooms, and technical facilities and of a lovely quiet landscape that provided a very productive working atmosphere, and the swimming pool and adjacent hiking paths that maintained our physical and mental health. Not least, it was a generous grant from the ZiF that initially allowed our group to convene and collaborate over a whole year.

Besides the contributors to this volume, our discussions also greatly profited from input by (associated) fellows and guest lecturers who contributed to and co-organized some of our workshops, as well as enriching our discussions with their take on cross-border labor markets. So, we would also like to specially thank Michele Battisti, Graham Hollingshead, Alexandra Kaasch, and Michael Neugart. Michael Piore and Frédéric Docquier gave inspiring keynote talks at our opening conference, and Michael Köster, former Deputy Head of the Employment Office of the City of Bielefeld, shared with us his practitioner's perspective on border-crossing labor markets. Last but not least, Mustafa Aksakal, Sevak Alaverdyan, Roland Bachmann, Lisa Carstensen, Laszlo Görke, Raimund Haindorfer, Philipp Harting, Zainab Iftikhar, Janroj Keles, Dirk Kohlweyer, Anna Krämer, Dries Lens, Mariya Mitkova, Christina Moll-Murata, Phoebe Morre, Friederike Maier, Béla Galgóczi, Judith Saurer, Sylvia Walby, Gerald Willmann, Bediz Yilmaz-Bayraktar, Sabrina Zajak, and Bénédicte Zimmermann gave papers at one or another of our workshops or weekly *jour fixe* meetings and significantly contributed to broadening and deepening our understanding of the phenomenon in question.

Finally, we wish to thank Linda Turner for her thorough language- and copy-editing of the whole book manuscript, and Annette Heinze for her dedicated administrative support during the production of this volume.

Figures and Tables

Figures

1.1 Number of enslaved people who made the Atlantic crossing 30
2.1 Modes of allocating labor—hypothetical historical connections 61
11.1 Interplay between national institutional change and transnational institution building 206
14.1 Trade vs. market 266
14.2 Model of market 269
14.3 Model of global markets 271

Tables

1.1 Four types of labor-power exchange (examples) 22
1.2 Composition of the world labor force, 1991 and 2018 38
9.1 Descriptive statistics, (*N* = 4680) 175
9.2 Output from the multinomial regression 179
14.1 Practices of comparison in general and on markets 272

Notes on Contributors

Patrik Aspers
is Chair of Sociology at the University of St. Gallen. He has previously worked at Stockholm University, Max Planck Institute for the Study of Societies in Cologne and Uppsala University. He has published numerous books and articles on fashion, theory and economic sociology and is currently writing a book on uncertainty reduction and leads a project on marketplaces.

Peter-Paul Bänziger
is a Senior Lecturer (Privatdozent) in the History Department of the University of Basel. His research focuses on the entangled histories of work and consumption, on the history of the body, and on the history of public health.

Martin Bühler
is a Research Manager at the University of Zurich and earned a Ph.D. at the University of Lucerne with a thesis on the emergence of global wheat markets. He was a visiting scholar at LSE (2018–2020) and his work focuses on the prerequisites for global markets.

Rebecca Gumbrell-McCormick
is a Senior Lecturer in the Department of Management at Birkbeck, University of London. She specializes in European and international industrial relations, trade unions and equality. A second edition of her book, *Trade Unions in Western Europe: Hard Times, Hard Choices* (with Richard Hyman), was published by Oxford University Press in 2018. Other recent publications include 'Was ist unser Ziel? Gewerkschaften und ihre politischen Projekte' {*'What are we here for?': Trade Unions and their Political Projects'*}, in Aulenbacher, B. et al. (eds.) *Mosaiklinke Zukunftspfade: Gewerkschaft, Politik, Wissenschaft*, (Munster): Westfälisches Dampfboot, 2021, '(How) Can International Trade Union Organisations Be Democratic?' (with Richard Hyman), *Transfer* 26(3), September 2020, and 'In Search of Global Labour Markets', (with Richard Hyman) *Journal of Industrial Relations* 62(2), April 2020.

Richard Hyman
is Emeritus Professor of Industrial Relations at the London School of Economics and Founding Editor of the *European Journal of Industrial Relations*. He also founded and coordinates the annual Industrial Relations in Europe Conference

(IREC). He has written extensively on the themes of industrial relations, trade unionism, industrial conflict and labor market policy, and is author of a dozen books as well as some two hundred journal articles and book chapters. His comparative study *Understanding European Trade Unionism: Between Market, Class and Society* (Sage, 2001) is widely cited by scholars working in this field. His book *Trade Unions in Western Europe: Hard Times, Hard Choices* (with Rebecca Gumbrell-McCormick), was published by Oxford University Press in October 2013 with a second edition in June 2018. A key theme in his current research is resistance to neoliberalism and austerity.

Sven Kesselring
is a Professor in 'Sustainable Mobilities' at Nuertingen-Geislingen University (HfWU), Germany. In 2005, he founded the international DFG research network Cosmobilities (www.cosmobilities.net). He was vice-president of the International Association for the History of Transport, Traffic and Mobility (t2m). Since 2021 he is a member of the climate change advisory board (Klima-Sachverständigenrat) of the Federal Government of Baden-Württemberg, Germany. He is co-editor of the journal *Applied Mobilities*, the *Networked Urban Mobilities* book series (Routledge) and *Studies in Mobility and Transportation Research* (Springer VS). Kesselring's research focuses on mobilities theory, sustainability, socio-technological change, new mobility concepts, corporate mobilities regimes, and future research.

Eleonore Kofman
is Professor of Gender, Migration and Citizenship and co-Director of the Social Policy Research Centre, Middlesex University London. She was co-Editor in Chief of *Work, Employment and Society* 2018–2021. She is co-Director of the Migration and Displacement stream in the UKRI funded Gender, Justice and Security Hub (2019–2024) in which she is project co-investigator for *Gendered Dynamics of International Labour Migration*. Her research interests are in theoretical and policy aspects of gender and migration, in particular family and skilled labor.

Ursula Mense-Petermann
is a Professor of Economic Sociology and the Sociology of Work at Bielefeld University, Germany. Her recent publications include articles in *Global Networks*, *Journal of Industrial Relations* and *Critical Perspectives on International Business*.

Sigrid Quack
is Professor of Sociology at the University of Duisburg-Essen and Managing Director of the Centre for Global Cooperation Research. She has written widely on globalization and institutional change, transnational governance, professions and expertise, as well as the comparative analysis of capitalism, gender relations, labor markets and employment systems. She was President of the Society of the Advancement of Socio-Economics (SASE) 2020–21 and Chairwomen of the European Group of Organizational Studies (EGOS) 2006–2008.

Alexandra Scheele
is University Lecturer at the Faculty of Sociology at Bielefeld University, Germany. Her current research focuses on care work and social reproduction, digital capitalism and gender inequalities at work. Important publications analyze the gender pay gap in a comparative perspective, the gendered division of labor and materialist theories. Latest publication: Scheele, Alexandra/Roth, Julia/Winkel, Heidemarie (eds.): *Global Contestations of Gender Rights*. Bielefeld: Transcript 2022.

Helen Schwenken
is Professor for Migration and Society and Director of the Institute for Migration Research and Intercultural Studies (IMIS), University of Osnabrück, Germany. Her areas of expertise are gender and migration, labor migration and social movement studies. She is co-editor (with Helge Schwiertz) of *Inclusive Solidarity and Citizenship along Migratory Routes in Europe and the Americas* (Routledge, 2022).

Karen Shire
is Professor of Comparative Sociology and Japanese Society at the University Duisburg-Essen and a member of the faculty of the International Max Planck Research School on the Social and Political Constitution of the Economy at the MPI for the Study of Societies in Cologne, Germany. Her research is on the making of cross-border labor markets in Europe and the Asia Pacific.

Marcel van der Linden
is Senior Research Fellow at the International Institute of Social History in Amsterdam, where he served for fourteen years as Research Director. He is the author or editor of some fifty books, including *Workers of the World. Essays toward a Global Labor History* (Leiden: Brill, 2008; French, German, Portuguese

NOTES ON CONTRIBUTORS XVII

and Spanish translations), and the two-volume *The Cambridge History of Socialism* (Cambridge: Cambridge University Press, 2022).

Thomas Welskopp (†August 19, 2021)
was a Professor of the History of Modern Societies at Bielefeld University, Germany. His research interests were on labor and labor movement history, comparative history of capitalism, political culture and social movements, and theoretical problems in history.

Tobias Werron
is Professor of Sociological Theory and General Sociology at Bielefeld University, Germany. His research focuses on competition, nationalism, globalization and practices of sociological theorizing.

Anna Zaharieva
is a Professor for Labour Economics at Bielefeld University, Germany. She gained her PhD from the University of Konstanz. Her research focuses on frictional labor markets, job matching, social networks and migration economics. Recent publications include articles in the *International Economic Review* and the *Review of Economic Dynamics*.

Introduction

In Search of the Global Labor Market: Conceptual Meanings, Empirical Evidence and Open Questions

Ursula Mense-Petermann, Thomas Welskopp and Anna Zaharieva

COVID-19 appears to be the true champion of globalization. No man-made structure or institution, not even supranational organizations, have so far matched its speed and ability to penetrate even the most remote corners of the globe. Ironically, this is precisely how "globalizers" in the world economy and in politics have shaped the public understanding of globalization for more than thirty years now. There is no need to be an outspoken neoliberal to accept the image of globalization as an irresistible force, an anonymous process that leaves only two choices: actively—enthusiastically even—embrace the development and profiting from its windfalls or recede into the provincial isolation of an impoverished backwater. Right now, people are flabbergasted to see a biopathological form of globalization easily disrupt, curb, or even suffocate man-made arrangements on the largest possible scales that no longer appear to be so irresistible. Analytically speaking, the effects of the pandemic have revealed the fragility, desultoriness, and vulnerabilities of global capitalism like an X-ray machine.

When the research group "In Search of the Global Labour Market" first planned this volume, we aimed both at an in-depth analysis and deconstruction of the term "global labor market" and at a dissection of the concepts, practices, and arrangements commonly associated with it. We did not need the "aid" of the virus to do so although it subsequently came as no surprise that the internationally recruiting meatpacking plants with their horrendous working and living conditions for migrant laborers mostly from Eastern Europe erupted into volcanic hotspots of the disease. Despite rosy visions of a universal win-win situation with globalization and the deregulation and liberalization of labor markets, the propagandists and protagonists of these processes have not met with unanimous acceptance or even agreement over the past few decades. Optimists promise a plethora of new opportunities, particularly for highly skilled experts to find attractive jobs anywhere in the world, whereas pessimists, among them many trade unions and the ILO, warn against the degradation of physical labor by subcontractors in the ever longer supply chain of Western trademark commodity production or the expansion of disempowered workers in the service sector deprived of their home resources and contacts by long range migration and repressive surveillance. The meatpacking scandals in Germany are just a case in point.

The title of this book *In Search of the Global Labor Market* may be read as a provocation. Even the staunchest adherents of the pure neoliberal creed would probably concede that the plural "markets" would be more accurate. Yet even then, the paragon would be the highly skilled, internationally trained, worldwide recruited and globally mobile expert moving with nonchalance within a community of like-minded people—a community dispersed in all major metropolises of the world. At this level, our initial hypothesis was that you would not really find distinct and *truly* global labor markets. Perhaps airline pilots, orchestra conductors, members of the entertainment industry, some investment bankers and professorial stars of the academic world, master cooks, and IT experts, although the latter tend not to leave their offices too often. And do we see a growing segment? Not always—the job of a sailor, for instance, has shrunk dramatically since the mid-twentieth century.

At an early stage, not only did we discover that the "global" could not be reduced to these somewhat marginal sectors of the economy in order to justify the discursive workload it has brought in its wake but also that simply speaking of cross-border relations could not replace the wider notion of the "global." This is not least because historically "cross-border" presupposes the existence of nation-states, a phenomenon not much older than the nineteenth century. In addition, new national borders only revealed regional patterns of labor migration that had not been transnational before there were these national borders to transcend.

Our project has since followed Karl Marx's motto: "All things are to be disputed" as a research strategy that has devoted much time and energy to finding out what the historical spectrum of "labor" has been, how we can conceive of "labor markets," what enables "labor" to cross borders, and what might and used to be the different readings of "the global." In a second step, we attempted to assemble combinations of the terms and test them on the basis of our empirical knowledge. We succeeded in uncovering fresh insights and some detailed answers to our questions whereas even more questions for further research arose during the process. This exciting intellectual journey of an interdisciplinary group of scholars is documented in this volume.

Embarking on this endeavor, we were able to draw on a wealth of literature from across pertinent disciplines that have addressed diverse aspects of the phenomenon in question. None of these, however, has taken global labor markets as a phenomenon sui generis and placed it center stage.

Academic economic research on globalization is largely conducted within the literature on international trade (the Heckscher-Ohlin model or the gravity model) and examines the impact of opening the economy and liberalizing trade for national welfare (e.g., Autor, Dorn, & Hanson, 2013). Even though the impact of openness on national labor markets is actively studied in this field, the scope of research is limited by the immobility of the labor power. Only a few recent studies explore a combined impact of trade liberalization and opening the borders for migration (e.g., Kennan, 2013). The analytical and computational challenges of modeling a multicountry framework with goods and worker flows as well as a lack of comparable empirical data across countries limit the number of contributions in this field (see the discussion in Clemens, 2011; Delogu, Docquier, & Machado, 2018).

Economic studies on migration explore the impact of immigration on labor markets in the receiving countries and the impact of emigration on the sending countries. The literature on emigration stressed the problem of brain drain and analyzed the impact of remittances on internal demand and consumption of sending countries (Beine, Docquier, & Rapoport, 2001; Docquier & Iftikhar, 2019; Dustmann, Frattini, & Rosso, 2015; Mountford, 1997).

Push and pull factors for migration have been studied in economic as well as sociological and anthropological streams of migration studies. Factors such as differences in earnings, better job prospects, and educational opportunities as well as stronger social protection in the receiving countries are traditionally analyzed by the economic literature (Borjas, 1987; Borjas, Kauppinen, & Poutvaara, 2019; Chiquiar & Hanson, 2005). A few economic studies (e.g., Battu, Seaman, & Zenou, 2011; Bauer & Zimmermann, 1997; Patacchini & Zenou, 2012) and, to a larger extent, sociological and anthropological contributions emphasized the importance of social networks as a driving force for migration (Aguilera & Massey, 2003; Behtoui, 2008; Elliot, 2001; Haug, 2008; Ooka & Wellmann, 2006; Portes, 1995; Verwiebe, Reinprecht, Haindorfer, & Wiesboeck., 2017; see also Zaharieva in this volume).

The concepts of "immigration" and "emigration" that dominate the relevant literature on labor markets and globalization, including migration studies (McGovern, 2007; Portes, 1995), underscore an emphasis on national labor markets as unit of analysis. Labor market research across disciplines to date have generally adhered to a national frame of reference (see, for example, Abraham & Hinz, 2018; Battisti, Felbermayr, Peri, & Poutvaara, 2018; Chassamboulli & Palybos, 2014; Heidenreich, 2004; Iftikhar & Zaharieva, 2019; see, however, also Pries, 2010; Quack, Schulz-Schaeffer, Shire, & Weiß., 2018). Sociological and politico-economic approaches are dominated by conceptions that link labor markets to the national institutional settings in which they are embedded and therefore lack conceptual tools that allow us to grasp cross-border labor markets (Mense-Petermann, 2020). Moreover, statistics are national and at least quantitative research has been caught in the chains of this limitation.

This said, there is in fact research addressing cross-border labor issues which, however, mainly concentrates on the European Union and examines European migration (Dølvik & Eldring, 2017; Zimmermann, 2005) and European employment policies (Heidenreich & Rice, 2016; Rogowski, Salais, & Whiteside., 2011; Singer & Bazzani, 2017). This offers in-depth analyses and critical discussions of European social policies and gives policy recommendations, but the authors neither argue within a labor market frame of reference nor address labor market issues in a global context.

With regard to unskilled or low-skilled labor, sociological, anthropological, and social geographical migration studies have delivered numerous in-depth empirical studies on labor migration in specific sectors such as care workers from the Philippines or Central and Eastern Europe working in Western European or other wealthy countries (Bludau, 2015; Choy, 2003; Connell, 2010; Jaehrling, 2008; Kingma, 2006; Trubek, 2005), maritime workers (Aspers & Sandberg, 2020; Galam, 2018; McKay, 2007; Swift, 2011), meat cutters from Central and Eastern Europe working in the German meat industry (Czommer, 2008; Refslund & Wagner, 2018; Wagner, 2015), or construction workers (Lillie, Wagner & Berntsen, 2014; Staples, Trinczek, & Whittall 2013) to give a few examples (Mense-Petermann, 2020). However, as Shire demonstrates in this volume, labor markets, let alone markets in general, have not been a key concept in interdisciplinary migration research to date. Although interdisciplinary labor migration studies have explored some labor market-related issues, such as skill mismatch (e.g., Creese & Wiebe, 2012) or "ethnic niching" (e.g., McKay, 2007), a labor market lens has rarely been applied in migration studies (Mense-Petermann & Schwenken in this volume).

On the other hand, and somewhat detached from the empirical analysis of different aspects of cross-border labor mobility, the term "global labor market" is widely used when it comes to accounting for current social phenomena as diverse as the ever-closer integration of China or India with their huge labor forces into the world economy,[1] the offshoring of specific operations of MNCs to countries with cheap labor forces,[2] or cross-border labor migration. A Google search for "global labor market" yields 167 million (!) results. In most of these cases, global or transnational labor markets are taken for granted by the media, consulting agencies, and other economic actors. Along the same

---

[1] http://www.economist.com/node/21556974.
[2] http://www.mckinsey.com/global-themes/employment-and-growth/the-emerging-global-labor-market.

lines, business-oriented studies of consultancy companies also assume global labor markets as a given (see Footnote 2). The concept of the global labor market—in the singular—in these references builds on a model economic understanding and relates a global labor force to global job offers.

When the global mobility of workers and the development of global labor markets become the topic of discussion by researchers in sociology, often "strong," partially prescriptive arguments dominate. This is the case in particular with regard to the development of a global, cosmopolitan, and mobile knowledge elite. According to Münch, their knowledge is entirely mobile and can be implemented anywhere in the world by its carriers, the top leaders of the cosmopolitan intellectual elite (1998, p. 186; Kanter, 1995). Another related argument is that of the "boundaryless career" (Arthur, 1994; Arthur & Rousseau, 1996), the existence of new career patterns that cross over both organizational and national borders, and also lead to the development of global labor markets for the highly qualified.

In most cases, "strong" assertions lack empirical backing, however. Pohlmann (2009), for example, has shown that the "battle for talents" is fought within MNCs and only to a very small degree on global labor markets. He therefore considers the emergence of external global labor markets for the highly qualified as a quantitatively important phenomenon to be somewhat unlikely. Rather, MNC-internal transnational mobility through global assignments seems to be the most frequent scenario for highly skilled professionals. Despite the initial surge in interest from labor and organizational sociology research in the transnational mobility of the highly qualified, it remains relatively unknown as to whether transnational mobility, particularly of these highly qualified individuals, really is of quantitative significance. Hence, the extent to which global labor markets have actually emerged in the advanced process of economic globalization, how these are structured, and what importance all this has for the working and living environments of the employees—notwithstanding some important contributions to the topic (see, for example, Adick, Maletzky, Pries, & Gandlgruber, 2014; Galgóczi, Keune, & Watt 2008; Kreutzer & Roth, 2006; Mense-Petermann, 2020; Pries 2010; Quack et al., 2018)—represent a pending research gap.

Historians address the question of the globalization of labor and labor markets from a different perspective. They point to long-lasting transregional patterns of labor exchange, even spanning continents, dating back as far as ancient times (Hansen, 2020). Modern constructions of a similar scale and scope sometimes let the older, premodern arrangements shine through. Thus, they question whether this can really be seen as an unprecedented new phenomenon. Contemporary historians, conversely, consider the global-scale change in work relations and the accompanying dissolution of regional or domestic-related recruiting patterns as a manifestation that first emerged after the "structural break-off" of the 1970s (Doering-Manteuffel & Raphael, 2012). This is doubtful, however, if a long-term historical approach is applied.

A deeper historical analysis and a broad comparative reappraisal of existing historical research on labor in its diverse forms and labor markets in their changing transnational manifestations is needed in order to challenge the "presentism" of currently circulating assumptions about the scope and characteristics of global labor markets. From a historical angle, such an undertaking has to involve a revitalization of the debate about the commonalities and differences between "free" and "unfree" labor, and the shades in-between, a more systematic study of slavery regimes and how they developed into different forms of serfdom which, in turn, have promoted a concept of labor that is traditionally rooted in the concept of service rather than labor, and the question who sells what on a labor market. The interdisciplinary take on the issue of global labor markets applied in this volume encourages this type of historical embedding of our research questions so far dominated by social scientific disciplines not geared to systematic probes of the past (see Rockman, 2009; van der Linden, 2011; Welskopp, 2014).

This sketchy overview of how research in different social sciences deals with the globalization of labor markets reveals that the concept of the global labor market—although widely used—is in urgent need of theoretical clarification and in-depth analysis. Considering that labor in this context is a subject of paramount importance, for people's identities, for social integration, and for economic welfare, it is more than astounding that the global labor market has rarely been explored as a phenomenon sui generis.

Going some way toward closing this research gap, this volume puts global labor markets center stage. It is based on the discussions of the international and interdisciplinary group of contributors to this volume who collaboratively worked on these questions within the research group "In Search of the Global Labour Market" at the Center for Interdisciplinary Research (ZiF), Bielefeld, during the academic year 2017/18. For a duration of ten months, academics from the fields of economics, history, industrial relations, management studies, migration studies, political science, social policy, and sociology met at ZiF to pool their expertise and perspectives. This book presents the manifold results of this intense collaborative exchange. These results are reported in four different parts of this volume that refer back to the guiding questions mentioned above.

Part 1 of the present volume deals with the issue of what exactly the "commodity" traded on global labor markets is. This is no trivial question, and it is vehemently debated across the social science disciplines. The basic question here is whether "free" wage labor has really been one of the key defining characteristics of capitalism—as Karl Marx and Max Weber have paradigmatically put it—or if the rocky road to "free" labor in the main industrializing countries of the West during the nineteenth century and—more importantly—the ever growing empirical evidence of the diversity of regional work arrangements worldwide in the past encourage new thinking about labor in capitalism which would not only broaden our understanding of the term "labor" itself but would also claim that forms of "unfree" labor were not only constitutive for the rise of capitalist economies but represented a systemic quality of capitalism as such (van der Linden, 2011; Welskopp, 2014). Only this could explain why certain arrangements of "unfree" labor have survived to this day although Marx, for instance, had termed them an anachronism even in his time and predicted their rapid demise. Moreover, whereas "chattel slavery" in the nineteenth century sense has almost disappeared right across the globe, other forms of "unfree" labor such as debt bondage, indentured or contract labor, and the posting of workers have proliferated at least in the peripheries of the industrial centers of the world, and seem to be of particular importance in the context of global labor markets. Part 1 brings together the sociological discussion on commodification or decommodification, as well as the debate on reproduction from a gender perspective, and the historians' debate on the meaning of "free" and "unfree" labor—which are not congruent—in order to allow the analysis to be both more detailed and precise. The part introduction by Richard Hyman and Thomas Welskopp further details this approach, and elaborates on the contribution of the four chapters in Part 1.

Part 2 focuses on the market concept and tackles the question of whether it is appropriate in the case of labor markets. While labor markets are taken for granted in economics, and also in industrial and in economic sociology, academics with a background in the sociology of work insist that labor markets are fundamentally different from commodity markets, and many migration scholars are even reluctant to refer to the market concept at all. The contributions in this part, therefore, offer a critical discussion of the analytical capacities of the market concept when it comes to accounting for the cross-border matching of workers to jobs. Moreover, a historical semantic analysis of the market term also historicizes the discourse on labor markets, and its embeddedness in the broader process of the emergence of nation-states. Peter-Paul Bänziger and Ursula Mense-Petermann, in their part introduction, give a detailed overview of these questions and the contribution of the four chapters.

Part 3 addresses the question of what enables a labor market to transgress national borders. It focuses on market makers, networks, and institutions that allow labor mobility across borders to take place and also contribute to (eventually) embedding cross-border labor into sustainable ways of working and labor relations. The part draws on theoretical traditions showing that labor markets can only come into existence as relatively stable economic and social phenomena when market actors have devices at their disposal enabling them to deal with and overcome the fundamental uncertainty inherent in any type of market exchange (Beckert, 2009). As Sven Kesselring and Karen Shire argue in their part introduction, features that help solve the coordination problems that are amplified in labor markets once they begin to cross national borders are key for cross-border labor markets to emerge.

Finally, Part 4 focuses on how the "global" in global labor markets might be understood. It brings together three contributions that deal with the different meanings that "the global" in this context can take. The term "global labor market" can be used to indicate quite different social phenomena: a specific scale beneath others (the local, the regional, the national, the world regional, and the global), real global flows of migration, global horizons, or perceptions of the global that influence actors' decisions and agency, or global institutions that regulate cross-border labor markets and act to protect migrant workers. The part introduction by Rebecca Gumbrell-McCormick and Eleonore Kofman further develops these different concepts and what they entail for our understanding of global labor markets.

Overall, the present volume aims at underscoring the importance of a global outlook in examining labor markets and calls for increased scholarly attention to this largely ignored phenomenon. It represents the collaborative efforts of the contributors to shed light on the transnational, and even global, features of labor markets that transgress national borders, and to lay the foundations for further research.

References

Abraham, M., & Hinz, T. (Eds.) (2018). *Arbeitsmarktsoziologie*. Wiesbaden: Springer Fachmedien Wiesbaden.

Adick, C., Maletzky, M., Pries, L., & Gandlgruber, B. (2014). *Cross-Border Staff Mobility: A Comparative Study of Profit and Non-Profit Organisations*. Basingstoke: Palgrave Macmillan.

Aguilera, M. B., & Massey, D. S. (2003). Social capital and the wages of Mexican migrants: New hypotheses and tests. *Social Forces, 82*(2), 671–701.

Arthur, M. B. (1994). The boundaryless career: A new perspective for organizational inquiry. *Journal of Organizational Behavior, 15*(4), 295–306.

Arthur, M. B., & Rousseau, D. M. (Eds.) (1996). *The Boundaryless Career: A New Employment Principle for a New Organizational Era*. New York, NY: Oxford University Press.

Aspers, P., & Sandberg, C. (2020). Sailing together from different shores: Labour markets and inequality on board merchant ships. *Global Networks*, 454–471. doi:10.1111/glob.12252.

Autor, D. H., Dorn, D., & Hanson, G. H. (2013). The China syndrome: Local labor market effects of import competition in the United States. *American Economic Review, 103*(6): 2121–2168.

Battisti, M., Felbermayr, G., Peri, G., & Poutvaara, P. (2018). Immigration, search and redistribution: A quantitative assessment of native welfare. *Journal of the European Economic Association, 16*(4), 1137–1188.

Battu, H., Seaman, P., & Zenou, Y. (2011). Job contact networks and the ethnic minorities. *Labour Economics, 18*(1), 48–56.

Bauer, T., & Zimmermann, K. F. (1997). Network migration of ethnic Germans. *International Migration Review, 31*(1), 143.

Beckert, J. (2009). The social order of markets. *Theory and Society, 38*(3), 245–269.

Behtoui, A. (2008). Informal recruitment methods and disadvantages of immigrants in the Swedish labour market. *Journal of Ethnic and Migration Studies, 34*(3), 411–430.

Beine, M., Docquier, F., & Rapoport, H. (2001). Brain drain and economic growth: Theory and evidence. *Journal of Development Economics, 64*(1), 275–289.

Bludau, H. (2015). Creating a transnational labor chain between Eastern Europe and the Middle East: A case study in healthcare. *InterDisciplines. Journal of History and Sociology, 6*(1).

Borjas, G. J. (1987). Self-selection and the earnings of immigrants. *The American Economic Review, 77*(4), 531–533.

Borjas, G. J., Kauppinen, I., & Poutvaara, P. (2019). Self-selection of emigrants: Theory and evidence on stochastic dominance in observable and unobservable characteristics. *The Economic Journal, 129*(617), 143–171.

Chassamboulli, A., & Palybos, T. (2014). A search-equilibrium approach to the effects of immigration on labor market outcomes. *International Economic Review, 55*(1), 111–129.

Chiquiar, D., & Hanson, G. H. (2005). International migration, self-selection, and the distribution of wages: Evidence from Mexico and the United States. *Journal of Political Economy, 113*(2), 239–281.

Clemens M. A. (2011) Economics and emigration: Trillion dollar bills on the sidewalk. *Journal of Economic Perspectives, 25*(3): 83–106.

Choy, C. C. (2003). *Empire of Care: Nursing and Migration in Filipino American History. American Encounters / Global Interactions*. Durham: Duke University Press.

Connell, J. (2010). *Migration and the Globalisation of Health Care: The Health Worker Exodus?* Cheltenham: Edward Elgar Pub.

Creese, G., & Wiebe, B. (2012). 'Survival employment': Gender and deskilling among African immigrants in Canada. *International Migration, 50*(5), 56–76.

Czommer, L. (2008). Wild west conditions in Germany? Low-skill jobs in food processing. In C. Weinkopf & G. Bosch (Eds.), *Russell Sage Foundation Case Studies of Job Quality in Advanced Economies. Low-Wage Work in Germany* (pp. 147–176). New York: Russell Sage Foundation.

Delogu M., Docquier F., Machado J. (2018) Globalizing labour and the world economy: The role of human capital, *Journal of Economic Growth, 23*, 223–258.

Docquier, F., & Iftikhar, Z. (2019). Brain drain, informality and inequality: A search-and-matching model for Sub-Saharan Africa. *Journal of International Economics, 120*, 109–125.

Dølvik, J. E., & Eldring, L. (Eds.) (2017). *Labour Mobility in the Enlarged Single European Market.* Bingley: Emerald Group Publishing Limited.

Doering-Manteuffel, A., & Raphael, L. (2012). *Nach dem Boom: Perspektiven auf die Zeitgeschichte seit 1970.* Göttingen: Vandenhoeck & Ruprecht.

Dustmann, C., Frattini, T., & Rosso, A. (2015). The effect of emigration from Poland on Polish wages. *The Scandinavian Journal of Economics, 117*(2), 522–564.

Elliott, J. R. (2001). Referral hiring and ethnically homogeneous jobs: How prevalent is the connection and for whom? *Social Science Research, 30*(3), 401–425.

Galam, R. G. (2018). Utility manning: Young Filipino men, servitude and moral economy of becoming a seafarer and attaining adulthood. *Work, Employment and Society, 33* (4), 580–95. doi:10.1177/0950017018760182.

Galgóczi, B., Keune, M., & Watt, A. (Eds.) (2008). *Jobs on the Move: An Analytical Approach to 'Relocation' and Its Impact on Employment.* Brussels: P.I.E. Peter Lang.

Hansen, V. (2020). *Das Jahr 1000: Als die Globalisierung begann.* Munich: Beck Verlag.

Haug, S. (2008). Migration networks and migration decision-making. *Journal of Ethnic and Migration Studies, 34*(4), 585–605.

Heidenreich, M. (2004). Beschäftigungsordnungen zwischen Exklusion und Inklusion. Arbeitsmarktregulierende Institutionen im internationalen Vergleich. *Zeitschrift für Soziologie, 33*(3), 206–227.

Heidenreich, M., & Rice, D. (2016). *Integrating Social and Employment Policies in Europe: Active Inclusion and Challenges for Local Welfare Governance* (1st ed.). Cheltenham, Gloucestershire: Edward Elgar Publishing.

Iftikhar, Z., & Zaharieva, A. (2019). General equilibrium effects of immigration in Germany: Search and matching approach. *Review of Economic Dynamics, 31*, 245–276.

Jaehrling, K. (2008). Polarization of working conditions: Cleaners and nursing assistants in hospitals. In C. Weinkopf & G. Bosch (Eds.), *Russell Sage Foundation Case Studies of Job Quality in Advanced Economies. Low-Wage Work in Germany* (pp. 177–213). New York: Russell Sage Foundation.

Kanter, R. M. (1995). *World Class: Thriving Locally in the Global Economy*. New York: Simon & Schuster.

Kennan J. (2013). Open borders. *Review of Economic Dynamics, 16*: L1-L13.

Kingma, M. (2006). *Nurses on the Move: Migration and the Global Health Care Economy. The Culture and Politics of Health Care Work*. Ithaca, New York: ILR Press.

Kreutzer, F., & Roth, S. (Eds.) (2006). *Transnationale Karrieren: Biografien, Lebensführung und Mobilität* (1. Aufl.). Wiesbaden: vs Verlag für Sozialwissenschaften.

Lillie, N., Wagner, I., & Berntsen, L. (2014). Posted migration, spaces of exception, and the politics of labour relations in the European construction industry. In M. Hauptmeier & M. Vidal (Eds.), *Comparative Political Economy of Work* (312–331). London: Macmillan Education UK.

McGovern, P. (2007). Immigration, labour markets and employment relations: Problems and prospects. *British Journal of Industrial Relations, 45*(2), 217–235.

McKay, S. C. (2007). Filipino sea men: Constructing masculinities in an ethnic labour niche. *Journal of Ethnic and Migration Studies, 33*(4), 617–633.

Mense-Petermann, U. (2020). Introduction to the special theme: Theorizing transnational labour markets. *Global Networks, 20*(3), 399–409.

Mountford, A. (1997). Can a brain drain be good for growth in the source economy? *Journal of Development Economics, 53*(2), 287–303.

Münch, R. (1998). *Globale Dynamik, lokale Lebenswelten: Der schwierige Weg in die Weltgesellschaft* (2nd ed.). *Suhrkamp-Taschenbuch Wissenschaft: Vol. 1342*. Frankfurt am Main: Suhrkamp.

Ooka, E., & Wellman, B. (2006). Does social capital pay off more within or between ethnic groups? Analysing job searches in five Toronto ethnic groups. In E. Fong (Ed.), *Inside the Mosaic* (pp. 199–226). Toronto: University of Toronto Press.

Patacchini, E., & Zenou, Y. (2012). Ethnic networks and employment outcomes. *Regional Science and Urban Economics, 42*(6), 938–949.

Pohlmann, M. (2009). Globale ökonomische Eliten? Eine Globalisierungsthese auf dem Prüfstand der Empirie. *KZfSS Kölner Zeitschrift für Soziologie und Sozialpsychologie, 61*(4), 513–534.

Portes, A. (1995). Economic sociology and the sociology of immigration: A conceptual overview. In A. Portes (Ed.), *The Economic Sociology of Immigration. Essays on Networks, Ethnicity and Entrepreneurship* (pp. 1–40). New York: Russel Sage Foundation.

Pries, L. (2010). *Erwerbsregulierung in einer globalisierten Welt* (1st ed.). Wiesbaden: vs Verlag für Sozialwissenschaften.

Quack, S., Schulz-Schaeffer, I., Shire, K., & Weiß, A. (Eds.) (2018). *Transnationalisierung der Arbeit*. Wiesbaden: Springer vs.

Refslund, B., & Wagner, I. (2018). Cutting to the bone: Workers' solidarity in the Danish-German slaughterhouse industry. In V. L. Doellgast, N. Lillie, & V. Pulignano

(Eds.), *Reconstructing Solidarity. Labour Unions, Precarious Work, and the Politics of Institutional Change in Europe* (pp. 67–82). Oxford, United Kingdom: Oxford University Press.

Rockman, S. (2009). *Scraping By: Wage Labor, Slavery, and Survival in Early Baltimore. Studies in Early American Economy and Society from the Library Company of Philadelphia.* Baltimore, Md.: Johns Hopkins Univ. Press.

Rogowski, R., Salais, N., & Whiteside, N. (Eds.) (2011). *Transforming European Employment Policy.* London, New York: Routledge.

Singer, R., & Bazzani, T. (Eds.) (2017). *European Employment Policies: Current Challenges.* Berlin: BWV Berliner Wissenschafts-Verlag.

Staples, R., Trinczek, R., & Whittall, M. (2013). "Posted workers": Zwischen regulierung und invisibilisierung. *Arbeit: Zeitschrift für Arbeitsforschung, Arbeitsgestaltung und Arbeitspolitik, 22*(4), 271–286.

Swift, O. (2011). Seafaring citizenship: What being Filipino means at sea and what seafaring means for the Philippines. *East Asia Research, 19*(2), 273–291.

Trubek, L. (2005). Health care and low-wage work in the United States: Linking local action for expanded coverage. In J. Zeitlin & D. M. Trubek (Eds.), *Governing Work and Welfare in a New Economy. European and American Experiments* (pp. 292–314). Oxford: Oxford Univ. Press.

van der Linden, M. (Ed.) (2011). *Humanitarian Intervention and Changing Labor Relations: The Long-Term Consequences of the Abolition of the Slave Trade.* Leiden, Boston: Brill.

Verwiebe, R., Reinprecht, C., Haindorfer, R., & Wiesboeck, L. (2017). How to succeed in a transnational labor market: Job search and wages among Hungarian, Slovak, and Czech commuters in Austria. *International Migration Review, 51*(1), 251–286.

Wagner, I. (2015). EU posted work and transnational action in the German meat industry. *Transfer: European Review of Labour and Research, 21*(2), 201–213.

Welskopp, T. (2014). *Unternehmen Praxisgeschichte: Historische Perspektiven auf Kapitalismus, Arbeit und Klassengesellschaft.* Tübingen: Mohr Siebeck.

Zimmermann, K. F. (Ed.) (2005). *European Migration. What Do We Know?* Oxford: Oxford University Press.

PART 1

What Is Meant by Labor Exchanged in Labor Markets?

∵

Introduction to Part 1
What Is Meant by Labor Exchanged in Labor Markets?

Richard Hyman and Thomas Welskopp

The battle cry "Labor is not a commodity" rang out across Europe and North America around the early 1870s when union-based resistance globally stiffened against the consequences of at least seven or eight decades of untrammeled commodification of labor by capital. Yet when the International Labour Organization (ILO) in its Philadelphia Declaration of 1944 famously insisted on this fundamental demand, it had by then become clear that the issues raised by this phrase were still far from being settled.

Since the present volume emphatically embarks on a search for the global labor market, it implies that there must be something out there rightfully called a "labor market." And this, in turn, requires at least a sufficient level of the commodification of labor which might explain the urgency in the appeal voiced by the ILO in 1944 almost as an admission of defeat.

Yet, for the research purposes of this volume, the empirical aspects and problems will inspire and direct our analysis: To what extent is a labor market a genuine market? What is actually exchanged in these markets? What is the kind of labor that is, in this sense, marketable? Are there limits to commodification or countertendencies of decommodification by regulation and/or resistance movements? Is the labor market just one of many arrangements for allocating labor and what does this mean for its role in capitalism?

The contributions to Part 1 are devoted to debates on some of these questions.

With his full-blown attack on what he calls mainstream labor economics and mainstream labor sociology, Marcel van der Linden raises the flag under which the entire venture of the present volume might be sailing. He exposes the tendency of both disciplines to consider jettisoning "historical," "legal," and other "anecdotal" evidence to be the prerequisite to achieve an allegedly pure "analytical" level of theorizing. Only from this decidedly ahistorical perspective, it was argued, was a valid comparative analysis of labor markets conceivable. Van der Linden instead insists on the historicity of labor regimes and the manifold patterns of allocation of labor, many of which have existed for centuries and are still with us. For him, the very term "labor market" is a misnomer since not labor per se but the temporal use of labor power would be what is the object of exchange here. Van der Linden establishes his disputable contention that a labor contract in fact works like a "hiring out" agreement rather than a sale. Thus, the researcher may be able to trace allocations by contract throughout history under varying circumstances and identify these as instances of labor markets which coexist side by side with multiple other forms of allocation of labor whose historical significance is subject to change over time.

Against this plea for an almost unlimited sectoral and temporal broadening of the concepts of labor and labor markets, Thomas Welskopp's contribution to this volume might superficially appear to be an exhibit from the time-honored museum of vintage German social history. Indeed, he maintains that wage labor as we know it—and "free" wage labor in particular—is the systematic corollary of capitalism as the dominant mode of economic activity in modern society. His rather narrow definition of wage labor as gainful employment does not in fact exclude all other forms of expending one's power to good use. Yet it focuses on—and attempts to explain—the mechanism by which societies under capitalism came to establish free wage labor as the hegemonic semantic formula for allocating labor. Welskopp argues that the ubiquitous subjectivization of individuals in modern society called for a worker who would be competent, diligent, proactive, self-responsible, and able to self-organize on the shop floor and beyond. "Free" came to mean "individuation" rather than "liberty." Only this, in fact, fueled new class tensions in an unknown intensity but—this is the main argument here—at the same time brought about the productive antagonism to which the unprecedented gains in productivity that capitalism displayed during the nineteenth and twentieth centuries must be attributed.

Whereas the preceding contributions controversially debate the role of "free" wage labor in capitalism and dispute whether the search for labor markets proper should be focusing on free contractual arrangements, Richard Hyman tackles the problem from a different angle. He starts out from "unfree" labor regimes, forms of forced labor which had been an issue addressed by the ILO for a long time now. Here the interests of colonial powers to protect brutal slave-like working relations blocked interference from the outside well into the postwar era. Yet modern states still—and increasingly—resort to violence to coerce certain groups of the population into forced labor relations with foreign contractors or intermediaries placing young, preferably female, migrants in precarious jobs abroad. Yet, within nation-states, an entirely state-run economy of convict labor and prison work has been jump-started during the past few decades which seems to reach ever new peaks with the privatization of the prison sector, as Hyman contends that in the US forced labor may be the post-decommodified labor regime most suitable for the globalized and financialized capitalism of our time.

Alexandra Scheele highlights the significant continuity of the gendered division of labor in society. For her, its systematic relation to capitalism remains obscure. It is much older than capitalism and covers all the vast areas of housework, subsistence work, and care work done at home in lieu of both pay and a labor contract. In Scheele's interpretation, this seems to point to ignorance and negligence on the part of capitalists and not so much to a sinister strategy to rake in windfall surplus value as some feminist schools of critique have it. Yet even where housework and care work are commercialized to an ever-higher degree on a global scale, and although these activities have recently begun to be upgraded into professions, ruggedly unequal gender structures have persisted and multiplied the number of low-paid, flexible, insecure, and constrained jobs that are often filled with collectively recruited precarious migrants.

Part 1 critically examines one of the essential core concepts of this volume which will be instrumental in our endeavor to embark on our search for the global labor market. The part —we hope—shows that the disputes over and clarification of terms have not been a waste of time but have both brought widely diverging disciplines under the umbrella of one joint project and provided us with a vocabulary everyone in the group is at least able to relate to.

CHAPTER 1

Labor Markets in History
A Global View

Marcel van der Linden

1 Introduction[1]

About eighteen centuries ago, the New Testament was written. Its Gospel of Matthew (20: 1–2) narrates the parable of "a householder who went out early in the morning to hire labourers for his vineyard" and who "after agreeing with the labourers for a denarius a day [...] sent them into his vineyard." Much earlier, in ancient Athens, there was a space known as *kolonos misthios*, probably on the west end of the agora, where those who wanted to hire themselves out as land laborers offered their services daily (Fuks, 1951). Indeed, in the ancient city of Rome, a large part of the male population—perhaps even the majority—had to rely on casual wage labor as dockers, porters, storemen, and construction workers (Brunt, 1971, p. 383). "Since the demand for labor fluctuated, workers must have been hired for varying lengths of time, from a day to weeks or even months, while some people were probably hired for the completion of a particular task. [...] Casual labor is inherently unstable, and this led to many in Rome living correspondingly unstable lives. Competition for jobs also likely kept wages low, resulting in widespread structural poverty in the city." Moreover, wage dispersion in the early Roman Empire was "indistinguishable from that in preindustrial Europe." And Roman labor contracts were "distinctly modern" (Temin, 2013, p. 114).

All the indications are that spot markets for casual labor have existed for thousands of years and are, therefore, much older than capitalism. Jan Lucassen (2018, p. 405) assumes that markets for wage labor emerged in the Middle East "between 2000 and 1000 BCE, when officials organizing work for temples turned into subcontractors." Meanwhile, labor markets have, as we know, become much more general, more extensive, and often more abstract.

---

1 I would like to thank my project co-participants and the project leaders Ursula Mense-Petermann, Thomas Welskopp, and Anna Zaharieva for the many useful discussions we have had. The project coordinator Annika Andresen helped me greatly, too. And Ad Knotter, Jan Lucassen, Alice Mul, and Matthias van Rossum kindly and critically read the first draft.

How did this transition come about? How did labor markets change from local to global? In this contribution, I offer a few preliminary thoughts on these questions.

My approach differs both from mainstream labor economics and mainstream labor sociology. Most labor economists nowadays deliberately ignore history. A major textbook declares, for example:

> The field of labor economics has long been recognized as an important area of study. But the content or subject matter of the field has changed dramatically in the past few decades. If you were to go to the library and examine a labor text published 30 or 35 years ago, you would find its orientation highly descriptive and historical. [...] To be sure, labor markets and unemployment were accorded some attention, but the analysis was typically minimal and superficial. This state of affairs has changed significantly in recent decades. Economists have achieved important analytic breakthroughs in studying labor markets and labor problems. As a result, economic analysis has crowded out historical, institutional, legal, and anecdotal material. Labor economics increasingly has become applied micro and macro theory.
> MCCONNELL, BRUE and MACPHERSON, 2017, pp. 3–4

The implication is, of course, that applied economic micro and macro theory must necessarily be ahistorical.

Labor sociologists are often less dogmatic than most labor economists. In a recent important contribution to the field, Bengt Furåker rightly argues that "labor markets are not only associated with capitalism, although we have a tendency to think of them in that way"; they also existed in "pre-capitalist and state socialist nations" (Furåker, 2005, pp. 1–2). But he nevertheless limits labor markets to markets for free wage labor:

> the labor market is a system for hiring labor power. I prefer the terms 'hiring' and 'hiring out' instead of 'buying' and 'selling', simply because I find the former more adequate to describe the characteristics of modern labor markets. A table or a chair can be bought and sold once and for all, which means that these objects cease to belong to their previous owner. Labor power is, however, different in this respect; it is not turned over to the employer but only for a limited period of time. [...] If, in the labor market, labor power is not the property of its bearer, slavery is the proper notion.
> FURÅKER, 2005, pp. 17–18

Contra the majority of labor economists and sociologists, I will argue that we can best understand the development of labor markets if we use a historical approach and do not limit ourselves to "free" wage labor but also include physically coerced labor (chattel slavery, etc.). First, I will attempt to clarify some of the relevant concepts, and then I will outline a few major trends from antiquity until the present.

2   Concepts

Obviously, a labor market is a type of market. A market is an actual (physical, concrete) or nominal (virtual) place where commodities are exchanged, that is, sold or hired out for money or a money equivalent. Let us first have a closer look at the most important components of this general definition.

To begin with, what are commodities and what is exchange? *Commodities* are, as Adam Smith already knew, "objects" that combine "value in use" (their utility) with "value in exchange" (their price) (Smith, 1776, p. 34). An object that has no utility for anyone cannot be a commodity; nor can an object that has no price. Karl Marx reintroduced this definition in the first chapter of *Capital Volume I*, giving it his own particular theoretical twist.

Commodities may be *real* or *fictitious*. In other words, not only objects intentionally produced for sale (cars, houses, or shoes) can be exchanged on markets; objects that are "just there" as gifts of nature can also become commodities (for example, the Amazonian rain forest, sandy beaches, or ivory).

Exchange—the act of reciprocal giving and receiving—in markets is always the exchange of money—or a good in kind as a general equivalent—for property rights concerning an object or service. Property rights are bundles of enforceable claims. Each property right is backed with the threat of public enforcement via some form of sanction—and, in the last instance, physical coercion. Property rights therefore presuppose the existence of a public authority with coercive power. Modern legal theory breaks property rights into the following rights and duties: "(i) the right to possess, (ii) the right to use, (iii) the right to manage, (iv) the right to the income of the object, (v) the right to the capital, (vi) the right to security, (vii) the right of transmissibility, (viii) the right of absence of term, (ix) the duty to prevent harmful use, (x) liability to execution, and (xi) the incident of residuarity." For full ownership of an object, a proprietor must have most (but not necessarily all) of these elements regarding that object (Honoré, 1961). There is no consensus on the question of which, if any, of these rights and duties are essential for property to exist.

Exchange can be temporary or permanent. A temporary exchange is hiring, while a permanent exchange is a sale. A sale is a transaction in which the original owner/proprietor of the commodity is replaced by another owner/proprietor in exchange for money; the property rights connected with the commodity are transferred from one person/institution/organization to another. Hiring is a transaction in which the original owner/proprietor remains the owner/proprietor but another party can—in exchange for money—use the commodity for a certain period of time. An exchange may take place under competitive or non-competitive circumstances. There is no competition if there is only one supplier and one buyer/renter, or if trade between suppliers and buyers/renters (in particular, prices and other aspects of commercial transactions) is heavily regulated, frequently by a public authority. There is competition if at least two suppliers or buyers/renters are bidding or haggling against each other (Aspers, 2005; North, 1977).[2]

If we turn to labor markets now, two additional questions arise: what is exchanged and who is exchanging? The term "labor market" is a misnomer. *No labor is ever exchanged* in labor markets. What is sold or hired out is the human capacity to labor (labor-power), not the labor itself. The old Aristotelian distinction between *dunamis* (potentiality) and *energeia* (actuality) is of crucial importance here. "The purchaser of labour-power consumes it by setting the seller of it to work. By working, the latter becomes in actuality what previously he only was potentially, namely labour-power in action, a worker" (Marx, 1976, p. 283).

Who is exchanging the labor-power? When we speak of labor markets, we usually think of contemporary exchanges in which free workers, mostly driven by economic necessity, hire themselves out to employers in exchange for a money wage.[3] The examples from antiquity mentioned above all involve such "voluntary" transactions. The implicit assumption of the present-day notion of labor markets is that the workers have to offer their labor-power *themselves*. This thought can, for example, be found in Karl Marx when he emphasizes that "labour-power can appear on the market as a commodity only if, and so far as, its possessor, the individual whose labour-power it is, offers it for sale or sells

---

2   Many examples of regulated markets can be found in Medieval Europe. See, for example, Casson, M. & Lee, J. S., 2011; Weber and Mayer-Maly, 1954. Attempts to break through such regulations have been reconstructed in, for instance, Kaplan, 1988.
3   Marx famously defined the free wage laborers ironically as "free in the double sense that as a free individual he can dispose of his labour-power as his own commodity, and that, on the other hand, he has no other commodity for sale, i.e. he is rid of them, he is free of all objects needed for the realization of his labour-power" (Marx, 1976, pp. 272–273). The "free wage earner" is therefore usually not free at all but is coerced by economic necessity.

it as a commodity." Only if the carrier of the labor-power is also the possessor of the labor-power is "the polarization of the commodity-market" possible, according to Marx (Marx, 1976, p. 271, p. 874). This is a highly questionable view. Why can't labor-power be sold by somebody *other* than the carrier? Is a slave market not a market where labor-power is sold?

In labor markets, the distinction between possessor and commodity may become blurred. The possessor can him- or herself become the commodity to be sold or hired out. The wage earner who offers his/her labor capacity for hire for, say, a month, is turning his/her own self into a commodity. But the enslaved person, who is sold or hired out by his or her proprietor, is also a commodity. Both slave markets and "free" labor markets meet the definition of a market. In both cases, there is a social structure for exchange of rights, which enables people, firms, and products to be evaluated and priced. In both cases, the actors are independent. This is not to deny, of course, that there are serious differences between the two types of market.

Just making the distinction between a "carrier" and a "possessor" of labor-power, we can already distinguish four different types of labor market exchange, namely markets in which the carrier of labor-power is also its possessor, and markets in which the carrier of labor-power is not its possessor. In both cases, the carrier's labor-power can be offered by the carrier him- or herself or by another person (see Table 1.1).

TABLE 1.1   Four types of labor-power exchange (examples)

	Lease	Sale
Carrier of labor-power is possessor of labor-power	"Free" wage labor Sharecropping	Self-sale[a] Sale of debt-peon
Carrier of labor-power is not possessor of labor-power	Slave for hire[b] Child laborer	Chattel slave

a Self-sale is an ancient phenomenon, even mentioned in the Codex Hammurabi (c. 1780 BCE). Hammurabi's case probably does not fit our definition of a market since it seems to have been a transaction between one seller and one buyer. Market-conform self-sales can be found in more recent centuries. See, for example, Patterson, 1982, p. 130; see also Dorn, 2011; Engerman, 2007, pp. 94–100; Hellie, 1982; Testart, 2001.
b Slaves for hire are slaves who, although the property of an owner, have to work for someone else, an employer. They were quite numerous in ancient Rome. In the eighteenth and nineteenth centuries, such slaves for hire could be found in various parts of the Americas and Africa. In Senegal, slave owners and employers even organized collective bargaining to negotiate slave wages (Mbodj, 1993).
SOURCE: OWN TABLE

3 Early Labor Markets

By far the most sizeable part of humanity performed subsistence labor up until the nineteenth century. In other words, they worked in order to provide for their own immediate consumptive needs. This was particularly true for the main economic sector, agriculture. As Chris Wickham wrote: "In human history, most cultivators have been peasants, who work the land autonomously, in family groups. [...] Peasant families control a given set of lands at any one time, cultivate it, rely on its produce to survive, and also give a part of the produce to a landlord if they have one, and/or to the state if it exists." (Wickham, 2005, p. 260) For instance, Evelyn Sakakida Rawski established for South China: "For at least the last millennium, Chinese agriculture has been dominated by many free, small-scale farmers, working under a system of private landownership. A Chinese peasant, if he did not own his land, aspired to eventually do so. Both tenants and landowning farmers were free to decide what to grow on their plots and to dispose of their own produce" (Rawski, 1972, p. 3). Consequently, for a very long time, labor-power commodification covered only a small section of the world's labor force. Take wage labor, for instance. There were, in fact, at least four basic forms of early wage labor: casual labor, particularly in agriculture (e.g., harvesting), but also in building, lumbering, etc.; artisanal labor, i.e., skilled work carried out from time to time but not continuously (metalwork and carpentry); military service—mercenaries constituted the first large group of wage earners; and artisans' apprenticeships—wage laborers who had to learn specific skills. All these have one thing in common: "free" wage labor was used in particular when the activities were of a temporary nature: temporary either in the sense of being seasonal work or carried out at a certain stage of the worker's life (in the case of apprentices) (van der Linden, 2008, pp. 42–45). Wage labor was frequently a side activity for peasants and artisans who also had other sources of "income" (subsistence labor, petty commodity production, etc.).

Conversely, slave labor was appropriate for activities carried out continuously. Slavery of shepherds was, for instance, the first form of economically significant slavery in ancient Greece.

> In contrast to arable farming and horticulture, [livestock farming] was an area of economic activity in which the amount of labor required remained relatively constant. This created the demand and favoured the deployment of a constant number of workers. 'Serfs', but also slaves certainly fitted better into this regime than impoverished free migrants, who

in all probability would only consent to contract out their services for a limited period.

AUDRING, 1985, p. 16

Enslaved and wage laborers often—but not always—did the same type of work. In Babylonia and Assyria, "free workers and slaves worked shoulder to shoulder in royal factories, in temple establishments, and in private industries." (Mendelsohn, 1943, p. 25) In ancient Rome,

> slaves were interchangeable with free wage labourers in many situations. [...] Roman slaves appear to be like long-term employees. The analysis of slave motivation and the wide distribution of slave occupations suggest that slaves were part of an integrated labor force in the early Roman Empire.
>
> TEMIN, 2013, p. 130

After Brazil had abolished slave trade in 1850, the coffee planters in the São Paulo region recruited Italian immigrants who worked in the fields side by side with Afro-Brazilian slaves (Stolcke & Hall, 1983). In North America, there were also frequently mixed labor forces (Steffen, 1979; Whitman, 1993; Schechter, 1994). At the waterfront of mid-eighteenth-century New York, "[s]laves toiled alongside unskilled white workers as teamsters, wagoners, dockers, stockmen, ropewalkers, and cartmen." (Rediker, 1987, p. 68) Moreover, a study of two nineteenth-century ironworks in New Jersey and Virginia concluded:

> Both slavery and free labor met the demands of entrepreneurs for flexibility. In a rural industrial setting, the methods by which proprietors attempted to create a disciplined labor force, whether slave or free, had much in common, particularly how they dealt with tradesmen. Both labor systems required ironmasters to strike a careful balance between encouragement and coercion, although slavery allowed for a wider range of options, especially punitive measures.
>
> BEZÍS-SELFA, 1999, p. 700

Even so, the labor markets for slaves and wage laborers were, to the best of my knowledge, always physically separated. Apparently, the difference between both forms of exchange was too large to allow for their integration.

Slave markets can take different shapes. For the Roman Empire, William Harris distinguishes four settings in which slave sales took place: small-scale "everyday" transactions; opportunistic markets of, for example, slave traders following the Roman army to buy captured enemy soldiers; periodic markets in small places; and large-scale trade in bigger cities, with Rome as the main trade center (Harris, 1980, pp. 125–126). Slave markets could also become extensive. The Greek geographer Strabo, who lived at the beginning of our era, reported on the tiny island Delos (3.4 km2), stating that it "could both admit and send away ten thousand slaves on the same day; whence arose the proverb, 'Merchant, sail in, unload your ship, everything has been sold.'" (Strabo, 1950, p. 329) Little is known about the slave trade between Japan, China, and Korea in the sixteenth and seventeenth centuries.

In precapitalist times, wage laborers were, to the best of my knowledge, never traded in large markets. But there was at least one exception: mercenaries. In China, military labor markets predate the emergence of the first imperial dynasty, the Qin, in 221 BCE (Lewis, 1990, pp. 54–66). As far as Western Europe is concerned, Erica Schoenberger (2008, p. 682) ascertained:

> Beginning in the tenth and developing through the twelfth centuries, then, the market for mercenaries was perhaps one of the better-developed branches of international trade. It was not a huge market; a mercenary army was rather more likely to run into the four digits than five. But they could be kept in the field for a long time and then dismissed [...] when they were no longer needed.

Labor markets could cover long distances. The Roman Empire sent British military units all the way to the Dacia region (contemporary Romania) during the first and second centuries CE (Ivleva, 2016, p. 161). The African slaves from the Swahili coast (the *Zanj*) who were forced to work in the salt marshes in south Iraq are well-known. Their fate became notorious because they rebelled (in 869) and founded a new, expansive city called al-Mokhtára ("the elect city"), just south of Basra, with elaborate defense works and home to a population of 50,000 or more. Only after fourteen years were these rebels defeated (Nöldeke, 1892; Popovic, 1999). Long-distance hiring of non-military wage laborers mainly occurred if these workers had special skills. We know, for example, that, in fourteenth- and fifteenth-century Anatolia, tile makers from Transoxiania (modern-day Uzbekistan, Tajikistan, and parts of Kyrgyzstan and Kazakhstan) were recruited owing to their unique blackline technique (Golombek, 1996; Samkoff, 2014). And, in the sixteenth century, German silver miners worked not only in the south of France, Southeast Europe, and Spain, but also in Santo Domingo (Haiti) and Venezuela (Probert, 1969, p. 102; Laube, 1975, p. 88; Denzer, 2005, pp. 79–81). It seems logical that the size of such labor markets remained limited.

On a global scale, labor markets for slaves remained of minor importance up until the eighteenth century. In China, for instance, slavery was rare: "there is little evidence that slaves formed a large part of the whole population at any time." (Pulleyblank, 1958, p. 220) In other parts of Asia, slavery remained a marginal phenomenon, too. "Although slavery existed in Mughal India [1526–1858], it was almost universally domestic slavery." (Habib, 1995, p. 197) "Agrarian slavery and serfdom were rare in India." (Roy, 2009, p. 149) In Tokugawa Japan [1600–1867], slaves were "primarily criminals and prisoners." (Leupp, 1992, p. 15) In the Ottoman Empire, "[m]arkets for slaves existed until the second half of the nineteenth century but most of the limited numbers of slaves were employed as domestic labour. Slave labour was virtually non-existent in agriculture, trade and manufacturing" (Pamuk, 2009, p. 123).

For a long time, free wage labor remained rare, too. In China, "[n]either the Qing nor the Ming [penal] codes showed much concern with hired labor, although its existence is attested to" (Moll-Murata, 2011, p. 175). In nineteenth-century Southeast Asia, "[f]ree (wage) labour had probably always been available in small (sometimes no doubt very small) numbers, but during the early modern period various forms of dependent or bonded labour were predominant" (Boomgaard, 2009, p. 59). Moreover,

> wage labour, whether semi-permanent or on a permanent basis, played an insignificant role in the economy. It occurred on an irregular basis in some larger centres in Java where, for instance, people did not have any association with land and sold their labour power.
> KAUR, 2004, p. 21

In India, "[b]ut few examples of large-scale migration or circulation before the eighteenth century involved wage work in permanent sites that employed hundreds of people together, such as the mills, plantations, canals, and railways of the nineteenth century" (Roy, 2009, p. 147). In the Ottoman Empire, "farms using year-round wage labour or servile labour were exceptional" (Pamuk, 2009, p. 121). In Germany, around 1800, free wage labor was still a "minority phenomenon" (Pierenkemper, 2009, p. 84).

There were, however, exceptions confirming this rule. In North Africa, in the fourth and fifth centuries, there were about 300,000 to 350,000 landless laborers,

> who moved on a seasonal basis from the North African towns and neighboring districts to areas where there was a high demand for [agricultural] labor. [...] Writing in the mid-fourth century, Optatus of Milevis claimed

that North African urban areas and periodic fairs were the main pools from which laborers could be recruited.

TEDESCO, 2018, pp. 413–414

More important were perhaps the Low Countries, where during the fifteenth and sixteenth centuries

arrangements in the country between employers and laborers were market-driven and based on a cash wage, paid daily, weekly, or monthly. Labour contracts in these areas were mostly formal and short-term—verbal agreements for the day and written ones for the year.

VAN BAVEL, 2011, p. 525

According to economic historian Jan de Vries, "the [Dutch] labour market already in the early sixteenth century was large and largely free of feudal constraints. [...] Wage labour played a larger role here than in many other European countries three hundred years later." (De Vries, 1993, p. 56) In the cities of Tokugawa Japan, free wage labor seems to have grown in importance, too (Leupp, 1992, pp. 123–154; Nagata, 2005, p. 16; Mathias, 2011, pp. 234–238).

In cases in which households could not work autonomously but were physically forced to labor, coercion could take many different forms. The number of variations of coerced labor is dizzying. One of these many variations was *unfree* wage labor, that is, a labor relation in which the workers receive wages but are tied to their employers through multiple obligations. Large numbers of unfree wage laborers could be found in South Asia and in preindustrial Europe. In Mughal India, the landless agricultural workers constituted between one-sixth and one-fifth of the rural population; they belonged to "the menial castes, compelled to serve the interests alike of peasants and of superior cultivators, and forming a vast rural semi-proletariat, maintained entirely through non-economic compulsions" (Habib, 1995, p. 197). For Europe, Charles Tilly has estimated that, in 1500, about 30 percent of the entire labor force consisted of proletarians, and, in 1900, almost 44 percent (Tilly, 1984, p. 36). The majority of these workers probably were, in so far as they were not casual laborers (either fully proletarianized or peasant workers whose households combined several sources of income), bonded wage laborers who were not allowed to hire out their labor power to an employer of their choice on their own initiative.

Moreover, research in recent years has revealed that many so-called free workers were really *bonded* laborers, far into the nineteenth century. Master and servant laws, apprenticeship arrangements, etc., ensured that workers were tied to their employers and had significantly fewer legal rights than the literature previously suggested. In this context, there has indeed been mention of "industrial serfdom" (Hay & Craven, 2004; Stanziani, 2014). The legal historian Thorsten Keiser has even argued that in nineteenth-century Germany, "multiple bonds [always] existed, for factory workers and craftsmen as well. For grown-up industrial workers, these bonds were completely removed only around 1900, for domestics [*Gesinde*] and agricultural labourers not until 1918" (Keiser, 2013, p. 404).

4   The Rise of Transcontinental Labor Markets

From the fifteenth century onward, labor relations began to change fundamentally on a global scale. This change has been gradual and uneven. The rise of colonialism was crucial. Colonialism, says Jürgen Osterhammel, is "a relationship of domination between an indigenous (or forcibly imported) majority and a minority of foreign invaders." Such an asymmetric relationship has two salient features. Colonial rulers make most decisions of consequence for the lives of the colonized people "in pursuit of interests that are often defined in a distant metropolis." And in making and implementing these decisions, the rulers assume that they are superior to the colonial subjects, and that they therefore have a "mandate to rule" (Osterhammel, 1997, pp. 16–17). Colonialism is far older than capitalism and may arise from many different motives: in addition to purely economic ones, the causes may be religious, political, demographic, or military. Early examples include the American Pre-Columbian empires or Han China (202 BCE—220 CE) which subdued parts of Korea, Vietnam, and Central Asia. The powers carrying out colonial projects have therefore certainly not been exclusively European or North American. The clearest recent example that illustrates this is Japan, which controlled a vast colonial territory between 1895 and 1945.

During the first four centuries, expansion to other continents was, however, mostly European in nature and impelled by two types of social forces: on the one hand, absolutist regimes in Spain, Portugal, and (to a somewhat lesser extent) France; and, on the other hand, merchant capitalists from the Netherlands and England. The first form of expansion was driven by the quest of monarchs and their aristocratic entourage to increase their wealth, and merchants were secondary and subordinate. The second type of expansion was the complete opposite: merchants took the initiative and the state facilitated them. This second form became dominant after about 1800.

With the growth of colonialism, we see—despite the dominance of non-commodified labor—the rapid growth of three types of transcontinental labor markets: indentured service, chattel slavery, and wage labor. The earliest important type was indentured labor. In this form of contract labor, an intermediary covers the cost of a worker's journey to a distant country. In return, the worker agrees to remain in the service of an employer at his/her new destination for a certain number of years (for example, three, five, or ten). Throughout this period, the worker is entirely subject to the authority of that employer and is not allowed to switch jobs. Workers violating the rules are treated as criminals, including possible incarceration. Although indentured laborers often accepted contracts "voluntarily" (compelled by material need), in many cases, their fate was regarded as simply a new state of slavery (Tinker, 1974). In particular, the English colonies in North America initially employed indentured servants. Precise numbers are not available, but "[a]n estimated 70 per cent of white migrants to England's American colonies in the seventeenth century were bound in indentured servitude as servants in agriculture or other employments, particularly in the staple-exporting colonies" (Wareing, 2017, p. 39).

In the course of the seventeenth and eighteenth centuries, colonists resorted less and less to indentured servants; these were increasingly replaced by African chattel slaves. There has been debate on the reasons for this. Here, it should be sufficient to say that slavery took the place of white servitude in two steps. First, slaves replaced indentured servants in "the unskilled field labor of staple-crop cultivation." And when slaves had been trained to perform skilled jobs, "this ultimately led planters to cease importing servants altogether" (Galenson, 1981, p. 174). The African continent became the main supplier of enslaved laborers not only in the Americas but also in the Middle East and South Asia. Between 1400 and 1900, some 10.3 million Africans were deported to the Americas. Moreover, 3.1 million Africans became victims of the trans-Saharan trade, while 1.3 million were shipped across the Red Sea, and just under a million across the Indian Ocean (Nunn, 2008, Table 11; Lovejoy, 2000, Table 7.1). The transatlantic slave trade peaked somewhere between 1750 and 1825 (see Figure 1.1). Over the following decades the number of victims declined, thanks to the British abolitionist campaign that increasingly resonated with other European potentates. The transcontinental labor market for chattel slaves was in all likelihood the deadliest labor market in history. The numbers of slaves embarking on ships differed vastly from those disembarking from ships, in effect indicating the number of enslaved Africans that perished *during* the voyage to the Americas from disease, abuse, murder, or suicide. Canadian historian David Eltis and his team gathered data on over 35,000 slave voyages; they arrived at the conclusion that in the period 1501–1866 one-seventh (14.5 percent) of the slaves who embarked "disappeared" (www.slavevoyages.org).

When the slave trade began to decline numerically in the nineteenth century, employers in subtropical and tropical countries resorted to indenture again. The immediate reason was the shortage of labor on sugar plantations following the abolition of slavery in the British Empire in 1834. Ex-slaves were reluctant to voluntarily engage in plantation labor, and this resulted in the search for other sources of labor. Many planters in the West Indies "initially turned their attention to Europe and Africa. Between 1834 and 1837, some 3000 English, 1000 Scottish and German, and 100 Irish labourers were introduced into Jamaica, with smaller numbers going to St. Lucia, on three- to five-year contracts." The failure of these and other experiments shifted attention to Asia (Lal, 2006, p. 48). South Asians and Chinese in particular, as well as Javanese, became important in this practice. It has been estimated that between 1801 and 1925 "about three million contract labourers were shipped out of China." (Pan, 1998, p. 61) A total of around 1.5 million indentured Indians emigrated to overseas destinations between 1834 and 1916 (Lal 1983). *Within* countries, indenture became more common as well. When, for example, around 1840 tea plantations were established in Assam, hundreds of thousands of indentured laborers were recruited in other parts of British India (Behal, 2014; Varma, 2017). Indentured migrations gradually diminished in the early decades of the twentieth century. By then, however, other migration flows were in progress.

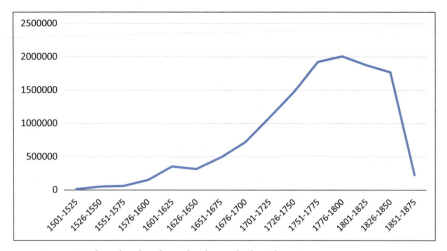

FIGURE 1.1   Number of enslaved people who made the Atlantic crossing
SOURCE: HTTP://WWW.SLAVEVOYAGES.ORG/ASSESSMENT/ESTIMATES

In the century from 1840 to 1940, three new migration systems emerged; in each of them, 50 to 60 million people were relocated (from North Asia, from Southeast Asia, and across the Atlantic Ocean) (McKeown, 2004). Migrants in these systems usually left not because of physical coercion but out of economic necessity—although some were kidnapped (shanghaied) and shipped out against their will.

The advance of global markets for free wage labor was, from a historical point of view, the result of a very long struggle between different systems of labor mobilization and various types of labor markets. Only the (partial) demise of the trade in slaves and indentured laborers ("coolies") made room for free labor markets. Nevertheless, we should still not forget that some long-distance labor markets existed before the breakthrough of global markets. As mentioned above, there were mercenaries, the Timurid tile makers in Anatolia, and the German silver miners in Santo Domingo and Venezuela.

Zooming in on the markets for free wage labor, we see two important trends. First, *labor markets for non-casual workers gain ground*, particularly in the agricultural sector. In China, during the early and middle Qing Dynasty, the majority of laborers were still hired on a short-term basis, although contracts of longer duration also existed.

> It was often the case that two labourers were hired by the year and three to five for the busy sowing and harvesting seasons. There had long been a labour market in the Chinese countryside and there are records of 'hiring markets' (*gongfushi* or *renshi*) existing in Kaiyuan in Fengtian, Linxian in Henan, Yanggao *xian* in Shanxi, Xinhui in Guangdong, and Shandong.
>
> SHI & ZHUOFEN, 2000, p. 144

In British India,

> [p]ermanent sites of hiring began to emerge from the eighteenth century, to receive migrant workers. Indigo factories of Bengal in the 1830s and 1840s, coal mines of Chota Nagpur and tea plantations of Assam somewhat later recruited workers who came from villages hundreds of miles away. From the end of the century, industrial cities recruited workers from longer distances and different regions.
>
> ROY, 2009, p. 150

In Southeast Asia,

> locally from the late eighteenth century, and across the region during much of the nineteenth, corvée obligations and fully fledged slavery were being increasingly abolished, while free wage labour took their place. This development was linked to three factors—population growth (which led to falling man–land ratios and therefore to cheaper labour), the continuing growth of international trade and measures taken by the colonial rulers.
> BOOMGAARD, 2009, pp. 59–60

In the late eighteenth century, William Marshall wrote about the annual hiring fair for farm laborers in Polesworth in the English West Midlands:

> The number of servants collected together, in the 'statute yard,' has been estimated at two to three thousand. A number, however, which is the less extraordinary, as Polesworth being the only place, in this district, and this the only day,—farm servants, for several miles round, consider themselves as liberated from servitude, on this day.
> MARSHALL, 1796, p. 18

A hundred years later, Peter Ditchfield pointed out that, in Yorkshire and Derbyshire, "statute fairs" used to be very common.

> The servants used to stand in rows, the males together and the females together, and masters and mistresses walked down the lines and selected those whom they considered suitable. The custom seemed to savour of slave-dealing, and the mingling of so many youths and maidens in a strange town without guardianship was not conducive to good morals.
> DITCHFIELD, 1896, p. 247

The tendential decasualization of wage labor meant that long-term employment was no longer the "privilege" of enslaved workers but increasingly involved wage earners. Why was this so? From an economic point of view, two factors deserve attention. The first (microeconomic) factor was already identified several decades ago by John Hicks: the more that free wage labor becomes a general phenomenon, unfree labor becomes more expensive because "they are competing sources: when both are used the availability of one affects the value (wage or capital value) of the other." (Hicks, 1969, p. 132) After all, the maintenance cost of a slave increases as the supply of slaves declines, while, conversely, an increasing number of wage laborers makes this form of labor cheaper. The second factor is macroeconomic: slaves have almost no purchasing power, but wage earners do. Twentieth-century capitalism based on mass consumption was only possible thanks to the growing buying power of the working classes in the metropoles. In fact, wage labor in the metropoles was, from this point of view, *a conditio sine qua non* for advanced capitalist prosperity.

A second trend was also of crucial importance: *the integration of local labor markets*. Apart from markets for mercenaries, free labor markets were mostly local. They were, borrowing a metaphor from the economist Arthur MacEwan, "like clearings in a forest, surrounded by a different and often hostile environment of other forms of socio-economic organization." As the clearings expanded and international trade increased, a network of long-distance connections between the separate clearings began to grow (MacEwan, 1991, pp. 115–116). Initially, this network concerned transport and the transfer of artisanal expertise but gradually it entered agriculture and manufacturing.

From the seventeenth century onward, the relative weight of transcontinental free labor markets grew. This was clearly most evident in the transport sector. One example is the Dutch East India Company that, during its years of operation (1602–1795), "may have sent over 900,000 or nearly a million individuals to the East." In addition, the organization recruited numerous free wage laborers (and slaves) as sailors in Asia, in particular for intra-Asian trade (Lucassen, 2004, p. 17). More in general there has, according to historian Matthias van Rossum, been a clear long-term trend in Asiatic maritime labor markets:

> The labour markets in Europe and Asia became increasingly entangled from 1500 onwards. This happened in partly overlapping stages: from almost entirely separated labour markets in maritime Europe and maritime Asia (before 1500); increasing connections between Asian and European maritime labour markets through intensified intra-Asiatic shipping (1500–1750); increasing integration in intercontinental shipping between Asia and Europe, including the recruitment of Asian sailors (1700–1800); increased and accelerated internationalization of recruitment of maritime labour in shipping in Asia (from the late eighteenth century onwards) and in intercontinental shipping (from the 1830s onwards); and finally, near-complete integration of European and Asian maritime labour markets, and the movement and settlement of Asian and European sailors in both Asia and Europe (1870 onwards).
>
> VAN ROSSUM, 2018, p. 260

During the eighteenth and nineteenth centuries, members of other occupational groups purposefully began to cross the oceans in search of work. Sometimes they kept in touch with their former colleagues in the sending country for a long time. J. T. Cumbler studied the mid-nineteenth century migration of English and Irish textile workers from Lancashire, England to Fall River, Massachusetts: "Lancashire's leading working-class newspaper during the late nineteenth century was the *Cotton Factory Times*. This weekly circulated widely among Lancashire textile workers and was used by workers on both sides of the Atlantic for information concerning the state of the trade, the cost of cotton in New York and New Orleans, wage rates in various sectors of the shire, strikes and union business, as well as political and social news of interest to the working class." (Cumbler, 1980, p. 284) There have been more examples: the skilled Scottish jute workers who, from the 1850s, moved to Bengal and helped to operate new jute factories there; the Belgian and English window glass makers who, in the 1870s and '80s, migrated to the United States; or the Italian workers (*golondrinas*) who seasonally helped with the harvests in Argentina.

The growth and geographical expansion of labor markets was often accompanied by an increasing influence of intermediators—these might be individuals (variously called crimp, jobber, *kangani*, *sirdar*, *baogongtou*, etc.), trade unions, commercial firms (temping agencies), or public institutions (labor exchanges). Intermediators tended to appear wherever "work must be done at many different locations, especially with heavy seasonal demand," or where the potential labor force was very heterogeneous, as in large and international ports (Granovetter, 1995, p. 122; Van der Linden, 1997). In fact, these intermediators have a very long history; they frequently seem to have played a role in ancient Rome, particularly in the transport sector (Mayer-Mali, 1956, p. 28). Labor intermediators reduced the transaction costs involved in labor recruitment. They always did at least one of three things: they recruited potential laborers in places outside the potential employers' information system (if laborers could be found in a huge urban labor pool or in remote places); they preselected potential laborers and thus reduced the employer's risk of hiring a man or woman not fit for the job; and they acted as interpreters in case of communication problems of a linguistic or other nature.

5   Segmentation, Integration, and Expansion

It is well known that labor markets under capitalism are segmented in multiple ways. Back in 1874, economist John E. Cairnes noted:

> What we find, in effect, is not a whole population competing indiscriminately for all occupations, but a series of industrial layers, superposed on one another, within each of which the various candidates for employment possess a real and effective power of selection, while those occupying the several strata are, for all purposes of effective competition, practically isolated from each other.
>
> CAIRNES, 1874, p. 66

However, the history of labor market segmentation goes back much further. We have seen that the markets for *slaves and wage laborers* have always been separate. Moreover, other forms of segmentation have a long history, too. *Gender divisions* are very old, and they have always had an impact on all labor relations. A study of *famuli* and *famulae* (unfree wage-laborers) on English estates in the thirteenth century reveals, for example:

> first, that sex was a major criterion in determining access to most positions; secondly, that there were far fewer opportunities for gainful employment open to women and girls; thirdly, that the *range* of jobs open to women was more restricted than that available to men; fourthly, that most women were recruited to service positions of an unspecified nature (e.g. 'one woman servant'), whereas adult males were usually employed in a specialist function; and finally, that there was a tendency for some women to be employed in personal services. It is among the permanent *famuli*, the unfree wage-labourers, that we find the first clear signs of occupational specialization and discrimination between the sexes that later came to typify free wage-labour under capitalism.
>
> MIDDLETON, 1979, p. 160

A third very old partition, mentioned above, is that separating *casual and permanent labor*, although the boundary between the two segments has not necessarily been impermeable. In China during the Qing period, day laborers "were not fundamentally different from labourers hired by the year; indeed, if there was sufficient demand, they too could become *changgong*" (Shi & Zhuofen, 2000, pp. 144–145).[4] Under capitalism, all these segmentations were maintained and sometimes amplified. For example, there are indications that, in Europe, female wage labor under precapitalist conditions was relatively extensive, then became much reduced, and increased again during the Industrial Revolution (Humphries, 1977; Middleton, 1988, pp. 26–29).

---

4 *Changgong* were workers employed for ten months or a year.

The arrival of the "modern" times of capitalism, colonialism, and nation-state building brought about at least one additional dividing line: the separation of workers according to their *nationalities*. For Europe, Stephan Epstein has argued that

> political integration rather than technical change was the principal driver of market integration after the Black Death. Political integration increased domestic stability, which was the precondition for trade; it established a quasi-customs union between formerly 'foreign' markets and reduced the incidence of local tariffs; it enabled weaker rural communities to establish markets and fairs against urban opposition; it stimulated the rationalization of road networks; and it improved market coordination. Each one of these developments was a result of political bargains, and political structures were therefore decisive for the speed and character of integration.
> EPSTEIN, 2000, p. 167

The national integration of labor markets occurred gradually. For some time, internal national markets remained "simply a loose collection of separate municipal markets" (Wood, 1994, p. 22). And the national borders often remained permeable for a certain period of time. Moreover, the growth of economic inequality between different parts of the world during the nineteenth and twentieth centuries led to a prosperity gap between the Global South and North. In general, it can be observed that "the more advanced a country is economically, the higher-priced will be its indigenous labor force" (Bonacich, 1979, p. 21). This situation, in combination with a growing labor reserve in the South, caused massive migration to the North. In the North, as a result, competition developed between the higher-priced workers of Northern origin and the lower-priced workers from the South. All other things being equal, employers will gravitate to the "cheap" workers since this will bring them higher profits. The higher-priced workers will oppose this. They may block immigration of "cheap" workers (for example, the White Australia policy; the exclusion of Chinese immigrants in California, etc.); they may lock "cheap" workers into certain low-wage sectors of the economy; or they may equalize wage levels by raising the wages of the lower paid workers. The first two options are usually accompanied by racist and xenophobic campaigns. Employers, in turn, can of course react to such strategies by moving their enterprises partly or entirely to runaway shops in the South.

Split labor markets got a further boost due to the rise of Northern welfare state arrangements. From the end of the nineteenth century, states in advanced capitalist countries took various steps to improve social security, such as introducing protective labor legislation and obligatory insurance, regulating working hours, etc. These measures required costly investments that stimulated "social protectionism" against foreign workers; newcomers had to be excluded from expensive social arrangements because they had not yet contributed—or not contributed enough—to financing them.

Through capitalist colonialism this splitting of labor markets began to extend beyond the territories of separate metropolitan nation-states. Matthias von Rossum writes about the maritime labor markets in Asia:

> In the eighteenth century, Asian sailors seem to have had a relatively good bargaining position, apparently better than that of European sailors. From the early nineteenth century onwards, increased European colonial interference in Asian societies—and especially in Asian labour markets—resulted in changing recruitment patterns, the breakdown of the negotiating positions, and the lowering of wages and working conditions for Asian sailors. Undermining the position of Asian sailors, colonial reforms advanced the position of employers and intermediaries, and increased their control over the Asian workforce. [...] Colonialism, in that respect, was not only an important factor in the increasing integration of labour markets, but at the same time in the increasing segmentation of these labour markets.
>
> VAN ROSSUM, 2018, pp. 260–261

The demise of colonialism and the new international division of labor that has spread across the globe since the 1960s have fundamentally changed labor markets. For a start, we have to take note of the increasing share of wage laborers in the world population: the percentage of pure wage dependents ("employees") rose between 1991 and 2018 from over 41 to over 51 percent (see Table 1.2).

The actual world working class, however, is considerably greater than the number of employees; in any case, contributing family members and most of the unemployed should be added to this figure, as well as an unknown share of own-account workers that in fact consists of false self-employed, i.e., those who are formally self-employed but in reality, have only one or two main clients and are therefore directly dependent on them.

Paralleling this trend, growing numbers of workers worldwide maintain direct economic contacts with one another, although many might be unaware of this. Transnationalization of labor processes, which began gradually in the 1960s and accelerated from the 1980s onward, has been crucial in this process. As a result, goods manufactured in one country are increasingly assembled

TABLE 1.2   Composition of the world labor force, 1991 and 2018[a]

	1991		2018	
	Number (1,000s)	%	Number (1,000s)	%
1. Employers (self-employed persons who engage staff on a regular basis)	60,600	2.5	104,000	3.0
2. Employees (persons in paid employment)	995,000	41.5	1,797,600	51.4
3. Contributing family workers (self-employed persons working in an establishment operated by a relative of the same household)	1,204,500	50.3	338,420	9.7
4. Own-account workers (self-employed persons without engaging employees)			1,052,600	30.0
5. Unemployed	134,900	5.6	188,200	5.4
6. Total labor force	2,395,100	99.9	3,498,600	99.5
7. Not in the labor force	1,247,900		2,164,100	

a The figures do not add up to 100 per cent, since members of producer cooperatives and workers not classifiable by status have not been included.
SOURCE: ILO WESO DATA FINDER (<HTTPS://WWW.ILO.ORG/WESODATA>), PLUS CALCULATIONS BY THE AUTHOR

from components produced in other countries, which in turn contain subcomponents made in still other countries. This process—also known as "slicing up" or "unbundling" supply chains—started at about the same time in North America (twin plants in Mexico and the United States) and East Asia, followed somewhat later by Europe, where Spain and Portugal joined the European Union in 1986, and where East European "socialism" collapsed in the early 1990s. Here, a crucial role is played by the Export Processing Zones (EPZs) which have mushroomed globally since 1959. In 1970, only seven countries had EPZs. In 1990, the World Bank counted 86 EPZs in operation in 27 countries, with a total of 533,900 employees. In 2000, the OECD estimated that there were "several hundred" EPZs in China, and observed that outside China, their number had grown from some 500 in 1996 to 850, employing 27 million people (World Bank, 1992; OECD Policy Brief, 2000). The World Free Zones Organization currently counts some 2,200 free zones around the world, with approximately 70 million workers.

Transnationalization has had sweeping effects for the world working class. First, a growing share of employees are part of global supply chains. In 1975, around 725,000 workers in the developing nations were employed in factories producing for the world market, in free production zones, and on other sites. In 1985, such workers numbered "more than 1.8 million, of which well over 50 per cent are women." (Potts, 1990, p. 5) The ILO's *World Economic and Social Outlook 2015* report estimated that

> in 40 countries representing 85 per cent of world gross domestic product and covering approximately two-thirds of the global labor force, the number of global supply chain-related jobs increased by 157 million or 53 per cent between 1995 and 2013, resulting in a total of 453 million global supply chain-related jobs in 2013.
> ILO, 2015

This equates to one-quarter of all employees globally.

While transnationalization has greatly boosted industrialization in the Global South, the jobs created are largely unskilled and substandard and are increasingly—particularly in the Global South—performed by women. The International Trade Union Confederation (ITUC) notes:

> Eighty per cent of world trade and 60% of global production is now captured by the supply chains of multinational companies. The majority of supply chain workers are trapped in insecure and often unsafe jobs with poverty wages and long hours. Informal work forced overtime and slavery are also found in the mix. A recent ITUC report shows that 50 of the world's largest companies directly employ just 6% of the workers in their supply chains—the remaining 94% are part of the hidden workforce of global production.
> <https://www.ituc-csi.org/supply-chains-resources-hub>

Second, international trade has risen considerably because, unlike in the past, goods today are no longer manufactured primarily in one place or, in any case, in one country, and therefore components need to be transferred. One of the consequences of this has been an upsurge in the number of jobs in transport and logistics—emphasizing flexibility and speed across long distances.

International delivery companies such as Fedex, UPS, and DHL have expanded. These corporations now have vast numbers of employees:

> UPS, for example, has a worldwide workforce of 395,000 employees, making it nearly the same size as the 400,000-strong US army. Fedex follows with a worldwide workforce of 300,000 employees, and DHL with 275,000. The combined standing and reserve force of the British army is 80,000.
> ALLEN, 2015

The final factor intensifying economic connections between workers from different parts of the world is migration. While the share of the total cross-border flow of migrants in the world population has been fairly consistent for decades (around three percent), three changes are remarkable. The proportion of international migrants in the world population increased from 2.8% to 3.5% between 2000 and 2020 (IOM 2019, pp. 19–51). According to a study by the World Bank, the proportion of world migration attributable to South–North migration rose from 16 percent to 37 percent between 1960 and 2000. Moreover,

> migrants widen their destination choices. [...] For example, migrants from East Asia and Pacific who once migrated elsewhere within the region now constitute sizable communities across the world. An increasing number of Africans make their homes in Europe and the United States.
> ÖZDEN, PARSONS, SCHIFF, & WALMSLEY, 2011, pp. 15–16

Finally, the share of women in international migration flows is progressively increasing, too. Not only have we witnessed the arrival of a new international division of reproductive labor (domestic servants, sex workers, etc.), but also global migrant streams of skilled women (Ehrenreich & Hochschild, 2002; Kofman & Raghuram, 2006).

These trends are accompanied by a massive return of casual labor markets, both in the industrializing Global South *and* in the Global North. During the twentieth century, in the South, the number of unemployed and underemployed has grown by leaps and bounds, particularly since the 1940s. In the late 1990s, economic historian Paul Bairoch estimated that in Latin America, Africa, and Asia, "total inactivity" was "on the order of 30–40% of potential working man-hours"—a situation without historical precedent, "except perhaps in the case of ancient Rome." (Bairoch, 1997, p. 778) In Europe, North America, and Japan, the average level of unemployment has always been significantly lower. Moreover, it has been determined mainly by the economic conjuncture, and it has therefore been cyclical, while "over-unemployment" in the Global South (this term is used by Bairoch) has a structural character. One of the first analysts who drew attention to this reality was Peruvian sociologist Anibal Quijano, who argued that the tens of millions of permanently "marginalized" workers in the Global South could no longer be regarded as a "reserve army" in the Marxian sense because their social condition lacked any "periodicity" and because they formed no "mass of human material always ready for exploitation," since their abilities were simply not compatible with those required by capitalist industry (Quijano, 1974; Marx, 1976, pp. 785–786). For the poor, begging, prostitution, crime, and casual labor are often the only options.

In the North, the standard employment relationship is currently being broken down—step by step, but somewhat consistently. In his Presidential Address for the American Sociological Association a few years ago, Arne Kalleberg summarized the causes as follows:

> The process that came to be known as neoliberal globalization intensified economic integration, increased the amount of competition faced by companies, provided greater opportunities to outsource work to low-wage countries, and opened up new labor pools through immigration. Technological advances both forced companies to become more competitive globally and made it possible for them to do so. [...] Unions continued to decline, weakening a traditional source of institutional protections for workers and severing the postwar business-labor social contract. Government regulations that set minimum acceptable standards in the labor market eroded, as did rules that governed competition in product markets.
>
> KALLEBERG, 2009

Overall, the balance of power has shifted in favor of employers. In OECD countries, the relative proportion of precarious workers has steadily increased at the same time. A 2004 report of the European Union already concluded "that in most countries precarious employment has increased over the last two decades." (EC, 2004, pp. 58–59) The same applies to the United States and Canada (Tremblay, 2008, p. 121).

Standard employment is becoming rarer in the advanced capitalist countries, and it seems to be even more a male privilege than was the case previously (Benería, 2001; Vosko, MacDonald, & Campbell, 2009). Consequently, labor relations in rich countries are beginning to look more like those in poor countries. *Precarization has become a global trend.* The current demolition of "social capitalism" confirms an insight into long-term developments that István Mészáros has stated as follows:

> The objective reality of *different rates of exploitation*—both within a given country and in the world system of monopoly capital—is as unquestionable as are the objective differences in the *rates of profit* at any particular time [...]. All the same, the reality of the different rates of exploitation and profit does not alter the fundamental law itself: i.e. the growing *equalization* of the differential rates of exploitation as the *global* trend of development of world capital.
>
> MÉSZÁROS, 1995, p. 891

The fierce, increasingly global competition between capitals now has a clear downward "equalizing" effect on the quality of life and work in the more developed parts of global capitalism.

6 Coda

The long movement towards decasualized labor markets seems to have reached its end. Three important trends accompany the rise of transnational labor markets: precarization, integration, and fragmentation. These tendencies are not absolute; there has always been a segment of the labor force with long-term employment (either in the form of slavery or tenured wage labour), and this will probably never change completely. Wage differentials between different segments of the world working class are still very considerable, both in terms of geography and of gender and ethnicity.

Moreover, a historical perspective reveals that labor markets are consistently "messy." In empirical reality, employers persistently combine several methods of labor recruitment, sometimes trying to tie down workers, and sometimes preferring loose connections. Naturally, there are patterns, but these patterns are usually far from law-like. As Sigmund Nosow said long ago: "Those working with labor market phenomena must ultimately face up to the problem that the deviations from the model of the economist are persistent, profound, and inexplicable through reference to this model" (Nosow, 1955, p. 233). Labor markets are very rarely fully transparent, competition is never perfect, and stable equilibrium prices do not exist.

Labor markets are power structures determining barriers for entry, accessibility of information, transactions, and outcomes. They include all forms of laborpower commodification and cannot be studied in isolation but are historically shaped exchange systems, path-dependent, embedded in a societal context, and—under capitalist conditions—linked to other economic subsystems, such as product and financial markets (Patnaik, 2006). If labor economics and labor sociology were to incorporate these insights, an integrated historical social science of commodified labor-power would become possible.

References

Allen, J. (2015). Studying logistics. *Jacobin*, 12 February.
Aspers, P. (2005). Markets, sociology of. In J. Beckert & M. Zafirovski (Eds.), *International Encyclopedia of Economic Sociology* (pp. 427–432). London: Routledge.
Audring, G. (1985). Zur sozialen Stellung der Hirten in archaischer Zeit. In H. Kreißig & F. Kühnert (Eds.), *Antike Abhängigkeitsformen in den griechischen Gebieten ohne Polisstruktur und den römischen Provinzen* (pp. 12–19). Berlin: Akademie-Verlag.
Bairoch, P. (1997). *Victoires et déboires III: Histoire économique et sociale du monde du XVIe siècle à nos jours*. Paris: Gallimard.
Behal, R. (2014). *One Hundred Years of Servitude. Political Economy of Tea Plantations in Colonial Assam*. New Delhi: Tulika.
Benería, L. (2001). Shifting the risk: New employment patterns, informalization, and women's work. *International Journal of Politics, Culture, and Society*, 15(1) (Fall), 27–53.
Bezís-Selfa, J. (1999). A tale of two ironworks: Slavery, free labor, work, and resistance in the Early Republic, *The William and Mary Quarterly*, 56(4) (October), 677–700.
Bonacich, E. (1979). The past, present, and future of split labor market theory, *Research in Race and Ethnic Relations*, 1, 17–64.
Boomgaard, P. (2009). Labour, land, and capital markets in early modern Southeast Asia from the fifteenth to the nineteenth century. *Continuity and Change*, 24(1), 55–78.
Brunt, P. A. (1971). *Italian Manpower, 225 B.C.—A.D. 14*. Oxford: Clarendon Press.
Cairnes, J. E. (1874). *Some Leading Principles of Political Economy Newly Expounded*. London: Macmillan.
Casson, M. & Lee, J. S (2011). The origin and development of markets: A business history perspective. *The Business History Review*, 85(1) (Spring), 9–37.
Cumbler, J. T. (1980). Transatlantic working-class institutions. *Journal of Historical Geography*, 6, 275–290.
De Vries, J. (1993). The labour market. In K. Davids & L. Noordegraaf (Eds.), *The Dutch Economy in the Golden Age. Nine Studies* (pp. 55–78). Amsterdam: NEHA.
Denzer, J. (2005). *Die Konquista der Augsburger Welser-Gesellschaft in Südamerika 1528–1556*. Munich: C.H. Beck.

Ditchfield, P. H. (1896). *Old English Customs, Extant at the Present Time* [...]. London: Methuen.

EC (2004). *Precarious Employment in Europe. A Comparative Study of Labour Market related Risks in Flexible Economies*. Brussels: European Commission.

Ehrenreich, B. & Hochschild, A. R. (Eds.) (2002). *Global Woman: Nannies, Maids and Sex Workers in the New Economy*.

Epstein, S. R. (2000). *Freedom and Growth. The Rise of States and Markets in Europe, 1300–1750*. London, New York: Routledge.

Fuks, A. (1951). κολωνος μισθιος: Labour exchange in classical Athens. *Eranos, 49*, 171–173.

Furåker, B. (2005). *Sociological Perspectives on Labor Markets*. Houndmills, New York: Palgrave Macmillan.

Galenson, D. (1981). *White Servitude in Colonial America. An Economic Analysis*. Cambridge: Cambridge University Press.

Golombek, L. (1996). Timurid potters abroad, *Oriente Moderno*, New Series, *15*(2), 577–586.

Granovetter, M. (1995). *Getting a Job. A Study of Contacts and Careers*. Chicago: The University of Chicago Press.

Habib, I. (1995). *Essays in Indian History. Towards a Marxist Perception*. New Delhi: Tulika.

Harris, W. V. (1980). Towards a study of the Roman slave trade. *Memoirs of the American Academy in Rome*, 36, 117–140.

Hay, D. & Craven, P. (Eds.), *Masters, Servants, and Magistrates in Britain and the Empire, 1562–1955*. Chapel Hill: University of North Carolina Press.

Hicks, J. R. (1969). *A Theory of Economic History*. London: Oxford University Press.

Honoré, A. M. (1961). Ownership. In A. G. Guest (Ed.), *Oxford Essays in Jurisprudence. A Collaborative Work* (pp. 107–147). Oxford: Clarendon Press.

Humphries, J. (1977). Class struggle and the persistence of the working-class family. *Cambridge Journal of Economics, 1* (September 1977), 242–258.

ILO (2015). *World Employment and Social Outlook 2015: The Changing Nature of Jobs*. Geneva, ILO.

IOM (2019). *World Migration Report 2020*. Geneva, IOM.Empire.

Ivleva, T. (2016). Peasants into soldiers: Recruitment and military mobility in the early Roman Empire. In L. de Ligt & L. E. Tacoma (Eds.), *Migration and Mobility in the Early Roman Empire* (pp. 158–175). Leiden, Boston: Brill.

Kalleberg, A. L. (2009). Precarious work, insecure workers: Employment relations in transition. *American Sociological Review, 74* (February), 1–22.

Kaplan, S. (1988). Les corporations, les 'faux ouvriers' et le faubourg Saint-Antoine au XVIIIe siècle. *Annales. Histoire, Sciences Sociales, 43*(2) (March-April), 353–378.

Kaur, A. (2004). *Wage Labour in Southeast Asia since 1840. Globalisation, the International Division of Labour and Labour Transformations.* Basingstoke: Palgrave Macmillan.

Keiser, T. (2013a). *Vertragszwang und Vertragsfreiheit im Recht der Arbeit von der Frühen Neuzeit bis in die Moderne.* Frankfurt am Main: Vittorio Klostermann.

Kofman, E. & Raghuram, P. (2006). Gender and global labour migrations: Incorporating skilled workers, *Antipode, 38*(2) (March), 282–303.

Lal, B. V. (1983). *Girmitiyas. The Origins of the Fiji Indians.* Canberra: Journal of Pacific History Monograph.

Lal, B. V. (2006). The Indenture system. In B. V. Lal (Ed.), *The Encyclopedia of the Indian Diaspora* (pp. 48–53). Singapore: Editions Didier Millet.

Laube, A. (1975). Zum problem des Bündnisses von Bergarbeitern und Bauern im deutschen Bauernkrieg. In G. Heitz, A. Laube, M. Steinmetz, & G. Vogler (Eds.), *Der Bauer im Klassenkampf. Studien zur Geschichte des deutschen Bauernkrieges und der bäuerlichen Klassenkämpfe im Spätfeudalismus* (pp. 83–110). Berlin: Akademie-Verlag.

Leupp, G. P. (1992). *Servants, Shophands, and Laborers in the Cities of Tokugawa Japan.* Princeton: Princeton University Press.

Lewis, M. E. (1990). *Sanctioned Violence in Early China.* Albany, NY: SUNY Press.

Lovejoy, P. E. (2000). *Transformations in Slavery. A History of Slavery in Africa.* Second Edition. Cambridge: Cambridge University Press.

Lucassen, J. (2004). A multinational and its labor force: The Dutch East India Company, 1595–1795, *International Labor and Working-Class History, No. 66*(Fall), 12–39.

Lucassen, J. (2018). Wage labour. In K. Hofmeester & M. van der Linden (Eds.), *Handbook of the Global History of Work* (pp. 395–409). Berlin: Walter de Gruyter.

MacEwan, A. (1991). What's 'new' about the 'new international economy'?, *Socialist Review, 21*(3–4) (July-December), 111–131.

Marshall, W. (1796). *The Rural Economy of the Midland Counties [...].* Second Edition, Vol. II. London: G. Nicol et al.

Marx, K. (1976). *Capital*, Vol. I. Trans. B. Fowkes. Harmondsworth: Penguin.

Mathias, R. (2011). Japan in the seventeenth century: Labour relations and work ethics. In K. Hofmeester & C. Moll-Murata (Eds.), *The Joy and Pain of Work: Global Attitudes and Valuations, 1500–1650* (pp. 217–243). Cambridge: Cambridge University Press.

Mayer-Mali, T. (1956). *Locatio conductio. Eine Untersuchung zum klassischen römischen Recht.* Vienna and Munich: Herold.

Mbodj, M. (1993). The abolition of slavery in Senegal, 1820–1890: Crisis or the rise of a new entrepreneurial class? In M. A. Klein (Ed.), *Breaking the Chains. Slavery, Bondage, and Emancipation in Modern Africa and Asia* (pp. 197–213). Madison: University of Wisconsin Press.

McConnell, C. R., Brue, S. L., & Macpherson, D. A. (2017), *Contemporary Labor Economics. Eleventh Edition.* New York: McGraw-Hill.

McKeown, A. (2004). Global Migration, 1846–1940. *Journal of World History*, 15 (2) (June), 155–189.

Mendelsohn, I. (1943). Free artisans and slaves in Mesopotamia, *Bulletin of the American Schools of Oriental Research*, No. 89 (February), 25–29.

Mészáros, I. (1995). *Beyond Capital. Towards a Theory of Transition*. London: Merlin Press.

Middleton, C. (1979). The sexual division of labour in feudal England, *New Left Review*, *113–114* (January-April), 147–168.

Middleton, C. (1988). The familiar fate of the *famulae*: Gender divisions in the history of wage labour. In R. E. Pahl (Ed.), *On Work. Historical, Comparative and Theoretical Approaches* (pp. 21–47). Oxford: Blackwell.

Moll-Murata, C. (2011). Work ethics and work valuations in a period of commercialization: Ming China, 1500–1644. In K. Hofmeester & C. Moll-Murata (Eds.), *The Joy and Pain of Work: Global Attitudes and Valuations, 1500–1650* (pp. 165–195). Cambridge: Cambridge University Press.

Nagata, M. L. (2005). *Labour Contracts and Labor Relations in Early Modern Central Japan*. London: Routledge.

Nöldeke, T., (1892) A servile war in the East. In T. Nöldeke, *Sketches from Eastern History*. Trans. J. Sutherland Black (pp. 146–175). London & Edinburgh: Adam and Charles Black.

North, D. C. (1977). Markets and other allocative systems in history: The challenge of Karl Polanyi. *Journal of European Economic History*, 6, 703–716.

Nosow, S. (1955). Toward a theory of the labor market, *Social Forces* 33(3) (March), 218–224.

Nunn, N. (2008). The long-term effects of Africa's slave trades. *Quarterly Journal of Economics*, 123(1), 139–176.

OECD Policy Brief (2000). *International Trade and Core Labour Standards*. Paris: OECD.

Osterhammel, J. (1997). *Colonialism. A Theoretical Overview*. Trans. S. L. Frisch. Princeton: Markus Wiener.

Özden, Ç., Parsons, C. R., Schiff, M. & W., Walmsley, T. L. (2011). Where on Earth is everybody? The Evolution of global bilateral migration 1960–2000. *The World Bank Economic Review*, 25(1), 12–56.

Pamuk, Ş. (2009). Changes in factor markets in the Ottoman Empire, 1500–1800. *Continuity and Change*, 24(1) 107–136.

Pan, L. (1998). Patterns of migration. In L. Pan (Ed.), *The Encyclopedia of the Chinese Overseas* (pp. 60–63). Richmond: Curzon Press.

Patnaik, P. (2006). The labour market under capitalism. *Social Scientist*, 34(1–2) (January-February), 9–20.

Pierenkemper, T. (2009). Der Auf- und Ausbau eines ‚Normalarbeitsverhältnisses' in Deutschland im 19. und 20. Jahrhundert. In R. Walter (Ed.), *Geschichte der*

Arbeitsmärkte. Erträge der 22. Arbeitstagung der Gesellschaft für Sozial- und Wirtschaftsgeschichte 11. bis 14. April 2007 in Wien (pp. 77–112). Stuttgart: Franz Steiner Verlag.

Popovic, A. (1999). *The Revolt of African Slaves in Iraq, in the 3rd/9th Century*. Trans. Léon King. Princeton: Markus Wiener Publishers.

Potts, L. (1990). *The World Labour Market. A History of Migration*. London: Pluto Press.

Probert, A. (1969). Bartolomé de Medina: The patio process and the sixteenth century silver crisis. *Journal of the West*, 8(1) 90–124.

Pulleyblank, E. G. (1958). The origins and nature of chattel slavery in China. *Journal of the Economic and Social History of the Orient*, 1(2) (April), 185–220.

Quijano Obregón, A. (1974). The marginal pole of the economy and the marginalised labour force, *Economy and Society*, 3(4) (November), 393–428.

Rawski, E. S. (1972). *Agricultural Change and the Peasant Economy of South China*. Cambridge, MA: Harvard University Press.

Rediker, M. (1987). *Between the Devil and the Deep Blue Sea. Merchant Seamen, Pirates, and the Anglo-American Maritime World, 1700–1750*. Cambridge: Cambridge University Press.

Roy, T. (2009). Factor markets and the narrative of economic change in India, 1750–1950, *Continuity and Change* 24(1) 137–167.

Samkoff, A. (2014). From Central Asia to Anatolia: The transmission of the black-line technique and the development of pre-Ottoman tilework. *Anatolian Studies*, 64, 199–215.

Schechter, P. A. (1994). Free and slave labor in the Old South: The Tredegar Ironworkers' Strike of 1847. *Labor History*, 35, 165–186.

Schoenberger, E. (2008). The origins of the market economy: State power, territorial control, and modes of war fighting. *Comparative Studies in Society and History*, 50(3) 663–691.

Shi Qi & Fang Zhuofen (2000). Capitalism in agriculture in the early and middle Qing Dynasty. In Xu Dixin & Wu Chengming (Eds.), *Chinese Capitalism, 1522–1840* (pp. 113–162). Houndsmills: Basingstoke.

Smith, A. (1776). *An Inquiry into the Nature and Causes of the Wealth of Nations*. Vol. I. London: W. Strahan & T. Cadell.

Stanziani, A. (2014). *Bondage. Labor and Rights in Eurasia from the Sixteenth to the Early Twentieth Centuries*. New York & Oxford: Berghahn.

Steffen, C. G. (1979). The pre-industrial iron worker: Northampton Iron Works, 1780–1820. *Labor History*, 20, 89–110.

Stolcke, V. & Hall, M. M. (1983). The introduction of free labour on Sao Paulo's coffee plantations. *Journal of Peasant Studies*, 10(2–3) (January-April), 170–200.

Strabo (1950). *The Geography of Strabo*. With an English Translation by Horace Leonard Jones, Vol. VI. Cambridge, MA: Harvard University Press & London: William Heinemann.

Tedesco, P. (2018). 'The missing factor': Economy and labor in late Roman North Africa (400–600 CE), *Journal of Late Antiquity, 11*(2) (Fall), 396–431.

Temin, P. (2013). *The Roman Market Economy*. Princeton: Princeton University Press.

Tilly, C. (1984). Demographic origins of the European proletariat. In D. Levine (Ed.), *Proletarianization and Family History* (pp. 1–85). Orlando: Academic Press.

Tinker, H. (1974). *A New System of Slavery. The Export of Indian Labour Overseas, 1830–1920*. London and New York: Oxford University Press.

Tremblay, D.-G. (2008). From casual work to economic security: The paradoxical case of self-employment. *Social Indicators Research, 88*(1) (August), 115–130.

van Bavel, B. J. P. (2011). Markets for land, labor, and capital in Northern Italy and the Low Countries, twelfth to seventeenth centuries, *The Journal of Interdisciplinary History, 41*(4) (Spring), 503–531.

van der Linden, M. (1997). Notes from an outsider. In P. C. van Royen, J. R. Bruijn, & J. Lucassen (Eds.), *"Those Emblems of Hell"? European Sailors and the Maritime Labour Market, 1570–1870* (pp. 349–362). St. John, Nfdl.: International Maritime Economic History Association.

van der Linden, M. (2008). *Workers of the World. Essays toward a Global Labor History*. Leiden and Boston: Brill.

van Rossum, M. (2018). Changing tides. Maritime labour relations in Europe and Asia. In K. Hofmeester & P. de Zwart (Eds.), *Colonialism, Institutional Change and Shifts in Global Labour Relations* (pp. 239–264). Amsterdam: Amsterdam University Press, 2018.

Varma, N. (2017). *Coolies of Capitalism. Assam Tea and the Making of Coolie Labour*. Berlin: Walter de Gruyter.

Vosko, L. F., MacDonald, M., & Campbell, I. (Eds.) (2009). *Gender and the Contours of Precarious Employment*. New York: Routledge.

Wareing, J. (2017). *Indentured Migration and the Servant Trade from London to America, 1618–1718*. Oxford: Oxford University Press.

Weber, W., & Mayer-Maly, T. (1954). Studie zur spätmittelalterlichen Arbeitsmarkt- und Wirtschaftsordnung. *Jahrbücher für Nationalökonomie und Statistik, 166*, 358–389.

Whitman, T. S. (1993). Industrial slavery at the margin: The Maryland Chemical Works, *Journal of Southern History, 59*, 31–62.

Wickham, C. (2005). *Framing the Early Middle Ages. Europe and the Mediterranean, 400–800*. Oxford: Oxford University Press.

Wood, E. M. (1994). From opportunity to imperative: The history of the market, *Monthly Review, 46*(3) (July-August), 14–40.

World Bank (1992). Industry and development division, *Export Processing Zones.* Washington, DC: World Bank.

CHAPTER 2

Free Wage Labor as the Most System-Relevant Mode for Allocating Work under Capitalism

Thomas Welskopp

1   Introduction: Free Wage Labor as the Key Element of Capitalist Productivism

This chapter takes on the task of solving the conundrum of why most theoretical approaches to capitalism declare "free" wage labor to be the dominant and congenial mode of allocation of the expenditure of labor power in this arrangement of economic activities, whereas obviously many other, "unfree," modes of the allocation of work have persisted from the past and new forms of constrained or even bonded labor have reemerged ever since (van der Linden, 2008; Welskopp, 2017b).

On the one hand, a variety of ways of allocating labor persisted simply because of the opportunistic character of capitalism. Thus, arrangements of labor relations, however free or unfree, have always been—and still are to this day—colonized from the outside by capital owners shying away from the intention to directly intervene in and reshape these production regimes as long as they are perceived to be working satisfactorily. On the other hand, the intrusion of capitalism into the spheres of production in the core countries of development brought about the fundamental *subjectification* of the position of workers since the socially closed sphere of the shop floor, resilient to these attempts at intrusion, eventually forced capitalists to (albeit grudgingly) respect, acknowledge, or even embrace their employees' workplace skills, dexterity, and abilities in the collective self-organization of production. The legally protected labor contract has to all intents and purposes been the most significant marker of this development, although this institutional arrangement had to be fought for globally in difficult disputes, tough collective bargaining, numerous lawsuits, and extensive—sometimes violent—industrial warfare. And it has never been uncontested to date.

Nevertheless, the conflict between capital and labor concerning commitment either to high-trust or suspicion-based regimes of work has still not been resolved definitively anywhere and instead has perpetuated the potentially explosive degree of tension in the productive antagonism I claim both to be central to the capitalist class relation and to be the force behind the huge surge in productivity that characterizes industrial capitalism. Indicators of the recent proliferation of attempts to retain—or return to—constrained or bonded labor regimes are, for example, discriminatory mechanisms for subliminally forcing labor relations, after a relatively free labor contract is concluded, toward increasingly restrictive conditions of employment at a later stage. A strong marker for this type of constellation is, for instance, measures to isolate a migrant workforce from their social resources by curtailing their right to free movement in the host country (Sarkar, 2017). This could be referred to as constrained labor, not as opposed to bonded labor but rather as the connecting part of a continuum ranging from free wage labor at one extreme to unfree labor at the other.

2   Relevance for the Sociological and Historical Analysis of Labor Markets

Irrespective of how large the share of free wage labor has ever been or currently is compared to all paid employment relations, and regardless of the meaning of "free" at different times and in different circumstances, it should be of relevance for understanding the issue of whether and how free wage labor is theoretically linked to capitalism. The question that arises is whether free wage labor, as Karl Marx and Max Weber attempted to demonstrate, is a defining element of capitalism as its dominant system-specific mode of allocating work.

This clarification seems to be necessary at a time when scholars of global labor history have been increasingly researching the most diverse forms of unfree labor in the past and present, with a special focus on the most disturbing regimes of exploitation and their social consequences that have come to light as recently as the past ten years. However, the flipside of this—certainly indispensable—research trend has been to neglect the question of what free wage labor actually was and still is. Even the majority of labor historians, scholars of industrial relations, and sociologists of work whose undisputed premise has for decades taken free wage labor to be the norm in capitalist employment relations are at a loss when asked to bring their tacit convictions in line with the findings of the new global labor history.

Yet this leaves us with a situation in which free wage labor as a kind of Weberian "ideal type" is either marginalized as the irreal "other" of the empirically identifiable realities of employment relations all over the world (including the traditional West) which are found essentially unfree. According to this reading, the notion of freedom is merely an ideological veil camouflaging the empirical fact that all dependent employment relationships are by definition unfree. This leads, on the one hand, to the contention that there is in fact no systematic interrelation between capitalism and free wage labor. This is sometimes bolstered by the claim that somehow free labor already existed several thousand years BC and has simply been with us ever since. On the other hand, employment relations deemed to be free are considered to not to be so free after all under closer scrutiny. Thus, if taken literally as freedom from all obligations, only casual or precarious labor counts as free whereas any commitments remove the element of freedom. Finally, even if critics concede that there has been a core of free employment relations developed in the West which experienced its heyday during the three decades of economic boom after the war, they still view it as nothing more than a short episode and always a minority epiphenomenon within capitalist development.

3   Marx and Weber's Concept of Free Wage Labor

The sharp polarization of positions may result from considerable confusion about how to understand the term "free." In most statements, freedom is perceived as a coherent, irreducible whole and basically used as a synonym for liberty. This loosely corresponds to the various classical liberal notions of personal or individual freedom although it should be noted at this early stage of my argument that, in liberal doctrines of this kind, individual independence based on profession and property is viewed as the precondition for and not the consequence of civil liberty. Yet it is difficult to sustain such an idealization when analyzing capitalist employment relations.

Let us not forget that Marx's definition of the "two freedoms" of the worker under capitalism has a decidedly sarcastic undertone:

> For the transformation of money into capital the money owner must be able [...] to locate the free worker in the commodity market, free in the dual sense that he has at command his labour power as his commodity as a free person [and] that he—on the other hand—lacks alternative commodities to sell, void and unbound, free from all means necessary to implement his labour power [by and for himself—T.W.].
>
> MARX, 1981, p. 183

In an argument based primarily on the question of individual motivation in capitalism, Weber makes a stunningly similar observation: The market transaction economy appeals to a disproportionally more intensive degree to the self-interest and enforces the freedom of selection according to efficiency [...] (of course: oriented at profitability) [and] therefore appears to be formally more rational (in the sense of the technical optimum) than any unmediated compulsion to work. This is conditional on the expropriation of the workers from all means of production and their relegation to the competition for open positions which entail remuneration by wage work, which means: the protection of the appropriation of the means of production by private proprietors.

> WEBER, 1980, pp. 86–87

For Marx, the positive effect of the existence of free wage labor is mainly focused on the fact that it transforms labor power into a commodity whose utilization is, for him, a key prerequisite for money owners to become able to turn into capitalists:

> The [...] precondition that the money owner can locate labour power as a commodity in the market is that its proprietor, instead of being able to sell commodities in which his work has been objectified, has to peddle his labour power itself as a commodity which only exists in his lively bodiliness.
>
> MARX, 1981, p. 183

The legal freedom of the worker makes it possible to draw a distinction between his person ("lively bodiliness") and his labor power and thereby enables him to act as a fully entitled market actor who can sell his labor power for a specified time and against financial remuneration to a capitalist buyer.

This transaction is sealed by a "free" contract:

> Labour power [can] enter the market as a commodity only insofar and because it is peddled or sold as a commodity by its own proprietor, the person whose labour power it is. For that its proprietor can sell it as a commodity, it is necessary that he has it at his command, that is to be the free owner of his labour capacity, his person. He and the money owner encounter each other in the market and enter into a mutual relationship on par with each other, distinguished only insofar that the one is the buyer, the other one seller, ergo that both are legally equal persons.
>
> MARX, 1981, pp. 181–182

Furthermore, for Marx, the unfettered freedom of the seller of his labor power was an essential precondition for a distinction between the laborer as a person, a human being, and his potential to expend his labor power. This was not only an advantage for the worker in terms of his self-image as a legally fully entitled (and protected) citizen—although this remained an imaginary concept for the majority of workers in the West for much of the nineteenth century—but also for the capitalists since their calculation of the most efficient production process in centralized manufacturing facilities relied on the figure of thought of "pure working activity" throughout working hours. This ideal was, of course, never attainable in reality since labor power can by no means be separated from the human being attached to it. "The continuation of this relationship," Marx wrote,

> requires that the owner of his labour power sells it only for a specified time-span, since if he sold it outright he would mutate from a free man into a slave, from a commodity owner into a commodity. He as a person must permanently relate to his labour power as his property and therefore his own commodity, and he is only able to do this insofar he conveys it to the buyer invariably on a temporary basis only for consumption, that is he does not relinquish it as his property.
> MARX, 1981, pp. 181–182

Weber expressed this phenomenon more bluntly and more precisely with a stronger emphasis on both the gain of discretionary freedom on the side of the employers and the opportunity to transfer social costs to the (private) sphere outside of the factory premises:

> Juxtaposed in opposition to the unmediated compulsion to work - care for the reproduction (family) and a part of the concern for selection (following the requirements for qualification) is here shifted to the persons in search of work themselves. Furthermore the capital demand as well as the capital risk is limited versus the utilisation of unfree labour and made more calculable. ...
> WEBER, 1980, p. 78

For Weber, free wage labor means a surplus of formal rationality and, therefore, modernity for capitalism

> by means of—under otherwise identical circumstances—a more pronounced shop floor rationality in terms of the free disposition of

management over the selection and allocation of workers, in contrast [...] to the emerging technically irrational barriers to progress and economic irrationalities, especially the interference by external private household and sustenance considerations. (p. 78)

Acknowledgement of the worker's personal freedom by the capitalist employer thus theoretically served the latter's interests best—although it took a long time of struggles, conflicts, and legal interventions if not to persuade the employers, then at least make them comply. Moreover, Marx starkly contrasts the formal "freedom" of settling the contract between the worker and future employer at least on paper and the remorseless tyranny the worker had to expect once passing through the factory gate:

> The former money owner takes the lead as a capitalist, the owner of labour power trails him as his worker; the one chuckling cryptically and keen on business; the other one shy, reluctant, like someone who has put his neck to risk and now has nothing to expect but a—brutal tanning.
> MARX, 1981, p. 191

Weber argued in a similar vein. Yet he was less interested in the labor market and contracts as legal and social institutions but more in how to force workers to work to capacity:

> Yet willingness to work (in the specific meaning of the execution of own dispositions or of those [ordered by] superiors) has always been determined by either a strong self-interest to achieve success or indirect respectively direct compulsion; to a very high degree work in the sense of the execution of disposition of others. This compulsion can consist in first the outright threat of physical force or other detriments, or second in the latent threat of unemployment in case of insufficient performance.—In the capitalist system, the most immediate bases of willingness to work are opportunities for high piece-rate earnings and the danger of dismissal.
> WEBER, 1980, p. 86

Finally, the separation of workplace and home, combined with the employers' ideal of ridding the shop floor of any interference due to workers' lifeworld needs which management attempted to enforce inside the workshops—albeit in vain—made it imperative for urban workers in particular to provide for their livelihoods through individual consumption. For Marx, this meant the closure of an economic system that turns even the basic needs of the common people into a major source of profit: "Production does not only provide want with material but provides material with a want. [...] Therefore, production produces not only a commodity for the subject but also a subject for the commodity" (Marx, 1983, p. 467). Weber saw in this a powerful propellant for the continued expansion of a fully developed market society: free wage labor was essential to capitalism because only the spread "of cash wages—promotes the expansion of the market for mass-produced goods" (Weber, 1980, p. 87).

On the one hand, Marx and Weber are both unequivocal in emphasizing the central systematic role of free wage labor in capitalism. For them, this is essential for conceiving a feasible theory of capitalism as the dominant mode of production in modern societies. Also, both insist on the systematic distinction between free and unfree labor in clear terms which might be helpful for a more sophisticated empirical analysis. Their main points are that there is a mode of allocating labor under capitalism which can be referred to as free labor, *that it is of strategic importance* for the modes of economic activity that constitute capitalism as a continuous flow of the interaction of diverse patterns of practice, and *that there is a qualitative difference* between free and unfree labor despite, as will be shown below, certain tendencies to converge within a large, complex, and shady middle ground.

On the other hand, the analysis has clearly demonstrated that "freedom" in the context of wage labor has never been a fixed term with an unambiguous meaning (Brass, 2014; Lucassen, 2018). On closer inspection, it is easy to get the impression that what we have here—as in other cases—is an empty signifier that circumscribes a contested terrain where many conflicting interpretations, projections, and claims have been colliding. This could give us some indication of why labor relations under capitalism have always been hotly debated and passionately disputed. The two more strongly opposing interpretations can be summarized by saying that for the employee "free wage labor" implies unrestricted freedom of movement, including choice of employment positions, whereas employers claim for themselves it means "freedom from" any form of responsibility for the worker as an individual outside the factory gates, including his physical integrity and social reproduction.

Not only does this concept of freedom fail to ring true with any association of liberty but it also points toward some kind of void, of the worker being left out in the cold to fend for himself. There is empirical evidence indicating that, in this and some other respects, "unfree" laborers might have been and might still be somewhat better off than their formally "free" colleagues. As Jean-Paul Sartre put it in 1943:

> I am responsible for everything [...] except for my very responsibility, for I am not the foundation of my being. Therefore, everything takes place as if I were compelled to be responsible. I am abandoned in the world ... in the sense that I find myself suddenly alone and without help, engaged in a world for which I bear the whole responsibility without being able, whatever I do, to tear myself away from this responsibility for an instant. (Sartre, 1956, Part 4, Chap. 1, III)

4 Free Wage Labor and the Transformative Experience of Self-Efficacy

I would like to advance the argument that the ideas and debates about the question of free wage work have accompanied the dawn of modern society. They have been a symptom of as well as a contributing factor to the overwhelmingly encompassing processes of *subjectification* on the new basis of the individual instead of within a social estate, a caste, a guild, or other clearly delineated and often legally defined collective entities (Reckwitz, 2006). Bourgeois society has, as is well known, created the whole ideology of liberalism around this complex of social change. The basic unit of liberal society was to be the individualistic individual, the (male) person independent from everyone and everything, supporting his claim to full political citizenship with/by private property or an elite education, and free to join others in—by definition—voluntary associations. Marx gleefully mocked the habit of competing political economists to make Robinsonades their basic unit and the point of departure of their theories.

He insisted that the ascent and recognition of the individual as a self-reliant person was only possible when the density of social relations and therefore embeddedness of the individual in society was most developed. Thus, according to Marx, the individual had emerged in a historical process that brought about modern society where—among other trends—the flows of communication had spread and accelerated on an unprecedented scale:

> Only in the eigthteenth century, in 'civil society', do the various forms of social connectedness confront the individual as a mere means towards his private purposes, as external necessity. But the epoch which produces this standpoint, that of the isolated individual, is also precisely that of the hitherto most developed social (from this standpoint, general) relations. The human being is in the most literal sense a *zoon politikon*, not merely

> a gregarious animal but an animal which can individuate itself only in the midst of society.
>
> MARX, 1983, p. 467

Thus, individualism only appears as the bourgeois ideological processing of impressions from and effects of a much wider, multifaceted structural change connected to the gradual spread of patterns of practice that are associated with bringing about modernity. The most important theoretical consequence for the question of free wage labor—a consequence that Marx only used as an argument to a very limited extent when speaking about the free market contract between worker and capitalist—is that *subjectification,* or *individuation* in modern society and its diverse modes of interaction has never been a bourgeois privilege but has always encompassed large and growing sections of society—including the workforce.

It follows on from this that all problems linked to different notions of freedom in the context of capitalist employment relations have been to date and still are multiple and often contested attempts by all sides to come to grip with the promises, challenges, and—frequently contradictory—real effects of *individuation*. This removes much of the unwarranted idealism from the notion of "freedom": it does not simply mean "liberty" in this context. For workers, *individuation* on the positive side promises independence from personal bonds, freedom of movement, self-reliance inside and outside the workplace, the right to team up in free associations, public appreciation of the value of their work, and recognition as fully entitled individuals and citizens (Welskopp, 2013).

Thus, this theory may be advanced as the answer to the initial question as to how far free wage labor is systematically endemic to the working of capitalism as a dominant mode of economic practice in modern society. This means of allocating labor has proved able to perform as the engine to the exponential growth of productivity that has marked the age of industrial capitalism since the beginning of the nineteenth century. Although sometimes contested, the multiplying communicative, organizational, and skill requirements of complex production processes has called for–or even presupposed existing arrangements of–a self-initiative and self-responsibility on the part of wage workers that has been transferred into new and overwhelming experiences of self-efficacy on the shop floor.

The emergence of a producers' ethics is testimony to how this experience has transformed workers from servants into socially and politically conscious subjects claiming recognition as bargaining agents and political citizens. Pride in skills, technical knowledge, specialized dexterity, combined with a strong sense of esprit de corps and camaraderie, has been observed in the core industries of industrializing countries worldwide. Here, the origins of the formation of strong shop floor-based unions and labor parties were much further removed from the point of production, the resources for strikes, and other forms of industrial strife, and the claim to civic respectability. Of course, the degree to which individuation translated into actual semi-autonomy on the shop floor or—beyond the factory gates—into a contentious program for social and political action varied over time and across a broad spectrum of industry-specific labor regimes. It also differed when viewed from a gendered perspective. However, there are clearly identifiable trends in the history of female employment that point in the same direction (Welskopp, 2019).

Yet, on the downside of *individuation*, the risks of having been disembedded from social safety nets traditionally provided by guilds, estates, masters, and higher authorities have loomed large particularly during the initial phases of industrialization in the West. The separation of workplace and home makes the organization of reproduction work a private affair, externalizing potential costs and risks for employers and placing the full burden of providing for their families on the workers themselves. Freedom of contract subjects the individual worker to the unmediated pressures of the business cycle. It is much easier to dismiss a redundant employee who is free as a person than to get rid of a serf. And finally, ideally, *individuation* places the individual worker in an unrestricted competition—with other workers but also with other means of allocating work (such as convict labor, forced labor, etc.) (Lichtenstein, 1996; Mancini, 1996). This unfettered exposure to competition was one of the main targets of the emerging international labor movement in the second half of the nineteenth century (Reick, 2015).

5   Points of Departure for Further Research

Using the concept of *individuation* as a key to the question of free wage labor opens multiple avenues of future research to empirically enrich the study of past and present labor markets. Thus, a vast body of existing scholarship on the history of work, of workers on the shop floor, on workplace solidarity, and on the formation or non-formation of unions that has lacked a common focus to date can be easily integrated into a more systematic synthesis contributing to a comprehensive historical theory of capitalism (Welskopp, 2017a). This requires a detailed analysis of past and present workplace and industrial relations—the "working parts" in the machine called capitalist class relations—under the auspices of trust-based versus suspicion-based low-trust labor regimes, the multiple transformations from one into the other and the fragile, transient compromises that are the effects of both cooperative and confrontative practices on the shop floor almost universally.

In addition, and in a complementary sense, the protracted and conflict-ridden historical process of the implementation and sustained establishment of free wage labor in the Western core regions of capitalist industrialization can be studied in a more refined and focused way. The perspective proposed here allows us to gain a much better understanding of the motivations, goals, perceptions, and resources of all groups of actors involved in this struggle as well as on the historical force of unintended consequences of social practices.

Finally, a synchronic and diachronic comparison of historical and current employment regimes under capitalism across the vast spectrum they cover over space and time will be possible and productive by using the concept of free wage labor as discussed here as an analytical benchmark for the development of a historical typology. This form of typology can serve as a heuristic to explore the diverse means of allocating labor in history and at present, with labor markets perhaps always having constituted a minor share only when viewed from both a socially segmental and a global angle.

Figure 2.1 shows my preliminary attempt to sketch such a typological heuristic. It is too complex to elaborate further in detail here, not only for reasons of space but also because it is still in the early stages of a program for a future research agenda. The heuristic serves, first, to do justice to the fact that labor regimes do not normally fit neatly into the one extreme of completely free wage labor or the other of completely unfree labor. Consequently, I have inserted two additional main categories: bonded and constrained labor which are intended to depict, on the one hand, the importance of personal bonds in shaping labor regimes even beyond outright slavery, and, on the other hand, the tendency to erode free contractual relations by situational constraints of a political, legal, racist, gender discriminatory, or regulatory (migration) nature (Sarkar, 2017, pp. 171–204).

The second dimension of this heuristic scheme concerns the historical perspective. I have attempted to sketch possible corridors of historical developments and connections which are, at this point, still hypothetical. Yet the integration of labor regimes governed by state institutions that hold legally unfree inmates in their custody and lease them out to private employers temporarily has already proven surprisingly productive, and the fact that this pattern of allocating labor is one of the three strands of the continuation of chattel slavery can already be established empirically. This is highly relevant for highlighting the assumption that free wage labor and the various shades of unfree labor may overlap in certain historical circumstances but that they have clearly distinct roots and there is one fundamental distinction. Whereas unfree

FREE WAGE LABOR AND CAPITALISM

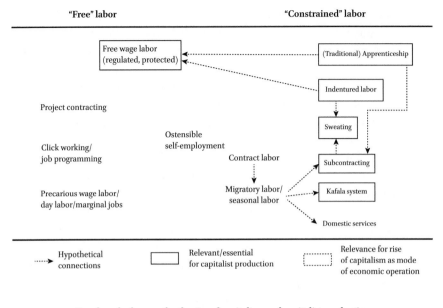

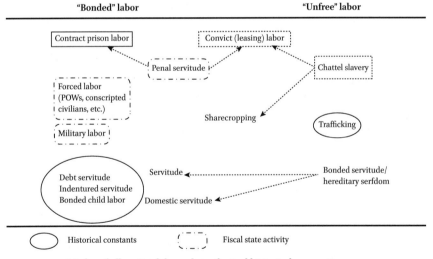

FIGURE 2.1 Modes of allocating labor—hypothetical historical connections
SOURCE: CREATED BY AUTHOR

regimes comprise the whole individual held in slavery or servitude, and work arrangements are only one—albeit important—aspect of the allocation of the individual's productive capacity, the work of free wage laborers is the main—if not only—subject of contractual labor relations, regardless of whether other aspects of the personality or livelihood of these persons are affected or infringed upon by their working conditions. Thus, economic dependency may be just as harsh even though it is not the same as legal deprivation and physical coercion.

Third, this heuristic could serve as a blueprint for research on the historical distinction between wage work and service (derived from servitude). This is largely uncharted territory and therefore constitutes a considerable challenge. Yet such an undertaking could well contribute to eliminating the conceptual confusion in the contested terrain of the history of work—and ultimately clarify what we find when we look for labor markets proper.

Finally, this heuristic is designed to facilitate an understanding of the relations of different forms of allocating labor to capitalism, on both a systematic and a historical level. I have attempted to show that free wage labor is indeed of key theoretical relevance for capitalism as a distinct set of productive practices, but that capitalism is opportunistic enough to assimilate slavery as a business plan or to prey on regional unfree labor regimes by colonizing these arrangements by extending global value chains. Yet these predatory endeavors have not *made* capitalism, as Sven Beckert and others would have it, nor have they been the source of the vast historical productivity gains defining capitalism as a system of productivism (Beckert 2014).

The present contribution provides a good argument for a more precise, deeper, qualitative distinction between free and unfree labor and for the contention that free wage labor has indeed turned out to be the dominant mode of allocating labor in capitalism, if we are talking about the Western core of capitalist industrialization and its extensions and about the direct intervention of capital in the organization of production processes.

References

Beckert, S. (2014). *King Cotton. Eine Geschichte des globalen Kapitalismus*. Munich: Beck.

Brass, T. (2014). Debating capitalist dynamics and unfree labour: A missing link? *The Journal of Development Studies, 50*(4) 570–582.

Lichtenstein, A. (1996). *Twice the Work of Free Labor: The Political Economy of Convict Labor in the New South*. London, New York: Verso.

Lucassen, J. (2018). Wage labour. In K. Hofmeester & M. van der Linden (Eds.), *Handbook Global History of Work* (pp. 395–409). Berlin, Boston: de Gruyter.

Mancini, M. J. (1996). *One Dies, Get Another: Convict Leasing in the American South, 1866–1928*. Columbia, SC: University of South Carolina Press.

Marx, K. (1981). *Das Kapital. Kritik der politischen Ökonomie*, Vol. 1: Der Produktionsprozess des Kapitals (1867), In Marx-Engels-Werke (MEW), Vol. 23. Berlin (GDR): Dietz.

Marx, K. (1983). Einleitung [zur Kritik der politischen Ökonomie], In Karl Marx. Friedrich Engels. *Ausgewählte Werke*, Vol. 11. Berlin (GDR): Dietz.

Reckwitz, A. (2006). *Das hybride Subjekt. Eine Theorie der Subjektkulturen von der bürgerlichen Moderne zur Postmoderne*. Weilerswist: Velbrück.

Reick, P. (2015). *'Labor Is Not a Commodity!' Contested Working-Class Discourse and the Movement to Shorten the Workday in Berlin and New York City in the late 1860s and early 1870s*, PhD-Diss. Free University Berlin.

Sarkar, M. (2017). Constrained labour as instituted process. Transnational contract work and circular migration in late capitalism. In *European Journal of Sociology, 58*(1), 171–204.

Sartre, J.-P. (1956). *Being and Nothingness: An Essay on Phenomenological Ontology* (first 1943). London, New York: Routledge.

Van der Linden, M. (2008). *Workers of the World. Essays toward a Global Labor History*. Leiden, Boston: Brill.

Weber, M. (1980). *Wirtschaft und Gesellschaft. Grundriss der verstehenden Soziologie* [1922], 5th ed., Tübingen: Mohr-Siebeck.

Welskopp, T. (2013). Anerkennung—Verheißung und Zumutungen der moderne. In A. Honneth, O. Lindemann, & S. Voswinkel (Eds.), *Strukturwandel der Anerkennung. Paradoxien sozialer Integration in der Gegenwart* (pp. 41–73). Frankfurt am Main, New York: Campus.

Welskopp, T. (2017a). Zukunft bewirtschaften. Überlegungen zu einer praxistheoretisch informierten Historisierung des Kapitalismus. *Praktiken des Kapitalismus, Mittelweg 26*, 81–97.

Welskopp, T. (2017b). ‚Kapitalismus und Konzepte von Arbeit. Wie systemisch zentral ist „freie Lohnarbeit" für den Kapitalismus? *Geschichte und Gesellschaft, 43*, 197–216.

Welskopp, T. (2019). ‚Kapitalismus und die Frage der „freien Lohnarbeit". In J.-O. Hesse, C. Kleinschmidt, R. Köster, & T. Schanetzky (Eds.), *Moderner Kapitalismus: Wirtschafts- und Unternehmenshistorische Beiträge* (pp. 31–48). Tübingen: Mohr Siebeck.

CHAPTER 3

Reflections on Violence
Some Contradictions of "Free Labor"

Richard Hyman

> You load sixteen tons, what do you get?
> Another day older and deeper in debt
> Saint Peter don't you call me, 'cause I can't go
> I owe my soul to the company store.[1]

∴

1 Introduction

Freedom of contract is commonly regarded as a defining characteristic of employment in modern capitalism. But as the previous chapters have indicated, what is meant by free labor is open to conflicting interpretations. In this chapter I address this ambiguity from the opposite direction, by exploring the contested meanings of forced labor; and I refer to the role of violence, broadly understood, in the making of labor markets. Drawing on Polanyi's discussion of fictitious commodities, I turn to the development of "decommodification" in postwar Europe and explore some of its limitations. Then I examine how economic globalization and financialization have led to a form of "post-decommodification." I suggest that what has become known as "modern slavery" can be seen an integral part of the business model of contemporary global capitalism but should be understood not as a distinctive (and aberrant) form of labor but rather as part of a continuum of modes of work and employment. In a brief conclusion, I discuss the role of the state in synthesizing violence and labor markets, asking whether and how resistance might be possible.

---

1 From the song 'Sixteen Tons', usually attributed to Merle Travis.

2   What Is Forced Labor?

Forced labor is a popular subject of research: Google Scholar provides over a million citations. The initial focus of studies using the concept was the treatment of labor in colonial regimes. The 1926 League of Nations Convention to suppress the slave trade and slavery was signed by forty countries and prescribed that member states should "take all necessary measures to prevent compulsory or forced labor from developing into conditions analogous to slavery." However, "under pressure from the colonial powers, the extraordinarily brutal regimes of coerced labour that, in the 1920s, were widely imposed by colonial authorities were removed from the Slavery Convention's orbit of concern" (O'Connell Davidson, 2015, p. 34). The issue was passed to the International Labour Organization (ILO), which in 1930 adopted Convention 29, the Forced Labour Convention. This was supplemented in 1957 by Convention 105 on the Abolition of Forced Labour and by the 2014 Protocol, both designed to strengthen enforcement procedures.

According to the original Convention, forced labor comprised "all work or service which is exacted from any person under the menace of any penalty and for which the said person has not offered himself voluntarily." Subsequently, the ILO has used slightly broader definitions; for example, it argued (2019) that

> forced labour can be understood as work that is performed involuntarily and under the menace of any penalty. It refers to situations in which persons are coerced to work through the use of violence or intimidation, or by more subtle means such as manipulated debt, retention of identity papers or threats of denunciation to immigration authorities.

The ILO stresses that the phenomenon is widespread. In 2005, it estimated that

> at least 12.3 million people are victims of forced labour worldwide. Of these, 9.8 million are exploited by private agents, including more than 2.4 million in forced labour as a result of human trafficking. Another 2.5 million are forced to work by the State or by rebel military groups. (2005, p. 10)

Subsequently, it estimated (2009, p. 32) that the total loss of income through unpaid (or underpaid) wages was about US$21 billion (€18 billion). It calculated (2014) that total profits obtained from forced labor amounted to US$150 billion (€130 billion), of which two-thirds derived from forced sexual exploitation. More recently, the ILO and Walk Free Foundation (2017) estimated that

16 million people were subject to forced labor in the private economy (just over half involving debt bondage) and a further 4 million were subject to state-imposed forced labor; while the numbers affected by the broader category of "modern slavery" were estimated at 40 million. (Note, however, that O'Connell Davidson raises important doubts regarding the "new abolitionists" and their statistics.)

Although the incidence of forced labor is thus perceived as extensive, it tends to be viewed officially as peripheral to "normal" capitalist work relations, for example primarily involving trafficking for sex work or agricultural labor in nonindustrialized countries. The 2005 ILO report concluded that more than three-quarters of those involved were in the Asia-Pacific region; the 2017 report also found that this region predominated in terms of total numbers, though the highest proportion of the population affected was in Africa.

Yet is involuntary labor so remote from "advanced" capitalism? Convention 29 contains a range of exceptions to the ILO definition of forced labor:

> any work or service exacted in virtue of compulsory military service laws for work of a purely military character; any work or service which forms part of the normal civic obligations of the citizens of a fully self-governing country; any work or service exacted from any person as a consequence of a conviction in a court of law, provided that the said work or service is carried out under the supervision and control of a public authority and that the said person is not hired to or placed at the disposal of private individuals, companies or associations; any work or service exacted in cases of emergency …, and in general any circumstance that would endanger the existence or the well-being of the whole or part of the population; minor communal services of a kind which, being performed by the members of the community in the direct interest of the said community, can therefore be considered as normal civic obligations incumbent upon the members of the community. … [2]

Similar provisions exist in the European Convention on Human Rights adopted by the Council of Europe in 1950: it prohibits slavery and forced labor but also excludes military service, prison labor, emergencies and "any work or service which forms part of normal civic obligations." These exemptions allow considerable elasticity in interpretation. For example, Topo (2016) shows how they

---

2 https://www.ilo.org/dyn/normlex/en/f?p=NORMLEXPUB:12100:0::NO::P12100_ILO_C ODE:C029.

can be used to deprive individuals of any effective choice of whether and how to work, which might be a reasonable test of whether labor is voluntary; in particular she discusses the conditionality increasingly attached to eligibility for social benefits ("workfare") but also identifies a range of other "gray areas" where work is at best quasi-involuntary. Another specific instance analyzed by Bales and Mayblin involves those held in immigration centers in the UK; they show (2018, pp. 18–19) that while work undertaken by detainees "holds several key features of regular employment," it "is not free; it is exploitative, coercive and undertaken within the broader constraints of immigration control and the threat of deportation."

This indicates that there is no binary divide between voluntary and involuntary, or free and unfree labor; rather, there are degrees of (un)freedom. Correspondingly, there are many varieties of violence and coercion. Physical violence is relatively straightforward to identify; threats of coercion may be less so; and the broader category of psychological violence is more diffuse still (Giaccone & Di Nunzio, 2015; Lawrence, 1970; Milczarek, 2010). But all occur within interpersonal relations, involving "abuse of power" as specified in the ILO Convention. However, it is increasingly recognized that coercion and violence can be embedded in the social framework within which interpersonal relations are played out.

Half a century ago, Galtung (1969, p. 173) distinguished between "personal" and "structural" violence: "personal violence shows. The object of personal violence perceives the violence. ... Structural violence is silent, it does not show." Subsequently, he insisted (Galtung, 1990, pp. 291–293) that "to discuss the categories of structural violence we need an image of a violent structure, and a vocabulary, a discourse" in order to interpret the underlying dynamics. He specifically analyzed "cultural violence" which, he argued, "makes direct and structural violence look, even feel, right—or at least not wrong." As Bauman has written (2001, p. 212), "when firmly institutionalized, coercion melts into the background of daily life, out of focus." There are clear parallels with Bourdieu's notion of "symbolic violence" (1984, 2001): cognitive structures, perhaps deliberately imposed, which encourage the perception of systems of domination and social damage as natural and inevitable. Similarly, Schroer (2000) has written of "soft violence." At this level, as de Haan argues (2008, p. 28), "violence is socially constructed because who and what is considered as violent varies according to specific socio-cultural and historical conditions." Hence, "it is more fruitful. both theoretically and methodologically, to consider definitions of violence to be essentially contested, to accept that valid arguments are feasible for either inclusive or restrictive definitions of violence" (de Haan, 2008, p. 38). In the context of industrial relations, the absence of alternatives to bad jobs or indecent work can be viewed as an expression of cultural and symbolic violence. If such alternatives are reduced, is labor increasingly unfree? I will return to these questions later.

3   Fictitious Commodities and Real Commodification

In the conclusion of his discussion of the sale and purchase of labor power, Marx (1976, p. 280) ironically described the labor market as

> a very Eden of the innate rights of man. It is the exclusive realm of Freedom, Equality, Property and Bentham. Freedom, because both buyer and seller of a commodity, let us say of labour-power, are determined only by their own free will. They contract as free persons, who are equal before the law. Their contract is the final result in which their joint will finds a common legal expression. Equality, because each enters into relation with the other, as with a simple owner of commodities, and they exchange equivalent for equivalent. Property, because each disposes only of what is his own. And Bentham, because each looks only to himself. The only force bringing them together, and putting them into relation with each other, is the selfishness, the gain and the private interests of each.

Shortly before the publication of *Das Kapital* in 1867, Maine (1861, p. 101) wrote of historical progress from a system of social relations predefined by feudal and familial constraints to one based on the "free agreement of individuals." The echoes in the passage from Marx quoted above may be more than coincidental. But whereas Maine viewed wholly positively the capacity of market actors "to settle rules of conduct for themselves with a liberty never allowed to them till recently," Marx stressed the contradictions between the form of "free agreement" and the reality of asymmetrical dependency. Equality before the law did not denote equality in practice. As many other authors emphasized, workers were often in competition with each other for jobs, entailing a downward pressure on wages; and because of their limited resources, even a short spell without work could entail severe deprivation, even starvation. Conversely, employers often possessed sufficient capital to survive longer without workers; and they could more easily act collectively.

Moreover, the freedom of "free labor" was double edged. While workers were free to sell their labor power—or as Kuczynski (2013) has insisted, the right to use it—for whatever wage they could obtain, with the rise of capitalism they were increasingly free from any alternative means of subsistence. This could be the consequence of the structural violence of unfettered market competition: for example, the independent Lancashire handloom weavers, whose products were undercut by cheaper factory production (Thompson, 1968) and who were therefore driven into dependent wage labor. But it could also be the outcome of the personal violence of landowners, capitalists, or governments. For example, the Highland clearances from the early eighteenth century involved the forcible dispossession of small-scale peasant tenant farmers and their replacement by large-scale sheep farms (Devine, 2018). This was one illustration of the violent face of the shift from status to contract: as clan chiefs, the Highland landowners had accepted some responsibility for the fate of their tenants; now in the guise of capitalist agriculturalists, they saw the relationship as essentially commercial. To survive, those driven from their traditional lands were forced to become "free" wage laborers.

Marx (1976, p. 895) described this "liberation" with bitter irony:

> the spoliation of the Church's property, the fraudulent alienation of the state domains, the theft of the common lands, the usurpation of feudal and clan property and its transformation into modern private property under circumstances of ruthless terrorism, all these things were just so many idyllic methods of primitive accumulation. They conquered the field for capitalist agriculture, incorporated the soil into capital, and created for the urban industries the necessary supply of free and rightless proletarians.

This coercive transformation was buttressed by the cultural violence of an emergent ideology which privileged economic self-interest over social obligation. Polanyi (1944, p. 92) examined the more general impact of "enclosures of the commons and consolidation into compact holdings" in rural Britain.

> The war on cottages, the absorption of cottage gardens and grounds, the confiscation of rights in the common deprived cottage industry of its two mainstays: family earnings and agricultural background. As long as domestic industry was supplemented by the facilities and amenities of a garden plot, a scrap of land, or grazing rights, the dependence of the laborer on money earnings was not absolute.

While beyond the scope of my discussion here, the violence of colonialism involved even more forcible and systematic dispossession.

The dynamic of enforced proletarianization was complemented by the transformation of social policy. As Polanyi discussed in detail, the Speenhamland system provided local financial support for the unemployed or low-paid and in theory (though not always in practice) obstructed the development of a "free" labor market. It reflected precapitalist status rights and obligations, in contradiction to the priority of contract enshrined in the new political economy. The New Poor Law of 1834 embraced Benthamite principles, requiring (again, not always in practice) that able-bodied paupers should receive support only in workhouses under circumstances of "less eligibility": their conditions should be inferior to the worst pertaining in the external labor market.

Polanyi (1944, p. 73) described labor, land, and money as "fictitious commodities" because while they were all subject to market forces, unlike real commodities, they were not produced for sale on the market. "To allow the market mechanism to be the sole director of the fate of human beings and their natural environment, indeed, even of the amount and use of their purchasing power, would result in the demolition of society." In the same year that Polanyi's book was published, the ILO in its Philadelphia Declaration affirmed as the first of its "fundamental principles" that "labour is not a commodity" (O'Higgins, 1997). For Marx, of course, labor as such was not a commodity; but in the context of capitalist employment, labor power—the capacity to perform productive work—was indeed commodified. It was the difference between the exchange value of labor power and the value of the products of the labor performed that provided the source of profit. Commodification involved a process whereby the specific activities of individuals with distinctive competences (concrete labor) became reduced to quantifiable, and hence marketable, phenomena (abstract labor). This was a development marginalizing the humanity of actually existing workers.

For Polanyi, the rise of industrial capitalism in the late eighteenth and early nineteenth centuries indeed imposed a commodity status on workers; but he argued that the resulting social dislocation necessarily precipitated a countermovement through "a spontaneous reaction" (1944, p. 149), and eventually a new framework of social rights was established. Subsequently, Esping-Andersen (1990) wrote of "decommodification," the protection of workers from the vagaries of market forces (and the imbalances of social power which they embedded).

In postwar Europe, "labor markets" became subject to a range of regulations which ensured that they constituted markets only in limited respects. Across the countries of what became the EU, employment regimes (or industrial relations systems) came to represent varieties of institutional structures which ensured that the employer-employee relationship was no longer primarily determined by market forces. Labor became recognized as a collective "stakeholder" with rights analogous to those of capitalists and shareholders.

Decommodification included important limits to the ways in which labor (power) could be bought and sold, often imposed through elaborate employment protection legislation which prescribed a wide range of substantive employment standards such as minimum wages, holiday entitlements, and maximum working hours, as well as extensive provisions regarding health and safety. All such "interference" with the labor market constrains the scope for "free agreement" between employers and workers, and for precisely this reason was strenuously opposed in the heyday of laissez-faire capitalism. Likewise, employment protection legislation restricted the employer's right to hire and fire, in contrast to the long-established US doctrine of "employment at will." In essence, employment was treated as a status rather than a mere contract, one which could be terminated only for good cause and through due process.

Public policy typically encouraged collective bargaining, and collective agreements usually had priority over individual employment contracts, further limiting the "freedom" of individual labor market actors. Moreover, centralized agreements and, in some countries, legal extension mechanisms resulted in high levels of bargaining coverage (even when union density was low). And almost universally, there were standardized national systems of workplace representation at least partially independent of management (underwritten by law or peak-level agreement): a reflection of the principle that a company is not simply the private property of its owners, that employment by a firm entails membership of a workplace community and requires a form of "industrial citizenship" of a democratic character.

This process was reinforced by extensive public welfare. As Esping-Andersen (1990) argued in coining the term "decommodification," the public provision of social welfare (or social security) systems, supporting citizens in circumstances of ill-health, injury, unemployment, and old age, protected the vulnerable from the vagaries of the labor market and reduced downwards competitive pressures on the standards of the core labor force. In the view of Marshall, writing four decades earlier, this represented the creation of a "social citizenship" by establishing the right to at least minimum standards of "economic welfare and security" and hence to enjoy "the life of a civilised being" (Marshall, 1950, pp. 10–11). This "social safety net" served to strengthen all employees in their relationship with the employer, since they were not forced to choose between working or starving and could therefore exert greater bargaining power. One may also note that state action, through progressive taxation and/or the provision of universal social benefits and services, modified the unequal outcomes which might otherwise be expected from the "free" operation of labor markets characterized by inequalities of power and resources.

Where did workers' rights come from? As noted above, Polanyi regarded the counter movement as "a spontaneous reaction"; but it would be a serious mistake to assume that national labor regimes were the outcome of some historical consensus on the architecture of employment regulation. In general, workers' rights were established in an uneven, sedimented, and contested process, involving long-term incremental adaptation and occasional radical innovation, with reverses as well as advances in decommodification. The systems emerging in each country typically reflected a contingent historical balance of class forces: rights were usually achieved as a negotiated accommodation between class interests or as a set of concessions by those in power to dampen protest from below.

Across Europe, the institutionalization of workers' rights—particularly as part of the various "postwar compromises" at a time when the balance of class forces was particularly favorable to labor movements—was a major social achievement. But such institutionalization has never been sufficient to prevent regression when circumstances change. One reason is that formal rights acquire substance only through a process of interpretation and application, and these compromises always involved a contradictory and hence unstable synthesis of status and contract, as many writers noted long ago (Fox, 1974; Hyman, 1987; Streeck, 1987; Supiot, 1990). Hence, the meaning of the rules which embody these rights is constantly reconstructed and renegotiated. As recent experience demonstrates, it is often easier for those who wish to weaken citizenship rights to erode their practical effect rather than to attack them frontally (Crouch, 2004; Streeck, 2009).

4   Globalization and Financialization: Post-decommodification?

Although decommodification was a common process across developed economies, particularly in western Europe, the dynamics and institutional outcomes were nationally specific. In all cases, the new regulatory regimes involved an accommodation between national labor movements and their interlocutors. Employers were primarily national in terms of corporate ownership and production strategies, often held the status of "national champions" and in most countries were willing to act collectively. Governments were to a large degree autonomous in social and economic policy and encouraged the rise of the Keynesian welfare state. These dynamics contributed to a marked diversity of national industrial relations models.

The world has changed. First, globalization—of which European economic integration is one important element—has removed the dominant capitalist agglomerations from national control. There are many ways of conceptualizing the historical development of globalization, including its technological foundations and its geographical scope. What is crucial is the transformation in its core dynamic. Its earliest forms involved international movements of commodities: raw materials, manufactured products, but also labor (including slave and semi-slave labor). The mid-twentieth century saw a qualitative shift to the dominant role of multinational corporations and the development of what may best be called global surplus value chains, in which corporate strategists subject actual producers to constant pressures to cut costs, creating new forms of insecurity. In the third, most recent phase, finance capital intensifies the dynamic of commodification.

The liberalization of financial markets has spawned an array of exotic fictitious commodities which Polanyi could never have imagined: derivatives, secondary markets, hedge funds, private equity, leveraged buyouts, credit default swaps. ... It is now possible, and indeed more effective, to generate a surplus without producing value. Money can be expanded without the production of commodities as traditionally understood: a process which McMurtry (1998) terms the cancer stage of capitalism. Corporations have themselves been transformed into commodities, increasingly bought and sold, creating new modes of insecurity: for growing numbers of workers (and their unions), it is no longer even clear who is the employer (Standing, 2011, p. 35).

An associated transformation involves the reconfiguration of the role of the state. The postwar compromises involved governments in multiple ways, as indicated above. Particularly but not exclusively in Europe, legislation created a web of individual employment rights, and also buttressed collective representation of worker interests through trade unions and works councils. Welfare regimes were central to Polanyi's "double movement." Macroeconomic regulation on Keynesian lines sustained near-full employment in many countries. Governments themselves became major employers, typically committed to supporting high labor standards. In recent decades, however, neoliberal globalization has provided an alibi for anti-social policies by governments that insist there is no alternative to submission to international markets (Weiss, 1998). On the one hand, government policies have been aimed at "rolling back the state," and restricting social protections to those that can be justified on grounds of productivity and competitiveness; on the other hand, new and repressive forms of intervention have been required to impose the sway of market forces. The EU, once often viewed as a defender of decommodification, has become one of the key drivers of this process: its "new economic governance" increasingly targets social welfare and employment protection; while the austerity packages ("shock therapy") imposed on the "programme" countries have coercively imposed escalating recommodification.

National economies and national labor markets are thus increasingly disembedded from effective social regulation; and the beneficiaries of financialized "shareholder value" capitalism have little interest in maintaining historic compromises. Keynesian macroeconomic management, one of the key foundations of the postwar settlements, presupposed the economic governance capacity of the nation-state; macroeconomic demand management has now been subordinated to the assumed inevitability of national "competitiveness." Where significant productive and infrastructural assets were in public hands, in most countries these have now been largely privatized.

These trends can be understood, within Polanyi's framework, as a counter-countermovement, a third phase involving the deliberate unravelling of the regulatory web constructed in previous decades. The norm of insecurity, widely believed to have been overcome in the mid-twentieth century, is increasingly reimposed. The crisis which began in 2007–2008 brought a rapid increase in unemployment, which in many countries persists. For many—and in some countries most—new labor market entrants, the only available employment opportunities are precarious: short-term contracts, bogus self-employment, agency work, zero hours contracts. ... What was once considered "atypical" employment is now increasingly typical.

The rise of the "platform economy" has brought a return to spot contracting in the labor market. According to the head of one major platform company,

> before the Internet, it would be really difficult to find someone, sit them down for ten minutes and get them to work for you, and then fire them after those ten minutes. But with technology, you can actually find them, pay them the tiny amount of money, and then get rid of them when you don't need them any more.
> MARVIT, 2014

The erosion of the "normal" employment relationship, with the advance of recommodification, has been one cause of growing income inequality and the expanding proportion of the workforce afflicted by the structural violence of no work on the one hand, overwork on the other, by increasingly precarious work, and often by indecent work in its many guises.

5   "Modern Slavery" as a Business Model

When, and how, does bad work constitute forced labor? Often, unfree labor is regarded as primarily a problem of "developing" countries, but one exported to "developed" economies through migration flows which themselves may be sustained through violence in the form of trafficking. It is also often seen as exclusively linked to what Andreas and Wallman (2009) term the "illicit economy," involving such activities as organized prostitution and the drugs trade. As Barrientos, Kothari, and Phillips put it (2013, pp. 1037–1038), "forced and unfree labour" is usually treated as "a separate and specific category of labor relations." By contrast, they insist that there is a continuum of

> relations and conditions of unfreedom. ... It is increasingly evident that contemporary labor relations often cannot in any useful sense be positioned on one side or the other of a clear dividing line between 'free' and 'unfree' labour.

Strauss (2012, p. 141) makes a similar point: "unfreedom ... needs to be understood as a continuum of exploitation to which any worker might be subject, but to which particular groups and individuals have particular vulnerabilities."

In her discussion of exploitative work, Phillips (2013, pp. 173–177) insists

> that forms of unfree labour need to be understood theoretically and empirically as ... the extreme end of a continuum of exploitative labour relations which underpins global production. ... This continuum runs from the forms of labour relations which most unambiguously would be characterized as "slavery" or "forced labour," involving a complete removal of the freedom and free will of a person, to those which are more fluid and combine clear dimensions of unfreedom with elements of freedom.

Likewise, Steinfeld (2009, p. 12) argues that

> rather than view compulsion in labor relations in terms of a binary opposition divided by type of pressure, it seems more plausible to think in terms of a combined scale of pressures, legal, physical, economic, social, psychological all running along a continuum from severe to mild, rather than falling into a binary opposition

—an argument also central to the discussion by Fudge (2019).

According to Crane (2013, p. 59), "the threat of violence is a definitional condition of modern slavery. Without it, labor practices may be inhumane and exploitative but will not constitute slavery because the victim has the opportunity to walk away." Yet as many writers have demonstrated, this "opportunity" may be precluded without the threat or exercise of direct physical violence. One contemporary example is the kafala system in the Arab Gulf states, Lebanon, and Jordan.

> The specific rules and regulations differ from country to country, but the basic elements are the same. Foreign nationals must have a local sponsor ... in order to obtain residence and work permits. During the term of service, the worker does not have the right to quit except under specific circumstances, and in most cases cannot change jobs or choose a new employer without the sponsor's consent. The employer, on the other hand, has the power to send the worker back to his or her country at any time. Within this framework, migrants are effectively bonded to their employers.
>
> FRANTZ, 2013, p. 1072

The cultural violence underpinning this system was exposed by the comments of a Kuwaiti "beauty blogger" who complained bitterly at new legislation which slightly improved the status of migrant workers:

> how can you have a servant at home who keeps their own passport with them? What's worse is they have one day off every week. ... If they run away and go back to their country, who will refund me?
>
> MICHAELSON, 2018, p. 2018

Lacking access to formally enslaved labor, employers may have many functional alternatives. Brown and van der Linden (2010, pp. 6–7) note that

> after the slave trade had gradually been abolished in Africa and the Americas, employers invented many tricks to guarantee the ongoing supply of bonded workers. For example, scholars of Africa are finding that colonial policies notwithstanding, precolonial slavery and ever more innovative forms of bonded labor are flourishing on the continent, revealing the complexities and subtleties of power relations that deliver the labor-power of the vulnerable to all manner of domestic and international employers.

This is not only a problem of distant history and faraway countries: it is important to recognise "the unclear divide between 'free' and 'unfree' work" and to question "the telos implicit in the understanding that 'unfreedom' belongs to the past, while 'proper' capitalism is based on 'free' wage labour" (Sarkar, 2017, p. 173). As Phillips argues, (2013, p. 178),

> entry into unfree labour relations may technically be "voluntary", but the key is the (il)legitimacy of the set of options which is available to a person at a given time. ... In contemporary global production, unfreedom is primarily constituted not by coerced entry but by precluded exit. These conditions are often established by indebtedness and/or the withholding of wages until the end of a contract, which may be combined with such abuses as imprisonment and restrictions on physical movement, threatened or actual violence (both psychological and physical, and both against a worker and against her family or co-workers) and/or the confiscation of documents and possessions. In a different but important sense, the preclusion of exit can arise from the workers' own perceptions of their obligations. Their need to support families, raise dowries, honour debts and so on are powerful disciplining mechanisms which can very effectively be harnessed to the cause of exploitation.

Unfreedom is often closely linked to the role of labor market intermediaries.

> There is a growing recognition that labour contracting is increasing, and that its worst forms are associated with the rise of unfree labour within contemporary globalised production. ... Labour contractors often charge migrant workers high fees for transport, training, provision of "documents", and also charge high "interest" on loans for these "services". These are often on top of large payments to agents for "travel" to the country of destination. Undocumented migrant workers have few channels for claiming their rights, and fear loss of work and deportation if they complain.
> BARRIENTOS, 2013, pp. 1059–1061

Hence, "bonded labour" is not simply a historical, third world problem; nor, in "developed" countries, is it simply associated with trafficking and people smuggling. Rather, "unfree labour ... is a stable feature of the contemporary global economy" (LeBaron & Phillips, 2018, p. 1). As Strauss insists (2012, pp. 137–138),

> the globalisation of production and capital flows, and the de- and re-regulation of national employment regimes to create flexible labour markets, mean that there are increasing interconnections between the demand for flexible, low-cost labour in the industrialised economies and a supply of workers unable to commodify their labour at home. ... Relations of unfreedom in the new global division of labour dissolve clear-cut distinctions between 'developed' and 'developing nations'. ... Far from a vestigial form of pre-capitalist exploitation, unfree labour is part of the continuum of exploitation.

Steinfeld (2009) discusses an extreme case of debt bondage in postwar Connecticut. In the UK, Skrivankova (2010) documents a number of recent cases. Crane (2013, p. 54) concludes that "slavery ... tends to enter stages of the supply chain where margins are narrow and where value is captured further downstream by larger and more powerful interests"; he terms this "value trap slavery." Agriculture is one major site of unfree labor. Rogaly (2008) describes its functioning in British horticulture, while Barrientos (2013, pp. 1062–1063) also explores the effects of the increased use of labor contractors in British agriculture, "particularly amongst those supplying supermarkets" and in South African producers for the UK market. A specific case involved a gangmaster who "employed South African workers who had been brought to the UK ostensibly as part of the Commonwealth Working Holidays Scheme and were, therefore, working legally." Travel to the UK was paid by

> loans with 100 per cent interest charges and the workers had to sign an agreement not to leave the gangmaster's employment until the loan was paid off. ... Once in the UK, most of the workers were housed in overcrowded accommodation by the gangmaster. They were paid below the minimum wage, discouraged from obtaining National Insurance numbers, and had deductions for transport, rent, loan repayments and sometimes other unspecified charges. They were often required to work long hours and continuous days.

Allain, Crane, LeBaron, and Behbahani (2013) also provide detailed documentation of the interlinkages between global value chains and "modern slavery," specifically examining construction, food and cannabis production. Forced labor, they argue, makes business sense for specific actors within these supply chains; not only do unscrupulous employers and intermediaries benefit, but so do the supermarket chains and consumers who enjoy lower costs than would otherwise be possible.

This implies that "modern slavery" is not an aberration but is rather integral to contemporary business models. As Brass argues (1999, p. 9), "unfree labour is not only compatible with relatively advanced productive forces but also fulfils the same role as technology in the class struggle: capital uses both to cheapen, to discipline, or as substitutes for free wage labour." The pressure which "modern slavery" can place on the wages and conditions of "free" labor across supply chains can itself be seen as a form of structural violence.

6 States, Violence, and Resistance

"Forced labour exploitation is often taken to be perpetrated by private individuals or firms in the 'private economy', whose actors and dynamics are deemed separate from states"; or else states tend to be "considered predominantly as the vehicles for responses to forced labour, rather than as actors who play a causal role in shaping the conditions that give rise to it" (LeBaron & Phillips, 2018, p. 2).

What counts (and does not count) as forced labor is usually specified in law, and statutory definitions vary considerably across jurisdictions (Skrivankova, 2010). Within the US, Steinfeld (2009, p. 4) shows that there have been very different understandings

> of when labor undertaken by contract amounted to "involuntary servitude". The courts in different states in the territories developed two quite distinct and inconsistent approaches to the problem. The first focused on the conditions of entry into the contract, the second focused on exit from the contract. Under the first test, if the contract was judged to have been entered into voluntarily then the contractual obligation to labor could be enforced against the body of the worker without infringing the prohibition against "involuntary servitude," the work having been undertaken "voluntarily". There could be no exit from such a labor contract, but the lack of a power to exit did not make the continued labor "involuntary", after all, what purpose did labor contracts serve in the first place if not to bind the worker to fulfill his "voluntary" undertakings. The courts in a second state disagreed violently holding that even work undertaken voluntarily would constitute involuntary servitude if a worker decided to leave in mid contract but was forced to continue work through the use of harsh legal remedies the master might invoke against the body of the worker. Continued work to avoid imprisonment or a beating could not be

described as "voluntary," and fell under the prohibition against "involuntary servitude."

In the UK, for most of the nineteenth century, the first of these statutory interpretations prevailed under the Master and Servant laws (Frank, 2010; Simon, 1954; Steinfeld, 2001). As Price (1986, pp. 39–42) indicates, these laws were used to impose social and industrial discipline. Although most commonly discussed as a mechanism for repressing strikes and trade unionism more generally, they could also prevent individual exit from the oppressive and exploitative enforcement of employment contracts. For example, coalminers and workers in other occupations who were commonly subject to 12-month contracts could suffer imprisonment with hard labor for individual breaches of contract, providing "a convenient instrument for quick punishment or intimidation over a wide variety of offences ranging from neglecting work to refusing overtime." This was not simply an anachronistic residue of feudal employment regulation: in the two decades before the repeal of the laws in 1875, in an era when capitalist wage labor was firmly established, prosecutions actually intensified. Perhaps exceptional within the modern EU is the 2018 "slave law" implemented by the Orbán government in Hungary, which allows employers to force employees to work overtime, but analogues of Master and Servant are still to be found elsewhere.

LeBaron and Phillips (2018), drawing empirically on recent US experience, focus on how state policy, through acts of commission or omission, can facilitate unfree labor both by increasing the pool of vulnerable workers and by enhancing the incentives to adopt a business model based on forced labor. Both are predictable outcomes of neoliberalism, a project founded on the at first sight paradoxical amalgam of "the free economy and the strong state" (Gamble, 1988). The "modernisation" of labor markets and social security systems, through the weakening or abolition of employment protection legislation and social safety nets and their replacement by recommodification and workfare, drastically restricts the options available to workers, forcing many into unwanted work situations. Reducing "burdens on business" by weakening regulatory regimes, cutting back on inspectorates and failing to prosecute (or imposing minimal penalties for) illegal practices makes resort to forced labor an increasingly profitable option. Much more actively, for several decades, the US government has created an elaborate "prison industrial complex" (Davis, 2003) based on forced labor.

An important aspect of state policy is the construction of migration regimes. LeBaron and Phillips (2018, p. 7) show how the tightening of US border controls, rather than preventing "illegal" immigration, has increased the cost of securing entry through traffickers and people smugglers. "The extent of the debt accrued in the context of a highly policed border enforcement regime augments the unfreedom that can be imposed on a migrant worker." Much more generally, variants of the kafala system have been implemented in many "developed" countries: work permits for many occupations are dependent on a specific job offer and may be revoked if the worker leaves the sponsoring employer (O'Connell Davidson, 2013, p. 183; 2015, p. 144). Those without a valid permit, or whose time-limited permit has expired, are particularly vulnerable to violent and abusive treatment by the employer. Well-grounded fears that complaints to the authorities may result in deportation can tie such workers to relations of forced labor. In the UK, government efforts to create a "hostile environment" for foreign workers (or those who may look foreign) clearly reinforce such unfreedom. More generally, one by-product of neoliberal globalization has been the political resurgence of the far right, often manifest in physical violence against migrants and refugees; this clearly diminishes free participation in the labor market.

Neoliberal policies replacing social protection by "workfare," and cutting back eligibility for, and the value of, welfare payments, inevitably encourage the growth of "indecent work." As O'Connell Davidson puts it (2014, p. 528), alluding to a comment by Marx in his 1844 Manuscripts:

> in a context where more and more people find themselves stripped of social protections and hurled onto weakly regulated or completely unregulated labour markets, prostitution once again begins to look like only "a specific expression of the general prostitution of the labourer."

According to the report of the UN Special Rapporteur on extreme poverty and human rights (Alston, 2018), the cumulative impact of successive cuts in the UK has been to drive some people into sex work. This induced the House of Commons Work and Pensions Select Committee (2019) to initiate an inquiry into the potential link between changes to the benefits system and the growth of "survival sex." Changes to the system of student financing—the replacement of grants by loans, and the sharp increase in fees—appears to have similar results (Roberts, Jones, & Sanders 2013; Sagar, Jones, Symons, Tyrie, & Roberts, 2015). According to Simpson and Smith (2019, pp. 709–710),

> it is estimated that around one in 20 university students are currently involved in some form of sex work in the UK. ... Given drastic increases in tuition fees—which are now over £9000 per year for undergraduate courses and on average £11,000 for postgraduate degrees—coinciding

with rising costs of student living, it is unsurprising that students are motivated by financial pressures to enter sex work.

Is forced labor the new normal, or can financialized global capitalism be re-regulated? As Sayer and Walker insist (1992, p. 3), "the old homilies are not enough." A century ago, Rosa Luxemburg wrote that "bourgeois society stands at the crossroads, either transition to socialism or regression into barbarism." The lineaments of the second alternative—economic subjugation, political oppression, environmental devastation, military aggression, and of course the expansion of unfree labor—are today even starker than when she wrote. Any new countermovement must embrace the principle that "capitalism is the reality, but not our perspective" (Urban, 2014, p. 41). To be effective, different modes of resistance must be mutually supportive, and informed by a vision of an alternative.

Neoliberalism emerged from the 2007–08 crisis—which surely demonstrated the practical bankruptcy of its recipes—stronger than ever (Crouch, 2011), partly because it serves powerful vested interests, but also because of the lack of widespread conviction, even among its opponents, that there is an alternative which is both practical and inspirational. There is a wall in our heads: neoliberalism has become the "common sense" of our times. To resist the spread of forced labor, a radically different logic is required, of sustainability, solidarity, equity, and dignity. How might this be propagated? We have to start from where we are and not from where we would like to be. The ideas of "free" markets are unquestioned by all but a small minority. But beliefs and understandings are always complex and contradictory. In concrete terms, most people do question the current economic system. They are perplexed by a financial dynamic which seems out of control. They are angry that failed bankers can still pay themselves obscene bonuses, that the rich still get richer while the rest of us suffer from cuts in real income and social supports, that decent jobs are increasingly becoming indecent, that extremely profitable corporations can exploit tax loopholes and tax havens to avoid paying their share. They are bewildered that hostile takeovers, which destroy jobs, are not only permitted but are actually encouraged by the European authorities. There is an upswell of popular anger and despair which often benefits the far right.

There are no simple answers, but any response must be constructed in part on decommodification from below. In the French-speaking world at least, the notion of a "social economy" has received growing attention on the left (Draperi, 2007; Laville, 2007). An imaginative response to the cancer stage of capitalism and its crisis ought to draw on such ideas, which could prefigure a transition from current political economy to a moral economy (Thompson,

1971). Creating a strategic vision which might counteract the advance of unfreedom is a massive challenge. It requires new forms of engagement with those most affected by the destruction of once seemingly secure freedoms and opportunities. But it also requires a willingness to move beyond the limits of pragmatism to the possibilities of utopia. In this, there is a crucial role for public intellectuals and engaged scholars, to show how there is an alternative to the new normality of forced labor.

References

Allain, J., Crane, A., LeBaron, G., & Behbahani, L. (2013). *Forced Labour's Business Models and Supply Chains*. York: Joseph Rowntree Foundation.

Alston, P. (2018). Statement on Visit to the United Kingdom, by Professor Philip Alston, United Nations Special Rapporteur on Extreme Poverty and Human Rights. https://www.ohchr.org/EN/NewsEvents/Pages/DisplayNews.aspx?NewsID=23881.

Andreas, P. & Wallman, J. (2009). Illicit markets and violence: What is the relationship? *Crime, Law and Social Change*, 52, 225–229.

Bales, K. & Mayblin, L. (2018). Unfree labour in immigration detention: Exploitation and coercion of a captive immigrant workforce. *Economy and Society*. doi: 10.1080/03085147.2018.1484051.

Barrientos, S. (2013). "Labour chains": Analysing the role of labour contractors in global production networks. *Journal of Development Studies*, 49(8), 1058–1071.

Barrientos, S. W., Kothari, U., & Phillips, N. (2013). Dynamics of unfree labour in the contemporary global economy, *Journal of Development Studies*, 49(8), 1037–1041.

Bauman, Z. (2001). *The Individualized Society*. Cambridge: Polity.

Bourdieu, P. (1984). *Distinction*. London: Routledge.

Bourdieu, P. (2001). *Masculine Domination*. Cambridge: Polity.

Brass, T. (1999). *Towards a Comparative Political Economy of Unfree Labour: Case Studies and Debates*. London: Frank Cass.

Brown, C., & van der Linden, M. (2010). Shifting boundaries between free and unfree labour. *International Labor and Working-Class History*, 78, 4–11.

Crane, A. (2013). Modern slavery as a management practice: Exploring the conditions and capabilities for human exploitation. *Academy of Management Review*, 38(1), 45–69.

Crouch, C. (2004). *Post-Democracy*. Cambridge: Polity.

Crouch, C. (2011). *The Strange Non-Death of Neoliberalism*. Cambridge: Polity.

Davis, A. (2003). *Are Prisons Obsolete?* New York: Seven Stories Press.

de Haan, W. (2008). Violence as an essentially contested concept. In S. Body-Gendrot & P. Spierenburg (Eds.), *Violence in Europe* (pp. 27–40). New York: Springer.

Devine, T. M. (2018). *The Scottish Clearances: A History of the Dispossessed.* London: Allen Lane.

Draperi, J-F. (2007). *Comprendre l'économie sociale: Fondements et enjeux.* Paris: Dunod.

Esping-Andersen, G. (1990). *The Three Worlds of Welfare Capitalism.* Cambridge: Polity Press.

Fox, A. (1974) *Beyond Contract: Work, Power and Trust Relations.* London: Faber.

Frank, C. (2010). *Master and Servant Law: Chartists, Trade Unions, Radical Lawyers and the Magistracy in England, 1840–1865.* Farnham: Ashgate.

Frantz, E. (2013). Jordan's unfree workforce: State-sponsored bonded labour in the Arab region. *Journal of Development Studies, 49*(8), 1072–1087.

Fudge, J. (2019). (Re)conceptualising unfree labour: Local labour control regimes and constraints on workers' freedoms, *Global Labour Journal, 10*(2), 108–122.

Galtung, J. (1969). Violence, peace, and peace research, *Journal of Peace Research, 6*(3), 167–191.

Galtung, J. (1990). Cultural violence. *Journal of Peace Research, 27*(3), 291–305.

Gamble, A. (1988). *The Free Economy and the Strong State: The Politics of Thatcherism.* London: Macmillan.

Giaccone, M. & Di Nunzio, D. (2015). *Violence and Harassment in European Workplaces: Causes, Impacts and Policies.* Dublin: Eurofound.

House of Commons Work and Pensions Select Committee (2019). *Universal Credit and Survival Sex: Sex in Exchange for Meeting Survival Needs.* Retrieved August 18, 2021, from https://publications.parliament.uk/pa/cm201919/cmselect/cmworpen/83/83.pdf.

Hyman, R., (1987). Strategy or structure? Capital, labour and control. *Work, Employment and Society, 1*(1), 25–55.

ILO (2005). *A Global Alliance against Forced Labour: Global Report on Forced Labour 2005.* Geneva: ILO.

ILO (2014). *Profits and Poverty: The Economics of Forced Labour.* Geneva: ILO.

ILO (2019). *What Is Forced Labour, Modern Slavery and Human Trafficking.* Retrieved August 18, 2021, from https://www.ilo.org/global/topics/forced-labour/definition/lang--en/index.htm.

ILO and Walk Free Foundation (2017). *Global Estimates of Modern Slavery: Forced Labour and Forced Marriage.* Geneva: ILO.

Kuczynski, T. (2013). What is sold on the labour market. In M. van der Linden & K. H. Roth (Eds.), *Beyond Marx: Theorising the Global Labour Relations of the Twenty-First Century* (pp. 305–318). Leiden: Brill.

Laville, J-L., ed. (2007). *L'économie solidaire: Une perspective internationale.* Paris: Hachette.

Lawrence, J. (1970). Violence. *Social Theory and Practice, 1*(2), 31–49.

LeBaron, G. & Phillips, N. (2018). States and the political economy of unfree labour. *New Political Economy* doi.org/10.1080/13563467.2017.1420642.

Maine, H. S., (1861). *Ancient Law: Its Connection with the Early History of Society, and Its Relations to Modern Ideas*. London: John Murray.

Marshall, T, H., (1950). *Citizenship and Social Class*. Cambridge: Cambridge University Press.

Marvit, M. Z., (2014). How crowdworkers became the ghosts in the digital machine. *The Nation*, 5 February.

Marx, K. (1976). *Capital*, Vol. 1. Harmondsworth: Penguin.

McMurtry, J. (1998). *The Cancer Stage of Capitalism*. London: Pluto Press.

Michaelson, R. (2018). Kuwaiti Instagram influencer causes uproar with comments on Filipino 'servants'. *The Guardian*, 23 July. Retrieved August 18, 2021, from https://www.theguardian.com/world/2018/jul/23/who-will-refund-me-kuwaiti-star-ignites-row-over-filipinos-days-off.

Milczarek, M. (2010). *Workplace Violence and Harassment: A European Picture*. Luxembourg: Publications Office.

O'Connell Davidson, J. (2013). Troubling freedom: Migration, debt, and modern slavery. *Migration Studies*, 1(2), 176–195.

O'Connell Davidson, J. (2014). Let's go outside: Bodies, prostitutes, slaves and worker citizens, *Citizenship Studies*, 18(5), 516–532.

O'Connell Davidson, J. (2015). *Modern Slavery: The Margins of Freedom*. London: Palgrave Macmillan.

O'Higgins, P. (1997). 'Labour is not a commodity': An Irish contribution to international labour law. *Industrial Law Journal*, 26(3), 225–23.

Phillips, N. (2013). Unfree labour and adverse incorporation in the global economy: Comparative perspectives on Brazil and India. *Economy and Society*, 42(2), 171–196.

Polanyi, P. (1944). *The Great Transformation*. New York: Rinehart.

Price, R. (1986). *Labour in British Society*. London: Croom Helm.

Roberts, R., Jones, A. & Sanders, T. (2013). Students and sex work in the UK: Providers and purchasers. *Sex Education*, 13(3), 349–363.

Rogaly, B. (2008). Intensification of workplace regimes in British horticulture: The role of migrant workers. *Population, Space and Place*, 14(6): 497–510.

Sagar, T., Jones, D., Symons, K., Tyrie, J. & Roberts, R. (2015). *The Student Sex Work Project: Research Summary*. Swansea: Centre for Criminal Justice and Criminology, Swansea University.

Sarkhar, M. (2017). Constrained labour as instituted process: Transnational contract work and circular migration in late capitalism. *European Journal of Sociology*, 58(1), 171–204.

Sayer, A. & Walker, R. (1992). *The New Social Economy: Reworking the Division of Labour.* Oxford: Blackwell.

Schroer, M. (2000). Gewalt ohne Gesicht. Zur Notwendigkeit einer umfassenden Gewaltanalyse. *Leviathan* 28(4), 434–451.

Simon, D. (1954). Master and servant. In J. Saville (Ed.), *Democracy and the Labour Movement.* (pp. 160–200). London: Lawrence and Wishart,

Simpson, J., & Smith, S. (2019). 'I'm not a bloody slave, I get paid and if I don't get paid then nothing happens': Sarah's experience of being a student sex worker, *Work, Employment and Society 33* (4), 709–718.

Skrivankova, K. (2010). *Between Decent Work and Forced Labour: Examining the Continuum of Exploitation.* York: JRF programme paper.

Standing, G. (2011). *The Precariat: The New Dangerous Class.* London: Bloomsbury.

Steinfeld, R. J. (2001). *Coercion, Contract, and Free Labor in the Nineteenth Century.* Cambridge: Cambridge UP.

Steinfeld, R. (2009). *Coercion/Consent in Labour.* Oxford: COMPAS Working Paper, 66.

Strauss, K. (2012). Coerced, forced and unfree labour: Geographies of exploitation in contemporary labour markets. *Geography Compass, 6*(3), 137–148.

Streeck, W. (1987). The uncertainties of management in the management of uncertainty, *Work, Employment and Society, 1*(3): 281–308.

Streeck, W. (2009). *Re-Forming Capitalism.* Oxford: Oxford UP.

Supiot, A. (1999). *Au-delà de l'emploi.* Paris: Flammarion.

Thompson, E. P. (1968). *The Making of the English Working Class.* Harmondsworth: Penguin.

Thompson, E. P. (1971). The moral economy of the English crowd in the eighteenth century. *Past and Present,* 50(1), 76–136.

Topo, A. (2016). Obbligo di lavoro e libertà di lavoro: Quando lavorare è un dovere "sociale". In M. Brollo, C. Cester and L. Menghini (Eds.), *Legalità e rapporti di lavoro: Incentivi e sanzioni.* (pp. 177–203). Trieste: Edizioni Università di Trieste.

Urban, H-J. (2014). Zwischen defensive und revitalisierung. *Sozialismus,* 11/2014, 35–41.

Weiss, L. (1998). *The Myth of the Powerless State.* Ithaca: Cornell UP.

CHAPTER 4

The Role of Gender in the Making of Global Labor Markets

Alexandra Scheele

1   Introduction

If we think of globalization, we think of a global exchange of goods and services and the disembedding of time and space. If we think of labor markets, we think of a public space where paid work is—in a more or less regulated way—bought and sold. If we think of migration, we think of men migrating from one country to another in the search for (better) jobs. What is, however, missing in the equation here is the "back stage of a global free market" (Hochschild, 2010) and the "female underside of globalization" (Ehrenreich & Hochschild, 2002, p. 3)—and thus the inclusion of gender.

The increasing globalization of production and the emergence of transnational and global production chains has led to flexible, informal, temporary, and insecure forms of predominantly female employment (Dannecker, 2019, p. 825). Women in the Global South are often found at the lower end of the hierarchy of the global division of labor. In the last few decades, more and more women have been on the move, and it is estimated that women make up about half of all international migrants worldwide. "Thanks to (...) 'globalization', women are on the move as never before in history" (Ehrenreich & Hochschild, 2002, p. 3). The feminization of migration is at the same time a feminization of labor, particularly in the service sector and healthcare, also as a result of the global care crisis.[1] This means—in short—that we are witnessing an increasing number of women migrating from their home countries to work in private households in other countries. Women migrate to the Global North to do the "women's work" that women there either cannot or do not want to do.

This development can be interpreted as the result of a worldwide gender revolution. Not only have women in Western societies officially been given equal opportunities—the right to vote, educational rights, matrimonial and

---

1 Here, I am not including the organized and partly forced migration of women for marriage, trafficking of women into the sex industry, or forms of "new slavery" (Femina Politica, 2016).

divorce rights, the right to work, and free disposal over financial resources, etc.—but also a large proportion of women want to work and to earn money and thus not only make use of their education (studies or vocational training) but also gain some kind of economic independence. In contrast to this "positive" assessment, Nancy Fraser (2009) argued several years ago that this development is related to the end of what she calls "state-organized capitalism" and the rise of neoliberalist capitalism. The latter requires a flexible workforce and employment opportunities for women all over the world.

Below I will provide a brief overview on global labor markets from a gender perspective. Although forms of female employment on national and global labor markets are manifold, I will focus on care work since female migration is largely related to a growing demand for care in most societies. I will begin by explaining the role of care work in a capitalist economy. Then I will show how the gendered division of labor and the attribution of care work as a female occupation led to a devaluation of care and care work—symbolically as well as in specific care arrangements. I will also discuss concepts pertaining to the particularities of female labor migration. In Europe, female migrants play a key role in securing a growing demand for care and help cushion the reproductive crisis but often work under precarious employment conditions. Therefore, finally, I will show how welfare and care regimes on the one hand and migration policies on the other hand limit opportunities to regulate irregular employment in the care sector. It should be noted that there is an abundance of research from postcolonial and intersectional studies as well as from (feminist) migration and economic studies on gender and the global division of labor (e.g., Sassen, 1991, Mohanty, 1986, Lutz, 2007). In this chapter, however, I am highlighting in particular the feminist Marxist "Bielefeld" approach as one of the prominent approaches to a critical social theory on the one hand, and the work of Arlie Hochschild on global care chains as one of the well-known perspectives adopted to grasp global interrelations of female migration on the other hand.

2 Care Work—A Blind Spot in Capitalist Economy

The gendered division of labor whereby women are responsible for unpaid care work while men pursue paid work is a global phenomenon. That is not to say that there are not huge regional or class-related differences regarding the meaning of "care" and how and to what extent care work is carried out. The general trend, however, appears to be that women care for children and other family members, prepare food, and keep the household clean. Although at a normative level care work is valued as the precondition for human existence and coined as the nucleus of society in the Western history of ideas, it is at the same time framed as women's work and devaluated in terms of recognition.

In Europe and North America, the starting point for the devaluation of care work lies in the industrialization and urbanization beginning in the late eighteenth century. In this process, the capitalist mode of production, which had previously only been found in some pre-industrialized commercial sectors, became the general principle of economic life. Wage labor on a contractual basis became a mass phenomenon and central feature of industrial capitalism (see Kocka, 2017, p. 82). Work became equated with market-related, productive work and detached from work in private households or in the family. Reproductive labor —care for children and elderly people, and domestic work including cleaning, cooking, and maintenance of the household— has been gradually split off and transferred to the private sphere. This separation of spheres into production and reproduction is largely accomplished through the gendered division of labor. By socially charging the "natural" differences between women and men, and providing them with meanings of femininity and masculinity, the division of labor becomes clear: due to their key characteristics, women are given the task of addressing basic human needs such as giving affection and ensuring secure emotional attachments. The positioning of the sexes in these different social spaces finds ideological legitimacy through gender classification. In a system where social structures are based on the gender dichotomy, differences between the sexes are overemphasized and placed in a hierarchical relationship of superiority and subordination (Scheele, 2019). Institutionalized forms and interpretive patterns of gender differentiation and inequality take effect at the subject and action level in an implicit but powerful interpretive "topography" of normative gender roles and allegedly gender-specific needs (Fraser, 1989, p. 12) and are simultaneously confirmed and reproduced by these (Scheele, 2010, p. 123).

This separation of "productive" (paid, public) and "unproductive" (unpaid, private) labor is linked to a discernible hierarchizaton of both spheres: the market economy takes precedence over other forms of economic activities, including reproductive labor in private households. This means that the valorization of capital takes precedence over the basic requirements of livelihood and "the logic of economic production overrides that of social reproduction" (Fraser, 2016, p. 103). Care activities become secondary to the "interests of one's own way of doing business" (Aulenbacher, 2015, p. 21). However, and this can be seen as an internal contradiction, the capitalist economy remains reliant "on other resources and services" (Aulenbacher, 2015, p. 22) such as nature and the constantly reproduced workforce but does at the same time undermine social-reproductive capacities. Nancy Fraser (2016, 103) calls this a crisis since capital's accumulation dynamic is destroying its own conditions of possibility.

In summary, the "structural carelessness" (Aulenbacher, 2015, p. 32) of capitalist economy is expressed by abstracting from the resources and services relevant for the "reproduction of labor power"—since these cannot be valorized profitably. This separation from all care activities that go far beyond the "private" sphere has been realized since the separation of spheres of industrialized modernity through gender segregation and gender division of labor. The gendered division of labor has become a social norm—and, in many cases, also a normality—through the corresponding ideological transformation, according to which women are better suited to care work and household activities.

3   Bringing Reproductive Labor and Care Back In

The gendered division of labor with the exploitation of reproductive labor and natural resources has been widely analyzed within feminist research and gender studies. Claudia von Werlhof, Maria Mies, and Veronika Bennholdt-Thomsen (1983) represent what is termed the feminist Marxist *Bielefelder Ansatz* (Bielefeld approach) or "subsistence approach" aiming to provide an alternative critique of capitalism by including aspects that have more or less been neglected within political economy as well as in the classical Marxist critique of capitalism. Based on their analyses of economies in countries of the Global South and the capitalist transformation of the subsistence economy in those countries, the above-mentioned authors criticize Marx's reductive concept of work and the fact that his primary concern was the exploitation of workers in the labor process. Instead, von Werlhof, Mies, and Bennholdt-Thomsen (1983) focus on the relevance of subsistence economy—an economy in which goods are only produced for their direct use and not for buying or selling—for the capitalist economy.

The authors showed that this kind of economy is not a traditional form of production which has been completely replaced by the production of commodities, but that it still exists and has only changed its character. Following the assumption that women are those who, in every era and in every society, have produced life on this planet and on whose work, consequently, all other activities depend, we can draw a structural similarity between women and peasants in subsistence economies. While women physically give birth to children and peasants harvest food from the soil, they both create the preconditions for capitalist production since the capitalist surplus relies on the work of non-capitalist producers. This kind of production of life in a double meaning can be manipulated and exploited but has never been part of capitalist production itself (Mies, 1983, p. 117). This is one element of what has been explained as primary accumulation (von Werlhof, 1978). Unlike Marx, the feminist researchers from Bielefeld argue that it is not the contradiction between capital and labor but rather the contradiction between capital and subsistence production—since only the latter is able to produce "life"—that marks the societal class (and, one might add, gender) conflict. The accumulation of capital relies not only on the exploitation of the waged laborer but also on the exploitation of the unpaid reproductive laborer (Mulvaney, 2013).

As a further consequence, care work itself and the women doing care work are devalued at the level of private households and within national contexts. The devaluation of care and care work takes place in many ways: first, the work carried out in private households, predominantly by women, is not regarded as "work" but as a leisure or unproductive activity. It does generate the future labor force but has no added value and its structure derives from the necessities of life. With the concept of life care (*Lebenssorge*), German philosopher Cornelia Klinger (2014) highlights the relevance of care work for human existence. By including the whole spectrum of care including love, recognition, self-care, education, and socialization—not only the "classical" aspects such as caring, cleaning, or cooking—she shows that care is not only an inevitable but a vital part of human existence. Klinger argues that focusing only on paid work ignores the social relevance of unpaid care work and "priceless" life care. She points to the affective dimensions of care activities, which can only be commodified to a very limited degree but are nevertheless indispensable for the functioning of the economic system. However, the separation of "life" and "work" makes it possible to externalize the "costs" of human life: Western modernity imagines a society in which no one is caring, and, at the same time, no one is in need of care (Klinger, 2014, p. 22).

In this regard and secondly, care work and housework done by women is not paid but considered to be "compensated" through male family wages. Both the attribution of care as a female activity and its devaluation are evidently inseparable and mutually reinforcing, even when these activities are being commodified and become paid work—either in private households or in public/private care facilities—it remains low-paid work. It is often considered as unskilled or low-skilled work since it is associated with the unpaid work women perform at home (Grimshaw, Fagan, Hebson, & Tavora, 2017, p. 8).

The second perspective representing the *Bielefelder Ansatz* is the term *Hausfrauisierung* (housewifization). With this term, the authors describe a historical double movement of making bourgeois and proletarian women to 'proper housewives' in Europe and the US on the one hand and the integration of the women worldwide into the into global production processes on the other hand (Mies 2014). The first is part of the capitalist developments in the 19th and 20th century, where the domestication of women—"first in the bourgeois class proper, then among the so-called petty-bourgeoisie and finally in the working class or the proletariat" (Mies, 2014, p. 103)—made them not only more and more dependent on their husbands, but also kept them away from political and economic rights. At the same time, "the creation of housework and the housewife as an agent of consumption" (Mies, 2014, p. 106) created new markets for household products and luxury goods. The *Hausfrauisierung* is closely linked to the process of colonization. Mies (1983, pp. 120–122) argued that the proletarianization of men and the *Hausfrauisierung* of women—both in the bourgeois class as well as in the working classes—in industrial countries in the Global North would not have been possible without the exploitation of resources and labor force in the Global South. Furthermore, the colonial rulers, too, tried to establish this model in the colonies. And here the second part of the movement becomes visible. Within the international division of labour, women—universally defined as housewives—became the "optimal labour force for the capitalist (and socialist) accumulation process on a world scale" (Mies, 2014, p. 116). Their work—even if it is commodified within capitalist production—is labeled as "domestic work" carried out by housewives who use their spare time to earn some extra money for the family. The label "housewife" legitimizes the devaluation and exploitation of the female work force (Mies, 1983, p. 118). In this context, it becomes obvious that the term *Hausfrauisierung* is not a paraphrase for specific domestic work but rather an analytical tool to better understand "unfree labor," in other words, unorganized labor with no regulation of working hours, extremely low wages, and no social or political rights (Werlhof, 1983).

Both, the devaluation of care and the exploitation of the female workforce not only in private households but also in the global division of labor continuous. Still, "women's labour market opportunities are limited and moulded by sex discrimination, gender inequalities in domestic labour, and the interplay of household and workplace power relations" (Grimshaw et al., 2017, p. 4).

4   Crisis of Social Reproduction

Over the past few decades, the gendered division of labor has undergone several changes: in most Western societies and welfare systems, the former prominent male breadwinner model has been modernized and partly replaced by an adult worker model. Especially at the EU-level, "[w]omen have been seen as an untapped labour reserve" (Lewis & Guiliari, 2005, p. 5) and a higher female labour-market participation is seen as "a means increasing both competitiveness and the tax base of the continental European social insurance welfare states" (ibid.). In addition, the increasing feminization of labor does not only stand for a growing number of women in gainful employment but also for a deregulation and partly precarization of formerly regulated employment relationships of men which undermine the concept of single income households (Spiegel, 2005). At the same time, legal achievements in gender equality, emancipatory processes for women, and increased female participation in market-based employment have created a vacuum in the field of "reproduction," what is termed a "crisis of (social) reproduction" (Jürgens, 2010) in many Western states. This means "a state in which the means for a society to regenerate itself are no longer available" (Mulvaney, 2013, p. 28). This affects childcare as well as care of the elderly and of dependents—plus self-care or the reproduction of labor power. Consequently, the gender equality norm of improving opportunities and conditions for female employment conflicts with society's need to provide care.

Throughout Europe, we see at the same time an increasing need for caregivers as an effect of the demographic development. The baby boom generation currently entering pension age combined with a higher life expectancy has led to a growing demand in long-term care provision. How this reproductive crisis is resolved varies across political systems and depending on societal resources, and it remains a contested arena between different actors (Scheele, 2002). Although many Western welfare states have developed facilities for the care of children and of elderly people, the main caring obligations remain a matter to be handled within the family or through formal or informal assistance. Although care work in welfare states is financially supported through insurance schemes and state support or by means of commodified work, care remains a female arena. This applies to all different types of care regimes.

Care regime approaches follow the prominent welfare state analysis by Gøsta Esping-Andersen (1990) who used the term "welfare regime" to compare different national policies and the interplay between the state, markets, and families/households regarding the provision of welfare. His early typology of three regimes—the liberal, the conservative, and the social democratic welfare regime—has not only been revised and broadened but has also been criticized by feminist researchers for not systematically including gender. As a result, not only have different gender regimes been identified but also different care regimes in terms of the social arrangement of care. Francesca Bettio and Janneke Plantenga (2004) divided European countries into five clusters: the family provided care which is typical of the Mediterranean countries Spain,

Italy, and Greece; a public-private mix of care provision in the UK and the Netherlands; a publicly facilitated private care model represented by Germany and Austria; a formalization of care through public financial resources for elderly people and services for children, as in Belgium and France: and high levels of formal (public) care services, as seen in the Nordic countries.

In the field of elderly care, in many countries the workforce of migrant women has become the main pillar for securing care, assistance, and support for this generation. Particularly where care arrangements are organized informally within families, care workers from other countries—in Western European Countries mainly from Central and Eastern European Countries, in North America from Latin America —are employed in private households to support people in need of care if households can afford this (Benazha/Lutz 2019). At this point, the private household often becomes part of a global labor market, in which migration and care regimes are closely linked and result in the phenomenon of global care chains. In the following section, I will take a deeper look at these forms of globalized labor relations.

5 Global Care Chains

Twenty years ago, Arlie Hochschild (2000) coined the term "global care chains" to explain how the increasing labor market inclusion of women in the Global North as well as in the Global South has created a new form of redistribution of reproductive labor. Hochschild describes how women in the "Global South" leave their families and travel to the Global North in order to find jobs—mainly in private households where they take care of children and older dependents. In their families of origin, they often hire other poorer women, sometimes also from other countries, to care for their children and dependent family members. This creates a "series of personal links between people across the globe based on the paid and unpaid work of caring" (Hochschild, 2000, p. 131).

The term "global care chain" has often been linked to the "global care drain" which itself relates to the widely used term "brain drain." This last term was used to highlight the fact that countries whose qualified elite leaves to move to other—richer—countries with better work and income conditions, lack opportunities for social development and economic progress. As Hochschild describes: "As rich nations become richer and poor nations become poorer, this one-way flow of talent and training continuously widens the gap between the two" (Hochschild, 2002, p. 17). A similar trend can be identified in the field of care, which Hochschild calls the "importation of care and love from poor countries to rich ones" (ibid.).

These global care chains have multiple effects: while for many women this is an achievement in terms of independence that their mothers could not even dream of, and so it can be interpreted as an emancipatory process and a means to greater gender equality, at the same time, it is also the result of a lack of employment opportunities in the country of origin. Arlie Hochschild (2010, p. 23) pointed out that "Marx's iconic male, stationary industrial worker has been replaced by a new icon: the mobile and stationary female service worker."

However, the vast majority of women migrating from one country to another are part of a workforce with no labor rights and labor power at all or only weak ones at best. This often is related to their precarious residence permit and to the kind of work—referred to as "women's work"—that they do. This precariousness is largely related to a subject that has been covered in the previous sections—the devaluation of cleaning and caring within the capitalist economy. Another issue is the fact that work in private households is not regulated but part of a "grey economy." Work contracts are frequently informal without any regulations on working hours, overtime pay, sick leave, or holidays. Migrant workers often work in 24-hour care jobs for several weeks and then go back home for a particular period of time before returning and continuing their work (Lutz 2007). This migration pattern has been called "circular migration" since it is not a permanent move from one country to another. It is also the effect of the "private" status of the employment relationship as well as of the often-limited citizenship rights.

This becomes evident if we look at the relatively precarious position of care workers for example from Eastern European countries, particularly from countries outside the EU. Although the European Union guarantees freedom of movement of people (and goods, services, and capital) between EU states, this is not the case for workers from countries outside the EU. Furthermore, with the EU enlargement in 2004 and 2007, the freedom of movement for citizens from the new Central and Eastern European member states was limited initially and only implemented in 2011 and 2014, respectively, for the two waves. Precarious citizenship rights and no work permits have a further negative impact on labor rights.

At a macro-economic level, however, economically weak countries benefit from the transfer of money linked to female migration. A large number of poor households in many countries rely on migrant remittances and in 2019, "remittance flows to LMICs became larger than foreign direct investment (FDI)" (World Bank, 2020, 7). It is expected that the remittance flows have been significantly dropped in 2020 due to the Covid-19 crisis (World Bank, 2020).

In contrast to the general positive economic impact of labor migration, global economic crises and the associated financialization processes have negatives effect on the conditions under which social reproduction services are provided, for example, in the wake of the financial crisis 2008 when families lost access to social infrastructure or had to fight against forced evictions from their houses in many European countries as well as in the US, when they were not longer able to pay back a loan or to pay the rent (Roberts, 2018). Also, the Covid-19 crisis has increased the burden of housework and its intensity and the need to provide home-based care, with women and girls carrying the greater load of these increased demands (UN Women 2020) and the closure of borders lead to a restriction of labor migration. This means that social reproduction must be considered in its global context since it is closely interwoven with the dynamics of global markets, financial, and migration regimes.

6   Conclusion

This chapter has aimed at analyzing the global labor markets from a gender perspective by focusing on the interrelation between productive and reproductive labor in capitalist economies and the gendered division between both spheres. It becomes obvious that the analysis of global labor markets needs to include commodified, more or less market coordinated work as well as often unpaid or low-paid care work in private households and commodified public or private care services.

Women still do most of the unpaid work in the area of home and care work worldwide. Care work has always been and still is a hidden part of modern capitalist markets and remains a "private" and predominantly unregulated form of labor, even when it becomes commodified labor. If the gendered division of labor is classified as a "natural" division of labor, it cannot be seen as a constitutive part of capitalist production but is systematically devalued and split off from other fields of work. The lack of recognition and regulation goes hand in hand with low wages and forms a typical labor market for (female) migrants. It becomes further apparent that the rise of female employment within national contexts is closely related to the increase in female migration on the global labor markets.

Consequently, the gendered division of labor not only leads to unequal opportunities between women and men but also between different groups of women, particularly between groups of women with and without full citizenship rights. At the same time, it is the cause of the undervaluation of women's paid work (Grimshaw et al. 2017, p. 8) as well as of the devaluation of the whole range of care and life concerns. Thus, "care" is, as Ute Gerhard (2014, p. 79) states, not only a descriptive collective term for a social practice of the division of labor but, at the same time, an analytical concept for the critique of social conditions.

References

Aulenbacher, B. (2015). Kapitalismus als Herrschaftszusammenhang und die Unterordnung des Lebens. In B. Aulenbacher, B. Riegraf, & S. Völker (Eds.), *Feministische Kapitalismuskritik* (pp. 13–53). Münster: Westfälisches Dampfboot.

Benazha, A. V., & Lutz, H. (2019). Intersektionale Perspektiven auf die Pflege: Geschlechterverhältnisse und Migrationsprozesse. In C. Rudolph & K. Schmidt (Eds.), *Interessenpolitik und Care - Voraussetzungen, Hürden und Perspektiven kollektiven Handeln* (pp. 146–160) Münster: Westfälisches Dampfboot.

Bettio, F., & Plantenga, J. (2004). Comparing care regimes in Europe. In *Feminist Economics, 10* (1), 85–113.

Dannecker, P. (2019). Globalisierung: Geschichte, Ansätze und Themen aus der Perspektive der Geschlechterforschung. In B. Kortendiek, B. Riegraf, & K. Sabisch, (Eds.) *Handbuch Interdisziplinäre Geschlechterforschung. Geschlecht und Gesellschaft* (pp. 823–832) Wiesbaden: Springer vs.

Ehrenreich, B., & Hochschild, A. R. (2002). Introduction. In B. Ehrenreich & A. Hochschild (Eds.), *Global Woman: Nannies, Maids, and Sex Workers in the Global Economy* (pp. 1–14). New York: Henry Holt.

Esping-Andersen, G. (1990). *Three Worlds of Welfare Capitalism*. Cambridge: Polity Press.

Femina Politica (2016). *Moderne Sklaverei und extreme Ausbeutung in globalisierten Arbeits- und Geschlechterverhältnissen, 25*(1). Opladen: Verlag Barbara Budrich.

Fraser, N. (1989). *Unruly Practices. Power, Discourse and Gender in Contemporary Social Theory*. Cambridge: Polity Press.

Fraser, N. (2009). Feminism, capitalism and the cunning of history. *New Left Review, 56*, 97–117.

Fraser, N. (2016). Contradictions of capital and care. *New Left Review*, 100, 99–117.

Grimshaw, D., Fagan, C., Hebson, G. & Tavora, I. (2017). A new labour market segmentation approach for analysing inequalities. Introduction and overview. In D. Grimshaw, C. Fagan, G. Hebson & I. Tavora (Eds.), *Making Work More Equal. A New Labour Market Segmentation Approach* (pp. 1–32). Manchester: Manchester University Press.

Hochschild, A. (2010). The back stage of a global free market. Nannies and surrogates. In U. Apitzsch & M. Schmidbaur (Eds.), *Care und Migration. Die Ent-Sorgung menschlicher Reproduktionsarbeit entlang von Geschlechter- und Armutsgrenzen.* (pp. 23–40). Opladen, Farmington Hill: Verlag Barbara Budrich.

Hochschild, A. R. (2000). Global care chains and emotional surplus value. In A. Giddens & W. Hutton (Eds.), *On the Edge. Living with Global Capitalism* (pp. 130–146). London: Jonathan Cape.

Hochschild, A. R. (2002). Love and gold. In B. Ehrenreich & A. Hochschild (Eds.), *Global Woman: Nannies, Maids, and Sex Workers in the Global Economy* (pp. 15–30). New York: Henry Holt.

Jürgens, K. (2010). Deutschland in der Reproduktionskrise. *Leviathan, 38* (4), 559–587.

Klinger, C. (2014). Selbst- und Lebenssorge als Gegenstand sozialphilosophischer Reflexionen auf die Moderne. In B. Aulenbacher, B. Riegraf, & T. Hildegard (Eds.), Sorge: Arbeit, Verhältnisse, Regime [Special issue]. *Soziale Welt, 20,* 21–39.

Kocka, J. (2017). *Die Geschichte des Kapitalismus* (3rd ed.). Munich: Beck.

Lewis, J. & Giullari, S. (2005). The adult worker model family, gender equality and care: The search for new policy principles and the possibilities and problems of a capabilities approach. *Economy and Society, 34* (1), 76–104.

Lutz, H. (2007). *Vom Weltmarkt in den Privathaushalt. Die neuen Dienstmädchen im Zeitalter der Globalisierung.* Opladen: Barbara Budrich.

Mies, M. (1983). Subsistenzproduktion, Hausfrauisierung, Kolonisierung. *Beiträge zur feministischen Theorie und Praxis, 6* (9/10), 115–124.

Mies, M. (2014). *Patriarchy and accumulation on a world scale: Women in the international division of labour.* London: Zed Books.

Mohanty, C. T. (1986). Under Western eyes. Feminist scholarship and colonial discourses. *Boundary 2. 12* (3), 333–358.

Mulvaney, K. (2013). For what it's worth: an examination of the persistent devaluation of "women's work" in capitalism and considerations for feminist politics. *GENDER - Zeitschrift für Geschlecht, Kultur und Gesellschaft, 5* (2), 27–44.

Roberts, A. (2018). Financialization and the production of gender and class relations. In A. Scheele & S. Wöhl (Eds.): *Feminismus und Marxismus* (pp 187–201). Weinheim, Basel: Beltz Juventa.

Sassen, S. (1991). *The Global City.* New Jersey: Princeton University Press.

Scheele, A. (2002). Von „Yettis" und „flinken Servicekräften". Zur geschlechtlichen Ausgestaltung des Dienstleistungssektors. In K. Gottschall, & B. Pfau-Effinger (Eds.), *Zukunft der Arbeit und Geschlecht. Diskurse, Entwicklungspfade und Reformoptionen im internationalen Vergleich* (pp. 249–266). Opladen: Leske und Budrich.

Scheele, A. (2010). Emanzipatorische Potentiale einer Zusammenführung von Arbeit und Politik. In M. Frey, A. Heilmann, K. Lohr, A. Manske, & S. Völker (Eds.), *Perspektiven auf Arbeit und Geschlecht. Transformationen, Reflexionen, Interventionen* (pp. 119–134). München: Rainer Hampp Verlag.

Scheele, A. (2019). Abwertung von Care-Arbeit durch Vergeschlechtlichung. In C. Rudolph & K. Schmidt (Eds.), *Interessenpolitik und Care - Voraussetzungen,*

Hürden und Perspektiven kollektiven Handelns (pp. 24–26). Münster: Westfälisches Dampfboot.

Spiegel, A. (2005). *Alltagswelten in translokalen Räumen: Bolivianische Migrantinnen in Buenos Aires*. Frankfurt/Main: iko.

UN Women (2020). Whose time to care: Unpaid care and domestic work during COVID-19. Retrieved August 18, 2021, from https://data.unwomen.org/publications/whose-time-care-unpaid-care-and-domestic-work-during-covid-19.

von Werlhof, C. (1978). Frauenarbeit: Der blinde Fleck in der Kritik der politischen Ökonomie. *Beiträge zur feministischen Theorie und Praxis, 1*, 18–32.

von Werlhof, C., Mies, M., & Bennholdt-Thomsen, V. (1983) *Frauen, die letzte Kolonie*. Reinbek bei Hamburg: Rowohlt.

World Bank (2020). COVID-19 crisis through a migration lens. *Migration and Development Brief no. 32*. World Bank, Washington, DC.

PART 2

The Market Concept and Its Heuristic Potential

Introduction to Part 2
The Market Concept and Its Heuristic Potential

Peter-Paul Bänziger and Ursula Mense-Petermann

This part of the collective volume builds on the discussions on "free" and "unfree" labor in the preceding part and is dedicated to a critical reflection on the notion of "market." Can we really speak of market exchange in the case of labor power? What are the similarities and differences between labor markets and markets for goods and services? What are the analytical strengths and weaknesses of the market term when it comes to scrutinizing (cross-border) labor markets and their embeddedness? Are there conceptual alternatives? These are all questions discussed in Part 2 of this volume.

In the capitalist societies of the twentieth and twenty-first centuries, market exchange as an institutional form gained momentum. However, market exchange is also an ideology with performative effects (MacKenzie, Muniesa, & Siu, 2007). The market term is at the core of neoliberal ideologies that advocate marketization and emphasize the advantages of the voluntary and rational choice of exchange partners as well as the efficiency of markets in terms of both individual and global utility maximization and allocation of resources. An undeniable performative effect of this is the fact that many workers have learned to see themselves as market participants and to act accordingly (see Bänziger in this part).

Markets feature center stage in what is known as new economic sociology. Scholars in economic sociology are interested in the non-market prerequisites of markets and in their embeddedness in institutional, cognitive, and cultural macrostructures (Beckert, 2009). From this perspective, in the first contribution to this part, Patrik Aspers discusses whether there is a uniqueness that labor markets have in comparison to other markets, or if we can use the same concepts and theories to explain trade in labor power as trade in other goods. Aspers argues that markets are structures for the exchange of rights under competition and puts forward three questions that have to be addressed in a market: 1. what is traded; 2. how things are done in the market; 3. how prices are set, although these questions can be dealt with in different ways. His contribution analyzes these three questions in relation to labor markets and sets up the hypothesis that although all markets are different, there is no need to have a specific market theory for labor. Combining a structural analysis of roles in markets with a phenomenological approach to deconstruct markets, he suggests that what is unique to labor markets is the actors' simultaneous enactment, and the switching between two roles: as seller and as objects of exchange.

In the second contribution in this part, Karen Shire discusses the contributions and limits of a market perspective on (cross-border) labor markets. This chapter connects to Aspers' contribution and argues that a firm market-sociological perspective is indeed useful for the analysis of labor markets because it introduces an actor-centered and process-oriented understanding of how labor markets are established and how they depend on non-market social relations and institutions for their survival. In order to make this perspective plausible and to provide a more substantial theory of the social order of (cross-border) labor markets, Shire stitches together a general sociological theory of labor markets out of the available fragments of market sociology, economic sociology, and labor sociology.

Two further contributions to this part explicitly address the cross-border dimension of (labor) markets. Peter-Paul Bänziger analyzes the coproduction of labor markets and nation-states between 1850 and 2000. He argues that labor markets did not emerge before the decades around 1900. Only the modern nation-state established a space for exchange of labor, defined the roles and rights of sellers and buyers, and made labor a commodity by standardizing and valuating different forms of it. At the same time, this process contributed to the consolidation of the nation-state itself. As Bänziger argues that it is questionable whether much has changed here to this day, his historiographical analysis critically examines the concept of "global labor markets."

Finally, Ursula Mense-Petermann and Helen Schwenken bring a market perspective into conversation with migration studies, and they identify the analytical potential and strengths as well as the "blind spots" of different market concepts. They critically review different strands of research on labor migration and the role that the market term assumes in these approaches. Building on this, Mense-Petermann and Schwenken propose that using a market concept as developed by the new economic sociology can be usefully adopted for analyzing cross-border labor migration and shedding light on aspects and dimensions of cross-border labor migration that are disregarded in contemporary migration studies.

Overall, Part 2 offers an in-depth discussion of the market concept in the context of cross-border labor.

References

Beckert, J. (2009). The social order of markets. *Theory and Society, 38*, 245–269.

MacKenzie, D., Muniesa, F., & Siu, L. (Eds.) (2007). *Do Economists Make Markets?* Princeton: Princeton University Press.

CHAPTER 5

What Is Unique about Labor Markets?

Patrik Aspers

1   Introduction

In contemporary capitalism, coordination of resources and factors of production is to a large extent done in markets. Consequently, markets are also used to find and select labor power (Polanyi, 1957), i.e., the power of human beings that can be put to work and thus used to accomplish certain ends. This power is hired out for a specific time or task, and it is extracted in an employment relation, often by means of hierarchy (organization), i.e., a superior decides what workers are supposed to be doing during the time they are hired.

Sociological research on labor markets rarely focuses on markets in general (see also Shire in this volume). Instead, issues of distributive outcomes of labor markets (Kalleberg & Sorensen, 1979) and the role of unions (Streeck, 2005) have largely dominated the literature to date. Wolfgang Streek points to underlying ideas that might explain this situation: "Generally, sociological research and theory maintain that the labor market is not really a market, in the sense of a universalistic, impersonal, color-and gender-blind mechanism matching supply of, and demand for, labor" (p. 254). Moreover, in the social scientific literature, labor markets are viewed as being different from other markets. A corollary is that the thematically related but diverse fields of sociology of work, sociology of labor markets, and sociology of markets appear to have limited interaction. Why this gulf between these fields exists is not clear, but it has not furthered our understanding of labor markets.

To increase our understanding, I suggest zooming in on the markets and deconstructing them. The distinct objects of trade make markets different from one another. Indeed, if we look at markets from this empirical end of the theory-evidence continuum, all markets are different. Seen from the other end, however, the most formal and abstract, all markets are identical. The scientific problem of market categorization involves identifying meaningful distinctions between types of markets that can increase our understanding and improve precision in empirical work.

In the present chapter, I argue that although there are some clear differences between labor and other objects of trade in markets, there is no need for a separate theory of labor markets. Such a theory would require a whole set of interrelated propositions that are specified and different than those in other markets. Nevertheless, there are differences that should be taken into consideration when analyzing the conditions of human beings in markets. Taking a phenomenological approach to deconstruct markets, I argue that what is specific about labor markets is that actors play two roles, as sellers and as objects of trade, switching between the two. However, this should not translate into a distinct "labor market theory." The two ideas of the similarity between labor markets and other markets and the uniqueness of human beings as being the seller as well as the object of trade run parallel in this chapter.

2   Markets

I will begin by analyzing what markets in general mean. Any market depends on the more fundamental institutional conditions, formal and informal (North, 1991), in which it is embedded (Polanyi, 1957). There are general laws, for example property rights, that apply to most markets, thereby providing a foundation to all markets. Most laws, for example property rights, apply to most markets. Laws are based on decisions and it makes sense to speak about organized (Ahrne, Aspers, & Brunsson, 2015), or at least partially organized (Ahrne & Brunson, 2011) markets. It is, furthermore, presumed that actors are free to make choices and to enter into a contractual relation, but not into relations that remove the right to draw up future contracts.

All markets are, by definition, ordered and ordering processes are of interest to both sociologists and economists (Nelson & Winter, 2002, p. 23). The following definition of a market aims to meet the different requirements mentioned in the literature: a market is a social structure for the exchange of owners' rights, in which individuals or organizations compete with one another via offers (cf. Aspers, 2011, p. 4). The market structure is based, in particular, on two roles: that of the buyer and that of the seller, each with their own interest to "sell at a high price" or to "buy at a low price" (Geertz, 1992, p. 226). The property rights (Carruthers & Ariovich, 2004) that actors exchange must be recognized. In order to have competition in a market, at least one side has to be characterized by competition. The competition between the parties may not revolve around money but around other variables, for example product differentiation or warranty policy (Chamberlin, 1953), and it implies that the actors have a choice to trade with others and also have the capacity to make these choices.[1] Choice, moreover, presumes that actors have the reflexive capacity to evaluate the options (Schutz & Luckmann, 1989).

There are three additional prerequisites for something to be a market. The first prerequisite refers to what is traded in markets. Markets presuppose the process of singularization of the offers traded to make them calculable (Callon & Muniesa, 2005). The second condition is about how things are done in the market. This is about the decided (formal) and grown (informal) institutions, which are part of the specific market's culture, including its "rules of engagement" (White & Eccles, 1987, p. 984) and "rules of exchange" (Fligstein & Mara-Drita, 1996, p. 15; Smith, 2007, p. 3; White, 2002, p. 2). This second prerequisite refers also to general market culture, for example a type of capitalism or a certain way of trading that is not specific of any particular market. The third prerequisite is about the value of the offer traded in the market. Given that actors know what is being traded, the economic value of the offers—the goods or services traded—can be, and must be, determined (Aspers & Beckert, 2011; Smith, 1989). Economic value is usually expressed in prices, with money being used as a means of accounting (Dodd, 2005). Below I use the three market prerequisites as the baseline of the analysis.

3 Markets and Labor

Using a substantive analysis of economic activities, Polanyi says that "Labor is another name for a human activity which goes with life itself" (Polanyi, 1957, p. 75). He does not see labor as a commodity, which is defined as "objects produced for sale on the market" (Polanyi, 1957, p. 75). Obviously, labor is possible to trade in markets, as are many other services. It is only by stipulating a definition that connects the purpose of making objects with market trade of these objects that labor becomes "fictitious," (Polanyi, 1957, p. 76). Polanyi's definition is thus more normative than scientific, and it does not account for the multitude of transactions that historically have taken place or are taking place under competition in markets. I fully agree with Polanyi that labor is central in life, but the normative semantics of his definitions make less sense.

Although some researchers, for example Arendt (1988), see differences between labor (the biological process of the human body) and work (the

---

1 As can be seen, my approach to markets does not see competition as a market "problem" as, for example, Shire (this volume) does. My point is that competition is essential to markets, although it might either appear to be an unintended consequence or the result of organization, depending on the type of market in question (Aspers, 2009).

making of unnatural things),[2] I will concur with Marcel van der Linden (this volume), who, like Marx and Polanyi, focuses on labor power, i.e., the capacity of human beings to accomplish something, a thing or a service. In labor markets, labor power is traded. Van der Linden points out that since this power cannot be packaged and traded like, for example, a bottle of wine, it is better to speak about "hiring out," and it is this hiring out that is meant by trading labor power. The thing for which one is hired out can be very specific, such as painting 20 square meters of a concrete wall per hour, or something more abstract, such as the development of a new marketing strategy for a company selling paint. If no labor power is traded, we either speak of forced labor, as in the case of slavery, or speak of voluntary work. What is traded in a given labor market is also normally what gives the name to this market. There are, hence, different labor markets, each specialized in a certain professional service that is traded, and which constitute a market category (Kennedy, 2005; 2008), such as taxi drivers, IT engineers, sociologists, or carpenters.

My point is that not only does it frequently happen that labor power is traded, but also labor markets meet the first prerequisite of a market, since it is clear enough to the parties what is in fact being traded. Let me therefore discuss the second prerequisite, namely that there are institutions that order the market (see Bänziger in this volume). In the economy, some type of "contract," formal or informal, is made between the seller and buyer, meaning that there are ways in which trade is done, many of which are grounded in formal laws. When there is a labor contract, we refer to hired labor force, i.e., the work done by someone who is paid for this service by someone else. The contract between the parties implies that the buyer has, for a limited domain of activities and for a specific period of time, the right to exercise hierarchical power (Ahrne, 1994;

---

2   The Oxford English Dictionary clarifies the distinction between labor and work. Labor refers to "the exertion of the faculties of the body or mind, especially when painful or compulsory" and work refers to "[s]omething that is or was done...an act, deed, proceeding, business" (Simpson & Weiner, 1989). Whereas labor focuses on the faculties of actor required and put into use to perform the act, work is what is actually done and being produced in the act. Neither of them, thus, focus on the product or the outcome per se.

   Work, to be more precise, is a human activity (Schutz & Luckmann, 1989, pp. 11–14), thereby excluding robots, that one is required to do, in contrast to hobbies or leisure activities that are "optional." Work produces something, although much work, and time spent on work, or the specific work activities a person is assigned, can indeed be "empty," meaning that there is little to do in relation to the work description and the number of hours spent at work (Paulsen, 2014). Moreover, to value labor as something positive is a recent phenomenon. Originally, in traditional societies and up until early modernity, when guilds were created, labor was avoided, and it was something to be done by slaves to the extent that this was possible (Lederer, 1932).

Luhmann, 2000; Thompson, Frances, Levacic, & Mitchell, 1991). The period of time may be very short or, in other cases, have no definite endpoint.

With hired labor under contract and paid labor for a given piece, the exchange is partial, meaning that the buyer is not, as in the case of slaves, in full control of the whole individual, or of the individual's full labor power. The human being is just renting out his or her capacity to work for a specific period of time or to do a certain thing.

Furthermore, in many labor markets, both sides have organized themselves, and there may be a whole range of established rules and institutions that regulate the work, rights to go on strike or take a vacation, the right to a pension, and many more aspects that are important in labor markets. It is not uncommon for parties in markets to be organized, however. Hence, the second prerequisite is also met.

The final prerequisite concerns the value of what is traded in a labor market. A whole range of alternatives to determine the value is available. In some cases, fixed wages have been determined in negotiations. But as long as actors have choices, there can still be competition between the individuals to get the process started, for example by credentials. Employers may also compete for the best workers. Some labor markets are characterized by centralized negotiations while in others, prices are set in direct deals between individual workers and employers; frequently, a combination of these two is used. In yet others, such as online markets, there may be bidding, or a race to the bottom (i.e., low wages) to get a job.

There is much more that can be said about pricing in labor markets, and this has to do with the type of market, and how they are ordered. Order in markets may be the result of either status or standard, although, in reality, we often observe a combination of these forms. The more work is standardized, the more easily exchangeable are the workers. Increasingly, simple service work is also standardized and can be purchased—or hired—on electronic platforms. Amazon Mechanical Turk (MTurk) exemplifies this type of platform, which is presented as

> a crowdsourcing marketplace that makes it easier for individuals and businesses to outsource their processes and jobs to a distributed workforce who can perform these tasks virtually. This could include anything from conducting simple data validation and research to more subjective tasks like survey participation, content moderation, and more. MTurk enables companies to harness the collective intelligence, skills, and insights from a global workforce to streamline business processes,

augment data collection and analysis, and accelerate machine learning development.³

In standard markets such as MTurk, work is compartmentalized, and thus made singularized (Callon & Muniesa, 2005) so that it resembles homogenous products. This is one condition for the imagined perfect market model presented by Knight (1921).⁴

The notion of status market can be used to capture another type of work, namely tasks that cannot be determined at the time the contract is signed. In status markets, order is essentially a function of buyers and sellers whose identities are ranked according to status. This means that there is a social structure, not only constituted by roles but also by identities, that the actors are able to identify and to discriminate between, as is the case with professional football clubs and players, for instance. What is traded in status markets may vary, but it is essentially a function of the trading parties coming together and "producing" whatever is the outcome of the work. In other words, what needs to be produced is not decided prior to the transaction but is an outcome of the combination of the person doing the work and the organization or other party that is paying for it. If this is the case, it is not possible to measure the output in terms of quality against a standard; it is rather a situation in which the parties are rubbing status off on one another (Podolny, 2005). Moreover, status is in the eye of the beholder; it is only possible to gain status if it is recognized by others. This means that actors gain status according to what other people think and value.⁵ A typical example is the world of academia in which people are hired to carry out research but essentially free to define what their research can and should be about. Markets for fashion photographers (Aspers, 2006)

---

3 Retrieved January 15, 2019, from https://www.mturk.com/.
4 The competition, potentially on both sides of the market interface, is increased. In this market, the work is quite similar to a thing being traded. Given the relatively much stronger position of buyers compared to sellers of labor power, sellers are normally in a weaker position. Since many of the tasks at MTurk are quite simple, and can be performed online, both the supply and demand can go global. In other words, globalization is one dimension of the increased competition, and the trend towards standardized, or rather, standard markets, is another.
5 Established institutions and people with status and affiliations to institutions come together and determine what is "good." Thus, although it is clear that actors attempt to influence their status by, for example, actions and organization, it is still other peoples' views that determine their status. Status, moreover, is relative so that some have more status than others. In a status market, the ranking of buyers and or sellers is more institutionalized (taken for granted) than the offers being traded.

and for authors of novels (Furst, 2017) are additional examples of this type of market.

We can conclude that on labor markets, as on any market, something is traded, there are rules for how this is done, and there are ways to set prices for what is being traded. One may argue that there is nothing unique about labor markets; they are just like other markets, seen from a formal point of view. However, if we look at the structural characteristics of markets, at the roles in particular, a different picture emerges. This is what I will outline now.

4   The Phenomenology of Labor Markets

What I argue is unique about labor markets is that the seller is both the object of trade[6]—what is traded—and the partner agreeing to the terms of the contract. Looking at this double role condition from the perspective of temporality, we see that the actor is, prior to being the object of trade, the seller of his labor power of trade. Subsequently, the actual work is performed, i.e., the specific tasks. The same actor, previously referred to as the seller, is then playing the role of worker or performer of the job or activity for which he or she is paid. In reality, this switching between "selling" and "working" may be a recurrent sequence of role switching, particularly with piece production, since there may be frequent renegotiations about the exact nature of the object traded and the working conditions.

However, role switching is not unknown in markets. It has been argued (Aspers, 2011) that one type of market is switch-role markets and another type is fixed-role markets. Switch-role markets are defined as markets in which actors constantly switch roles between being either sellers or buyers, for example, many financial markets. These are different from fixed-role markets in which the actors are identified as being either sellers or buyers. An actor may switch, for instance, between being a seller and a buyer at a flea market, but no actor switches between being a buyer and a piece of art, for example. Moreover, in many markets, you can rent things, such as a car but one can never become the car.

Consequently, what is really unique about labor markets is not the switching between roles per se, but the switching between selling one's labor power and being this very object of trade, labor power. In other words, what we

---

6   This contention is based on the assumption that labor power—as the precise object of exchange—can only analytically separated from its bearer, the individual. In practice, the individual is still and always involved when it comes to make use of the object of exchange.

human beings are renting out is our labor power, i.e., our physical and mental capacities for a certain time. That there is a phenomenology of being rented out, and that we switch this role on and off makes this market different from other markets for us as human beings. But not necessarily from the perspective of market theory.

If, however, we look at this trade from an objective point of view, i.e., from a distance and not accounting for the subjective perspective of the market actors, only small differences can be detected between trading in human labor power and trading in shares of companies or in tomatoes, for instance. The fact that human beings are playing two roles is not of major importance. If, in contrast, we take the point of view of the actor, the objective account is not accurately mirroring what is happening, and above all, what people are experiencing, in labor markets. Departing from phenomenology (Heidegger, 2001b; Husserl, 1960), i.e., analyzing how things appear to the actors, represents a radically different vantage point than the objective one.

5   The Human Being as an Object of Trade

Several authors in this volume agree to the classic view that human beings' labor power is not separate from their beings. This statement is, by definition, tautologically true. What I do here is examine this statement phenomenologically in order to see what it means for people in practice. From a phenomenological point of view, the object of trade is not neutral but ultimately inseparable from a human being, with capacities, emotions, interests, and much more, who is able to reflect on his or her situation while being in the situation, and while doing other things. It is actually the individual doing things. Thus, while on the job, performing the tasks assigned, one can reflect on the conditions, for example, the content of the work, the pay, security at the workplace, and future prospects in the current position. Talking to others at the workplace and making use of one's network (cf. Granovetter, 1974) are two means of comparing one's current situation with other potential jobs. Thus, this reflection depends to a large extent on what others do or do not do in markets.

Furthermore, in their everyday routine life, human beings, or at least many of them, are evaluated by others in the markets. In labor markets, this is indeed existential, since the object of trade is inherently "the individual." What is evaluated and exposed to competition is one's self. As mentioned above, the labor contract means that an individual, as a worker, is subject to the hierarchy and the power of the employer. The point is that the other side of the market ultimately decides whether someone is selected or not, for the position or the opportunity. An actor is consequently not in control of his or her identity. Hence, by being selected, or not, one is either in or out of the market. Nowhere is this existential dimension more pronounced than in the aesthetic sector (Menger, 2014), where job and identity are almost identical (Aspers, 2015; Furst, 2017).

6   Switching

It is true that labor can be existential—but so are most human activities. It is interesting that human beings can play two roles in a market. But the fact that we switch practices and registers structures the different experiences and is central to our reflexive capacity (Giddens, 1991; Mische & White, 1998). The argument here is not just that the potential of switching is of importance, although this is true, but that the actual switching itself is the very essence of human reflexivity. In other words, the person who is hired at the only factory in town at the age of 15 and whose father and grandfather are working at the same place is less likely to reflect on being in a particular market—since this is what "everyone does" (cf. Durkheim, 1984)—than those having several different jobs or contracts perhaps also in different markets.[7] The difference between the two or more domains is the key to bringing about reflexivity.

The most important aspect is to look at the potential and consequence of switching between roles while at the same time being "one" person, albeit with two market identities. Harrison White spells out the role of switching for identities: "Identities trigger out of events—that is to say, out of switches in surrounding—seeking control over uncertainty and thus over fellow identities" (White, 2008, p. 2).

I do not wish to point at switching as an empirical phenomenon only. Switching is an ontological constitutional component of human beings and their capacity to reflect. Ontologically, the individual concerned is in between roles (Aspers & Kohl, 2013; Heidegger, 2001b). If we follow Martin Heidegger, we do not come as one unit but become a unit as a result of dispersion (*Zerstreuung*) of the different activities into which we are thrown (*geworfen*). These different activities make up what Heidegger calls a *Dasein* (1978). *Dasein*, the term used by Heidegger to characterize being human, is not only ontologically dispersed, it is also dispersed in its own activities: caring (*Sorge*)

---

7 This is not the same thing as evaluating the conditions of mobilization and social resistance, for example in terms of unions or other social movements.

for something, doing something, questioning, and other types of activities (Heidegger, 2001b, pp. 56–57). Work is, of course, a central activity to which Heidegger explicitly refers. Hence, man is not first what many people today would call self, and then falls apart as a result of social interaction (Heidegger, 2001a, p. 333). It is in fact the other way around: the dispersion is the condition of the self. Man, according to Heidegger is this "conglomerate" who finds himself "dispersed." More elaborated reflection is a consequence of actors gaining several different identities, and not a given trait of humans.[8]

7 Conclusion

In this chapter, I argue that the field of labor market research has neglected the question of what a market is. The main question posed in this chapter is whether or not there should be a specific market theory for labor. The short answer to this question is "no." However, this is not to say that labor markets are like any other market. The question of what nevertheless sets labor markets apart from other markets leads us to our own being: being is work and work is being; this is a statement to which many would subscribe. It can be argued that being is largely constituted in labor. This condition was taken as the point of departure for a phenomenological analysis. The main point presented in this chapter is that switching in labor markets facilitates reflexivity, which in turn opens up the analysis to existential questions.

Finally, I argue that labor markets should be more central to sociological studies. Moreover, by going beyond the merely descriptive analyses of labor markets, we can gain a more in-depth understanding of labor markets. We can thus move beyond the economic view of actors who are taken for granted or the sociological focus on unions and collective bargaining.

References

Ahrne, G, Aspers, P., & Brunsson, N. (2015). The organization of markets. *Organization, 36*, 7–27.

Ahrne, G. (1994). *Social Organizations. Interaction Inside, Outside and between Organizations*. London: Sage.

---

8 Reflection is a condition, but in contrast to the egological approach (Tengelyi, 2012), I see reflection as a result of the dispersion of identities (cf. Heidegger, 1975 p. 226). Mead (1934, pp. 354–79) presents similar ideas.

Ahrne, G., & Brunsson, N. (2011). Organization outside organizations: The significance of partial organization. *Organization, 18*, 83–104.
Arendt, H. (1988). *The Human Condition*. Chicago: Chicago University Press.
Aspers, P. (2006). *Markets in Fashion, A Phenomenological Approach*. London: Routledge.
Aspers, P. (2009). How are markets made? Cologne: Max Planck Institute for the Study of Society, *Working Paper, 3*/09.
Aspers, P. (2011). *Markets*. Cambridge: Polity Press.
Aspers, P. (2015). Phenomenological identity theory in economic sociology. In P. Aspers & N. Dodd (Eds.), *Re-Imagining Economic Sociology* (pp. 252–274). Oxford: Oxford University Press.
Aspers, P., & Beckert, J. (2011). Introduction. In J. Beckert & P. Aspers (Eds.), *The Worth of Goods* (pp. 3–40). Oxford: Oxford University Press.
Aspers, P., & Kohl, S. (2013). Heidegger and socio-ontology: A sociological reading. *Journal of Classical Sociology, 13*, 487–508.
Callon, M. & Muniesa, F. (2005). Economic markets as calculative collective devices. *Organization Studies, 26*, 1229–1250.
Carruthers, B. & Ariovich, L. (2004). The sociology of property rights. *Annual Review of Sociology, 30*, 23–46.
Chamberlin, E. (1953). The product as an economic variable. *Quarterly Journal of Economics, 67*, 1–29.
Dodd, N. (2005). Reinventing monies in Europe. *Economy and Society, 34*, 558–583.
Durkheim, É. (1984). *The Division of Labour in Society*. London: Macmillan.
Fligstein, N., & Mara-Drita, I. (1996). How to make a market: Reflections on the attempt to create a single market in the European Union. *The American Journal of Sociology, 102*, 1–33.
Furst, H. (2017). *Selected or Rejected? Assessing Aspiring Writers' Attempts to Achieve Publication*. Uppsala: Uppsala University.
Geertz, C. (1992). The bazaar economy: Information and search in peasant marketing. In M. Granovetter & R. Swedberg (Eds.), *The Sociology of Economic Life*. (pp. 225–232). Boulder: Westview Press.
Giddens, A. (1991). *Modernity and Self-Identity, Self and Society in the Late Modern Age*. Cambridge: Polity Press.
Granovetter, M. (1974). *Getting a Job, A Study of Contacts and Careers*. Cambridge, Mass.: Harvard University Press.
Heidegger, M. (2001b). *Sein und Zeit*. Tübingen: Max Niemeyer Verlag.
Heidegger, M. (1975). *Die Grundprobleme der Phänomenologie, Gesamtausgabe, II. Abteilung, Vorlesungen 1923–1944*, Vol. 24. Frankfurt am Main: Vittorio Klostermann.
Heidegger, M. (1978). *Metaphysische Anfangsgründe der Logig im Ausgang von Leibniz, Gesamtausgabe, II. Abteilung: Vorlesungen 1923–1944*, Vol. 26. Frankfurt am Main: Vittorio Klostermann.

Heidegger, M. (2001a). *Einleitung in die Philosophie, Gesamtausgabe, II Abteilung: Vorlesungen*, Vol. 27. Frankfurt am Main: Vittorio Klostermann.

Husserl, E. (1960). *Cartesian Meditations, An Introduction to Phenomenology*. Haag: Martinus Nijhoff.

Kalleberg, A. L., & Sorensen, A. B. (1979). The sociology of labor markets. *Annual Review of Sociology, 5*, 351–379.

Kennedy, M. (2005) Behind the one-way mirror: Refraction in the construction of product market categories. *Poetics, 33*, 201–226.

Kennedy, M. (2008). Getting counted: Markets, media, and reality. *American Sociological Review, 73*, 270–295.

Knight, F. (1921). *Risk, Uncertainty and Profit*. Boston: Houghton Mifflin Company.

Lederer, E. (1932). Labor. In E. Seligman (Ed.), *Encyclopedia of the Social Sciences*, Vol. 7 (pp. 615–620). New York: Macmillan.

Luhmann, N. (2000). *Organisation und Entscheidung*. Opladen: Westdeutscher Verlag.

Mead, G. (1934). *Mind, Self, and Society, From the Standpoint of a Social Behaviorist*. Chicago: Chicago University Press.

Menger, P.-M. (2014). *The Economics of Creativity: Art and Achievement und Uncertainty*. Cambridge Ma: Harvard University Press.

Mische, A., & White, H. (1998). Between conversation and situation: Public switching dynamics across network domains. *Social Research, 65*, 695–724.

Nelson, R. R. & Winter., S. G. (2002). Evolutionary theorizing in economics. *The Journal of Economic Perspectives*, 16, 23–46.

North, D. C. C. (1991). Institutions. *The Journal of Economic Perspectives, 5*, 97–112.

Paulsen, R. (2014). *Empty Labor: Idleness and Workplace Resistance*. Cambridge: Cambridge University Press.

Podolny, J. (2005). *Status Signals, A Sociological Study of Market Competition*. Princeton, NJ.: Princeton University Press.

Polanyi, K. (1957). *The Great Transformation*. Boston: Beacon.

Schutz, A. & Luckmann, T. (1989). *The Structures of the Life-world*, Vol. II. Evanston: Northwestern University Press.

Simpson, J., & Weiner, E. (1989). *The Oxford English Dictionary*. Oxford: Oxford University Press.

Smith, C. (1989). *Auctions, The Social Construction of Value*. Berkeley: University of California.

Smith, C. (2007). Markets as definitional practices. *Canadian Journal of Sociology, 32*, 1–39.

Streeck, W. (2005). The sociology of labor markets and trade unions. In N. Smelser & R. Swedberg (Eds.) *The Handbook of Economic Sociology* (2nd ed., pp. 254–283). Princeton: Princeton University Press.

Tengelyi, L. (2012). Action and selfhood: A narrative interpretation. In D. Zahavi (Ed.), *The Oxford Handbook of Contemporary Phenomenology* (pp. 265–286). Oxford: Oxford University Press.

Thompson, G., Frances, J., Levacic, R., & Mitchell, J. (1991). *Markets, Hierarchies and Networks*. London: Sage.

White, H. (2002). *Markets from Networks, Socioeconomic Models of Production*. Princeton: Princeton University Press.

White, H. (2008). *Identity and Control: How Social Formations Emerge*. Princeton: Princeton University Press.

White, H., & Eccles, R. (1987). Producers' market. In J. Eatwell, et. al. (Eds.), *The New Palgrave: A Dictionary of Economic Theory and Doctrine* (pp. 984–986). London: Macmillan.

CHAPTER 6

The Contributions and Limits of Market Theory for the Study of Labor Markets

Karen Shire

1 Introduction[1]

Labor markets have been surprisingly undertheorized in sociology despite the central meaning of the exchange of labor for the rise of industrial capitalism and the development of market societies. As historians note, "free" labor markets are "recent social inventions," (Tilly & Tilly, 1994). The first century of their existence began with an unanimous critique of the "free" exchange of labor by the classical sociologists (Streeck, 1992, pp. 41–46) but has ended with most research about labor markets using the concept in largely descriptive terms, to "denote geographical areas or occupational and industrial groups, as well as groups of workers defined by ethnicity, race, sex, and levels of education and skill" (Kalleberg & Sorensen, 1979). Several important exceptions focus on explaining historical institutional constructions of labor markets (Fligstein, 2002), their core institution, the employment relation (Streeck, 1992), and how corporate actors shape their cross-national variations (Streeck, 2005). As Streeck noted a decade and a half ago, the economic sociology of labor markets has paid too little attention to explaining how labor market exchanges operate: "… although economic sociologists have insisted on the essential significance of social relations for the operations of labor markets, formal rules and institutions regulating such relations have not been at the center of sociological inquiry" (Streeck, 2005, p. 256).

---

[1] The author would like to thank Heidi Gottfried, Sigrid Quack, and Richard Hyman, who have all urged me in their own ways to foreground the problem of reproduction in the regulation of cross-border labor. This chapter builds on—and attempts to go beyond—an initial theorization of cross-border labor markets in Shire, 2020. Research for this chapter was supported by the ZiF Research Group "In Search of the Global Labour Market," and the extremely stimulating exchanges with its interdisciplinary and international members, and coordinators, sociologist Ursula Mensa-Petermann, historian Thomas Welskopp, and economist Anna Zaharieva.

Yet these important theoretical interventions into a largely descriptive field of social inquiry have limited the study of regulations to national institutions and practices. The operation of cross-border labor markets, defined as the exchange of labor across territorial jurisdictions, is under-researched in the sociology of labor and labor markets. Both the rise of circular migration and cross-border subcontracting of labor have formalized intentionally temporary labor mobility and established regular and repeated exchanges of labor across national borders. The aim of this chapter is to draw on economic sociology, political economy, and labor sociology to develop a specific theory of labor markets, and on this basis, to consider some of the important dimensions of cross-border labor markets.

The argument proceeds as follows. In the section below, I review the contributions of the old and new sociology of markets for theorizing the specificity of labor markets. As a general theory of markets, however, it underplays the relevance of the specificities of labor markets. The next sections discuss three specificities of labor markets: the nature of what is sold, the nature of the employment contract, and the transformation of labor power into labor effort. The final section turns to consider how this theory of labor markets can contribute to studying the operation and possible regulation of cross-border labor exchanges.

2 Contributions of the Old and New Sociology of Markets for Studying Labor Markets

Markets in the tradition of economic sociology are defined as the *voluntary and competitive* exchanges of ownership over objects produced for sale (Weber, 1922, 1978; Aspers, 2011). Markets differ empirically in the nature of the objects traded, a point which leads Aspers (this volume) to view labor markets and the exchange of labor power as no different theoretically from other markets and commodities. In this chapter, I argue for a specific theory of labor markets, based on the fundamental difference in the nature of labor power and its competitive exchange.[2] Max Weber, over a century ago, in his short essay in *Economy and Society* on "The Market: Its Impersonality and Ethic," characterizes markets as highly impersonal social exchanges, diffusing only where trade is sought with persons who do not share the same social context. Their

---

2   The specificity of labor markets also concerns the voluntary nature of labor exchanges, but this point is already addressed by Hyman (this volume, 1971, 1987; see also Streeck, 1992).

impersonality ties their stability, in his view, to the development of a "market ethics" to guide social action in markets. "Market ethics" enable a competitive exchange to "free itself most successfully from illimited dickering and return, in the interest of the parties, to a relative limitation of fluctuation in prices and exploitation of momentary interest constellations" (Weber, 1978, p. 637). What Weber tells us is that market actors develop an interest in curbing the very competition that is at the core of the market form of exchange. Weber suggests two ways in which competition can lead to market failures: the first, emphasized in the above passage, is disorder ("illimited dickering"), and the second, discussed in subsequent passages of his work on market ethics, is through the formation of monopolies. Both too much and too little competition pose risks to the stability of markets.

Competition divides the interests of and creates antagonisms between sellers and buyers of commodities, but the interests of market actors are also joined in efforts to insure the survival and order of markets. Their tendentially converging interests in market survival motivate market actors to negotiate rules and to embed their exchanges in macrostructures and social institutions (Beckert, 2009), or as Aspers (this volume, 2011) states, to create a market culture establishing "how things are done in the market." Anticipated in Weber's work, the contribution of the new sociology of markets is in how it ties together the making of markets, with their *regulation* through rules, often with a legal status, but also through formal and informal institutions and practices. The new sociology of markets recognizes that the regulation of competition is particularly important in labor markets "because they provide the only source of income for a vast majority of the population" (Beckert, 2009, p. 259).

An older tradition in economic sociology and political economy, however, views the regulation of competition in labor markets in relation to the nature of what is exchanged. Labor is not a commodity in that it is not produced for sale. Moreover, what is sold in the labor market is not the laborers themselves, but the promise of their labor power, yet the use of labor power cannot be separated from the laborers, who retain their agency in expending their labor. Yet labor markets treat labor power as if it were a commodity for the purpose of market exchange. This fiction, of treating labor as if it were a commodity, entails risks, not only to the stability of labor markets, but to the existence of laborers, and the stability of society as a whole (Polanyi, 2001 (1944)). The central institution of labor markets, the employment contract, is designed to minimize these risks, to markets, to laborers, and to society as a whole (Streeck, 1992). Yet employment contracts are not like other contracts of sale. Even where work is relatively standardized, the contingencies of production make detailed contracts of who and what forms of labor will be exchanged unrealistic. As the indeterminacy of employment contracts suggests, the exchange of labor power is not completed in the market, but in the sphere of production, the social relations of which are characterized by the private authority of employers. The next sections aim to build a theory of labor markets in relation to these fundamentally different structural properties of the competitive exchange of labor power.

3   A Theory of Labor Markets

3.1   *Labor Is Not a Commodity Like Any Other*

As acknowledged by both Aspers and van der Linden (this volume), a central issue in the operation of labor markets concerns the nature of what is sold (see also Kuczynski, 2009). Following Marx (Marx, 1977 (1867)), what is sold in contemporary labor markets is not the laborer him or herself, but his or her capacity to labor, summarized in the concept of labor power. Unlike other commodities traded in markets, however, labor power is not produced for sale. Labor power is treated as if it were a commodity, but this is no more than a necessary fiction for enabling labor power to be exchanged in markets (Polanyi, 2001 (1944), p. 75). Moreover, human beings who enter the labor market as seller of their labor power cannot be separated from their labor (Kuczynski, 2009).

What all this means is that what is at stake in labor markets is fundamentally different from what is sold and bought in "normal" markets, where the objects traded are produced for sale, and the transaction is completed with the transfer of ownership. From the perspective of buyers, labor exchanges do not end with ownership; in fact, the transaction does not end in the market. What is exchanged is the promise of temporary control over the use of labor power, but at a later time and in the workplace, not the marketplace. From the perspective of sellers, the exchange is not just about earning a livelihood, but because their labor power will be used in a workplace, under the private authority of owners/managers, what is at stake is the reproduction of life itself, in its corporal, social, symbolic, and aspirational (as well as material) dimensions.

Thus, the problem of restricting competition which Weber tells us is inherent to the operation of markets is not only about the stability of markets but also about the stability of human and social life. Minimizing the risk to reproduction of the competitive exchange of human labor involves offsetting the private authority of owners/employers, and thus requires social movements and public authorities. To the extent that competition in labor markets is not restricted, their operation threatens the conditions for life in its existential and social dimensions. In the dramatic terms of Polanyi, what is at risk in the treatment of labor as if it were a commodity like any other is the destruction of an individual worker, and ultimately, the demolition of society itself (Polanyi, 2001 (1944), p. 76).

Expressed in his concept of the "double movement," for Polanyi (2001), the history of labor markets is at once the history of their regulation, and their origins in the age of nation-building and industrialization have formed labor markets as national institutions. To the extent that labor is mobile across national borders, it enters into and out of specific jurisdictions. Yet even in the most regulated labor markets historically, the rules and practices restricting competition have never applied uniformly across all groups of workers or sectors of wage labor. As Vosko (2010) shows, the normalization of employment relations guaranteeing the conditions of social reproduction proceeded by restricting children and women from entering labor markets, and migrants from making claims to social protections covering native workers.

With the expansion of market societies, restrictions on the treatment of women's labor, as if it were a commodity, was rooted in a gendered division of labor, with women responsible for "non-commodified" unpaid labor in the domestic sphere (see Scheele in this volume), while making their livelihoods dependent on the institution of marriage, rather than markets. Throughout the advanced capitalist economies, in some cases well into the 1970s, restrictions on married women's labor market participation were enforced through "marriage bars" requiring the permission of their husbands for engaging in an employment relation (Walby, 1990). As women's employment expanded in the wake of the second wave of feminist movements in the 1970s, new employment opportunities opened to women continued to assume their dependence on marriage for livelihoods, and thus entailed far fewer restrictions on competition and control (Rubery, Smith, & Fagan, 1999; Walby, 1997).

In the case of migrant labor, immigration restrictions contribute to increasing competition and the authority of owners/employers over the use of labor. The creation of segments of low wage and potentially exploitative work for migrant labor is tolerated even by social actors and public authorities involved in the regulation of labor markets, since segmentation also functions to preserve the more protected segments of labor, and legitimated by cross-country wage differentials and the absence of employment opportunities in countries of origin (Piori, 1979). As a consequence, destination-country labor markets shift the responsibility for social reproduction of noncitizen labor to the country of origin (Vosko, 2010).[3]

---

3   The combination of temporary visa and limited-term contracts mean that even where migrants contribute to and are covered by employment and social protections, their return

The labor movement and trade union representation historically played a central role in restricting competition in labor markets (Streeck, 2005), yet in the more conservative gender regimes, and restricted migration countries, the membership logic of trade union representation meant they tended to restrict their activities to regularly employed native worker and male breadwinner members (Gottschall & Schröder, 2013). Recent research shows that unions engage in the representation of migrant workers' interests only when these overlap with the interests of their native and core members (see Heinrich, Shire, & Mottweiler, 2020 for a summary of recent research). The extensive literature on challenges facing national unions as workforces diversify indicates that capacities and interests in regulating cross-border labor exchanges remain underdeveloped (see Gumbrell-McCormick & Hyman, 2013 for a recent summary and discussion).

Aspers (this volume) acknowledges the unique nature of labor power, while arguing that the concept of switching, common to markets where actors switch between selling and buying objects, can account for this uniqueness. For Aspers, labor power is a different kind of commodity because the seller of labor power is also the object of trade, but labor power is still a commodity. In this section, I build on Polanyi's argument about the fictional nature of treating labor as if it were a commodity. Because labor power is not produced for sale but is a human capacity, subjecting labor power to unrestricted competition in labor markets is a risk to social reproduction and social stability. The fundamental question in the making of cross-border labor markets concerns the less fettered competition in the sectors and segments of migrant labor. In circular migration exchanges, sending countries bear the responsibility for shouldering these risks. Evidence suggests, however, that sending countries do view themselves as market actors but little research has focused on their regulatory capacities and engagement.

---

to their home country limits or even excludes their capacity to make claims, for example, for pensions. In many circular migration corridors, requirements for workers to pass health checks restrict the population of migrants to those who are proven to be able-bodied, and unlikely to make claims for health care in destination countries. Restrictions on the migration of family members, typical in many guest-worker schemes, mean that dependents (and their care and educational needs) remain in countries of origin. The most dramatic example is the case of domestic workers, who leave their children and parents at home in the care of other family members, while they care for the children and elderly of their foreign employers (for a summary of this extensive literature, see Kofman & Raghuram, 2015; Scheele in this volume).

3.2 An Employment Contract Is Not the Same as a Contract of Sale

The central institution regulating the exchange of labor power under competitive conditions is the employment contract (Streeck, 2005). From a broader labor sociological perspective, employment contracts are different from other contracts of sale, and these differences yield coordination problems specific to the market exchange of labor power. In the case of contracts of sale,

> [...] the economic relations between buyer and seller are, in fact, fully specified: the contract stipulates what (qualitatively and quantitatively) specified thing shall pass from the ownership of the seller to that of the buyer, as well as under what conditions and at what price. The contract of sale thus reciprocally defines the spheres of disposition over the item sold [...] (to) [...] bring about a precise social disjunction: what was previously under the legal and actual disposition of the one is now placed at the disposal of the other. Herein lies the peace-making and assuring function of contractual rights for both sides.
>
> OFFE, 1985, p. 21

Similarly, employment contracts attempt to outline the quantity and quality of labor power promised to the buyer in exchange for a wage, but even under conditions of relatively standardized work, they can never exactly specify the work to be performed. In contracts of sale, "the seller loses every legal and physical power of disposition over the item sold [...] what was previously under the legal and actual disposition of the one is now placed at the disposal of the other" (Offe, 1985, p. 21).[4] This is not the case, however, in labor markets, where the seller of labor does not lose her power of disposition over her labor power, even under the most despotic controls of the labor process.

Van der Linden (this volume) suggests that instead of a transfer of ownership implied by the act of selling, that we speak instead of laborers "hiring out" the use of their labor power. This shift in terminology might seem to render labor markets more like rental or leasing markets, where ownership is transferred for a specific period of time (Kuczynski, 2009). This analogy, however, breaks down as soon as we consider the different structural dimensions of labor market exchanges.

First of all, the price of wages for the use of labor power is not equivalent to the price of monthly rent for the use of housing (Kuczynski, 2009). In Marx's

---

4 This also applies to the rental markets for property, or other commodities, which I discuss below.

labor theory of value, wages represent a share of the value created by labor; however, renters do not create value, but rather depreciate the value of the property they use. Wages might also be considered as the cost of reproducing labor at a socially acceptable standard, and thus roughly equivalent to rent as the cost of maintaining or replacing the value of property use. More importantly, however, there are power differences in the relative position of buyers and sellers in labor and rental markets. The analogy of renting and hiring suggests an equivalence between the owner of a housing property and the owner of labor power, and between the homeless person renting a home and an employer hiring a laborer. In terms of the asymmetries in employment versus property relations, the structural position of employers on the demand side of labor markets is more equivalent to housing property owners on the supply side of rental markets. The asymmetric dependencies between sellers and buyers in rental and labor markets are exactly reversed.

This point is made in Offe's analysis of social relations in labor markets:

> An asymmetry between the two sides of the market is based on the fact that (at least on average, and in the long term) the buyers of labor can more easily make themselves independent of supply than is the case with the suppliers of labor with respect to the demand side.
> OFFE, 1985, p. 189

Like employers, the sellers of rental property can more easily make themselves independent of tenants than a renter, who risks homelessness. Moreover, employment contracts (unlike sales contracts) "do not stipulate the totality of the relations that arise between contracting parties" (Offe, 1985, p. 21). By obligating laborers to exert an indeterminable capacity to labor, employment contracts instate the authority of employers in the social relations of production. Looking to the case of cross-border labor markets, the terms of migration must also be considered alongside the terms of the employment contract. One of the classic ways in which immigration restrictions exacerbate the subordination of migrant labor beyond the employment contract is by tying a visa to a specific employer. Tied visas amplify the "normal" asymmetries of the employment relation, since workers have no legal right to exit an employment relation without losing their right to work in the destination country. Losing a job means losing residency and facing forced deportation.

In the circular cross-border labor markets that characterize migration, an additional dimension of subordination is tied to the role of private intermediaries, who conclude employment contracts on behalf of migrant workers. In this case, migrants do not sell their labor, but are sold—by intermediaries.

Most of the important sending states now require migrants to use the services of intermediaries to whom they have delegated the responsibility for managing the out- and return migration of their citizens. Sending state licensing requirements attempt to regulate the activities of intermediaries, yet the delegation of migration governance to intermediaries often results in new mechanisms subordinating migrants beyond the employment contract and beyond immigration controls. The most frequent form of subordination is debt bondage, that can result from exorbitant fees charged to migrants by intermediaries for arranging their jobs abroad, or from interest charged on loans to finance travel and other costs of migrating and working abroad. While intermediaries derive profits from fees and credit, both depend on migrants being paid. Intermediaries are in competition however, with other intermediaries and other sending countries, and have an interest in keeping pay low enough to capture a large share of the migrant labor market. Market share in turn, depends on supplying enough migrant labor power. Intermediaries are thus concerned about their reputation among the migrants and their communities. If intermediaries fail to protect migrants from poor employment and mobility conditions, migrants may refuse their services in the future, or warn off potential migrants in their home communities. Thus, the interests of intermediaries—and the recruitment and placement industry they are part of—are in part aligned with migrants' interests in decent employment and working conditions, and in part opposed as profit derives from fees and interest paid on loans, which contribute to asymmetries in the employment relation.

3.3 *The Transformation Problem*

The third specificity of labor markets concerns the completion of the exchange of labor in the transformation of labor power into expended labor effort. The sale of labor power is the promise of labor to be expended; however, the expending, which completes the transaction, is not done in the relations of the market but in the relations of production. The labor market itself is a product of these relations of production. The transformation problem as discussed in the sociology of labor (Deutschmann, 2002) is a problem of gaining and maintaining the cooperation of labor in the labor process under conditions which ideally give employers/managers unilateral authority over the organization of work. Solutions range from attempts to completely control labor effort to higher degrees of autonomy in the labor process. The power of labor in production is shaped by structural differences in specific production processes but, more importantly, by the associational power resources (Wright, 2000) of labor to resist unilateral control and to mobilize public authorities to intervene in regulating labor standards. Even in the advanced industrial economies, where many of the ILO conventions are ratified and implemented in labor law and industrial relations, the private authority of employers and limited public resources of labor inspectorates still restrict the enforcement of labor standards and leave much up to the negotiation of efforts between workers and supervisors in specific work contexts (Burawoy, 1979).

The tied visas of migrant labor discussed in the previous section make managerial unilateralism more likely in the organizations of production with high concentrations of migrant labor. Violations of labor standards and contractual conditions are difficult to contest, even if migrants are aware of their rights and have recourse to dispute resolution procedures, since to do so comes at the risk of deportation. In particular, the temporary contracts used in many contemporary cross-border labor markets mean that migrants have little access to associational resources, such as in the form of trade union membership and representation. Recent research suggests that migrant labor conditions are more dependent on societal resources[5] and social movements with a human rights approach than on traditional forms of industrial action (Zayak, 2013; Piper & Grugel, 2015). The power of employers in shaping labor markets for low-wage migrant labor is increasingly challenged by civil societal campaigns of blaming and shaming, which seem more effective in motivating the intervention of public authorities than labor union advocates (Mense-Petermann, 2020).

Labor markets as arenas of social exchange are largely shaped by the organizations of work and production to which they supply labor. The completion of the market exchange in the inherently contradictory transformation of labor power means that the dynamics of labor markets cannot be understood through a theory that limits its scope to what happens in the market, or which ignores how markets are shaped by organizations of production. The contribution by Mense-Petermann in this volume makes a similar argument, in an analysis of how markets for migrant labor in the meat processing industry in Germany have evolved.

4   Theorizing Cross-Border Labor Markets

Labor is not a commodity produced for sale, employment contracts are not the same as sales contracts, and the exchange of labor is not completed in the market, but in the private sphere of production. These specificities of labor markets

---

5 See the special issue of the *Global Labor Journal*, 2018, Vol. 9 (2, 3) on the power resources of global labor.

generate risks, which threaten the stability of labor markets yet, more importantly, they threaten human existence and the stability of society. Although the employment contract introduces restrictions on competition, it also subordinates the laborer within the employment relation. The transformation of labor power into labor effort in the labor process reveals the contradictions in the private authority of production, and the inseparability of labor power from the laborer. The risks posed to reproduction through subordination and managerial unilateralism are amplified in migrant labor markets, particularly where immigration restrictions increase vulnerabilities to extreme exploitation.

The brief references made above to the actors and dynamics of emerging cross-border labor markets suggest the relevance of a theory of labor markets for identifying pathways to regulating migration markets. One regulatory pathway is the mobilization of the interests of sending states in protecting migrant labor. Increasingly, outmigration is part of national development strategies, and thus a matter of great political importance. A second pathway involves regulating the activities of labor market intermediaries in the recruitment, contracting, and control of migrant labor. Sending states outsource much of the responsibility for operating migration markets to these private actors, but how well they meet national public interests in protecting migrant labor is questionable. A third pathway points to the role of civil society advocacy, social movements, and relatively unconventional forms of activism such as blaming and shaming which may mobilize public authorities on both the sending and receiving sides to intervene in regulating exploitative labor practices. Fourth, as the central institutions of labor markets, the employment contracts used to engage migrant labor deserve far more scrutiny in relation to immigration controls and intermediation.

In conclusion, critical migration research often assumes that migrant labor is doomed to suffer the consequences of the neo-liberalization of global production. The sociology of markets, however, suggests that market making is always tied to market regulation. The theory of labor markets developed in this chapter identifies the risks specific to the exchange of labor power, and the actors and instruments involved in the operation of labor markets and, thus, generates a number of insights into the pathways that might be pursued in securing the reproduction and improving the standards of global labor.

References

Aspers, P. (2011). *Markets*. Cambridge: Polity.
Beckert, J. (2009). The social order of markets. *Theory and Society, 38*, 245–269.

Burawoy, M. (1979). *Manufacturing Consent. Changes in the Labor Process under Monopoly Capitalism*. Chicago: University of Chicago Press.

Deutschmann, C. (2002). *Postindustrielle Industriesoziologie. Theoretische Grundlagen, Arbeitsverhältnisse und soziale Identitäten*. Weinheim and Munich: Juventa Verlag.

Fligstein, N. (2002). *The Architecture of Markets: An Economic Sociology of Twenty-First-Century Capitalist Societies*. Princeton: Princeton University Press.

Gottschall, K. & T. Schröder (2013). „Familienlohn"—Zur Entwicklung einer wirkmächtigen Normierung geschlechtsspezifischer Arbeitsteilung. *WSI Mitteilung*, 3, 161–170.

Gumbrell-McCormick, R. & Hyman, R. (2013). *Trade-Unions in Western Europe: Hard Times, Hard Choices*. Oxford: Oxford University Press.

Heinrich, R., Shire, K., & Mottweiler, H. (2020). Fighting (for) the margins: Trade union responses to the emergence of cross-border temporary agency work in the European Union. *Journal of Industrial Relations*. doi:10.1177/00228569900649.

Hyman, R. (1971). *Marxism and the Sociology of Trade Unionism*. London: Pluto Press.

Hyman, R. (1987). Strategy or structure? Capital, labor and control. *Work Employment & Society*, 1(1), 25–55.

Kalleberg, A. L., & Sorensen, A. B. (1979). The sociology of labor markets. *Annual Review of Sociology*, 5, 351–379.

Kuczynski, T. (2009). What is sold on the labor-market? In M. van der Linden & K. H. Roth (Eds.), *Beyond Marx. Theorising the Global Labor Relations of the Twenty-First Century* (pp. 305–318). Leiden: Brill.

Marx, K. (1977 (1867)). *Capital* (B. Fowkes, Trans. Vol. 1). New York: Vintage Books.

Mense-Petermann, U. (2020). Interest representation in transnational labour markets: Campaigning as an alternative to traditional union action? *Journal of Industrial Relations*, 62(2), 185–209. doi:10.1177/00228569900642.

Offe, K. (1985). The political economy of the labor market. In K. Offe (Ed.), *Disorganized Capitalism* (pp. 10–51). Oxford: Oxford University Press.

Piori, M. (1979). *Birds of Passage: Migrant Labor and Industrial Societies*. Cambridge: Cambridge University Press.

Piper, N. & J. Grugel (2015) Global migration governance, social movements, and the difficulties of promoting migrant rights. In C.-U. Schierup, R. Munck, B. Likić-Brborić, & A. Neergaard (Eds.) *Migration, Precarity, andGglobal Governance: Challenges and Opportunities for Labor* (pp. 261–78). Oxford: Oxford University Press.

Polanyi, K. (2001 (1944)). *The Great Transformation. The Political and Economic Origins of Our Time* (2nd ed.). Boston Beacon Books.

Rubery, J., Smith, M. & Fagan, C. (1999). *Women's Employment in Europe: Trends and Prospects*. London: Routledge.

Shire, K. (2020). The social order of transnational migration markets. *Global Networks*, 20 (3), 434–453.

Streeck, W. (1992). Revisiting status and contract: Pluralism, corporatism and flexibility in social institutions and economic performance. In *Social Institutions and Economic Performance. Studies of Industrial Relations in Advanced Capitalist Economies* (pp. 41–75). New York: Sage.

Streeck, W. (2005). The sociology of labor markets and trade unions. In N. J. Smelser & R. Swedberg (Eds.), *The Handbook of Economic Sociology* (pp. 254–283). Princeton: Princeton University Press.

Tilly, C., & Tilly, C. (1994). Capitalist work and labor markets. In N. J. Smelser & R. Swedberg (Eds.), *The Handbook of Economic Sociology* (pp. 283–312). Princeton, NJ: Princeton University Press.

Vosko, L. F. (2010). *Managing the Margins: Gender, Citizenship, and the International Regulation of Precarious Employment*. Oxford: Oxford University Press.

Walby, S. (1990). *Theorizing Patriarchy*. Oxford: Basil Blackwell.

Walby, S. (1997). *Gender Transformations*. London, Routledge.

Weber, M. (1922) Wirtschaft und Gesellschaft, in Grundriss der Sozialoekonomie, III Abteilung. Tuebingen: J.C.B. Mohr Verlag.

Weber, M. (1978). The market: It's impersonality and ethic (frament). In G. Roth & C. Wittich (Eds.), *Economy and Society* (Vol. I). Berkeley: University of California Press.

Wright, E. O. (2000). Working class power, Capitalist class interests, and class compromise. *American Journal of Sociology, 105*(4), 957–1002.

Zajek, S. (2013). Transnational private regulation and the transformation of labor rights organizations in emerging markets: New markets for labor support work in China. *Journal of Asian Public Policy*, 6(2), 178–95. doi: 10.1080/17516234.2013.814309.

CHAPTER 7

An Object of Analysis Rather Than a Research Tool

The Coproduction of Labor Markets and Nation States in the Decades around 1900

Peter-Paul Bänziger

1   Introduction

In the capitalist societies of the twentieth and twenty-first centuries, markets appear to have become the predominant mode of allocation of services, goods, and labor. But what exactly do we mean when we say "market"? There are essentially two modes of using the concept: as an object of analysis and as a research tool. In the past few decades, the latter mode has become widely accepted in social scientific as well as in historiographical literature. It is now common practice to describe a wide range of allocation and exchange processes as market-like—from the medieval crusades and early modern knowledge exchange (Füssel, Knäble, & Elsemann, 2017) to modern migration practices. (In this volume, the complexities of current migration regimes are discussed by Mense-Petermann and Schwenken, and Shire, amongst others.) At the same time, however, the market concept is tightly bound to (neo-)classical economics and to a related set of policies that have become hegemonic in the past three or four decades. By using this as a research tool, we risk contributing to the political project of portraying human action as market action and making the world a marketplace. This is a project that the dominant strands within economic departments and many others more or less consciously adhere to. It is all the more astonishing that the far-reaching socio-theoretical and epistemological implications of the market concept have barely been discussed in the social scientific and historiographical literature.

Certainly, we cannot write about the past without applying concepts we use in the present-day world. Historiography is necessarily anachronistic to some extent. Yet the very concept that is at stake is of great importance. It makes a difference whether a heuristic tool is deeply rooted in hegemonic discourses, as with the concept of market, or in critique. Consequently, in the present chapter, I begin by doing what my training as a historian qualifies me best for. Instead of simply using the market concept as a research tool, I apply the first of the above-mentioned perspectives and conceive of (labor) markets as objects of historiographical analysis first of all. Most notably, this means delineating the historical contexts in which markets—and labor markets in particular—emerged. Thus, we will eventually be able to use the market concept as a more precise research tool. Rather than adhering to the economists' endeavor to searching for abstract similarities in distant times and places, such a concept can help us to analyze societies in which (labor) markets have indeed become the predominant mode of allocation—that is, mainly, present-day societies. In other words, by analyzing precisely how markets have been established, we avoid fortifying the current hegemony of market thought that is based completely on an ahistorical concept of market.

In the first section of this chapter, I propose analyzing the history of markets from a post-structuralist point of view: essentially, a historical structure of allocation was a market because some of the contemporaries considered it to be a market, whatever the specific meanings may have been. We therefore have to take account of the fact that it is not until the second half of the nineteenth century that we can find the concept of labor markets in the sources. Against this background, I argue in the following section that labor markets emerged in close relation to a far-reaching societal transformation at the turn of the twentieth century: the largely intertwined consolidations of the nation state and of a new mode of conceptualizing and institutionalizing labor as "work." In this context, the hitherto isolated application of the concept gave way to concerted efforts to establish labor markets. Finally, in my conclusion, I ask to what extent labor markets were denationalized in the past few decades. While the nation state did not lose its pivotal role, I argue, we should not underestimate the performativity of the discourse on "global labor markets" and of related institutional practices in the present world and—perhaps even more—in the future. This is just one of the nuances the historiographically sensitive market concept I delineate in this chapter allows us to perceive.

2   A Post-structuralist Approach to the History of Labor Markets

It is well-known that Karl Polanyi (1957) carved out "reciprocity," "redistribution," and "market" as the trinity of allocation modes. Such a high level of abstraction entails a serious analytical problem: It renders almost self-evident the conclusion that we can find markets wherever there is neither a central redistributive agent nor a reciprocal exchange between a limited number of actors. This is essentially how the vast majority of the literature proceeds. In order to avoid the socio-theoretical shortcomings mentioned above, and to ultimately gain a more nuanced market concept, I propose beginning the analysis at the micro level of structures of allocation rather than at the macro level of Polanyi's taxonomy. Structures of allocation consist of materialized "structures for exchange" in the broadest sense, including tacit practices and discursive "rules of exchange." Every market—ranging from a farmer's market in a medieval country town to an early modern stock exchange or an online trading platform—is such a structure, regardless of the specific mode allocation processes are taking place within it.

However, the question arises why these exemplary structures of allocation are markets? Is there something they share that allows us to regard them as concretions of a general idea? Can we say, for instance, that all of them are "structures for the exchange of rights under competition" as Aspers (this volume) argues? We are unable to do this. The meanings of the concept of market have changed considerably over time and varied widely between different places—a fact that is often overlooked in sociological, anthropological, and historiographical literature. In particular, a nexus with present-day ideas of "competition" has only gained momentum in the course of the past three centuries. Speaking about a "competition problem" that a market needs to solve is therefore hardly a suitable description for medieval and early modern markets. Yet the lack of competition does not allow us to conclude that these markets were in any way less "real" markets than the stock exchanges of the late nineteenth and twentieth centuries or the present-day online trading platforms.

What all of these examples have in common is the concept itself: Contemporaries did in fact refer to these structures of allocation as markets. This does not appear to apply, however, to the crusades, to early modern practices of knowledge exchange, or to certain patterns and practices of migration (see Mense-Petermann & Schwenken, and Shire in this volume). In clear contrast to the previous examples, these lack any contemporary reference to the concept of market. From a post-structuralist point of view, this perspective can be generalized: Ultimately, a certain structure of allocation is a market as soon as at least one of the contemporaries uses this term to describe it. Since none of us live in a solipsistic world, this extreme case is unlikely to occur. Words never pop up out of nothing. Nevertheless, for a historian, the following question is of crucial interest: To what extent do isolated references in the sources suffice to call a structure of allocation a market?

In order to find an answer to this question, we can look at labor markets as a case in point. Today, both theories and practices of labor are linked to the concept of market. In historiography and in social sciences, as in economics, the existence of labor markets is rarely challenged. If anything, the question is whether there is just one (local, national, regional, or global, as the case may be) labor market with different sections, or distinct markets for different types of labor or industries. At the same time, labor has become a commodity in everyday life. The undeniable effect of job interviews, for instance, is that we learn to conceive of ourselves as market participants and to act accordingly: to present ourselves—and not only our labor power—as commodities an employer would like to acquire (see Aspers in this volume). It is somewhat unlikely that most of us will attempt to subvert as widely as possible the market-like behavior imposed on us from "outside" as Miller (2002) supposes with reference to the quantification of academic labor. Similar performative effects can be attributed to the information about the state of the labor market that the mass media provide us with on a regular basis. Even when unemployment is high and jobseekers know very well that being hired is rarely a matter of bargaining, they are encouraged to act as if they were on a marketplace— one with too many market stalls and too few customers in this case.

However, while there is no doubt that labor markets exist in present-day societies, very few people living in the eighteenth or nineteenth centuries viewed labor and/or themselves as marketable commodities. Despite his reputation as one of the founding fathers of market-praising economics, not even Adam Smith thought of labor allocation as a purely market-like process. On the one hand, as he famously put it, "the higgling and bargaining of the market" would eventually create a "sort of rough equality" between labor and commodities. On the other hand, he insisted that it was solely the value of goods "which varies, not that of the labour which purchases them." (Smith, 1814 [1776], p. 46, p. 49) Much like the contemporary quest for the intrinsic value of labor, such a characterization did little to encourage conceptualizing labor as a commodity. This is precisely what Karl Marx, in contrast, is well known for. Occasionally, he used the concept in Volume 1 of his *Kapital*. He did so in a mostly theoretical manner to describe the commodification of labor under capitalist conditions. In Chapter Four, for instance, he argues that the money owner finds "the labor market as a particular section of the commodity market" (Marx, 1973 [1867], p. 183; my translation).

In the second half of the nineteenth century, Marx was not the only one to write about labor markets. As Marcel van der Linden (this volume) argues with respect to the United Kingdom, the concept was gradually taken up by other authors during the same period. Prior to that—and in contrast to theorizations of town markets, which can already be found in antiquity—, hardly anyone seems to have seen labor allocation as market-like. Even by the time Marx wrote his *Kapital*, the concept appears to have had very little reverberation outside of economic literature. Instead of relying on empirical cases, Marx himself discussed labor markets mainly from a theoretical point of view (Welskopp, 2017, p. 202). As mentioned above, he was interested in the historical emergence of commodified labor and aimed to provide a theory of capitalist labor. He was not interested in the functioning of contemporary structures of labor allocation: in institutions, discourses, or practices. This helps me answer the question I raised above: While the use of the concept of market is necessary, it does not suffice by itself. In order to call a historical structure of allocation a market, some ideas of what a market is and what it should serve for must be at least to some extent implemented in it (although, as Streng [2017] for instance shows, not always as prominently as in the paradigmatic account by Garcia [1986]). As I argue in the next section, labor markets, in this broader sense, only emerged at the turn of the twentieth century.

3   Work, the Nation State, and Labor Markets

Labor historiography of the past two decades has shown that labor as work, as we largely know and practice it to this day, emerged around 1900 (see Conrad, Macamo & Zimmermann, 2000). In the course of a few decades, work became a mode of earning a living that was, first, based on a new ethos of joyful efficiency (see Bänziger & Suter, 2017). It replaced both the bourgeois deontology of family-oriented industriousness, which was deeply rooted in contemporary religious beliefs, and the proletarian concept of labor as an inescapable toil. Second, labor as work was conceived of as both a precondition for and a duty deriving from the privilege of national citizenship. Third, it was defined and differentiated from "non-work" by social and labor sciences that came into existence largely during the very process. The scope of this new type of knowledge was, again, the nation state, which at the same time reinforced its relevancy by legal codification. Fourth, in close relation to these processes, the welfare institutions emerged. They provided the "citizen workers" with a certain degree of public support while reinforcing the exclusion of other modes of making a living as non-work and thus, ultimately, non-national (and vice versa). Fifth, not only on the level of ideology, work became predominantly male. The women's share of the factory workforce was gradually reduced, and the remaining female laborers were further relegated to subordinate and temporary jobs. Even if it was difficult to be accomplished in everyday working life, housekeeping—not (wage) work—became the duty of the female citizen (for the Swiss case, see Wecker, 1997).

To sum up the current state of research, in the decades around 1900, work became based on a new ethos, linked to national citizenship, defined by scientific knowledge, supported by welfare institutions, and masculine gendered. In every respect, the nation state provided the ultimate horizon of thought and action while, through this very process, it was itself consolidated to a considerable extent. Work was essentially national work, and the nation a workers' nation. This far-reaching societal transformation was fostered by two further aspects historiography has not yet systematically considered: the formation of "consumer societies" and the mobilization of labor by a process of "marketization." In other words, within the boundaries of the nation state, (male) workers ultimately became "free" both to consume and to search for jobs. For the sake of brevity, I will not elaborate in detail on consumerism here (see Bänziger, 2020). Nevertheless, I would like to mention some of its core aspects as these are at least partly linked to the process of marketization.

First, a growing significance of mass consumer goods in production and, at least on the European continent, a turn towards protectionist measures brought about an increasingly pronounced need for domestic markets for these goods. The recent historiography of marketing practices has clearly shown how the managements of companies have gradually shifted the focus from production and costs to sale. Not only did they "nationalize" products—as in the famous case of Swiss chocolate (Rossfeld, 2007)—but they also began addressing domestic consumers as a target group. Not least against this background, imagining the nation state as a marketplace, and thus popularizing the idea of an essentially national economy, gradually became popular. Second, in and well outside the booming urban centers, new types of commercial entertainment emerged. These partly replaced and transformed the luxury and amusement practices of the nineteenth-century bourgeois classes. While the social framework of the latter had been the family and the local community, it now became a broader—although not homogeneous—public.

Third, not only in the context of protectionism, nationalist ideas of a self-sustaining domestic economy gained societal relevance. In addition to the transformation of troublesome labor into nationally important work, which in return entitled the workers to consume, they helped to cast a positive light on emerging consumerist practices. Buying mass-produced domestic goods and enjoying local commercial entertainment became both a reward for the efforts of the (male) workers and the (female) citizens' duty (see Kühschelm, 2022). In other words, "national consumerism" was an acceptable way of spending the few hours of non-work—hours now called "free" time: time to choose from what is offered by the domestic economy. It replaced the bourgeois values of moderation (if not abstinence) and Christian charity (Maß, 2017) while at least partly substituting the family and community focus by an orientation towards the "whole" nation. Consumption and entertainment in public gradually lost the negative connotations that had previously been attached to them.

At the turn of the twentieth century, national work was not only accompanied by—and rewarded through—national consumerism. It was also to be allocated in a way that corresponded to the needs of the domestic economy. In principle, earning a living has no distinct geographical limits (ultimately, the scope is almost global). Yet there have almost always been attempts to territorialize the respective practices. For most of European history, these were based on varying types of bondage—service, slavery, and other forms of "unfreedom" (see Part 1 of this volume). The territory of labor as work, however, was defined by the boundaries of the nation state. One of the pivotal questions emerging within this context was how to best mobilize and allocate labor. In the twentieth century, the answers given were mainly of two types. First, in interwar vocational counseling, for instance, the aim was to put the "right person" in the "right place." Psychology, physiology, sociology, and other sciences promised to provide the knowledge that would eventually make this possible (Bachem, 2013, Saxer, 2011). We may call these structures of labor allocation the scientific or social engineering mode. This was closely connected to the above-mentioned process of scientification of labor. From a more abstract point of view, it can be conceived of as a redistributive mode of labor allocation.

Second, in the decades around 1900, structures of labor allocation emerged that were based on contemporary market theory. Rather than conflicting with the scientific ones, they incorporated them in many countries and in most periods of the twentieth century. Thomas Buchner (2013), one of the first historians to have applied a post-structuralist perspective to labor markets, argues that it was not until the 1890s that German national economics and politics "discovered" the labor market (much like unemployment, see Zimmermann, 2001). In 1897, for instance, the journal *Der Arbeitsmarkt* (The Labor Market) was established. Since their earliest discussions, national economists portrayed the labor market as imperfect, disordered, and an unknown entity because there were no market institutions. It particularly lacked appropriate regulation. As a result, work-related institutions such as employment offices began systematically setting up market structures. They collected data on labor markets on the national, regional, and local levels; they segmented these markets by gender, profession, and qualification; they identified the individuals and practices to be included or excluded; they attempted to ensure the mutual exclusiveness of the roles of sellers and buyers; and they objectified labor by separating the commodity from the seller. Furthermore, the offices themselves were designed to constitute specific marketplaces. At the same time, there was a shift from poverty reduction to market regulation in labor policy. Hence, much like Michel Callon (1998) argued for markets in general, labor markets were embedded in economics to a considerable extent.

This is not to say that, in the interest of a smoothly functioning labor market, contemporary employers, for their part, voluntarily stopped preventing as far as possible the labor force from moving autonomously. If the level of direct coercion was nevertheless reduced in the decades around 1900, this happened mainly for three reasons. First, since the mid-nineteenth century a variety of company-based housing and other services allowed for "soft" types of bondage such as the obligation to work in the landlord's factory. This process was fostered by an increased need for skilled labor. Second, due to the growing influence of the labor and abolition movements and as a consequence of a broader democratic participation, the rights of the labor force became an issue of public interest. This is one major reason why enforcing bonded labor contracts by means of legal procedures was increasingly difficult (Welskopp, 2017). Third, and just as importantly, the consolidating nation state was willing to optimize the distribution of resources within the national economy. The institutionalization and regulation of labor markets was a key aspect of this process.

To sum up my argument so far, labor markets did not emerge until the decades around 1900. Contemporary economics and labor-related institutions did not simply discover and institutionalize markets that had already existed. Nor did the nation state nationalize them. Rather, these forces made a vital contribution to a "marketization" of labor in the context of a more general process: the production of national work.

Against this background, the question arises whether the emergence of the market mode of labor allocation—both in its ideal and institutional dimensions—was more than a historical coincidence. On the one hand, and in view of the increasing importance of markets within contemporary economics and economies alike, one is tempted to argue that applying the concept of markets to the realm of labor was only a matter of time. Indeed, once economists had learned to see the world as a marketplace, they could easily compare the hiring of day laborers or the colonial slave trade to the transactions on town markets or exchanges. Or as Marx (1973 [1867], p. 282) put it: "For slave-trade read labour-market, for Kentucky and Virginia, Ireland and the agricultural districts of England, Scotland, and Wales, for Africa, Germany."

On the other hand, however, we should take the fact seriously that, before the new mode of work emerged in the context of the consolidating nation state, the concept of labor market was barely used at all. This is not surprising. As mentioned above, for the bourgeois classes of the nineteenth century, work was an end in itself as well as a service to the family and to the community, and ultimately to God. Thinking of it in terms of competition or price was completely inconceivable. The same applies to the labor of the other classes. Dealing with it as with a commodity, the price of which was to be freely bargained between the seller and the buyer, would have sounded ridiculous to their ears. In accordance with the differentiation between the roles of the master and the servant in Christian morality at the time, few of them could have imagined treating their laborers as equals. Yet it is hardly surprising that they had no interest in Marx's endeavor to lay open the structural similarities of slave and factory labor, either. Some argued that, in order to ultimately overcome this strongly perceived gap, the laborers needed to adopt the bourgeois work ethos first of all. Others, less interested in the fate of the laboring classes, were convinced that the only way of guiding them was through coercion. And all of them shared a preference for fixing wages and working conditions by agreement with other factory owners (and not with the unions, of course) instead of establishing rules and other institutions that would have allowed for bargaining and competition. Markets, at least in Europe, were designed for the allocation of goods, not of labor. In any case, competition and profit orientation—and its symbol, the stock exchange (Engel, 2016)—had to be confined within narrow limits.

The historical role of the consolidating nation state was precisely to overcome the modes of allocation that had prevailed well into the second half of the nineteenth century. Ever since mercantilism, the nation had been the main target of economic thought. Yet it was not until the decades around 1900 that the nation state permeated its territory to an extent that allowed for a practical implementation of this thought. It was not until then, in other words, that what we now call a domestic economy came into existence. This consisted not only of uniform commodity markets but also of common factor markets. Even if we do not need to follow Polanyi (1957) in his strict demarcation from traditional economies, he rightly pointed to the spatial dimension in the history of markets. He argued that setting up domestic markets was of crucial importance for the emergence of what he calls a market society. This process largely depended on the weakening of local bonds that tended to restrict markets. As Fernand Braudel (1979) argued, only the powerful modern states were able to open territories of a sufficient size for a vast variety of market transactions. In the United Kingdom, in France, and in Prussia, this happened back in the eighteenth and early nineteenth centuries. Yet here as elsewhere, decades passed before theory became practice (see Stanziani, 2012). In particular, this applies to staple foods (Streng, 2017) and labor.

Of course, the emergence of labor markets was also based on earlier transformations, as the example of Switzerland shows. Along with freedom of trade, freedom of domicile had been a widely debated topic well before the founding years of the federal state after the successful revolution of 1848. Yet while the restrictions for the Jewish population were abolished in 1866, the practical implementation of the new rights took several decades. For instance, it was only with the new federal constitution of 1874 that male citizens moving to another municipality were granted full political rights. A similar process can be identified in Germany, where freedom of movement was granted by the constitutions of the North German Federation (1867) and of the German Reich (1871). And even in the United Kingdom and in the United States of America, the freedom to accept and cancel contracts was not granted to workers until the decades around 1900 (Welskopp, 2017, pp. 204ff.).

But what about the decommodification that the emerging welfare states (or, as in Switzerland, the liberal-conservative states with welfare institutions) of the early twentieth century are often lauded for? Undoubtedly, they provide the citizen workers with a specific form of freedom: they free them from subjecting themselves to every type of exploitation—but not from labor market participation. It is precisely by preventing the workers from becoming a commodity themselves—from "convert[ing] himself from a free man into a slave," as Marx (1973 [1867], p. 182) wrote—, that the welfare states give them the opportunity to sell their labor power in the market. In much the same way as labor protection laws and collective bargaining, welfare institutions thus enable market participation of laborers by contributing to what Callon (1998, p. 44) has stated for markets in general: "that the very nature of competition is to rarefy competition." Seen from this perspective, decommodification is not the antipode of commodification.

At the same time, it is important to note that labor markets were not only, as Callon indicates, produced by "the state." While they were made possible by the emerging (welfare) state, they also contributed to the consolidation of the latter to a considerable extent. As with other aspects of the history of the new type of work, there was, in other words, a coproduction of labor markets and of the nation state. This, of course, was a historical coincidence. There is no timeless link between labor markets and nation states. What seems to be uncontroversial, however, is that there must be some form of power strong enough to prevent local bonds and obligations from becoming dominant. In theory, therefore, labor markets with a global scope are possible. To what extent they actually came into existence in the twentieth century is an empirical question I will now tentatively discuss in the concluding remarks.

4   Conclusion: A Denationalization of Labor Markets?

The coproduction of labor markets and of the nation state notwithstanding, the scope of the marketization of labor in the twentieth-century Atlantic world needs to be put into perspective. We must keep our eyes open for other modes of labor allocation (and, of course, allocation of goods). In the course of the working lives of a considerable share of the male citizen workforce of the twentieth century, for instance, the "right" place they had once been attached to remained the only one to stay in. They would never have seen themselves as labor market participants. Today, however, as mentioned above, labor markets are no longer only a conceptual tool of economics and other academic disciplines. They have become a general mode of conceiving of and institutionalizing labor allocation. Even the laboring subjects are supposed to think of themselves as market participants. And many of them do so in their everyday lives.

Interestingly, marketized labor thus seems to have become hegemonic in a time that is shaped by the latest wave of denationalization: the production of transnational labor markets on the regional level such as in the European Union, the reduction of tariffs and the re-regulation of trade by modes of global governance, and the "opening" of national economies for transnational capital. These processes went hand in hand with the advancement of austerity policies and monetarism at the expense of Keynesianism. In many parts of the former third world, this involved an end to import substitution and industrialization policies. All of this fostered the emergence of a new global reserve army. Thus, at first sight, an intensified marketization of both goods and production factors and recent denationalization processes seem to have occurred in close relation to each other.

However, even if the global level is gaining momentum, there is no doubt that labor markets are still mostly based on national institutions. In other words, while labor was increasingly subjected to marketization in the course of recent globalization processes, the labor markets themselves have not been denationalized. Rather, the concept of labor market, together with the nation state, has diffused even more around the world. Nevertheless, we should not underestimate the performativity of the widespread discourse on "global labor markets" and of related institutional practices in the present world and—perhaps even more so—in the future. In particular, they encourage the laboring subjects to act and think in a way that is both market-oriented and global. And, indeed, a global class of highly qualified people has emerged in the past few decades. At the other end of the spectrum however, transnational labor allocation resembles the structures of mid-nineteenth century far more than what economists denote as a market (see Mense-Petermann & Schwenken, and Shire in this volume).

The history of (labor) allocation structures I have delineated in this chapter not only allows us to describe such recent transformations with greater precision. It also reveals that, due to the coproduction of labor markets and of the nation state, labor markets have indeed played an increasingly important role in the last 150 years. At the same time, they differ fundamentally from earlier modes of labor allocation. By describing the latter based on the established heuristic of market sociology, we may certainly be able to discern some similarities. For instance, we might conclude that guild or bourgeois apprenticeship practices also featured market-like aspects. In doing so, however, we risk masking the peculiarities. We overlook that what resembles a market at first sight was strongly embedded in reciprocal, and often familial, obligations. In some cases, we even find ourselves on the wrong track. If anything, competition, for instance, was of marginal importance within structures of labor allocation well into the second half of the nineteenth century. Reconstructing precisely how structures allowing for—or even enforcing—competition were established in the subsequent decades not only helps us to be historically more accurate. It also prevents us from fortifying the present hegemony of market thought that is based on an ahistorical understanding of markets.

References

Bachem, M. (2013). Beruf und Persönlichkeit. Zuordnungsroutinen der Berufsberatung in der Schweiz um 1920. *Geschichte und Gesellschaft, 39*(1), 69–85.

Bänziger, P.-P. & Suter, M. (Eds.) (2017). *Histories of Productivity. Genealogical Perspectives on the Body and Modern Economy*, New York: Routledge.

Bänziger, P.-P. (2020). *Die Moderne als Erlebnis. Eine Geschichte der Konsum- und Arbeitsgesellschaft, 1840–1940.* Göttingen: Wallstein.

Braudel, F. (1979). *Civilisation matérielle, économie et capitalisme. XVe-XVIIIe siècle.* Paris: Colin.

Buchner, T. (2013). Arbeitsmärkte ordnen oder konstruieren? Öffentliche Arbeitsnachweise in Deutschland (circa 1890 bis 1914). *Vierteljahrschrift für Sozial- und Wirtschaftsgeschichte, 100*(3), 292–310.

Callon, M. (1998). Introduction: The embeddedness of economic markets in economics, In M. Callon, (Ed.). *The Laws of the Markets* (pp. 1–57). Oxford: Blackwell,

Conrad, S., Macamo, E. & Zimmermann, B. (2000). Die Kodifizierung der Arbeit: Individuum, Gesellschaft, Nation, In Kocka, J. & Offe, C. (Eds.). Geschichte und Zukunft der Arbeit (pp. 449–475). Frankfurt a. M., New York: Campus.

Engel, A. (2016). »Ist nämlich der ganze Spekulationsverkehr erst einmal in einen krankhaft erregten Zustand hineingeraten … « Pathologien der Börse im späten 19. Jahrhundert. *Jahrbuch für Wirtschaftsgeschichte, 57*(2), 333–365.

Füssel, M., Knäble, P., & Elsemann, N. (Eds.) (2017). *Wissen und Wirtschaft. Expertenkulturen und Märkte vom 13. bis 18. Jahrhundert.* Göttingen: Vandenhoeck & Ruprecht.

Garcia, M.-F. (1986). La construction sociale d'un marché parfait. *Actes de la Recherche en Sciences Sociales, 65*(1), 2–13.

Kühschelm, O. (2022). *Einkaufen als nationale Verpflichtung. Zur Genealogie nationaler Ökonomien in Österreich und der Schweiz, 1920–1980.* Berlin: De Gruyter Oldenbourg.

Marx, K. (1973 [1867]). *Das Kapital. Kritik der politischen Ökonomie,* Vol. 1. Berlin: Dietz.

Maß, S. (2017). Useful knowledge. The monetary education of children and the moralization of productivity in the nineteenth century. In P.-P. Bänziger & M. Suter (Eds.), *Histories of Productivity. Genealogical Perspectives on the Body and Modern Economy* (pp. 74–91). New York: Routledge.

Miller, D. (2002). Turning Callon the right way up. *Economy and Society, 31*(2), 218–233.

Polanyi, K. (1957). *The Great Transformation. The Political and Economic Origins of Our Time.* Boston, Mass: Beacon Press.

Rossfeld, R. (2007). *Schweizer Schokolade. Industrielle Produktion und kulturelle Konstruktion eines nationales Symbols 1860–1920.* Baden: hier + jetzt.

Saxer, D. (2011). Persönlichkeiten auf dem Prüfstand. Die Produktion von Arbeitssubjekten in der frühen Berufsberatung. *Historische Anthropologie, 19*(3), 354–371.

Smith, A. (1814 [1776]). *An Inquiry into the Nature and Causes of the Wealth of Nations,* Vol. 1. Edinburgh: Oliphant, Waugh & Minnes.

Stanziani, A. (2012). *Rules of Exchange. French Capitalism in Comparative Perspective, Eighteenth to Early Twentieth Centuries.* Cambridge: Cambridge University Press.

Streng, M. (2017). *Subsistenzpolitik im Übergang. Die kommunale Ordnung des Brot- und Fleischmarktes in Frankreich (1846–1914).* Göttingen: Vandenhoeck & Ruprecht.

Wecker, R. (1997). *Zwischen Ökonomie und Ideologie. Arbeit im Lebenszusammenhang von Frauen im Kanton Basel-Stadt 1870–1910.* Zürich: Chronos.

Welskopp, T. (2017). Kapitalismus und Konzepte von Arbeit. Wie systemisch zentral ist "freie Lohnarbeit" für den Kapitalismus?. *Geschichte und Gesellschaft, 43*(2), 197–216.

Zimmermann, B. (2001). La constitution du chômage en Allemagne. Entre professions et territoires, Paris: Ed. de la Maison des sciences de l'homme.

CHAPTER 8

Analytical Capacities and "Blind Spots" of the Market Concept in Analyzing Cross-Border Labor Migration

Ursula Mense-Petermann and Helen Schwenken

1 Introduction

Patrick McGovern (2007), a labor migration scholar and an economic sociologist, considers the study of labor migration to be a test case for labor market approaches more generally. Migration processes have a number of "anomalies" for those "approaches that treat labour primarily as a commodity" (ibid., p. 218). Although interdisciplinary labor migration studies have explored some labor-market-related issues, such as patterns of labor migration and recruitment (e.g., Ye, 2014), skills mismatch (e.g., Creese & Wiebe, 2012), or "ethnic niching" (e.g., McKay, 2007), the labor market as a concept has only been addressed peripherally in migration studies (Pries, 2010, p. 730). There are some exceptions, however (see Bade, 2000; Bauder, 2006). On the other hand, research explicitly focusing on labor markets has remained tied to the concept of national labor markets (Mense-Petermann, 2020). The phenomenon of cross-border—let alone "global"—labor markets has been largely neglected to date.

This chapter addresses the question of how the functioning of the labor market, and particularly its cross-border dynamics, have been conceptualized in different disciplines and from interdisciplinary perspectives. We aim to bring a "market perspective" from economic sociology into conversation with migration studies and to discuss whether "market" is an appropriate analytical concept for understanding cross-border matching of workers to jobs—in other words: labor migration.

As we will elaborate on in more detail below, in migration studies, neoclassic economic models have for a long time been the dominant paradigm for explaining the driving forces of labor migration. Later, in particular in the sociology of migration, other concepts such as "chains" or "networks" gained more prominence than "labor markets." Hence, "market" is a contested concept when it comes to analyzing cross-border labor migration.

This chapter will discuss the analytical capacities and strengths as well as the "blind spots" of market concepts. We intend to bring together the different perspectives productively, without, however, promising a new unified theory. In the remainder of this chapter, we will first review the interdisciplinary migration literature and discuss the role labor markets have played in different strands of this research. This includes a critical discussion of the market concept, particularly with regard to its appropriateness for analyzing cross-border labor migration. Building on this discussion, we argue that using a market concept, not as in neoclassic models but as developed in the new economic sociology, can be usefully adopted for examining cross-border labor migration. Such an understanding of labor markets has a number of strengths: (1) it sheds light on the problems of commodification and (the lack of) decommodification of labor power at a transnational scale; (2) it is able to account for the complex constellations of actors in different roles that are involved in creating cross-border labor markets and (3) for the processes of the making of such labor markets; (4) it emphasizes the embeddedness of (cross-border labor) markets in institutional, cultural, and cognitive macro-structures (Beckert 2009) and makes it possible to empirically analyze the relevant macro-structures in which particular cross-border labor markets are embedded. As institutions as well as migration regimes and cognitive orientations such as imaginations of certain destination countries or ideal-type workers come into focus here, using this particular market concept also helps explain the structure of migration flows.

2 Migration Studies and the Concept of Labor Markets

In response to the question of what role the labor market concept plays in explaining work-related migratory movements in migration studies, essentially, the debate moves between two poles: migration is labor market driven and migration impacts labor markets.

In literature from economic labor migration studies (which were also widely received in the other social sciences), the market concept takes center stage. This research was dominated by an instrumentalist view of the migrant worker. The latter is seen not as an individual with all of his or her emotions, relatives, and networks but merely as labor power. The influential wage differential theory (Borjas, 1989; Tadaro, 1969), for example, considered higher or lower wages on cross-border labor market settings to be the key explanatory factor for migration. Scholars in development studies, in particular development economy, examine the implications of emigration on local and national labor markets in countries of origin (e.g., ETF, 2012), studying who leaves and the effects of the outflow. Is it a loss of highly skilled workers, we might ask, as much of the brain drain literature argues, in particular with reference to sectors such as health, or is it the exodus of the "relative surplus population" (referred to by some authors as a "global reserve army" in analogy to the Marxist "reserve army" argument, e.g., Foster, McChesney, and Jonna, 2011)?

Most contributions, however, analyze the effects of immigration on receiving countries' labor markets, namely a potential negative effect on the wages and unemployment level of nonmigrants within the neoclassical framework with the assumption of a competitive labor market (Ben-Gad, 2004; Borjas, 1999, 2003; D'Amuri, Ottaviano, & Peri, 2010; Dustman, Frattini, & Preston, 2013; Dustmann, Fabbri, & Preston, 2005; Manacorda, Manning, & Wadsworth, 2012). These neoclassical economic analyses of cross-border labor markets in terms of emigration and immigration have, however, met criticisms from different perspectives. As a reaction to the dominance of neoclassic migration theories, Michael Piore (1979) formulated a counterargument in his book *Birds of Passage*, adopting an institutionalist approach. Piore sees labor migration as a demand-driven process and thus understands that labor power is extracted from countries with a labor surplus. In the receiving countries, the labor market is segmented, with migrants frequently occupying the less desirable sectors and positions. Piore's line of argumentation influenced much of the labor migration research in the 1980s and 1990s, in which the segmentation approach was considered to explain a great deal of what could be observed.

Moreover, and this also applies to Piore's approach, what is used here is the national frame of reference: cross-border labor migration is seen as *immigration*, and the focus is on the impact of immigration on receiving countries' *national* labor markets. Consequently, in these accounts the *transnational* characteristics of cross-border labor markets are not addressed at all.

From a migration sociological perspective, Pries (2010, p. 732), for instance, emphasizes that the neoclassical theory reaches its limits when it comes to explaining why it is not the poorest in a country who tend to migrate although they would profit most from wage differentials, but rather sections of the middle classes. Also, as a whole, migration flows do not go from the poorest to the richest countries. Economic approaches to cross-border labor markets, thus, fail to explain the structure of empirically observable migration flows.

From a migration systems approach (Kritz, Lim, & Zlotnik, 1992) and later from the migration transformation approach (Castles, 2010), scholars were calling to leave this national container model behind. Instead, their theories did not emphasize the (imagined) functioning modes of the labor market but instead drew a larger, structural picture of global inequalities and how labor migration is a part of this. Consequently, the focus was not so much on the mobile individuals or employers and their (economic) motivations but rather on the flows of labor. The labor migrant in this perspective is thus drawn into these flows and moving according to prescribed corridors. Since the mid-1990s, migration studies scholars have increasingly moved toward explanations on the meso level, namely the important role of chains, networks, and channels (see, for instance, Yeates, 2004: see also, more broadly, the literature on transnational migration, for example, Glick Schiller, Basch, and Blanc-Szanton, 1992, in which networks play a crucial role). It is essentially argued that migrants are moving along beaten paths and that social and other forms of networks span between sending, transit, and receiving countries.

The previously undisputed idea that a person who moves then becomes an immigrant was also complicated by the discovery of many more complex migration patterns. In this perspective, the enabling labor migration infrastructures such as licensed recruitment agencies or informal labor brokers were also part of the picture. Here, the concept of "migration infrastructures" by Xiang and Lindquist (2014) is instructive. These authors define migration infrastructures as "the systematically interlinked technologies, institutions, and actors that facilitate and condition mobility" (p. 124). The conceptual idea behind this proposal is to move away from a perspective that only considers people as agents: "it is not migrants who migrate, but rather constellations consisting of migrants and non-migrants, of human and non-human actors" (p. 124). Following Xiang and Lindquist's text, a new interest in the organizational specifics of intermediaries could be observed (e.g., the 2018 Special Issue "Exploring the Migration Industries" of the *Journal of Ethnic and Migration Studies*, Vol. 44, Issue 4). In a similar vein, a research group around Manuela Bojadzijev and Sandro Mezzadra coined the term "logistification of migration" (Altenried, Bojazijev, Höfler, Mezzadra, & Wallis, 2017) in order to better understand today's regimes of mobile labor that are characterized by an (im-)material infrastructure, including own-account self-employed migrants that often makes formal recruitment and employment superfluous.

Another critical issue regarding much of migration economics' conceptualization of cross-border migration as market-driven is that it neglects the role of states. Yet, a web of laws and policies limits and regulates mobility. This becomes relevant in particular when we look at the countries that position themselves as market makers and actors on "global labor markets." One example is the competition between the labor-sending states Indonesia and the Philippines in the care and domestic work sector. The Philippine state, for instance, introduced a "supermaid" program to make "their domestic workers" competitive with those from other states by training them in ways that are demanded by more up-scale employers, such as the handling of electronic domestic devices or knowledge in health care.

We also see arguments in the same line from migration and border regime approaches (see Pott, Rass, & Wolff, 2018 for an overview): It is neither abstract labor market forces nor easily identifiable actors that determine who works where but, rather, the interplay between various actors, and political and economic conditions. The global visa regime and how mobility is governed, as well as discourses (for instance, on security, narrated reputation of certain countries or skills by members of certain nationalities) do indeed have a bearing on how cross-border labor markets work. Restrictive policies are also often detrimental to the interests of employers when politicians follow (assumed) voter interests. This contradicts some of the assumptions of earlier schools of thought arguing that labor follows demand, and that business dominates politics.

There are also other problems with the market concept that are not specifically migration related. We will examine two of them here: first, the dual structure (buyer and seller) and second, the voluntariness of the exchange that both form part of the market concept. As regards the dual structure of markets, a glance at empirical cross-border labor markets shows that most of the cases involve some form of intermediary, such as non-profit or for-profit recruiters, temporary agencies, subcontractors, or occur within organizations, for instance, multinational companies. The involvement of intermediaries transforms the dual structure (buyer–seller) into a three- (or more) party relationship. Frequently, market organizers are also involved: "To regard market and organization as opposites is rarely useful, however, and may even be misleading" (Ahrne, Aspers, & Brunsson, 2015, p. 8). Instead, Ahrne and his colleagues propose discussing the organization *of* markets. And they emphasize: "Like formal organizations, markets can be more organized, less organized and differentially organized." (ibid.). What becomes clear from this observation is that understanding cross-border labor markets as a dual structure neglects the complexity of the cross-border exchange of labor power. Given the complex structure of actor settings and the great importance of organization, the question arises as to how market exchange and organization relate to one another. The question is whether there is a market at all, and whether the concepts used in migration studies, namely "chain," "network," "channel," "infrastructures," and "logistics" are not better suited for capturing the embeddedness of the labor exchange into far-reaching (in geographical and temporal terms) interactions.

The other feature of the market concept, namely the voluntariness of exchange, is also problematic in the case of labor migration. As has been shown in Part 1 of the present volume, some cross-border matching of workers to jobs takes place in the form of forced labor, slave labor, or human trafficking (see Bales & Mayblin, 2018; Carstensen, 2019; LeBaron & Phillips, 2018; see also van der Linden, Hyman, and Scheele in this volume). Even when matching takes place on the basis of voluntarily signed employment contracts, one party often capitalizes on the vulnerability of another, namely the workers (see Welskopp in this volume). The concept of vulnerability that is key for understanding the social structure of much cross-border exchange of labor power for money is a "blind spot" of the market concept. This market concept, going back to Max Weber, implicitly posits exchange at eye level:

> Actors on both sides of the market interface have partly similar and partly conflicting interests: while they must both be interested in the exchange of a good, they have conflicting interests regarding the price and other specifications of the contract from which a price struggle between them emerges that results if the exchange is to take place in a compromise between the exchange partners.
> BECKERT, 2009

However, particularly in migration settings, job offers cannot always be evaluated by workers at the time of signing the employment contract because intermediaries capitalize on an information asymmetry between workers and intermediaries (e.g., Xiang, 2007; Valiani, 2012). Here, the pertinent question is how and why these labor markets are stabilized despite the information asymmetries.[1] Migrants often feel obliged to fulfill their own and family's expectations by sending remittances back home or having to pay back debts resulting from their migration investments.

Finally, another critical factor with regard to using the neoclassical labor market concept in migration studies is that not all migration is labor migration. There are very different reasons for migrating: many migrants initially move without economic motivation, although most do end up working and their migration consequently has economic effects. This calls into question the term "labor migration" because it assumes an intention that may—at least for some migrant groups - be misleading. However, a labor *market* perspective is still highly valuable here because the personal motivation for crossing a border is irrelevant and what counts is that a person de facto engages in work and is therefore part of a labor market. This is also reflected in the current

---

1   In his seminal article "The Market for Lemons," George Akerlof (1970) demonstrated that information asymmetries in markets tend to lead to an erosion of the relevant market.

ILO definition of labor migration (ILO 2018), which includes all noncitizens who take up gainful employment, irrespective of the initial migration mode or intention. Earlier definitions of labor migrants only counted those who were recruited or came with the intention to work.

Thus, sociological migration studies teach us that instead of applying an abstract market model to explain the matching of migrant workers to jobs, it is important to differentiate between the modes of labor migration and the channels, which both differ significantly and have an impact on the position in the labor market. We need to distinguish between (at least) four channels: (a) people who migrate because they have been actively recruited in their country of origin by for-profit recruiters or by state agencies. Some states, like the Philippines (Rodriguez, 2010) have even established sophisticated institutions for this purpose and also actively market their citizens abroad; (b) people who, on the basis of information from various potential sources, expect better income or working conditions in regions other than their home country and therefore migrate (this has been the assumption of most economic labor migration theories), (c) people with family, friends, or other people they know who motivate or inspire them to go abroad for work; and (d) people who cross borders involuntarily and are forced to work in a foreign country.

These various channels and terms of migration put the migrant in very different labor market positions. Some come documented, others undocumented. Some already have a job offer or contract, while others don't. Some come documented and with a contract but are still vulnerable because their status is dependent on their employer (for instance, under the *kafala* system). Some might have their credentials recognized, while others have to work below their skill level. Some have to repay smugglers, save for a family reunification, or send remittances back home, and are in a weak bargaining position on the labor market, while others with professions in demand are able to negotiate where and under what conditions they want to work. Care should be taken, however, to avoid making simplistic assumptions such as correlating a high skill level with a better bargaining position. Even health professionals and IT specialists run the risk of being exploited and put into a disadvantageous position on the labor market (see, for example, Xiang's 2007 study on the practice of "benching" Indian IT specialists).

Migration channels and structural labor market positions are inextricably linked: the more legally and socially precarious the cross-border mobility is, the weaker the person's bargaining position on the labor market. Research that brings together aspects of the market and a migration studies perspective therefore needs to systematically evaluate the modes under which a person migrates in order to shed light on cross-border labor market structures and their dynamics.

These critical debates on the shortcomings of migration economic conceptualizations that put labor markets at the center of migration theory, have—unfortunately—led to an overall neglect of the concept of labor markets in current migration studies. The role and functioning of the labor market today is by no means at the center of most migration studies literature or migration theories, even those on labor migration. Interdisciplinary migration studies have mainly focused on issues such as migratory patterns of movement and recruitment, the impact of migration on national labor markets, the skills mismatch of migrants' employment compared to their education, skills, and jobs prior to migration, the segmentation of labor markets along lines of race and migration status, and, following gender studies research, also gender in conjunction with race and migration status. Yet cross-border labor markets as a phenomenon sui generis have not been addressed.

To sum up, there are (at least) two critical points that arise in connection with the market concept when this is applied for analyzing cross-border labor migration. First, the market concept as used in migration economics has proven unable to explain the structure of empirically observable migration flows. Second, emphasizing the importance of intermediaries who act as market makers or market organizers the question arises whether we can in fact speak about a "market" at all.

Despite this critical assessment of the market concept adopted on cross-border labor markets, there are, however, also good reasons for viewing cross-border labor migration through a market lens as one element of a comprehensive analysis, which will be discussed in the following section. The question, here, is shifted from *whether* the market lens is a useful analytical tool to *what kind* of market concept to apply to the analysis of cross-border labor markets and what kind of research questions it might be able to answer.

3   An Economic-Sociological Concept of (Cross-Border) Labor Markets

The disciplines of economics and economic sociology share an understanding of markets as constituted through four elements: 1) objects to be exchanged, 2) buyers and sellers, 3) competition (and through this, price determination), and 4) voluntary character of transactions (see Aspers, 2011; Beckert, 2009; Engels, 2009).

Yet, since the mid-1980s, scholars in economic sociology have been critically discussing the market concept of neoclassical economics and have developed more comprehensive and complex concepts of markets (see Aspers and Shire in this volume; see also, as above, Aspers, 2011; Beckert, 2009; Engels, 2009). Contributions from the sociology of markets have accounted for this complexity by emphasizing the importance of market makers (Abolafia, 1998) or market organizers (Ahrne et al., 2015) and intermediaries, and identifying different kinds of actors involved, namely "profiteers," i.e., actors who make a profit from organizing a market (e.g., a stock exchange, or organizations from what is termed the "migration industry", Gammeltoft-Hansen & Nyberg Sørensen, 2013), and "others," i.e., actors who engage in market making on behalf of others who may be (negatively) affected by the relevant market (e.g., NGOs) (ibid). The idea of market making by actors other than buyers and sellers is particularly useful for examining cross-border labor markets. Yet these market concepts have rarely been used so far to conceptualize cross-border labor migration (for exceptions, see Aspers & Sandberg, 2020; Mense-Petermann, 2020; Shire, 2020). In the remainder of this section, we will, therefore, discuss the question of what the analytical strengths and weaknesses of such a market concept are when it comes to conceiving of cross-border labor migration.

The new sociology of markets stresses "that markets are highly presuppositional arenas of social interaction in which actors are confronted with profound coordination problems." (Beckert, 2009, p. 246). In order to emerge, markets depend on cognitive, cultural, and institutional macrostructures (Beckert, 2009) that shape the actions of market actors. These macro-structures represent the nonmarket prerequisites of markets and have to be socially constructed in order to enable markets to emerge (Engels, 2009). Yet the existence of these macro-structures cannot be taken for granted at the supranational or transnational scale. Sociological approaches to labor markets have stressed their embeddedness in specific institutional settings such as the production system (where decisions on production are made), the system of industrial relations (in which decisions on the level and structure of remuneration are made), the social security system (as an area of employment, as an alternative to wage labor, and as a reason for taxation and/or social insurance contributions), the gender regime or household system (as an alternative to wage employment), and the education system (that provides qualifications and skills that equip workers for wage labor) (Heidenreich, 2004, p. 210, with reference to Bosch, 2010; Rubery & Grimshaw, 2003; Schmid, 1997b). Yet all these institutions occur at the national level and so the question arises of how and which macrostructures are socially constructed that enable cross-border labor markets to emerge and function (for the following, see also Mense-Petermann, 2020).

Engels (2009) has elaborated three subprocesses of the social construction of markets, namely the social construction of marketable objects, the social construction of competition, and the social construction of market-specific orientations and action repertoires of market actors (Engels, 2009; see also Mense-Petermann, 2020). Regarding the subprocess of the *social construction of marketable objects* (commodification), Engels emphasizes that in order to be marketable, objects have to be "qualified" and "classified," i.e., attributed certain qualities and grouped into different classes of similar products (Engels, 2009, p. 72). Furthermore, marketable objects need to have an exchange value, i.e., a price.

The many empirical studies that Engels has reviewed for her article show that often extensive investments by market external actors, i.e., market makers such as states, are necessary to assure the marketability of objects (Engels, 2009, p. 75). In the same vein, Ahrne et al. (2015) stress that states or intermediaries frequently act as market organizers, for instance, by setting standards (see also Fligstein, 2001). In the case of cross-border labor markets, the question, therefore, arises whether there are actors and/or institutions that make labor power (as a commodity) comparable, valuable, and exchangeable transnationally. One example would be the above-mentioned efforts of states like the Philippines to develop and to brand the employee category of "supermaid" and to certify the package of qualifications this brand represents. For-profit recruiters can act in the same capacity, as Bludau (2015) has shown in her study on Czech nurses recruited to work in Saudi Arabia.

In the case of cross-border labor markets, the social construction of marketable objects is particularly pertinent as labor markets are not "ordinary" markets like any product or services market because the "commodity" exchanged is a "fictitious commodity" (Polanyi, 1957; see also Shire in this volume). Consequently, the social construction of labor markets does not only consist of commodification of labor power, but—in the sense of Polanyi's "double movement"—inevitably has to take into account processes that set limits on the commodification of labor power, i.e., *decommodification*.

The focus of a study on cross-border labor markets, therefore, would be on the question as to what extent transnationally mobile workers are covered by national and/or transnational labor laws and social security provisions, and subject to negotiations and collective agreements in national or transnational arenas of industrial relations. Due to the specifics of the international system of industrial relations (see Cotton & Gumbrell-McCormick, 2012; Gumbrell-McCormick in this volume), however, the capacity of the relevant parties to act on behalf of migrant workers at the transnational scale is limited, and workers often sit in a legal limbo as Lillie (2016) has shown for posted workers in the

EU construction and meat industries (see also Mense-Petermann, 2020, and in Part 3 of this volume).

The second subprocess of the social construction of markets is the *social construction of competition*. As with marketable objects, competition cannot be conceived of as a given. In fact, market participants have to develop a sense of what competition on a specific market means, who their competitors are, and how they can relate to them (Engels, 2009, p. 70).

An economic sociological perspective on cross-border labor markets therefore focuses on the questions of how market actors have broadened their search strategies for labor power or for jobs beyond their home country's national border, and whether or not and why they have concentrated on specific other countries and localities. The role of border regimes of the prospective host countries, and of other institutions and actors who restrict or enable crossing borders in search of jobs or labor power also comes to the fore in this perspective. It is, for example, no coincidence that the German meat industry mainly employs workers from Eastern European countries (see Mense-Petermann, 2020, and in Part 3 of this volume). In fact, this is due to EU legislation, namely the "free movement of services" that enabled German meat producers to contract out slaughtering and meat cutting to Eastern European service providers after the accession of the relevant countries to the EU. Workers are recruited mainly through personal networks in the hometowns or regions of the subcontractors.

A third subprocess of the social construction of markets is the social construction of *market-specific cognitive orientations and action repertoires*. This subprocess addresses the question of actor constitution in markets. Economic analyses often presuppose actors who are willing and able to make decisions as rational choices, but this is not at all self-evident (Engels, 2009, p. 79). Specific markets necessitate competent actors with specific cognitive orientations and action repertoires for that market (Engels, 2009, p. 70).

Hence, the focus of analysis in the case of cross-border labor markets is directed toward the processes in which the willingness of workers to migrate transnationally emerges, the processes in which the willingness to take on a job in a specific industry in a specific country is evoked, and, generally, the roles and identities of employers, intermediaries, and workers. In the above-mentioned example of the meat industry, it is again through personal networks that the willingness to migrate to Germany to work in the meat industry arises. Workers from Eastern European countries already employed in the German meat industry tell their contacts at home about the opportunity to work in Germany and inform them about the relevant migration channels.

Hence, the economic sociological market concept allows us to shed light on the precise nonmarket prerequisite for market exchange in cross-border labor migration.

4 Discussion and Conclusion

In the previous sections, we first demonstrated that the neoclassical market concept as adopted in migration and development economics has a series of weaknesses, namely its inability to explain empirically observable migration flows or to address the transnational properties of cross-border labor markets. Current migration studies scholars with a more sociological or anthropological background have therefore generally refrained from using the market concept at all. However, we have argued that using a market concept as developed in the new economic sociology might be better suited for the analysis of cross-border labor markets. This form of "market perspective" has a number of strengths.

First of all, it sheds light on the process of *commodification* of labor power and the problems that might occur in this regard in cross-border labor markets. The existence of standards and classifications—such as vocations - that allow us to evaluate and compare labor power across national borders is not at all self-evident. Since this is not the case for most occupations, cross-border labor markets are most likely to emerge on the one hand for unskilled work and on the other hand for high-skill professions which require (globally comparable) university degrees. For other occupations, such as, for instance, health care work, market organizers (Ahrne et al., 2015) are needed to invest heavily in building training facilities and developing curricula for educating designated migrants for the demands of prospective employers in the host country (as, for example, the Philippine state did). Consequently, this approach also highlights the importance of market organizers such as states, for-profit recruiters, and temporary agencies, as well as that of restricting and facilitating institutions and regulations, including border regimes.

An economic-sociological market perspective thus points to the conditions of possibility of cross-border labor markets and is able to explain why these labor markets occur in some sectors but not in others. Whereas migration scholars have produced a whole range of in-depth empirical studies on particular cross-border labor markets and how they have emerged and function, without however using the market lens, these questions have not been addressed in this research to date.

The market concept as proposed in this chapter, however, does not only allow us to focus on the prerequisites for cross-border labor markets to emerge and to function, but it also contains a critical potential because it sheds light on the problem of the objectivation of human labor power and on subjecting human labor power to market forces. The economic-sociological theory of markets suggests that markets also depend on actors with market-specific cognitive orientations and identities. Hence, the processes of developing these orientations on the part of the migrant workers, for example, perceiving oneself as the "seller" of one's labor power, and evaluating the "worth" of one's labor power, come to the fore here (see also Bänziger in this volume).

An economic-sociological perspective on markets, adjusted to labor markets (see Shire in Part 2 of this book) also raises the question of decommodification or the lack thereof. Cross-border labor markets are characterized by multilayered embeddedness at the national, world-regional, and global scales. One consequence of this regulatory complexity and inherent legal limbos is a high vulnerability of migrant workers and a lack of decommodifying institutions.

A further strength of the economic-sociological market concept is that it allows us to differentiate the market exchange of labor power (as a voluntary exchange) from other forms such as trafficking or modern forms of slavery, and therefore gives us a much better picture of cross-border labor migration.

To sum up, it is the market concept of economic sociology that is particularly suited to being combined with the migration studies perspective because it accounts for the relevance of multiple actors, also beyond the traditional labor market actors, and the complexities that characterize cross-border labor markets.

Some of the more recent innovations in labor migration studies, such as the concept of migration infrastructure, tie in well with the impulses on the conceptualization of markets from new economic sociology. What is needed in addition are the insights from migration studies on the bigger picture of global dynamics of both migration systems and historical legacies and on the functioning of the regulation of migration in which a major role is still played by states. When we apply these concepts together, it becomes clear that the relationship between migration and labor markets is a recursive one, not an either-or, as has been dominant thinking in migration studies for a long time now. Thus, to end with a quote from Bauder's insightful work: "migration flows regulate labor markets, and labor markets shape migration flows" (Bauder, 2006, p. 15).

References

Abolafia, M. Y. (1998). Markets as cultures: An ethnographic approach. *The Sociological Review*, *46*(1), 69–85. doi:10.1111/j.1467-954X.1998.tb03470.x.

Ahrne, G., Aspers, P., & Brunsson, N. (2015). The organization of markets. *Organization Studies*, *36*(1), 7–27. doi:.10.1177/0170840614544557.

Akerlof, G. A. (1970). The market for "lemons": Quality uncertainty and the market mechanism. *The Quarterly Journal of Economics*, *84*(3), 488. doi:10.2307/1879431.

Altenried, M., Bojazijev, M., Höfler, L. I., Mezzadra, S., & Wallis, M. (Eds.) (2017). *Logistische Grenzlandschaften: Das Regime mobile Arbeit nach dem 'Sommer der Migration'*. Münster: Unrast Verlag.

Aspers, P. (2011). *Markets*. Cambridge: Polity Press.

Aspers, P., & Sandberg, C. (2020). Sailing together from different shores: labour markets and inequality on board merchant ships. *Global Networks*, *20*(3), 454–471.

Bade, K. J. (2000). *Europa in Bewegung. Migration vom späten 18. Jahrhundert bis zur Gegenwart*. München: Beck Verlag.

Bales, K., & Mayblin, L. (2018). Unfree labour in UK detention centres: Exploitation and coercion of a captive immigrant workforce. *Economy and Society*, *47*(2), 191–213. doi:10.1080/03085147.2018.1484051.

Bauder, H. (2006). *Labor Movement: How Migration Regulates Labor Markets*. Oxford, New York: Oxford University Press.

Beckert, J. (2009). The social order of markets. *Theory and Society*, *38*(3), 245–269. doi:10.1007/s11186-008-9082-0.

Ben-Gad, M. (2004). The economic effects of immigration—a dynamic analysis. *Journal of Economic Dynamics and Control*, 28(9), 1825–1845.

Bludau, H. (2015). Creating a transnational labor chain between Eastern Europe and the Middle East: A case study in healthcare. *InterDisciplines*, 6(1), 95–120. doi:10.4119/UNIBI/indi-v6-i1-133.

Borjas, G. J. (1989). Economic theory and international migration. *International Migration*, *13*(3), 457–485.

Borjas, J. (1999). The economic analysis of immigration. In O. Ashenfeler, & D. Card (Eds.), *Handbook of Labor Economics*, Vol. 3A (pp. 1697–1760). North-Holland: Elsevier.

Borjas, J. (2003). The labor demand curve is downward sloping: Reexamining the impact of immigration on the labor market. *Quarterly Journal of Economics*, November, 1335–1374.

Bosch, G. (2010). Strukturen und Dynamiken von Arbeitsmärkten. In F. Böhle, G. G. Voß, & G. Wachtler (Eds.), *Handbuch Arbeitssoziologie* (pp. 643–670). Wiesbaden: VS Verlag für Sozialwissenschaften.

Carstensen, A. L. (2019). *Das Dispositiv Moderne Sklavenarbeit: Umkämpfte Arbeitsverhältnisse in Brasilien*. Frankfurt: Campus Verlag.

Castles, S. (2010). Understanding global migration: A social transformation perspective. *Journal of Ethnic and Migration Studies, 36*(10), 1565–86. doi:10.1080/1369183X.2010.489381.

Cotton, E., & Gumbrell-McCormick, R. (2012): Global unions as imperfect multilateral organizations: An international relations perspective. *Economic and Industrial Democracy, 33*(4), 707–728. doi:10.1177/0143831X12436616.

Creese, G., & Wiebe, B. (2012). 'Survival employment': Gender and deskilling among African immigrants in Canada. *International Migration, 50*(5), 56–76. doi:10.1111/j.1468-2435.2009.00531.x.

D'Amuri, F., Ottaviano, I. P., & Peri, P. (2010): The labor market impact of immigration in Western Germany in the 1990s, *European Economic Review, 54*, 550–570.

Dustmann, C., Fabbri, F., & Preston, I. P. (2005). The impact of immigration on the British labour market. *The Economic Journal, 115* (507), F324–F341. doi:10.1111/j.1468-0297.2005.01038.x.

Dustmann, C., Frattini, T., & Preston, I. P. (2013). The effect of immigration along the distribution of wages. *Review of Economic Studies, 80*, 145–173. doi:10.1093/restud/rds019.

Engels, A. (2009). Die soziale Konstitution von Märkten [Special issue]. *Kölner Zeitschrift für Soziologie und Sozialpsychologie,* (49), 67–86.

ETF, European Training Foundation (2012). *Union for the Mediterranean Regional Employability Review. The Challenge of Youth Employment in the Mediterranean.* Brussels. Retrieved August 18, 2021, from https://www.etf.europa.eu/sites/default/files/m/3B779523E600440FC1257B1E0055F27D_UfM%20regional%20employability%20review.pdf.

Fligstein, N. (2001). *The Architecture of Markets: An Economic Sociology of Twenty-First Century Capitalist Societies.* Princeton, NJ: Princeton Univ. Press.

Foster, B. J., McChesney, W. R., & Jonna, R. J. (2011). The global reserve army of labor and the new imperialism. *Monthly Review.* Retrieved August 11, 2019, from https://monthlyreview.org/2011/11/01/the-global-reserve-army-of-labor-and-the-new-imperialism/.

Gammeltoft-Hansen, T., & Sørensen, N. N. (Eds.). (2013). *Routledge Global Institutions Series: The Migration Industry and the Commercialization of International Migration,* Vol. 69. London, New York: Routledge.

Glick Schiller, N., Basch, L., & Blanc-Szanton, C. (1992). Transnationalism: A new analytic framework for understanding migration. In N. Glick Schiller, L. Basch, & C. Blanc-Szanton (Eds.), *Towards a Transnational Perspective on Migration: Race, Class, Ethnicity and Nationalism Reconsidered.* (pp. 1–24). New York: New York Academy of Sciences.

Heidenreich, M. (2004). Beschäftigungsordnungen zwischen Exklusion und Inklusion. Arbeitsmarktregulierende Institutionen im internationalen Vergleich. *Zeitschrift für Soziologie, 33*(3), 206–227.

ILO, International Labour Office (2018): Guidelines concerning statistics of labour migration. ICLS/20/2018/Guidelines. Retrieved July 29, 2021, from https://www.ilo.org/wcmsp5/groups/public/---dgreports/---stat/documents/meetingdocument/wcms_648922.pdf.

Kritz, M. M., Lim, L. L., & Zlotnik, H. (Eds. 1992). *International Migration Systems: A Global Approach*. New York: Clarendon Press.

LeBaron, G., & Phillips, N. (2018). States and the political economy of unfree labour. *New Political Economy, 24*(1), 1–21. doi:10.1080/13563467.2017.1420642.

Lillie, Nathan (2016): The right not to have rights: Posted worker acquiescence and the European Union labor rights framework. *Theoretical Inquiries in Law, 17* (1). doi:10.1515/til-2016-0003.

Manacorda, M., Manning, A., & Wadsworth, J. (2012). The impact of immigration on the structure of wages: Theory and evidence from Britain. *Journal of the European Economic Association, 10*(1), 120–151. doi:10.1111/j.1542-4774.2011.01049.x.

McGovern, Patrick (2007). Immigration, labour markets and employment relations: Problems and prospects. *British Journal of Industrial Relations, 45*(2), 217–235. doi:10.1111/j.1467-8543.2007.00612.x.

McKay, S. C. (2007). Filipino sea men: Constructing masculinities in an ethnic labour niche. *Journal of Ethnic and Migration Studies, 33*(4), 617–633. doi:10.1080/13691830701265461.

Mense-Petermann, U. (2020). Theorizing transnational labour markets—A research heuristic based on the new economic sociology. *Global Networks, 20*(3), 410–433.

Piore, M.J. (1979). *Birds of Passage: Migrant Labor and Industrial Societies*. Cambridge: Cambridge University Press.

Polanyi, K. (1957). *The Great Transformation*. Boston: Beacon Press.

Pott, A., Rass, C., & Wolff, F. (2018, Eds.). *Migration Regimes: Interdisciplinary Approaches to a Key Concept*. Wiesbaden: Springer.

Pries, L. (2010). Internationalisierung von Arbeitsmobilität durch Arbeitsmigration. In F. Böhle, G. G. Voß, & G. Wachtler (Eds.), *Handbuch Arbeitssoziologie* (pp. 729–747). Wiesbaden: vs Verlag für Sozialwissenschaften.

Rodriguez, R. M. (2010). *Migrants for Export: How the Philippine State Brokers Labor to the World*. Minneapolis, London: University of Minnesota Press.

Rubery, J., & Grimshaw, D. (2003). *The Organization of Employment: An International Perspective. Management, Work and Organisations*. Basingstoke, Hampshire: Palgrave Macmillan.

Schmid, G. (1997a). Beschäftigungswunder Niederlande? *Leviathan.* (25), 302–337.

Schmid, G. (1997b). Arbeitslosigkeit und Beschäftigung in Europa. In Statistisches Bundesamt (Ed.), *Statistische Informationen zum Arbeitsmarkt* (pp. 15–39). Stuttgart: Metzler-Poeschel.

Shire, K. (2020). The social order of transnational migration markets. *Global Networks, 20*(3), 434–453.

Tadaro, M. P. (1969): A model of labour migration and urban employment in less developed countries. *The American Economic Review, 59*(1), 138–148.

Valiani, S. (2012). *Unequal Exchange: The Global Integration of Nursing Labour Markets*. Toronto: University of Toronto Press.

Xiang, B. (2007). *Global "Body Shopping". An Indian Labor System in the Information Technology Industry*. Princeton: Princeton University Press.

Xiang, B., & J. Lindquist (2014). Migration infrastructure. *International Migration Review*, 48, 122–148. doi:10.1111/imre.12141.

Ye, J. (2014). Labour recruitment practices and its class implications: A comparative analyses of constructing Singapore's segmented labour market. *Geoforum,* 51, (Jan), 183–190. doi:10.1016/j.geoforum.2013.10.011.

Yeates, N. (2004). Global care chains. Critical reflections and lines of enquiry. *International Feminist Journal of Politics, 6*(3), 369–391.

PART 3

What Enables Labor to Cross Borders?

Introduction to Part 3
What Enables Labor to Cross Borders?

Sven Kesselring and Karen Shire

The contributions in this part examine the actors and practices that enable labor to cross borders and contribute (gradually) to embedding cross-border labor in transnational labor regulations. Mobility studies have emphasized infrastructures, organizations, and networks enabling labor to cross borders (transport, digital communication, and global production chains) and highlighted the formal organization of mobility (recruitment, bilateral agreements, and immigration policies). While building on this work, the contributions in this part turn to examine the practices that contribute to sustainable forms of labor and working relations, as well as the practices that undermine these as they operate across borders. All of the contributions consider how the making of labor markets is tied to building institutions governing cross-border labor exchanges, including networks, rules, and new forms of governance. The issues raised include how actors deal with distance and manage the multiple networks and scales involved in cross-border exchanges of labor and global labor organizations. These three chapters address the questions of what does and does not work, what the contradictions are, and what the new constellations and figurations are. The authors explore what prevents a labor force from crossing borders, what enables them to do so, and how labor relations are gradually embedded in multiple scales of regulation.

For both employers and workers, the cross-border exchange of labor entails more uncertainties and asymmetries. These cannot be reduced through established recruitment and placement practices since language barriers and a lack of information about how labor exchanges and placements operate represent serious obstacles. In addition, those practices may also implicitly favor native or later generations of migrant workers who are better adapted to national labor markets. Social networks of migrants have long been studied in relation to how they operate to enable individuals to cross borders but, as Anna Zaharieva shows, migrant networks are an important factor in enabling new migrants to find jobs at their destinations. Analyzing data from the Socio-Economic Panel (SOEP) study, she shows that recent immigrants are more likely to find jobs through referrals by social contacts than are native workers and earlier generations of migrants. Social networks are particularly important in matching less educated migrants or in matching men, but less so in matching women, for recruitment into part-time jobs, or for finding jobs in smaller companies. Comparing her results with those of studies in other national labor markets, Zaharieva suggests that social networks enable employment (as well as migration itself) by reducing the uncertainties potential migrants may experience when seeking a job in their desired destination. Given that referrals are most common for low-skilled jobs, a possible problem with matching through social contacts is that migrants are routed and locked into low-quality jobs with lower wages and with higher risks of underemployment and occupational mismatch.

One of the important insights of this collaborative volume is that global labor markets per se barely exist. The studies compiled in this volume show that labor mobility is more often regionally bound, involving a limited number and cluster of proximate countries, linked by economic asymmetries (mobility from poorer to richer nations) and by bi- and multi-lateral agreements specific to certain occupations or industries. Ursula Mense-Petermann advocates for a concept of transnational rather than global labor markets, and for an empirical approach to overcome the methodological nationalism of labor market theories and research and the resulting lack of research on cross-border exchanges of labor. In a study of how a specific cross-border labor market—for unskilled, low-wage, migrant labor in the German meat industry—Mense-Petermann shows how labor markets are made by powerful market actors who take advantage of international as well as national regulations to fashion labor to its profit-making advantage, though not without opposition. The transition from an earlier craft to a Taylorist mode of production created a strong demand for low-skilled labor, unavailable in Germany. Demand shifted to foreign labor, which was originally sourced through bilateral guest worker agreements, then, as these agreements were ended, through cross-border subcontracting, also on the basis of bilateral agreements. Many of these agreements were no longer necessary with the expansion of the European union, and with the availability of posted workers through the principle of the freedom of services (provided by the same subcontractors in the new EU member states who had already supplied labor through bilateral agreements). Social protests, government reforms, the expiration of transition measures for the freedom of mobility from new member states, and the responses of powerful employers to all of these pressures eventually forced foreign subcontractors to "patriate" their businesses to Germany and to subject themselves to German labor and employment regulations. As the extensive news coverage of meat industry workers during the COVID-19 crisis in Germany has shown, migrant workers were then employed on a contract basis, and still subject to extreme exploitation despite coverage by German laws. The contribution by Mense-Petermann underlines how transnational labor markets are *made*, and how the asymmetries between the positions of those selling their labor power and those buying labor power place employers in a powerful position to determine and change the contractual conditions of exchange. Her contribution shows both how national states remain important actors in the making of cross-border labor markets and also how they must increasingly operate through a myriad of cross-border mechanisms and at multiple levels of (local, national, and supranational regional) labor market governance.

The multiple scales and opportunities for transnational regulation of cross-border labor markets is the subject of the third chapter in this part by Sigrid Quack. As the contribution by Mense-Petermann has already shown, transnational labor markets are only possible once the rules of the game are established, but not all transnational labor regulations result in sustainable transnational labor markets. Drawing on theories of institutionalization and her previous work on transnational institution building, Quack argues that processes of creating and destroying labor regulations may proceed unevenly in different directions of change (top-down or bottom-up), at different scales (local, regional, national, supranational, or even global) and across what she identifies as the five domains of labor regulation (commodification, competition, control, reproduction/welfare, and standardization of knowledge). Institutional change is always gradual if meaningful, but it can be consequential. Quack emphasizes the opportunities for emerging regulations of transnational labor markets to improve labor conditions and balance the asymmetries of power inherent to the market exchange of labor. As Mense-Petermann's empirical work also suggested, transnational labor markets are likely to be sector specific and governed within an assemblage of territorially defined and non-territorial rules, which Quark, drawing on Trubek, Mosher, & Rothstein (2000), calls an "interlocking mosaic" of transnational labor regulations. In contrast to national labor markets (which Quack reminds us also contain a myriad of sector-specific rules, exceptions, and gaps in coverage), the making of transnational labor regulations is an actor-driven and negotiated process of gradual institutional change, which is "carried out in a loosely coordinated way, in the absence of a centralized authority" (see Quack in this volume) but with potentially transformative consequences for improving protection and addressing the exploitative conditions faced by many cross-border workers.

Overall, Part 3 presents a rich set of empirical analyses and conceptualizations of how transnational labor markets, and their regulation are possible. It demonstrates that the making of markets is at once a process of institution building across multiple scales of action and governance.

References

Trubek, D. M., Mosher, J., & Rothstein, J. S. (2000). Transnationalism in the regulation of labor relations: International regimes and transnational advocacy networks. *Law & Social Inquiry, 25*(4), 1187–1211.

CHAPTER 9

The Role of Social Networks for Job Search in National and Transnational Labor Markets

Anna Zaharieva

1   Introduction

When the labor market becomes transnational and opens its borders to foreign labor, there are several search channels and mechanisms matching foreign workers to jobs. These include international personnel agencies, referrals from social contacts, direct formal applications to positions advertised online and in the international press, among others. The contribution of employment agencies to cross-border mobility was already highlighted by Karen Shire (in this volume). The focus of the present study is on the role of social networks for job search leading to employment opportunities for foreign workers. Existing literature on referral hiring (Granovetter, 1995; Dustmann, Glitz & Schönberg, 2016) shows that social networks are often used as a job search channel in situations of high uncertainty and asymmetric information between workers and potential employers. A comparison of national and transnational labor markets shows that in order to consider jobs in a foreign country, potential migrants need to collect information about the job platforms used in the relevant country, the application standards, the culture of conducting job interviews, and the process of applicant selection. Also, companies need to compare foreigners' skills and qualifications with those of local workers and evaluate the language proficiency of foreign candidates. Consequently, it is to be expected that cross-border matching is associated with more uncertainty and more asymmetric information compared to the local national labor market and that informal search channels such as intermediate organizations and social contacts become relatively more important in the international context. Existing literature examining the migration decisions of foreign workers supports this expectation and shows that greater uncertainty makes workers and companies more dependent on social networks in cross-border matching. However, very little is known about whether the importance of social networks persists for migrant workers after their arrival in the host country. Therefore, this study uses German empirical data (Socio-economic Panel SOEP) to explore which worker and company characteristics are positively or negatively associated with referrals via social networks paying special attention to the incidence of referrals in the group of immigrant workers living in Germany. The findings are contrasted with comparable studies analyzing the labor market integration of immigrants and their job search strategies in other countries.

2 Referral Hiring of Migrants and Cross-Border Commuters

As a point of departure, this section reviews the literature analyzing the impact of social networks on the decision to migrate, the integration of recent migrants in the destination country, and cross-border commuting of foreign workers. When we consider the impact of social networks in the context of migration, there are several aspects that should be highlighted. First, social contacts may provide useful information about jobs and accommodation in the destination country and reduce the cost of moving for potential migrants. For these reasons, Haug (2008) classifies social networks in the destination country as a pull factor increasing the probability of migration. In her empirical study, she analyzes the migration propensity from Bulgaria to Western Europe and identifies several groups of potential migrants: long-term migrants and labor migrants (15%) with a high probability of permanent resettling, short-term migrants and tourists (15%), and nonmigrants or stayers (70%) without any intention of traveling to Western Europe. She finds that 64% of long-term migrants and only 30% of nonmigrants have relatives or friends abroad. Thus, having relatives or friends abroad is identified as an important factor influencing the intention to emigrate.

In an earlier study, Bauer and Zimmermann (1997) consider migration of ethnic Germans. Specifically, they use SOEP data on families whose ancestors left Germany and settled abroad while the offspring generation returned to Germany after World War II. This offspring generation forms the pool of immigrants and they were interviewed several years after migration to Germany. Bauer and Zimmermann (1997) find that 73% of these immigrants live close to relatives and friends and 77% have friends from the same country of origin, indicating the important role of networks for the newly arrived immigrants. Overall, Bauer and Zimmermann (1997) and Haug (2008) provide empirical support for the idea that social networks in the destination country increase the probability of migration for potential migrants.

One of the reasons for the positive link between the presence of social contacts in the destination country and the probability of migration is that social contacts may provide useful information about job opportunities. Ooka and Wellmann (2006) examined the importance of social networks in relation to the job search strategies of five immigrant groups living in Toronto: British, German, Jewish, Ukrainian, and Italian. They find that Jewish immigrants have the highest rate of using personal contacts when searching for jobs (54%), followed by Italians (51%), Germans (45%), British (44%), and Ukrainians (40%). In another study with Canadian data, Goel and Lang (2009) find that, in 32% of cases, recent immigrants with a close tie in Canada found their first job via a network referral; in contrast, the corresponding figure was only 19% for recent immigrants without a close social tie in Canada. Note that recent immigrants are defined as those who arrived within the last five years.

Elliot (2001) considers recent Latino immigrants to the United States. He finds that 81.1% of recent immigrants from this group were hired through the informal channel. The corresponding figure is somewhat lower for established immigrants (in the US for more than five years) and equal to 72.8%. It drops to 61.9% for Latino individuals born in the US. For comparison, the percentage of native US nationals finding jobs via the informal channel is 51.1%. First, these findings indicate that referral hiring is relatively frequent in the US, with about a half of jobs generated via this channel. Second, these results suggest that immigrant workers in the US are more likely to rely on their social networks in the job search process compared to natives, but this effect diminishes as workers assimilate in the destination country. Specifically, the percentage of informal hires among ethnic minorities decreases as time passes after their arrival. Third, Elliot (2001) finds that immigrants with no or "moderate" English language skills relied more frequently on insider referrals than immigrants with good English. This shows that referral hiring reduces uncertainty with respect to the language skills and facilitates cross-border matching between workers and companies.

In a related study, Aguilera and Massey (2003) analyze employment outcomes of male Mexican migrants in the United States. One important feature of their data is that they have information on documented and undocumented migrants. Most of the respondents in their sample are temporary and seasonal workers. They find that 60% of documented migrants and 71% of undocumented migrants found their job with a help of a friend or a relative. These figures are substantially higher than the average percentages of referral hires observed for established immigrants living in the US for more than five years. This finding illustrates that the importance of social contacts in the job search decreases as workers register and settle down in the destination country. However, this result should be interpreted cautiously as most workers in the sample are unskilled and unskilled workers are more likely to rely on their family and friends in their job search even in the national context. Aguilera and Massey's evidence is also in line with the crucial role of the foreign language highlighted by Elliot (2001) since they find that 51% of undocumented Mexican migrants in the United States do not speak or understand English.

Battu, Seaman, and Zenou (2011) find a similar assimilation effect of immigrant workers in the United Kingdom. They find that the less assimilated the ethnic unemployed workers are, the more likely they are to use their network as their main method of job search. Moreover, they report that ethnic workers who obtained their current job as a result of their personal network are in a lower-level job as a result. This indicates that faster accession to jobs provided by social networks goes hand in hand with a wage penalty and worse job quality. In a follow-up study, Patacchini and Zenou (2012) approximate social proximity with geographical proximity and show that a higher population density of the same ethnic group living within a 30-minute drive has a strong positive impact on the employment rate of workers from this ethnic group. This effect decreases for longer distances of 60 minutes' drive and vanishes completely for larger distances of 90 minutes' drive. Thus, social networks tend to operate in local labor markets and lose their relevance with longer distances within the same country.

Behtoui (2008) considers recruitment channels of native and immigrant workers in Sweden. He finds that 42% of Swedish natives found their most recent job via the informal hiring channel. At 37%, the corresponding figure is lower for immigrant workers, which is different from the situation in other countries. This finding suggests that formal matching mechanisms are relatively efficient in Sweden, so that immigrant workers are less dependent on referrals from their network compared to in other countries. This could be partly explained by the fact that firms are legally obliged to register all vacancies with the public employment agency in Sweden. Concerning wages, Behtoui (2008) shows that native workers obtain higher wages if they are recommended via the network. In contrast, immigrant workers receive significantly lower wages upon being referred for the job. Although the impact of referrals on wages is an active research field and the empirical evidence is mixed, this finding seems to suggest that native workers in Sweden tend to rely on professional recommendations, whereas immigrant workers draw upon the network of family ties.

One of the more recent studies on cross-border mobility and social networks was conducted by Verwiebe, Reinprecht, Raindorfer, and Wiesboeck (2017). The authors collected information on workers from the Czech Republic, Slovakia, and Hungary who were commuting to jobs in Vienna and surrounding areas. They find that 66% of commuters in their sample found their job with the help of a friend or a relative. Further, Verwiebe et al. (2017) confirm the prediction that language seems to be one of the factors increasing dependence on social connections. Applicants with limited or no language proficiency were the ones who looked for jobs via networks in particular.

Summarizing a number of main results reviewed in this section, we can see that social networks become a more important search channel when migrant workers and border-crossing is involved compared to native workers searching for jobs in their home country. Moreover, one of the reasons for this effect is the uncertainty associated with a poor knowledge of foreign languages by the prospective job candidates which makes them more dependent on their social networks. This effect can be expected to be stronger for low-skill workers as their language skills and international experience tend to be limited compared to high-skill workers. At the same time, the importance of social networks is diminished as immigrant workers settle down in the destination country and learn the language of this country.

3   Empirical Evidence from Germany

In this section, we explore the role of social networks for job search in Germany with a particular focus on comparing immigrant and native workers. Existing research for Germany is mostly based on descriptive statistics and summarized in short policy reports such as Drever and Hoffmeister (2008) and Brenzel et al. (2016). Whereas the first study uses data from a large-scale household survey (SOEP), the latter provides descriptive evidence from the perspective of companies based on the IAB (Institute for Employment Research) Job Vacancy Survey. At the same time, more rigorous econometric analysis encompassing several data waves is still missing in the literature. This study fills the gap by estimating a pooled multinomial logit regression over the years 2010–2013 based on the SOEP data (Goebel et al. (2018)). The sample is limited to full- and part-time employees aged 18 to 67 who started a new job in the period 2010–2013. Note that both types of transitions—from unemployment into employment and between two employers—are included in the sample. This generates a pooled cross section of 4,680 observations. The time period between 2010 and 2013 is characterized by a relatively favorable situation in the German labor market as the negative consequences of the financial crisis had been largely overcome and the refugee crisis had not yet begun.

The data show that there are three large search channels that workers use when looking for jobs in Germany and several minor ones which we merged together into a single fourth channel for the purpose of the present study. The first channel can be characterized as independent job search when workers find relevant vacancy information in the printed press or on the internet and directly apply to open positions without intermediaries. In Germany, about 22.5% of new hires are attributed to this channel. The second channel involves support from intermediary organizations, such as public and private employment agencies, including headhunters. This is the channel with the smallest share generating 10.7% of all new hires. The third channel reflects situations when relatives, friends, and other social contacts transmit information about vacancies and give recommendations. This is the channel generating 26.7% of new job matches. Brenzel et al. (2016) report a similar figure of 29% for referral hires in Germany. In the remaining cases, the worker returned to their previous employer, was selected from a list of internal candidates, or did not report the exact search channel. When all these cases are merged as the fourth channel, it comprises 40.1% of new hires.

These statistics reveal that referral hiring is less important in Germany compared to other countries in the European Union and to the United States. For example, Pelizzari (2010) reports that the average percentage of referral hires in the EU is 38%. Moreover, referral hiring is more widespread in southern Europe with up to 47% in Portugal and Italy (Addison & Portugal, 2002; Pistaferri, 1999). Bentolila, Michelacci, and Suarez (2010) document the incidence of referral hiring in the United States, which is about 50%, higher than in most European economies. The same conclusion is obtained in the seminal study by Granovetter (1995) and in the overview articles by Marsden and Gorman (2001) and Topa (2011).

Table 9.1 shows the composition of the sample. Note that the sample consists of newly hired workers in the years 2010–2013. The average worker in the sample is 37.7 years old and has completed 13 years of schooling. A total 46.1% of the sample consists of male workers, with the remaining share females. Natives comprise 88.8% of the sample and are defined as workers holding German citizenship from birth. The remaining group of 11.2% includes foreign citizens and those who obtained German citizenship at some later stage. In addition, 29.4% of the employees in the sample are working part-time and a large share of 55.4% are commuting to work. This category includes daily and weekly commuting. The geographical dimension is captured by the variable West which comprises 77.1% of employees. In terms of industrial composition, we can see that 46.2% of workers are employed in the service sector with other large industries being manufacturing, construction, and trade. Finally, the company size is captured by four binary variables: very small companies with less than 20 employees, medium-sized companies with 20–200 employees, large companies with 200–2000 employees, and very large companies with more than 2,000 employees.

TABLE 9.1   Descriptive statistics, (N = 4680)

Variable	Mean	Industry	Mean %	Company size and year	Mean %
Education	13.010	Agriculture	0.016	≤ 20 employees	0.284
Age (years)	37.670	Energy	0.015	20–200 empl.	0.286
Age^2	1537.3	Manufacturing	0.154	200—2,000 empl.	0.205
Male %	0.461	Construction	0.124	> 2,000 empl.	0.225
Native %	0.888	Trade	0.146	Year=2010	0.219
Part-time %	0.294	Transport	0.056	Year=2011	0.266
Commuting %	0.554	Finance	0.027	Year=2012	0.265
West %	0.771	Services	0.462	Year=2013	0.251

SOURCE: OWN CALCULATIONS, DATA: VERSION 32, SOEP, 2017, DOI:10.5684/SOEP.V32.1

The outcome variable—successful search channel—has four categories where $j = 1$ stands for employment agencies, $j = 2$ stands for printed press and internet, $j = 3$ stands for referral hiring via social networks and $j = 4$ includes all the remaining channels. This study therefore uses a pooled multinomial logit regression for the analysis with $j' = 2$ as a reference category. Let $P\{Y = j\}$ be the probability of observing search channel j, so that $P\{Y = j\}/P\{Y = j'\}$ is the odds ratio indicating a relative probability of using channel j versus channel j'. The corresponding regression coefficient α_{jl} can then be interpreted based on the following equation:

$$\alpha_{jl} = \frac{\partial}{\partial x_l} \ln \frac{P\{Y = j\}}{P\{Y = j'\}}$$

Hence $\alpha_{jl} > 0$ indicates that higher values of explanatory variable x_l make it relatively more likely that a given person found a job by means of channel j rather than channel j'. In contrast, $\alpha_{jl} < 0$ makes it relatively less likely. The estimated coefficients α_{jl} for $j = 1, 3,$ and 4 are summarized in Table 2. This table shows that educated workers are relatively less likely to use employment agencies and social contacts as intermediaries in their job search. Thus, direct online applications are the primary search channel for workers with higher education. In addition, public employment agencies and social networks are relatively less important in western Germany compared to the eastern part.

Male workers are referred more often by their social contacts than female workers. The estimation shows that a man with average characteristics has $P\{Y=2\} = 20.1\%$ probability of finding a job via the internet and $P\{Y=3\} = 30.0\%$ probability of finding a job via referrals. Therefore, the log odds ratio for men becomes ln $0.201/0.300 = -0.4$ This is different for women, with the probability of finding a job via the internet equal to $P\{Y = 2\} = 25.0\%$ and the probability of finding a job by referral equal to $P\{Y = 3\} = 24.1\%$. Thus, the log odds ratio for women becomes ln $0.25/0.241 = 0.037$. This leads to a difference in the log odds ratio equal to $\alpha_{3_f} = 0.437$. This finding is generally consistent with the idea that women lack professional networks compared to men. It is also supported by the previous empirical research for the United States in Marsden and Gorman (2001) and Elliot (2001), and in Behtoui (2008) for women in Sweden. Marsden and Gorman (2001) present several possible explanations for this effect. First, women are frequently more mobile when it comes to following their spouse to a different geographic location, which reduces the size of their professional and social networks. Second, women tend to be overrepresented in occupations with more bureaucratic hiring processes and standards such as administration. And, finally, women have a lower probability of participating in social and professional organizations, which is an important source of network formation.

Further, German empirical data reveal that jobs in smaller companies are more frequently filled via social networks compared to applications via the internet. This result is in line with the recent evidence in Rebien, Stops, and Zaharieva (2020) using company-level data of the German Federal Employment Agency. Interestingly, employment relationships involving daily, or weekly commuting are substantially less likely to be created by means of referral hiring. This means that social networks create jobs with shorter distances and travel times in the national labor market context. One possible explanation for this finding is given in Marsden and Gorman (2001, p. 478) who conclude that informal job search methods "are better suited to providing information about local employment opportunities, while formal techniques such as advertisements have a wider catchment area." Note, however, that there is some contradiction with the empirical evidence of Verwiebe et al. (2017). Whereas we find that workers commuting to jobs within the borders of their home country are less likely to rely on their contacts in the job search process, Verwiebe et al. (2017) show that the opposite is true for cross-border commuters. This comparison suggests that it is not the distance per se but rather the change in the labor market environment beyond the border, such as different regulations and institutions, that creates additional uncertainty and makes workers more dependent on their social networks and intermediaries in cross-border matching.

Next, the data reveal that part-time jobs are more often found through social contacts than full-time jobs. This raises a more general question as to whether the quality of the job is correlated with the search channel. Alaverdyan and Zaharieva (2019) analyze match qualities of newly hired workers in Germany over a period 2000–2014 (SOEP). They find that social networks lead to occupational mismatch more often than other channels. In their study, occupational mismatch is a self-reported variable indicating that the worker's existing skills are not required to perform the job. Among workers who applied formally via the internet, 69% report that their qualification is well matched with the job requirements. In contrast, the corresponding figure is only 46% among workers who obtained help from their social connections. This result is in line with Battu, Seaman, & Zenou (2011), and another similar finding is reported by Bentolila et al. (2010) for the United States. Although social contacts reduce unemployment duration by one to three months in their study, these are associated with wage decreases of at least 2.5% due to occupational mismatch. This evidence reveals a trade-off from using social contacts in the job search: even though social contacts lead to new jobs faster and allow workers to find employment, these jobs are more likely to be associated with occupational mismatch, part-time jobs, and lower wages. In the next step, we address the primary research question of the present study and explore the impact of ethnic background on referral hiring. From a theoretical perspective, there are two counteracting arguments. On the one hand, immigrant workers are likely to have a smaller social and professional network in the destination country compared to native workers born in this country. This argument seems to suggest that referral hiring should be less widespread among immigrant workers. On the other hand, the probability of receiving a job offer conditional on application is typically lower for immigrant workers compared to natives. Possible explanations for this effect include more uncertainty concerning the recognition of foreign qualifications, lower language proficiency of immigrant workers, and direct discrimination. If this latter effect is sufficiently strong, then immigrant workers may be in greater need of help from their social networks than native workers. In this case, we should expect there to be a higher share of referral hires among immigrant workers compared to natives.

The estimation results in Table 9.2 reveal that native workers are referred less often by their social contacts than immigrant workers. The estimation shows that a native worker with average characteristics has $P\{Y = 2\} = 22.9\%$ probability of finding a job via the internet and $P\{Y = 3\} = 26.1\%$ probability of finding a job via referrals. Therefore, the log odds ratio for native workers becomes ln 0.229/0.261 = −0.131. This is different for immigrant workers with the probability of finding a job via the internet equal to $P\{Y = 2\} = 20.8\%$ and the probability of finding a job by referral equal to $P\{Y = 3\} = 32.1\%$. The log odds ratio for foreign workers then becomes ln 0.208/0.321 = −0.433, which leads to a difference in the log odds ratio equal to $\alpha_{3l} = -0.304$. This result supports the descriptive evidence presented in Drever and Hoffmeister (2008) for Germany. It is also in line with studies for other countries (Ooka & Wellmann, 2006; Elliot, 2001; Aguilera & Massey, 2003) with the exception of Behtoui (2008).

In a complementary study, Alaverdyan and Zaharieva (2019) use SOEP data over a longer period (2000–2013) and split the group of immigrant workers into direct migrants who were born abroad and later migrated to Germany and indirect migrants born in foreign families already living in Germany. Their results indicate that the share of referral hires for indirect migrants is somewhere between that for native workers and that for direct immigrants. This suggests that social networks become less important for the second generation of migrants, indicating some degree of assimilation. Overall, we conclude that migrant workers are more likely to rely on their social networks in their job search than native workers in Germany, which could be a natural reaction to the lower probability of employment associated with direct applications.

4   Conclusions

The present study considers the role of social networks for migration and cross-border matching of workers and companies. On the basis of the empirical data for Germany over the years 2010–2013, we show that referrals via social networks are more often used by less educated workers, by males, and by workers in part-time jobs and small companies, especially in eastern Germany. Moreover, the incidence of referral hiring is higher for immigrant workers compared to natives. Related literature comparing native and immigrant workers shows that these effects are similar in other developed countries such as the United States and the United Kingdom, but the frequency of referral hiring is substantially higher in the US. Other related studies also indicate that social contacts in the destination country are likely to increase the probability of migration and cross-border commuting. One possible explanation for this effect is that migration and cross-border matching are likely to be associated with greater uncertainty and more asymmetric information for both workers and companies. Social contacts reduce this uncertainty by providing additional information about job candidates to companies and about

TABLE 9.2 Output from the multinomial regression

Variable x_l	Empl. Agencies Coefficients α_{1l}	Referrals Coefficients α_{3l}	Other channels Coefficients α_{4l}
Education	-0.145***	-0.0655***	0.0224
	(-6.11)	(-3.85)	(1.49)
Age	-0.105**	-0.0531	-0.0104
	(-2.89)	(-1.80)	(-0.37)
Age²	0.00150***	0.000648	0.000219
	(3.31)	(1.73)	(0.62)
Male	0.151	0.437***	0.214*
	(1.17)	(4.46)	(2.40)
Native	-0.190	-0.305*	0.0270
	(-1.08)	(-2.26)	(0.20)
Agriculture	1.092*	0.665	0.799*
	(2.33)	(1.56)	(1.96)
Energy	-0.661	-0.518	-0.526
	(-1.29)	(-1.47)	(-1.81)
Manufacturing	0.178	-0.0488	-0.224
	(1.11)	(-0.37)	(-1.87)
Construction	0.212	0.155	0.0432
	(1.13)	(1.05)	(0.31)
Trade	-0.253	0.213	-0.199
	(-1.43)	(1.66)	(-1.60)
Transport	-0.125	0.262	0.0694
	(-0.46)	(1.33)	(0.37)
Finance	-0.932	0.451	0.597*
	(-1.48)	(1.48)	(2.28)
≤ 20 employees	0.129	0.265*	-0.536***
	(0.73)	(2.09)	(-4.63)
20– 200 employees	0.163	-0.0766	-0.520***
	(0.95)	(-0.61)	(-4.69)
200–2,000 employees	0.231	-0.228	-0.440***
	(1.27)	(-1.66)	(-3.74)
Part-time	0.261	0.318**	0.198*
	(1.90)	(3.03)	(2.05)
Commuting	-0.0402	-0.323***	-0.250**
	(-0.35)	(-3.69)	(-3.11)
West	-0.713***	-0.374***	-0.375***

TABLE 9.2 Output from the multinomial regression (cont.)

Variable x_l	Empl. Agencies Coefficients α_{1l}	Referrals Coefficients α_{3l}	Other channels Coefficients α_{4l}
	(-5.43)	(-3.46)	(-3.73)
Year=2011	0.182	0.224	0.209
	(1.14)	(1.82)	(1.86)
Year=2012	0.00322	0.0324	0.0209
	(0.02)	(0.26)	(0.19)
Year=2013	0.0763	0.203	0.118
	(0.47)	(1.63)	(1.04)
Constant	3.068***	2.266***	0.937
	(3.95)	(3.70)	(1.62)

t Statistics in parentheses. *p < 0.05, **p < 0.01, ***p < 0.001
Reference outcome: j^l = 2—Internet and printed press
Reference categories: industry=services, company size≥ 2,000 employees, year=2010
SOURCE: OWN CALCULATIONS, DATA: VERSION 32, SOEP, 2017, DOI:10.5684/SOEP.V32.1

vacancies and job characteristics to potential migrants. This reduction of uncertainty is particularly important for low-skill workers with low language proficiency. At the same time, there is a caveat associated with network hiring since this channel often leads to low quality jobs, wage penalties, and occupational mismatch.

Moreover, German empirical data reveal that the importance of social networks is diminishing for the second generation of migrants. This effect is also supported by other studies, indicating a lower rate of referral hiring as more time passes after the immigrant's arrival in the destination country, indicating some degree of assimilation. Finally, German data show that referral hiring is less common for jobs involving long-term commuting; thus, social networks tend to operate in local labor markets and lose their relevance with longer distances within the same country. Contrasting this finding with the fact that referral hiring is used more often for cross-border matching of workers and companies, we can conclude that it is not the distance per se but rather the change in the labor market environment beyond the border, such as a different language, different regulations and institutions, that makes workers more dependent on their social networks and intermediaries in cross-border matching.

References

Addison, J. T., & Portugal, P. (2002), Job search methods and outcomes. *Oxford Economic Papers, 54*(3), 505–533.

Aguilera, M. B., & Massey, D. S. (2003). Social capital and the wages of Mexican migrants: New hypothesis and tests. *Social Forces, 82*(2), 671–701.

Alaverdyan, S., & Zaharieva, A. (2019). Immigration, social networks, and occupational mismatch. *SOEPpapers on Multidisciplinary Panel Data Research 1033.* Berlin: DIW Berlin, The German Socio-Economic Panel (SOEP).

Battu, H., Seaman P., & Zenou, Y. (2011). Job contact networks and the ethnic minorities. *Labour Economics, 18*(1), 48–56.

Bauer, T., & Zimmermann, K. (1997). Network migration of ethnic Germans. *The International Migration Review,* 143–149.

Behtoui, A. (2008). Informal recruitment methods and disadvantages of immigrants in the Swedish labour market. *Journal of Ethnic and Migration Studies, 3,* 411–430.

Bentolila, S., Michelacci, C., & Suarez, J. (2010). Social contacts and occupational choice. *Economica, 707*(305), 20–45.

Brenzel, H., Czepek, J., Kubis, A., Moszall, A., Rebien, M., Röttger, C., Szameitat, J., Warning A., & Weber, E. (2016). Stellen werden häufig über persönliche Kontakte besetzt. IAB-Kurzbericht, 4(2016).

Drever, A. I., & Hoffmeister, O. (2008). Immigrants and social networks in a job-scarce environment: The case of Germany. *International Migration Review, 42*(2), 425–448.

Dustmann, C., Glitz, A., & Schönberg, U. (2016). Referral-based job search networks. *The Review of Economic Studies, 83*(2), 514–546.

Elliot, J. (2001). Referral hiring and ethnically homogeneous jobs: How prevalent is the connection and for whom?. *Social Science Research, 30,* 401–425.

Goebel, J., Grabka, M. M., Liebig, S., Kroh, M., Richter, D., Schröder, C., & Schupp, J. (2018). The German Socio-Economic Panel (SOEP). Jahrbücher für National Ökonomie und Statistik/*Journal of Economics and Statistics* (online first).

Goel, D., & Lang, K. (2009). Social ties and the job search of recent immigrants. *NBER Working Paper, No. 15186.*

Granovetter, M. (1995). *Getting a Job: A Study of Contacts and Careers.* Chicago: University of Chicago Press.

Haug, S. (2008). Migration networks and migration decision-making. *Journal of Networks and Migration Studies, 34*(4), 585–605.

Marsden, P. V. & Gorman, E. H. (2001). Social networks, job changes and recruitment, *Sourcebook of Labour Markets: Evolving Structures and Processes, 19,* 467–502.

Ooka, E., & Wellman, B. (2006). Does social capital pay off more within or between ethnic groups? Analyzing job searches in five Toronto ethnic groups. In E. Fong (Ed.), *Inside the Mosaic* (Chapter 9). University of Toronto Press.

Patacchini, E., & Zenou, Y. (2012). Ethnic networks and employment outcomes. *Regional Science and Urban Economics, 42*(6), 938–949.

Pellizzari, M. (2010). Do friends and relatives really help in getting a good job? *Industrial and Labor Relations Review, 63*(3), 494–510.

Pistaferri, L. (1999). Informal networks in the Italian labor market. *Giornale degli Economisti e Annali di Economia, 58*(3–4), 355–375.

Rebien, M., Stops, M., & Zaharieva A. (2020). Formal search and referrals from a firm's perspective. *International Economic Review, 61*(4), 1679–1748.

Topa, G. (2011). Labor markets and referrals, *Handbook of Social Economics, 1*, 1193–1221.

Verwiebe, R., Reinprecht C., Raindorfer R., & Wiesboeck, L. (2017). How to succeed in a transnational labor market: Job search and wages among Hungarian, Slovak, and Czech commuters in Austria. *International Migration Review, 51*(1), 251–286.

CHAPTER 10

Transnational Labor Markets and the Role of Market Makers—The Case of Eastern European Service Contract Workers in the German Meat Industry

Ursula Mense-Petermann

1 Introduction[1]

The terms *"global labor market"* and *"transnational labor market"* are widely used when it comes to accounting for current social phenomena such as the ever closer integration of China or India with their huge labor forces into the world economy,[2] or the offshoring of specific operations of MNCs to countries with cheap labor forces.[3] A Google search (July 2, 2018) for *"global labor market"* produces about 159 billion (!) results, and for *"transnational labor market"* another 6.4 million.

In most of the cases, global/transnational labor markets are taken for granted by the media, consulting agencies, and other economic actors, as well as by many scholars. At the same time, there has been very little research to date on global/transnational labor markets as phenomena *sui generis*. It is astounding that the *"global/transnational labor market"* has rarely been subjected to theoretical clarification and systematic research. In fact, the vast majority of labor market research today still applies a national frame of reference and examines specific national labor markets.

The present chapter ties in with a sociological approach that questions whether the national institutional complexes that have been at the center of sociological labor market theories suffice in explaining newly emerging

---

[1] This chapter builds on research conducted in the context of the ZiF Research Group "In Search of the Global Labour Market." I am grateful for helpful comments and feedback from the fellows of the Research Group, particularly Karen Shire, on presentations and earlier drafts of this chapter.
[2] http://www.economist.com/node/21556974.
[3] http://www.mckinsey.com/global-themes/employment-and-growth/the-emerging-global-labor-market.

transnational labor markets. In this chapter, it is suggested that such border-crossing labor markets are differently embedded and structured compared with national ones. On the other hand, truly global labor markets rarely exist. This is also why, in the remainder of this chapter, I will use the term *"transnational labor markets"* instead of *"global labor markets"* because most cross-border labor markets embrace workers competing for a job from only a very limited number of countries. And one challenge for a more sophisticated understanding of transnational labor markets lies in explaining the structures of specific transnational labor markets in light of this.

In this chapter, I suggest that a close analysis of transnational labor markets ideally begins by conducting an empirical study of specific transnational labor markets and inductively developing theories on this basis. Yet transnational labor markets are not at all self-evident. On the contrary, they are unlikely to emerge because of a lack of order at the transnational level that is one of the most important non-market prerequisites for markets to function (Aspers, 2011; Beckert, 2009; Engels, 2009). Moreover, it is a very demanding process to overcome the obstacles that prevent a labor force from crossing borders, not least, for example, restrictive border regimes. Therefore, a useful starting point for examining transnational labor markets is to identify the *conditions-of-possibility* of specific markets of this type. The main proposition I am advancing in this chapter is that powerful *market makers* who organize transnational labor markets and institutionalize the "rules of the game" are the most important prerequisite for transnational labor markets to emerge.

The chapter provides an empirical reconstruction of the emergence of one specific transnational labor market, namely the labor market that matches Eastern European workers to jobs in the German meat industry. It draws upon an in-depth qualitative case study conducted during the working phase of the ZiF Research Group "In Search of the Global Labour Market" (2017–2018). For this case study, interviews have been conducted with representatives of one large focal meat producer, one subcontractor who acts as service provider for the meat producer, several workers from Poland, Romania, and Bulgaria working at the meat producer's premises, a representative of the Union for Food, Beverages, and Catering (Nahrung-Genuss-Gaststätten, NGG), and of various organizations that belong to the *migration industry* as it is known (Gammeltoft-Hansen & Nyberg Sorensen, 2013)—actors and organizations that facilitate the border-crossing mobility of workers.

Section 2 below provides an empirical reconstruction of the process of making this labor market, the most important market makers, and the four different employment regimes under which foreign workers have been recruited to work at the meat producers. Then the findings are discussed in Section 3.

Finally, in the Conclusion (Section 4), we consider more generally what this case study teaches us about the making of transnational labor markets and their specific features compared with purely national labor markets.

2 The Case Study—Eastern European Workers in the German Meat Industry

In this section, the making and several reorderings of the transnational labor market that matches Eastern European workers to jobs in the German meat industry will be reconstructed. The German meat industry is highly concentrated: The three largest producers of pork and beef account for the slaughtering of over 50 percent of all slaughtered pigs in Germany.[4] The top ten German meat producers have a joint market share of almost 80 percent (Friedrichsen & Huck, 2018). The case study focuses on an area in Germany that hosts one of these very large slaughterhouses and meat producers controlling a considerable market share, as well as several other midsize abattoirs, meat producers, and cold cut producers. Since these companies do not run their production lines with their own employees but instead outsource the production work to subcontractors, a few of these service providers have also relocated to the area. The meat producer observed in this study and the associated organizational field are typical of the German meat industry in that—as is evident from earlier studies (Wagner, 2015; Czommer, 2008) and from the press and television[5]—the production model of subcontracting and employing mostly Eastern European workers is also largely used by other producers (see also DGB, 2017).

2.1 *The Establishment of the Industry of Meat Production*
The making of the transnational labor market that matches Eastern European workers to jobs in the German meat industry is inextricably linked to the

---

4 In Germany, the amount (in tonnes) of slaughtered pigs is five times as high as that of cattle and of poultry.
5 See, for instance, the German television features "Der Mann für alle Fälle—Ein Subunternehmer aus der Fleischbranche packt aus," broadcast in Germany on WDR on 31 January 2018 (https://www1.wdr.de/fernsehen/die-story/sendungen/ein-mann-fuer-alle-fae lle-100.html), and "Deutschlands neue Slums—Das Geschäft mit den Armutseinwanderern," broadcast on ARD on 2 September 2013 (https://gloria.tv/video/EVDX3g6Lshrk2RgF3gtLyx knw). These both report on the practices of large meat producers and their subcontractors that are in line with what is described here, as well as on the working and living conditions of contract workers.

making of meat production as an *"industry."* In Germany, slaughtering, meat cutting, and meat and cold cut production were all crafts carried out by self-employed butchers up until the late 1960s. It was not until the 1970s that a meat industry developed. One reason for this was a change in consumer preferences: With growing wealth in the 1960s, consumers tended to buy cutlets and schnitzel and other premium parts, and no longer bought the heads, the paws, or the tails of slaughtered animals. However, these parts represent a substantial share of the worth of the whole animal, and ways to utilize and make profit out of them were sought.

This led to a division of labor between meat production and cold cut and sausage production: Two different industries developed in which the meat producer is responsible for the slaughtering, meat cutting, and production of various raw meat products and, at the same time, acts as supplier of downstream products for the cold cut and sausage industry. This division of labor and the concentration of slaughtering in centralized abattoirs employing wage labor made it possible to adopt a Taylorist mass production model in the emerging meat industry in the 1970s. The focal meat producer of the present study was a pioneer here. Today, this meat producer, like the other large producers, is slaughtering tens of thousands of animals per day. The plant is equipped with conveyors that carry the slaughtered animals and meat cuts along the production line to the packaging department.

This model of production no longer relies on skilled butchers but on unskilled labor. Each worker only has to make one specific cut or hand move. Hence, through inventing and developing industrialized meat production, the meat producer at the same time also created a labor market for unskilled slaughterers, meat cutters, and packagers. With rising demand for the cheap meat products that constituted the output of this mass production model, the meat producer was soon in need of several thousand unskilled workers.

In order to recruit these large numbers of unskilled workers, the meat producer was competing with other industries employing unskilled workers who, however, were offering higher pay and better working conditions. Meat cutting is extremely hard and exhausting work that has to be carried out at very low temperatures in the workshop. Therefore, the meat producer has been experiencing a critical labor shortage that could only be resolved by tapping into foreign labor forces. The production model of industrialized mass meat production and employment of unskilled labor soon spread within the whole sector and became the dominant production paradigm. Hence, a transnational labor market in the meat industry was created.

2.2 Recruiting Unskilled Labor for Industrialized Meat Production—The Four Employment Regimes of the Transnational Labor Market in the Meat Industry

Due to its Taylorist production model, the meat producer offers unskilled work that can be learned on the job without much training. In this case, consequently, we observe job standardization instead of skill standards that prevail in vocational and professional labor markets. Yet how did the meat producer manage to tap into foreign labor forces? Since the establishment of industrialized meat production, recruitment of unskilled labor from foreign countries has taken place under the following four different employment regimes:

(1) In the early stages of industrialized meat production, the unskilled work was done by so-called *Gastarbeiter* (guest workers), mainly from Turkey. Employment of *Gastarbeiter* took place under the specific recruitment program of the German government that—on the basis of bilateral government agreements—enabled workers from Italy, Spain, Yugoslavia, etc., and also from Turkey to come to Germany to take up jobs in the German economy. *Gastarbeiter* were employed on regular employment contracts under German labor laws and German social security provisions, so employment relations were regulated at the host country national level. However, matching took place cross-border under a bilateral government agreement, in other words, an international border regime.

(2) During the 1980s, however, the *Gastarbeiter* program was abolished and—due to the substandard working conditions resulting in a very high labor turnover—the industry was continuously facing labor shortages. Therefore, the focal meat producer of this empirical case study further developed its production model in such a way that contracting out of slaughtering and meat cutting to foreign service providers became possible. In accordance with German law on subcontracting (Sections 631 ff. of the German Civil Code) and regulations against abusive use of subcontracting, contracting out requires service providers to send entire teams of workers with their own foremen to carry out a clearly defined job on the premises of the main contractor. No mixed teams of service providers' and main contractor's employees are permitted, nor service providers' employees under the supervision of the main contractor's foremen. Service providers are responsible for organizing their teams and have to take over the role of employer. Consequently, the meat producer had to install separate conveyor belts for the different stages of meat processing so that these could then be carried out by teams from specific service providers using each particular belt, also supervised by these providers. Service contracts are defined as a specific amount (defined by weight or

piece) of meat to be processed (for example, to extract the shoulder bone or to cut schnitzel) in a fixed period of time. Therefore, the meat producer had to organize clear-cut interfaces between the production stages in order to assess service providers' performance.

Once the production line had been set up accordingly, during the 1980s, the focal meat producer of this study began to contract out slaughtering and meat cutting to teams of Eastern European workers on the basis of contracts for work. These workers were permitted to work in Germany for a limited period of time under bilateral contingent agreements that the German government negotiated with several Eastern European countries. Here again, we see the employment relation regulated by national law and social security systems. However, unlike under the *Gastarbeiter* regime, under the contingent regime, employment relations were governed by home country regulations. And again, matching took place cross-border and under a bilateral government agreement. Hence, a second employment regime in the German meat industry, applied from the 1980s through to the beginning of the 2000s, was contracting out meat processing under contingent agreements.

(3) With the EU enlargements of 2004 and 2007, the freedom to provide services throughout the EU also applied to service providers from the Central and Eastern European acceding countries. However, as Germany applied the 2-3-2 regulation of the clause on a transition period restricting free movement in the EU for citizens of the new member states, workers from these countries could not seek employment in Germany until 2011 or 2014, respectively. Hence, posting of Eastern European workers in the German meat industry under the freedom to provide services—first from Poland, and then also from Romania and Bulgaria—was gaining momentum. The system of contracting out meat processing under the posting regime was able to build on relations established under the contingent regime: Some for-profit service providers had been working as contingent workers during the 1980s and 1990s, and under the freedom to provide services, they were now able to capitalize on these experiences and on existing network contacts. The majority of contracted workers came from the same countries as under the contingent regime.

Hence, the third employment regime that was applied in the years from 2004 to 2014 was constituted by Eastern European service providers posting workers in the German meat industry under home country employment contracts (see also Wagner, 2015; Czommer, 2008). Posting in the EU means a "temporary movement of labour between member states with the aim of encouraging more competition in European service markets" (Maslauskaite, 2014, p. 1). Posted workers' employment relations are embedded in the two national contexts of their respective home and host countries. Therefore, Wagner (2015, p. 204) states that "[p]osting follows a transnational pattern because the posted workers' employment relationship in the host society is mediated by their employer instead of by the host country." For Lillie, this existence "between labor markets and regulatory systems, outside the jurisdiction of a particular national system" (Lillie, 2016, pp. 40–41), leads to posted workers being *stateless* in the sense that they are "nominally entitled to a set of labor rights, but unable to claim these rights in practice because labor rights, like human rights generally, are exercised via national industrial relations systems, and posted workers are partially outside these systems" (pp. 40–41). This situation has led to highly problematic working conditions in the sectors concerned, particularly in the meat industry, characterized by "underpayment, highly flexible working times, employment insecurity, lack of proper work clothes for the cooling chambers and substandard housing arrangements" (Wagner, 2015, p. 205; see also Maslauskaite, 2014).

At this stage, the media, social organizations located in the area where the meat producer is located, and, last but not least, NGG and DGB, the German Trade Union Confederation, began to *blame and shame* the meat producer and the service providers alike for the intolerable working and living conditions of workers under this employment regime. They drew attention to the scandalous fraud and exploitation in this transnational labor market and put pressure on politicians at the local community level, at the level of the German federal states, and at the national level.

(4) In 2014, a further shift in employment regimes took place. NGG finally succeeded in negotiating a minimum wage with the employer organization ANG (Nahrung und Genuss) that was declared collectively binding for the German meat industry in August 2014. Although up until the end of 2017 this collectively negotiated minimum wage was still less than the statutory minimum wage introduced in 2015, this prompted a major reordering of the transnational labor market in question.[6] With a collectively

---

6 The announcement by the German government to implement a statutory minimum wage which did not exist up until 2015 was certainly the most important reason why employers

binding minimum wage in place, posted workers who were working in the German meat industry, too, had the right to be paid this minimum wage. Moreover, with the introduction of the decree to include the meat industry in the sectors that are covered by the German Posting Law, the main contractor liability clause that forms part of this law also applies to German meat producers. The clause stipulates that primary contractors, in this case the meat producers, are fully liable for the payment of the minimum wage and contributions to social security funds for workers working under their service contracts in cases where any service provider in a subcontractor chain fails to pay wages or contributions. In addition, since 2011 and 2014, respectively, the free movement of individuals within the EU fully applies to the new member states from the EU enlargements of 2004 and 2007, respectively. Since then, posting is no longer the only possibility for employing workers from these countries in Germany.

These amendments have prompted massive changes in the transnational labor market under review: Since 2014, the focal meat producer of this study forces its service providers to run subsidiaries in Germany and to employ their workers under German labor law and social insurance provisions. For fear of being prosecuted under the main contractor liability clause for wages or social insurance contributions not being paid by foreign subcontractors, the meat producer has ensured that it has more control and a stronger grip on what subcontractors are doing when they are operating in Germany in accordance with German law.

Furthermore, *blaming and shaming* by the media and through local protest movements, as well as pressure by the government, have led to a voluntary commitment to improve the working conditions in German meat production signed by the six largest meat producers and many smaller producers in 2015. In this document, all signees agree to abolish posting and to contract out meat processing only to service providers who employ their workers under German employment and social security laws.

Since then, all contracted workers at the focal meat producer of the present case study were employed by German employers under German labor law, German social security provisions, and the collective agreement for the meat industry. This means that they benefit from the full protection and social security of the German labor law and welfare state, and also a remarkable increase in wages. At first glance, and in terms of the legal entities who act as employers,

---

gave up resistance against collective bargaining. Negotiation of a collective agreement with minimum wages lower than the subsequently introduced statutory minimum wage allowed undercutting of the statutory minimum wage for a transition period of two years.

there has also been a major shift because the employers are now German companies. Yet the actors involved have not changed. The CEOs of the German subsidiaries that employ the workers today are the same individuals who were running the Polish, Romanian, or Bulgarian service providers under the posting regime.

Also, as reported by several interviewees, fraud and exploitation of workers are still prevalent in this labor market. Contracted workers are still uninformed about their rights and lack a sufficient command of German to become informed and claim what they are entitled to. Moreover, most of them seem to be reluctant to consult the information centers and helplines of the union and of other social organizations for fear of being fired when their employer learns about this.

3   Discussion

3.1   *"Coproduction" of Industries and Labor Markets*
The case study presented shows that labor markets do not develop independently from the sectors in which they are embedded. On the contrary, the case study reveals that the making of the transnational labor market observed here went hand in hand with the establishment of the meat production industry. The large meat producer, together with the other large producers, became the main *maker* of this transnational labor market because they had developed a production model that depended on large numbers of unskilled workers who were willing and able to submit to a Taylorist work regime and accept the extremely hard and exhausting working conditions and poor wages that the meat producers offered. These workers could not be recruited from the native German population. Therefore, the meat producers had to tap into foreign labor forces and to organize a transnational labor market that matches Eastern European workers to the jobs the meat producers were offering.

While matching theory predominantly focuses on skills, the present case study sheds light on the importance of industries and their production models that rely on specific modes of using labor power. Matching in this context not only refers to a fit of worker and job in terms of skills but also more broadly with regard to being willing and able to accept the wages offered and put up with the working conditions (see also Piore, 1979).

Moreover, production models are embedded in the broader development of value chains. In this case, the meat producers have not only developed a Taylorist production model for themselves but also helped establish a value chain in which large retailers who distribute the huge amounts of cheap meat products that constitute the output of mass meat production are in a position to put a great deal of pressure on the producers. On the other end of the chain, farmers who fatten pigs in huge numbers and *produce* them in a standardized manner so that they fit into the standardized production lines of the meat producers have established a *price cartel*[7] that does not allow the meat producers to play out their own buyer power against them. As pigs cannot be transported over long distances, the meat producers cannot switch to suppliers from afar. Therefore, as an unintentional consequence of developing the mass meat production industry, the meat producers have contributed to creating a situation in which they are squeezed between the price cartel of the farmers and the huge buyer power of a handful of dominant retail chains. Given the tight connections and couplings of the elements of this value chain as well as the huge financial investments of the meat producers in their production model, this is a lock-in situation that delimits the dynamics in the relevant labor market. The meat producers could not switch to an economy of scope and quality production that would allow them to offer skilled jobs, pay higher wages, and improve working conditions. Instead, the meat producer observed in this study is following the Taylorist path and—according to this logic—planning to substitute as much labor power with technology, namely robots, as possible. In packaging and minced meat production, automation has already gained momentum.

3.2 *Power, Counter Power, and the Scales and Modes of Strategizing*

Notwithstanding the described lock-in situation, the focal meat producer and its peers are still the most important *profiteers* (Ahrne, Aspers, & Brunsson, 2014) and by far the most important and powerful organizers of this labor market. Even though the meat producers are not legally the workers' employers, the companies are the actors that have the greatest impact on the quantitative and qualitative demand for labor power. Moreover, the meat producers define the main conditions and factors affecting the working conditions and wages of the workers: The focal meat producer of this study prescribes the conditions and prices for service contracts and defines the service contracts in such a way that they put enormous pressure on subcontractors to reduce labor costs as the only "screw" they can turn in order to secure profits. The meat producer does not open competitive bidding but offers ready-made contracts to service providers who may accept or refuse these terms and conditions. Yet most of

---

[7] The interviewee from the meat producer of this study put it like this (interview P, pp. 6–7). He refers to the Association of Cattle and Meat Producers (Vereinigung der Erzeugergemeinschaften für Vieh und Fleisch e.V., VEZG) who issues a weekly price recommendation to which all members are expected to adhere.

them have to accept the contracts as they only have this one client. Thus, the meat producer defines the room for maneuver of service providers with regard to wages and working conditions.

The meat producers also set the legal and regulatory frameworks under which their service providers may employ workers. It was the meat producers who organized and enforced the different employment regimes described above and, since 2014, forced service providers to run subsidiaries in Germany and to employ their workers under German labor law and social insurance provisions.

As earlier research has already shown, as the responsible union, NGG has been virtually unable to counter this power (Wagner, 2015). It is also important to note that contract service workers are not subject to representation by the works' council of the meat producer. Under the posting regime, contracted workers remained in their home countries' wage and social security system with no statutory or generally binding minimum wage in the German meat industry in place. For a long time, no collective agreement was negotiated in the meat industry because employers were reluctant to do so and employers' associations in the industry were fragmented or virtually nonexistent (Wagner, 2015; Czommer & Worthmann, 2005). Since 2014, however, there is a collectively negotiated minimum wage that has been declared generally binding by the government. This has prompted a major reordering of the transnational labor market in question.

NGG has been able to gain more power by extending the scales and modes of strategizing (Mense-Petermann, 2021; see also Wagner, 2015). The union was continuously pushing employers to negotiate a collective agreement for the meat industry but also began to combine this with two other strategies. First of all, at the local level, NGG started to collaborate with other actors from civil society, like local protest movements and local branches of welfare organizations. These actors coordinated activities that were targeted at *blaming and shaming* the meat producers who were then *under fire* as bad corporate citizens. Second, at the level of the federal state and at national level, NGG and DGB, the German Trade Union Confederation, joined together to put pressure on politicians. The latter were then pressuring the large German meat producers to improve wages and working conditions (see DGB, 2017). Hence, union organizations and NGOs were gaining more power and importance as market makers due to multiscale and multimode strategizing. They have succeeded in initiating a major reordering of the transnational labor market in question. Yet, within these power struggles, they have certainly profited from state policies such as the implementation of a statutory minimum wage in Germany, and more regulation of meat producers' practices by including the meat industry in the sectors covered by the German Posting Law, subjecting producers to the main contractor liability clause.

What emerges from this is that the large meat producers remain the most powerful actors in defining the *"rules of the game"* and in negotiating the order of this transnational labor market. Yet the nation state emerges as a powerful counterpart that can be mobilized to enter the "game" through strategies of joining forces and *blaming and shaming* by union organizations and NGOs. This, however, requires extensive efforts and investments, in terms of organizational, financial, and time resources, by the latter.

However, while the legal and social situation has improved greatly, the actual working and living conditions of Eastern European workers in the German meat industry have not changed that much: Interviewees report continuing fraudulent and abusive behavior of service providers towards their workers.[8] They expect them to do overtime without extra pay: Working about 60 hours a week is standard practice. Many workers are still not aware about their rights, for example, to elect a works council, and those who had been reluctant to do so for fear of losing their job. No service provider covered by this study had a works council. Workers who still claim their rights, for instance with the support of the union NGG, are pushed by their employers to refrain from complaining and threatened with being fired (see also DGB, 2017).[9]

4 Conclusion

The case of the transnational labor market that matches Eastern European workers to jobs in the German meat industry is interesting in itself—at least from a German point of view—as it is characterized by substandard wages and working conditions as well as by employment practices that are taking place in a legal limbo to say the least. Not only does it undermine German labor and wage standards, but it also entails the emergence of a new deprived underclass in the regions where large meat producers are located.

---

8   This is supported by the results of labor inspections in 30 slaughterhouses in Northrhein-Westphalia in October 2019 which revealed extensive violations of labor laws and safety at work provisions.

9   In Spring 2020, after completion of this manuscript, the Corona pandemic proved to be a *game changer* in favor of the critics of the contracting system. The high rates of infection among cross-border subcontracted contract workers in the meat production industry has led the German government to prohibit contract labor in the sector from January 2021. This has paved the way for a further shift of the employment regime under which Eastern European workers are working in the German meat industry.

Yet the case study also allows for some more general and theoretical insights into the specifics of transnational labor markets compared with national ones: Transnational labor markets are embedded in a complex and multilayered set of institutions (see also Quack in this volume). While the nation-state certainly continues to be of major importance also as the institutional context for transnational labor markets, not least because it regulates access of foreign labor forces through its border regime, transnational labor markets are also embedded in transnational institutional settings like, in this case, the EU.

Yet these institutions do not *make* transnational labor markets. Actors are needed who create and enact these institutions. An actor-centered perspective on transnational labor markets, their emergence, structure, and functioning as applied in this chapter has proven very useful for capturing these actors and their strategizing (for markets in general see Ahrne, Aspers, and Brunsson, 2014). A labor market analysis that concentrates on the actors who *make* a labor market first of all reveals that employers and/or employees may not be the main actors in a labor market. While most (labor) market definitions presuppose a two-sided or dual exchange relation with competition at least on one side of this relation (Weber, 1972), the present case study shows that the situation may be much more complex with third or even more parties involved in the exchange. In this case, more parties become involved by differentiation of the employer role. Employer functions such as defining jobs, recruiting workers, deciding on modes of and issuing contracts, negotiating wages and working conditions, providing workplaces, working equipment and tools are distributed among different types of actors, namely the meat producers, the subcontractors, and, in some cases, also specialized recruiters.

Second, the actor-centered approach of the present case study also reveals the power relations in the labor market. As has been demonstrated, the meat producers—although not formally party to the labor power exchange proper—are the most powerful actors constructing and shaping this transnational labor market. A stress on power relations as a constitutive element of markets (Abolafia, 1998) helps to uncover the extraordinary power asymmetry as the main structural feature shaping the functioning, dynamic, and outcomes of this transnational labor market.

Given the lack of preexisting and stable institutional orders at the transnational scale and the many obstacles that they have to overcome in order for transnational labor markets to emerge, they need powerful market makers to organize them. In the case of the meat industry, a highly concentrated sector with only a few but all very large producers, the latter have assumed this function. In other cases, such as elderly and health care, either state agencies, as in the case of the Philippines (Choy, 2003), or for-profit recruiters (Bludau 2015) perform this role. Temporary agencies can also function as market makers (Imai, 2009; Peck, Theodore, & Ward, 2005; Shire et al. 2018). Further research, therefore, should take a comparative perspective and systematically explore different types of *makers* of transnational labor markets and the impact of these different types on geographical structures, wages, and working and living conditions in these markets.

References

Abolafia, M. (1998). Markets as cultures. An ethnographic approach. *The Sociological Review, 46*(1), 69–85. doi:10.1111/j.1467-954X.1998.tb03470.x.

Ahrne, G., Aspers, P., & Brunsson, N. (2014). The organization of markets. *Organization Studies, 36*(1), 7–27. doi:10.1177/0170840614544557.

Aspers, P. (2011). *Markets*. Cambridge: Polity Pess.

Beckert, J. (2009). The social order of markets. *Theory and Society, 38*(3), 245–269. doi:10.1007/s11186-008-9082-0.

Bludau, H. (2015). *Creating a TransnationalLlabor Chain between Eastern Europe and the Middle East: A Case Study in Healthcare*. Advance online publication. doi:10.4119/UNIBI/indi-v6-i1-133.

Choy, C. C. (2003). *Empire of Care: Nursing and Migration in Filipino American History*. Quezon City: Ateneo de Manila University Press.

Czommer, L. (2008). Wild West conditions in Germany?! Low-skill jobs in food processing. In G. Bosch & C. Weinkopf (Eds.), *Russell Sage Foundation Case Studies of Job Quality in Advanced Economies. Low-wage Work in Germany* (pp. 147–176). New York: Russell Sage Foundation.

Czommer, L., & Worthmann, G. (2005). *Von der Baustelle auf den Schlachthof. Zur Übertragbarkeit des Arbeitnehmer-Entsendegesetzes auf die deutsche Fleischbranche.*: IAT-Report 2005/03.

DGB (2017). *Zur Situation in der deutschen Fleischindustrie Standpunkte und Fallbeispiele*. Deutscher Gewerkschaftsbund.

Engels, A. (2009). Die soziale Konstitution von Märkten. [Special issue]. *Kölner Zeitschrift für Soziologie und Sozialpsychologie*, 49, 67–86.

Friedrichsen, J., & Huck, S. (2018). *Nichtorte der Fleischindustrie: Fakten und Hintergründe zum Schlachten in Deutschland*. Berlin: WZB.

Gammeltoft-Hansen, T., & Nyberg Sorensen, N. (Eds.) (2013). *The Migration Industry and the Commercialization of International Migration*. New York/London: Routledge.

Imai, J. (2009). The expanding role of temporary help agencies in Japan's emerging external labor market. *Japanese Studies, 29*(2), 255–271.

Lillie, N. (2016). The right not to have rights: Posted worker acquiescence and the European Union labor rights framework. *Theoretical Inquiries in Law, 17*(1), 39–62. doi:10.1515/til-2016-0003.

Maslauskaite, K. (2014). Posted workers in the EU: State of play and regulatory evolution. Policy Paper 107. Jacques Delors Institute (Notre Europe). Retrieved August 18, 2021, from https://institutdelors.eu/en/publications/posted-workers-in-the-eu-state-of-play-and-regulatory-evolution/.

Mense-Petermann, U. (2021). Interest representation in transnational labour markets. Campaigning as an alternative to traditional union action? *Journal of Industrial Relations, 62*(2), 185–209.

Peck, J., Theodore, N. & Ward, K. (2005). Constructing markets for temporary labour: employment liberalization and the internationalization of the staffing industry. *Global Networks, 5*(1), 3–26.

Piore, M. J. (1979). *Birds of Passage.* Cambridge: Cambridge University Press.

Shire, K., Heinrich, S., Imai, J., Mottweiler, H., Tünte, M., & Wang, C. C. (2018). Private labour market intermediaries in cross-border labour markets in Europe and Asia: International norms, regional actors and patterns of cross-border labour mobility. In S. Quack, I. Schulz-Schaeffer, K. Shire, & A. Weiß (Eds.), *Transnationalisierung der Arbeit* (pp. 155–183). Wiesbaden: Springer Fachmedien Wiesbaden.

Wagner, I. (2015). EU posted work and transnational action in the German meat industry. *European Review of Labour and Research, 21*(2), 201–213. doi:10.1177/1024258915573187.

Weber, M. (1972). *Wirtschaft und Gesellschaft* (5th ed.). Tübingen: Mohr.

CHAPTER 11

Emergence and Demise of Labor Market Institutions

A Transnational Perspective

Sigrid Quack

1   Introduction[1]

In a book part that centers primarily on transnational labor markets in the making, and, therefore, on the establishment of related institutions, a chapter focusing on the processes by which social institutions emerge and cease to exist may initially come as a surprise. However, emerging cross-border labor market institutions do not automatically prevail of their own accord or because they are more effective than those that previously existed within customary, delineated spaces such as the region or the nation state. Nor does the global diffusion of policy models of labor market deregulation or reregulation automatically undermine preexisting regional or national institutions. Rather, these changes must be propagated by certain groups of actors and must be tolerated, if not actively supported, at least by the dominant actors in the spaces under question. As a result, preexisting institutions may be entirely displaced, and hence cease to exist entirely. Yet they may also be transformed and integrated into regulatory structures that span different scales, inserting them in transnational systems.

In this chapter, I argue that a transnational perspective on gradual institutional transformation is necessary for understanding the making of cross-border, world regional, or, in some instances, even global labor markets. It is only through emerging transnational institutional assemblages that specific cross-border flows of companies, jobs, and/or individuals/workers become a transnational or global labor market (Quack, Schulz-Schaeffer, Shire, & Weiß, 2018). Following Djelic and Quack (2003, 2018), this kind of transnational perspective

---

1   Many thanks to Linda Jayne Turner for her diligent copy editing and proofreading of the paper. Sections 3 and 4 of this contribution build on Quack (2005) and apply the framework developed there to transnational labor markets. I would also like to thank David Antal for his very knowledgeable, accurate, and attentive translation of these sections from the German text. Jonathan Zeitlin provided very helpful comments on an earlier version of this paper.

combines the analysis of processes of institutionalization and deinstitutionalization, transnational referring here to features and processes that extend beyond nation state borders and also involve non-state actors. Accordingly, we need to examine the development of institutions beyond national state boundaries in conjunction with institutional change within previously contained national or regional entities. An analysis of gradual institutional transformation involves looking at formal and informal rules of the game as well as exploring the struggles of state, private, and civil society actors over what rules should prevail and be legitimate, not only for the exchange or hire of labor power in a market but also for the constitution of such a labor market. This perspective allows us to capture how assemblages or sets of formal and informal institutions emerge on a transnational or global scale. It also enables us to identify instances where evolving regulations remain largely decoupled from each other.

It is proposed in this chapter to conceptually distinguish between transnational regulation of labor and transnational labor markets. While transnational regulation is a constitutive element of transnational labor markets, not every transnational regulation of labor makes a transnational labor market. In order for a transnational labor market to emerge, multidimensional and multiscalar processes of institutionalization and deinstitutionalization of rules governing labor need to be assembled in recognizable sets of transnational labor regulation.

To develop this argument, the chapter begins with a short review of what are typically considered to be labor market institutions and a proposal for how to expand the concept when applying it to an analysis of transnational labor markets. In a second step, the nexus between processes of institutionalization and deinstitutionalization is examined from two different streams of institutional theory, represented by Lepsius (1997) and Berger and Luckmann (1980). In a third step, a conceptual framework is presented for studying the complex entanglements between transnational institution-building on the one hand and national and subnational institutional change on the other hand and this is illustrated with examples from the field of labor regulation. In a fourth step, it is emphasized that from such a transnational perspective, shifts in the boundaries between the jurisdictions of different institutional arrangements are constitutive elements of institutional change. The last section links this dynamic institutional analysis to assemblage approaches. Overall, the chapter proposes that instead of searching for a pre-given global labor market, we are better advised to study the fluid transnational institutional assemblages emerging from the coevolving dynamics of institutionalization and deinstitutionalization across multiple territorial and regulatory scales and their resulting institutional assemblages.

2   Labor Market Institutions: From National to Transnational?

Markets for the allocation of labor, for instance, the hire or sale of labor power in exchange of money, can only function if they are politically and socially embedded (see Aspers and van der Linden in this volume). Institutional devices are key to guide and stabilize mutual expectations about the (e)valuation of quality and price, the rules of competition as well as of cooperation in markets (Beckert, 2009). Following Shire (in this volume), three types of institutions can be analytically distinguished that provide coordination in labor markets: those preparing labor (commodification), those regulating contractual arrangements between individuals selling labor power and the buyers of labor power (competition), and those providing rules about the use of labor power in production (control). As labor is not directly produced for sale on markets, the functioning of labor markets also presupposes social institutions that support human reproduction outside and independent of the labor market, whether it be by means of welfare states, international aid, or family networks (reproduction and welfare). Finally, labor markets require a set of institutions that provide for a standardization of jobs, work tasks, and knowledge needed to enable the allocation of different categories of qualifications to different types of jobs in these labor markets (standardization of knowledge).

Research on the forms, functions, and outcomes of labor market institutions has largely focused on the nation state.[2] Conventional wisdom dates the emergence of formalized labor market institutions in the US and Europe to the period of the formation of the nation state at the end of the nineteenth century (introduction of the first social welfare institutions) and the run-up to World War I and the interwar period (labor law, unemployment exchanges, and insurance) (for a critical discussion, see Bänziger in this volume). The formation of these institutions had been preceded and promoted by transnational epistemic networks of labor lawyers and social reformers and led to the establishment of the International Labour Organization (ILO) at the Paris Peace Conference in 1919. Yet, the subsequent institutionalization of

---

[2] Social institutions governing specific aspects of cross-border mobility of tasks and employees have existed much longer. These date back at least to the long-distance trading system of the guilds and merchant houses in medieval Europe and the rise of the Dutch and British East India Companies (Braudel, 1992; Quack, 2009).

mandatory social benefits, unemployment insurance, labor legislation, and wage-setting institutions took place predominantly within national borders. Particularly during the period following World War II, international regulation of industrial relations, as undertaken by the ILO, relied on national laws and collective bargaining, and the national effectiveness of regulation.

In the past decades, these internationally coordinated national systems of labor market institutions have faced challenges in a number of areas, including from international economic integration, sectoral and technological shifts in production, as well as changing approaches towards regulation. While one strand of academic literature portrays globalization as undermining national labor market institutions and the global sphere as largely un- or under-regulated, other authors have called for giving up the strong binary between national and global regulation in favor of studying the "interlocking mosaic" of national and transnational institutions governing labor relations (Trubek, Mosher, & Rothstein, 2000, p. 1187). This contribution aims to bridge the gap between these two lines of thought by combining the study of institutionalization and deinstitutionalization from a transnational perspective.

This requires a broadening of perspective in terms of actors, forms, and scales of regulation. In addition to national public regulators and bargaining parties, there are now also labor activists and NGOs mobilizing across borders for better working conditions, unions coordinating in European and World Works Councils, private intermediaries and companies developing rules that facilitate cross-border mobility of tasks and workers, to mention only a few of the multiple actors involved in building transnational institutions governing labor relations. In addition to public forms of regulation, various types of social regulation developed by private and civil society actors, often not legally binding but nevertheless guiding actors' behavior, need to be considered separately and in interaction with public regulation. Better knowledge is also required about how regulatory arrangements governing the exchange of labor power in markets and labor relations more broadly become increasingly entangled across different jurisdictional scales, ranging from the subnational to the national to the world regional and global.

Against this backdrop, the following sections propose a conceptual framework for analyzing transnational labor market making as a process of gradual institutional transformation. It is suggested that focusing on coevolving processes of institutionalization and deinstitutionalization provides a productive lens for the systematic study of the evolving mosaic of informal and formal rules that govern transnational labor markets across different scales.

3   Processes of Institutionalization and Deinstitutionalization

New institutional rules do not come out of the blue. They are created by social actors, and their effectiveness requires social acceptance and recognition by the actors involved. Nor do new rules often arise in an institutional vacuum. On the contrary, certain forms of control and coordination with which they compete normally already exist. If the new rules are successful, they displace, transform, or change the established ones. The transformation of these rules of the game can thus be understood as a constant process by which patterns of social coordination and expectations are institutionalized and deinstitutionalized. But how do these processes of replacing old institutions with new ones work? What phases can be distinguished and what factors affect the course of these processes?

Processes of institutionalization and deinstitutionalization are addressed in the literature from a macro- and micro-sociological perspective. Representing the macro-sociological stance, Lepsius (1997) assumes the coexistence of different and sometimes contradictory guiding social principles. Their institutionalization involves spelling them out as practical behavioral orientations ("rationality criteria"); elaborating an action context in which these rules are claimed to be authoritative as a behavioral norm; and using sanctions or internalization to implement the guiding idea they embody. The institutionalization of a certain guiding idea always entails conflicts with other guiding ideas. Institutional change under normal conditions is therefore manifested as an "ongoing process of institutionalization and deinstitutionalization of guiding ideas" (Lepsius, 1997, p. 63). In this "institutional struggle" (Lepsius, 1995, p. 399), legal admissibility and economic possibility are decisive factors for the institutionalization or deinstitutionalization of a guiding idea, as is the organizational and mobilizing capacity of the responsible actors. Ultimately, the way in which the conflicts between the individual institutions are regulated by mediation structures determines the character of societal systems. Although Lepsius does not explicitly address this point, social disputes about the institutionalization and deinstitutionalization of certain guiding ideas are also conceivable in these mediating institutions. The discussion about transnational labor governance itself can also be considered as a dispute about the positive and negative implications of various coordination and mediation mechanisms and, hence, as institutional policy across different institutional domains such as labor law, citizenship rights, and migration control.

Whereas Lepsius (1995, 1997) assumes the existence of abstract guiding ideas, Berger and Luckmann (1980) draw on their inquiries into the sociology of knowledge to explore how the everyday actions of individuals produce institutional guiding principles through institutionalization or make them disappear through deinstitutionalization. Berger and Luckmann distinguish between three phases of institutionalization (see also Tolbert and Zucker, 1996). In the first phase, habitualization, actors develop specific patterns of thought and behavior to solve specific tasks. Faced with new problems arising from the cross-border mobility of companies, tasks, and individuals, actors will first attempt to respond by activating their repertoire of routines for finding solutions and/or will try to interpret and stretch institutional rules in such a way that the routines become feasible. However, this response is not merely reactive. Individual actors can also experiment with new patterns of action and habitualize them by reciprocal typification in a local area. Many different habitualized patterns of action coordination can thereby coexist in the institutional niches of a societal entity, be it at the regional or national level. Through extension and reinterpretation, local experiments can be accommodated at least temporarily under the umbrella of the given institutional framework.

In the second phase, objectivation, efforts to legitimize patterns of thought and behavior are made in arguments that can (but need not) contribute to their acceptance and adoption by other actors beyond the local context. Whereas the actors participating in habitualization still remember the sense of the rules, this must first be made comprehensible to new actors. To persuade other actors, promoters must explain and justify the superiority of their own solutions over existing institutional rules. Advocating an alternative proposal as the more efficient, appropriate, or otherwise better model may take a long time and can require a wide audience. In many cases, however, it is possible to identify specific key situations in which existing institutions were challenged by an influential group of actors or the public for the first time. To become objectified, locally habitualized forms of action coordination must surmount numerous obstacles. First, the question is whether locally developed patterns or orientations of action are capable of addressing enough horizons of "dormant" interest and experience among other social actors to win them over to the new guiding idea. The next hurdle may be open conflicts of interest and power between different groups with different ideas. Norms and values can also trigger rejection and mental roadblocks. Finally, functional complementarities between different institutional subsystems cause a certain rigidity.

In the first two phases (habitualization and objectivation), newly emerging forms of governance serve as orientation for possible changes in the behavior of actors not involved in developing the alternative model for coordinating action. The emergence of a new local model for coordinating action can call into question previously generally accepted institutions, especially if the fundamental legitimacy of the guiding ideas sedimented in them has already begun to dissolve and if the new patterns of action make existing weaknesses and shortcomings apparent. In many cases, guiding ideas for new patterns of action coordination remain semi-institutionalized, with groups of actors developing, justifying, and advocating proposals for coordinating action in societal subareas. Locally practiced forms of governance can become "fashionable" and encourage imitation, but they are not yet generally accepted. The very coexistence of alternatives suggests that they can be fleeting. Nonetheless, they may become the basis for subsequent change in formal institutions.

Complete institutionalization calls for sedimentation, which is the third phase. In other words, it requires internalization and naturalization as a social fact. Berger and Luckmann (1980) focus on cognitive processes of reciprocal typification and on their routinization and transmission through socialization processes. Organs for imposing sanctions arise when such internalization processes are not sufficient for the generally binding transfer of rules that are relevant throughout society. To Berger and Luckmann, however, the social cement of institutional order consists primarily in its linguistically mediated legitimation. This legitimation explains the institutional order by assigning normative status to its objectified sense of cognitive validity and its pragmatic imperatives. Legitimation as secondary objectivation of what it means to coordinate action takes the form of generalized guiding ideas (in Lepsius's sense), particularly because it shifts from establishing individual rules to explaining symbolic worlds of meaning.

The approaches taken by Lepsius (1995, 1997) and by Berger and Luckmann (1980) also diverge with respect to the conceptualization of deinstitutionalization. Lepsius (1995, 1997) describes deinstitutionalization as a top-down process that begins when actors institutionalize alternative guiding ideas in competition with the prevailing rules by specifying criteria of rationality and their scope of application. By contrast, Berger and Luckmann see deinstitutionalization primarily as a bottom-up process in the course of which actors critically probe the unquestionability and legitimacy of existing institutions in light of new constellations of problems that keep surfacing. Because everyday actions and knowledge are closely interwoven, deinstitutionalization usually occurs through parallel processes in which new forms of action and coordination are habitualized in local contexts as society's support for institutional rules gradually declines.

However, a common feature of the two approaches is that they cast institutionalization and desinstitutionalization as processes rather than as states of being. Despite being rooted in very different sociological theories, they highlight the scope that actors have in principle when it comes to their interpretation and action in institutional contexts. Critically pointing to what Wrong

(1997, p. 25) called the "oversocialized conception of man in modern societies," both approaches underscore that actors have to appropriate, interpret, and adapt the institutional rules anew. What exactly does rule X mean in situation Y, and in what form and within what limits is it applicable? The actors face this question regardless of whether they have a strongly instrumental orientation to the calculation of benefit or a cognitive-normative orientation to action shaped by socialization processes. This implies ongoing critical reflection on even the normatively most powerful or cognitively most self-evident institutions, be they legally binding rules or voluntary standards. The action-related orientation to these institutions includes independent (hence, potentially idiosyncratic) instances of interpretation and adaptation. Internalization of institutionalized rules therefore does not necessarily lead to conformity; it can also become the grounds for learning and innovation processes. Both approaches take social heterogeneity into account as a source of institutional change, and they allow for the possibility that actors belong to different institutional realms and therefore have not only one but multiple repertoires of institutional logics to choose from in cross-border settings.

Taken together, the two approaches offer concepts for analyzing top-down and bottom-up processes of institutionalization and deinstitutionalization that can be productively applied to rules and rights governing labor relations across different scales, including subnational, national, and transnational ones. But how can we capture the coevolution of these processes and their entanglement across different territorial and jurisdictional scales? For this purpose, it is helpful to consider theories of gradual transformative change of institutions.

4 Gradual but Consequential Institutional Transformation

Rather than perceiving economic globalization as an exogenous and homogenous force that produces radical ruptures in national labor market institutions, the concept of gradual institutional transformation, as developed by Djelic and Quack (2003, p. 309), suggests that economic globalization comes in many faces and that it is likely to trigger a "succession and combination, over a long period, of a series of incremental transformations" that "could lead in the end to consequential and significant change." According to the authors, this type of gradual institutional change is particularly likely to unfold as a combination of deinstitutionalization and reinstitutionalization at the interface of national and transnational regulation (Figure 11.1). Their "stalactite model" depicts institutional change as the "aggregation and crystallization through time of a multiplicity of smaller processes of transformation" (p. 22) composed of three analytically distinct effects: transnational institution building, trickle-down and trickle-up institutional change.

One of the key tenets of the model is that transnational, in the sense of cross-border and multi-actor institution building does not take place in a "vacuum" but rather unfolds as a recombination from existing bits and pieces, often drawing on, working around, combining, reinventing, or reinterpreting institutional logics and arrangements that already exist somewhere. As institution building in the transnational sphere brings together a wide range of actor groups, they have a great variety of institutional repertoires at their disposal, be it from their home countries or other contexts, including preexisting international organizations, supranational institutions, and transnational communities in the same or other policy fields. Consequently, we can expect that existing institutional rules at the sectoral, subnational, and national level will to some extent frame the emergence of transnational institutions governing labor relations, as will existing international organizations and transnational communities through diffusion and recombination. As there are typically several templates available and regulatory preferences are likely to diverge, contestation and negotiation will be the rule rather than the exception in these framing processes of transnational institution building. As institutional density of the international sphere rises, transnational institution building will increasingly go hand in hand with deinstitutionalization of previously existing rules.

The two other effects highlighted in the model refer to the ways in which globalization and transnational institution building impact on national and subnational institutions. As part of economic globalization, enhanced

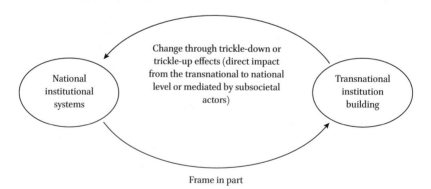

FIGURE 11.1   Interplay between national institutional change and transnational institution building
SOURCE: DJELIC & QUACK, 2003, P. 306

cross-border mobility of companies, tasks, and individuals is likely to produce what Djelic and Quack (2003) call trickle-down and trickle-up effects on institutions governing labor relations in national contexts. Both effects result from confrontation, competition, and conflict between incumbent and challenger rules. Trickle-down effects occur when emergent or established transnational institutions challenge nationally or subnationally enshrined institutions. These trickle-down effects can occur through legally binding or what are termed informal voluntary channels. In supranational institutions such as the EU or NAFTA, or international organizations, such as the ILO, collectively agreed laws and conventions, if ratified, have to be implemented in national law. International organizations and transnational communities can also develop standards, guidelines, and other forms of regulation that, although without binding force, can challenge existing institutions if promoted as normatively preferable models.

While trickle-down effects imply a direct impact of transnational institution building on national or subnational institutions, trickle-up effects have indirect impacts that are mediated by subsocietal actors. Trickle-up effects can but do not necessarily arise from transnational institution building. They can equally be triggered by actors from other national institutional contexts challenging preexisting incumbent rules in a given jurisdiction. For example, multinational companies might not only apply home country industrial relations or human resource management systems in foreign subsidiaries but begin promoting them as superior models in their host countries through professional or industry associations. Global companies dominating specific sectors, such as Amazon in logistics or Facebook in social media, export low workplace standards and anti-works council politics and thus influence sectoral models of labor relations in other countries.

Trickle-down and trickle-up effects work through five mechanisms identified by Streeck and Thelen (2005, p. 31): displacement, layering, conversion, drift, and erosion. The first three in particular refer to coevolving processes of institutionalization and deinstitutionalization. *Displacement* refers to processes of institutional change in which previously subordinate or downstream institutional arrangements eventually become dominant institutions. If new institutional elements are added to existing institutions and help structurally change or displace old institutions by rapidly gaining legitimacy, this process is called *layering*. *Conversion* characterizes the redirection of an institution to new goals, functions, and purposes that might bring it in competition with existing institutions. The two other mechanisms mentioned by Streeck and Thelen refer primarily to deinstitutionalization: gradual institutional change can also occur through *drift*, i.e., neglecting to adapt to shifting contextual conditions or strategically deciding not to do so, formally maintaining institutions while they lose their grip of social reality. *Exhaustion* is a process in which an institution entirely passes away, erodes, and disappears, although in a gradual way because no actions are taken to maintain and stabilize it. Still, these are all relevant because they may prepare the ground for alternative institution building.

In sum, the theory of gradual transformative institutional change provides a useful conceptual framework to analyze coevolving processes of institutionalization and deinstitutionalization. Applying it systematically across different scales to specific realms of labor regulation can help to reconcile prevailing contradictory assessments of emerging transnational mosaics versus deregulation in the literature. What might look like the passing away of an institution in a national labor market may well be part of transnational institutions in the making, for example, the development and implementation of transnational standards. Unlike with previously prevailing national labor market institutions, the boundaries of transnational institutions are not given a priori. Instead, they are determined as part of the process of institutional emergence and change. Consequently, we need to develop a basic understanding of the processes through which the boundaries of institutional authority are drawn and redrawn for the present study.

5 Shifting, Overlapping, and Contested Boundaries of Institutional Authority

Lepsius (1997) highlights that the institutionalization of guiding social principles in rules always requires a demarcation of the action context in which they are claimed to be authoritative as behavioral norms. In labor market research, this action context has all too often been defined a priori as the nation state. Yet, even within nation states, only a few institutional rules, such as constitutional standards and criminal law, hold for all members of society, and the application of those rules is spelled out in each case by an array of specific interpretations (for instance, by courts) for particular contexts of action. Division of labor and social differentiation in developed industrial nations means that most institutionalized rules refer to specific groups of actors and defined contexts of action, such as distinct economic sectors, individual forms of enterprise or organization, or specific economic activities.

This is even more so the case in functionally specialized policy fields of the world system, and it is further exacerbated in the highly fragmented field of transnational labor regulation. In this context, it is therefore useful to distinguish between territorial and non-territorial jurisdictional boundaries of institutional authority. Territorial boundaries demarcate the validity of an institutional rule in reference to geographical space. Non-territorial boundaries do so in terms of objects or groups of addressees of institutional rules. For example, while the ratification process of ILO conventions refers to and reconfirms territorial boundaries for ratification in the respective state, transnational labor standards of the Fair Labor Association (FLA), drawing on the ILO core labor standards, establish and operate on the basis of non-territorial jurisdictional boundaries defined by membership of leading companies to the FLA and relationships with their suppliers.

Gradual institutional transformation at the intersection of the national and transnational sphere often involves drawing and redrawing both territorial and non-territorial jurisdictional boundaries of institutional authority. Institutionalization of rules, particularly in the objectification and sedimentation phase, often occurs through the expansion of the action context in which they are claimed to be authoritative as behavioral norms. As a mirror image, deinstitutionalization involves the weakening, contraction, or disappearance of the boundaries that constitute such an action context. Another approach in which gradual institutional transformation may redraw the boundaries of institutional authority is through layering, a process in which new institutional elements are added to existing institutions in ways that change the meaning and legitimacy of the former ones without necessarily fully displacing them. Hence, an examination of establishing boundaries of institutional authority is central for understanding processes of institution building, as is the study of shifting boundaries of institutional authority for processes of institutional change.

Empirical examples of the above processes abound. Transnational standard setting for working conditions may start by delineating potential addressees through categorization of activity or sector, thereby establishing non-territorial boundaries for which authority is being claimed in a global realm that is imagined as geographically borderless, exemplified by the demand for better labor standards for all workers in global supply chains of the garment industry. Yet these rules might still be translated into territorially defined processes when it comes to implementation on the ground (Zajak, 2017). In the process of deinstitutionalization, displacement or erosion of existing institutions often begins with a critique of existing demarcations of the authority of institutional rules and realigns these demarcations. For instance, private staffing firms had been pushing to expand the boundaries within which agency work would be acceptable in many countries prior to the ILO Convention on Private Employment Agencies (1997) which finally removed the ban on fee-charging employment services (Shire et al., 2018). A good example of layering is the European Posting of Workers Directive which seeks to establish a regulatory framework for workers sent by their employer from one to another EU member state to work under a service contract. Wagner (2015) shows how this European directive intersects with national and company-level institutions in complex ways that redraw boundaries between categories of workers and lead to the deinstitutionalization of host country rules while providing only minimum protection at other institutional scales.

Due to the multifaceted and overlapping nature of institutional boundaries, transnational labor regulation offers plenty of scope for strategic action. For employers, union representatives, and labor activists alike, redrawing the territorial and non-territorial jurisdictional boundaries of institutional rules governing labor relations makes a significant difference. Historical instances of the struggle for the abolition of forced labor are indicative in this respect. The international labor standards developed by the ILO in its early period were tailored to the situation in industrialized Western nations. A "colonial clause" in the ILO's constitution of 1919 "granted the metropolitan powers the right to exclude, in part or entirely, their overseas territories from the ratification of norms …" (Maul, 2007, p. 480). A distinctive "Native Labour Code" constituted the colonies as "an area of separate and ultimately less stringent regulation" and workers in the colonies as subjects rather than citizens (Maul, 2007, p. 481). In a countermove, proponents of a complete abolition of all forms of forced labor mobilized to tear down these territorial limitations of the ban. Success came in gradual steps: while the 1930 Forced Labour Convention obliged its signatories to abolish forced labor "in all its forms" irrespective of the territory in which it was performed, it contained detailed definitions of what forms of labor were not deemed to fall under the category of forced labor, and its ratification by many of the leading powers took more than two decades.

Shifts of the boundaries of institutional authority can also occur in less publicly discussed and more invisible ways. Such a shift can sometimes be the factor that makes gradual institutional change possible. Changes that the actors would most probably have rejected, as a whole at some point, are more likely to be accepted by other initially hostile actors if they occur through incremental learning and adaptation processes. Some of the preceding examples of deinstitutionalization processes originated in regulatory islands or "regulatory gaps." Actors habitualized new patterns of behavior and coordination in societal spaces that were not subject to the dominant regulation for the given contexts of action (e.g., companies with their own internal collective bargaining agreements) or that had a low overall degree of institutional structuring (e.g., standard setting and regulation in the international arena). The question of jurisdiction arose only in the second step, the point when promoters began to advance arguments and justifications for widening the application of the rules to action context beyond the niches in which they had been developed. The legitimacy of dominant regulations was questioned, often in a way that did not reject them entirely but critically questioned their jurisdictional boundaries. Yet regulatory islands or gaps are not the only place to begin changing the boundaries between the jurisdictions of different institutional rules. Actors can also develop behaviors and coordination patterns diametrically opposed to prevailing rules. It is often actors on the periphery who try out new strategies. Old (national) sectorial boundaries of labor regulation become increasingly blurred, and new transnational or global assemblages of labor regulation emerge.

6   Institutional Assemblage: A Heuristic Device in Search of Transnational Labor Markets

How can the preceding analysis contribute to a better understanding of what constitutes a transnational market? In this concluding section, it is proposed that we should conceptually distinguish between transnational regulation of labor and transnational labor markets. While transnational regulation is a constitutive element of transnational labor markets, not every transnational regulation of labor makes a transnational labor market. Transnational regulation of labor can unfold in a loosely coordinated or uncoordinated way along the different dimensions of labor relations, as we have seen from the analysis of processes of institutionalization and deinstitutionalization, and it unfolds across different scales. There may be countervailing developments of deregulation and reregulation across the five key dimensions of labor governance identified as commodification, competition, control, reproduction/welfare, and standardization of knowledge. In each of these dimensions, the institutionalization and deinstitutionalization of rules unfolds in a piecemeal fashion, often driven by different actors and developed in various international organizations and transnational fora. The picture is further complicated by the fact that the territorial and non-territorial jurisdictional boundaries of such transnational regulation of labor vary greatly, with some calling for global authority while many others demand more limited cross-border, world regional, or sectoral authority.

Following this line of argument, the emergence of transnational labor markets is characterized by growing density and increasing interaction of rules governing a specified type of labor relation along several (not necessarily all) of the dimensions: commodification, competition, control, reproduction/ welfare, and standardization of knowledge. For a transnational labor market to emerge, actors need to invest significant work into assembling various processes of (de)institutionalization of rules into what Trubek, Mosher, and Rothstein (2000, p. 1187) call "interlocking mosaics" of transnational labor regulation. The institutional work performed by the German meat producer in the region analyzed by Mense-Petermann (this volume) that intertwined formal and informal layers of institutions into three successive arrangements of rules governing locally situated but transnationally operating labor markets for meat cutters is just one example of this. There are many other actors involved, however, some of them addressed in contributions to this volume, such as intermediaries, networks, unions, or national, European, and international public agencies. Most of this assemblage work is carried out in a loosely coordinated way, in the absence of a centralized authority, and does not follow a rational master design.

Therefore, we suggest that the concept of assemblage is a useful heuristic in search of transnational labor markets. The concept of assemblage is now widely used in various disciplines for research into emergent decentralized and heterogeneous processes that compose diverse elements into some form of provisional socio-spatial social order (Acuto & Curtis, 2014; Anderson, 2011; Markus & Saka, 2006). The approach highlights the labor required to assemble, reassemble, and disassemble diffuse socio-material practices into a common world built from heterogeneous parts. Most assemblages emerge bottom-up and can therefore be linked to the above-mentioned understanding of Berger and Luckmann (1980) of institutionalization (processes). However, within nested formations of different assemblages, those coming into being at larger scales (such as the global or European) will begin to act as resources or limitations for assemblage work at smaller scales (such as the cross-border or even local). Collier (2014) advocates the concept of global assemblage as a tool for analyzing translocal interactions between regulations at different scales and invites researchers to further explore how assemblages gain or lose stability.

The conceptual framework developed above suggests that stabilization of assemblages of transnational regulation of labor occur through two types of boundary work. The first process of boundary work refers to non-territorial jurisdictions, the second to territorial ones (Bueger, 2014). Non-territorial jurisdictional boundary work seeks to stabilize the identity of the assemblage by increasing its internal homogeneity and the clear definition of its boundaries in terms of mutually recognized objects, actors, and forms of regulation that fall within its realm or not. The claims of validity of the assemblage rules are homed in respect to the types and dimensions of labor regulations covered.

Various illustrations of such processes of categorization, characterization, and sorting are provided in the literature on the historical emergence and change in regulation of slavery and forced labor by international and national authorities (Maul, 2007). Studying recent developments in human trafficking, Strauss (2017) shows how a recategorization and recharacterization of objects of regulation led to political-legal approaches of criminalization gaining priority over human and labor rights approaches.

In contrast, boundary work on territorial jurisdictions seeks to increase internal homogeneity of the assemblage by more clearly defining its spatial boundaries. Within a transnational assemblage of labor regulations, boundary work can seek to establish where transnational regulation is authoritative and where it is not. The classical example is the national ratification process of ILO conventions. Yet territorial demarcation of institutional authority can take varied forms. In the field of transnational regulation of labor conditions for garment workers in supply chains, claims for global validity of core labor standards prevailed prior to the Accord on Fire and Building Safety in Bangladesh and extra-territorial lawsuits in support of the victims of fire accidents in Bangladesh factories led to a nested reterritorialization of institutional claims for validity of rules.

Territorial and non-territorial boundary work can be mutually reinforcing in stabilizing transnational assemblages of labor regulation. A case in point is the International Convention Concerning Decent Work for Domestic Workers. With this convention, the ILO significantly redefined the non-territorial boundaries of the application of international conventions by including informal work undertaken in domestic settings in its definition of work. By subsequently claiming global validity of this redefinition of what constitutes work, the ILO exerted pressure on its member states to follow its recategorization in national legislation, so far, however, only with limited success (Albin and Mantouvalou, 2012). Yet both types of boundary work can also be used to disassemble, and it can interact in ways that destabilize an assemblage as Wagner (2015) argues for the European Posted Workers Directive.

Taken together, the proposed concepts from institutional and assemblage approaches provide heuristic devices for analyzing the emergence of transnational labor markets in systematic and comparative ways that avoid the traps of methodological nationalism. The study of transnational labor markets should therefore focus on intertwined processes of institutionalization and deinstitutionalization: gradual but transformational processes of institutional change of labor regulation along the dimensions of commodification, competition, control, reproduction/welfare, and standardization of knowledge; the assembling of decentralized elements of transnational labor regulation into provisional socio-spatial orders; the boundary work that stabilizes or destabilizes institutional assemblages of transnational labor regulation.

Given the fluid and emergent features of transnational institution building in the labor field highlighted in this chapter, is it possible to have "a global labor market"? Obviously, the answer depends on how "global" is defined (see Kofman; Gumbrell-McCormick; and Bühler and Werron in this volume). If a "global" labor market is conceived of as an institutional space with homogenous rules applied across the globe, the answer is "no" because there is little reason to believe that such a densely coordinated and centralized institutional realm will emerge in the foreseeable future. However, if a "global" labor market is understood as an assemblage of institutional rules governing labor relations within a more specified jurisdiction, such as a profession or occupation, there may be some examples emerging, such as global labor markets for seafarers, football players, or artists. Overall, however, labor markets that transcend national borders are more likely to take the form of transnational labor markets, understood as institutional assemblage discussed in this paper, and should therefore be further explored by future research.

References

Acuto, M., & Curtis, S. (Eds.) (2014). *Reassembling International Theory. Assemblage Thinking and International Relations.* Basingstroke: Palgrave MacMillan.

Albin, E., & Mantouvalou, V. (2012). The ILO convention on domestic workers: From the shadows to the light. *Industrial Law Journal, 41*(1): 67–78.

Anderson, B., & McFarlane, C. (2011). Assemblage and geography. *Area, 43*(2): 124–127.

Beckert, J. (2009). The social order of markets. *Theory and Society, 38*(3): 245–69.

Berger, P. L./Luckmann, T. (1980). Die gesellschaftliche Konstruktion der Wirklichkeit. Eine Theorie der Wissenssoziologie. Frankfurt am Main: Fischer Taschenbuch Verlag. (Original work published 1966).

Braudel, F. (1992). *Civilization and Capitalism, 15th-18th Century, Vol. III: The Perspective of the World.* Berkeley. University of California Press.

Bueger, C. (2014). Thinking assemblages methodologically: Some rules of thumb. In M. Acuto, & S. Curtis (Eds.), *Reassembling International Theory* (pp. 58–66). Basingstroke: Palgrave MacMillan.

Collier, S. J. (2014). Assemblages and the conduct of inquiry. A conversation with Stephen J. Collier. In M. Acuto & S. Curtis (Eds.). *Reassembling International Theory.* Basingstroke: Palgrave MacMillan: 32–38.

Djelic, M.-L., & Quack, S. (2018). Globalization and business regulation. *Annual Review of Sociology, 44,* 123–142.

Djelic, M.-L., & Quack, S. (Eds.) (2003). *Globalization and Institutions: Redefining the Rules of the Economic Game*. Cheltenham: Edward Elgar.

Lepsius, M. R. (1995). Institutionenanalyse und Institutionenpolitik [Special issue]. *Kölner Zeitschrift für Soziologie und Sozialpsychologie, 35*. Politische Institutionen im Wandel: 392–403.

Lepsius, M. R. (1997). Institutionalisierung und deinstitutionalisierung von rationalitätskriterien. In Göhler, G. (Ed.), Institutionenwandel. Leviathan, [Special issue] *Zeitschrift für Sozialwissenschaft, 16*/1996. Opladen: Westdeutscher Verlag: 57–69.

Marcus, G. E., & Saka, E. (2006). Assemblage. *Theory, Culture & Society, 23*(2–3), 101–106.

Maul, D. R (2007). The International Labour Organization and the struggle against forced labour from 1919 to the present. *Labor History, 48*(4): 477–500.

Quack, S. (2005). Vom Werden und Vergehen von Institutionen—Vorschläge für eine dynamische Governanceanalyse. In G. F. Schuppert (Ed.): *Governance-Forschung* (pp. 346–370). Baden-Baden: Nomos.

Quack, S. (2009). "Global" markets in theory and history: Towards a comparative analysis. [Special issue]. *Kölner Zeitschrift für Soziologie und Sozialpsychologie*.

Quack, S., Schulz-Schaeffer, I., Shire, K, & Weiß, A (Eds.) (2018). *Transnationalisierung der Arbeit*. Wiesbaden: Springer.

Shire, K., Heinrich, S., Imai, J., Mottweiler, H., Tünte, M., Wang, C.-C. (2018). Private labour market intermediaries in cross-border labour markets in Europe and Asia: International norms, regional actors and patterns of cross-border labour mobility. In S. Quack, I. Schulz-Schaeffer, K. Shire, & A. Weiß (Eds.), *Transnationalisierung der Arbeit* (pp. 155–183). Wiesbaden: Springer.

Strauss, K. (2017). Sorting victims from workers: Forced labour, trafficking, and the process of jurisdiction. *Progress in Human Geography, 41*(2), 140–158.

Streeck, W., & Thelen, K. (Eds.) (2005). *Beyond Continuity—Institutional Change in Advanced Political Economies*. Oxford: Oxford University Press.

Tolbert, P. S., & Zucker, L. G. (1996). The institutionalization of institutional theory. In Clegg, S. R., Hardy, C., & Nord, W. R. (Eds.), *Handbook of Organization Studies* (pp. 175–190). London: Sage.

Trubek, D. M., Mosher, J., & Rothstein, J. S. (2000). Transnationalism in the regulation of labor relations: International regimes and transnational advocacy networks. *Law & Social Inquiry, 25*(4), 1187–1211.

Wagner, I. (2015). The political economy of borders in a 'borderless' European labour market. *JCMS: Journal of Common Market Studies, 53*(6), 1370–1385.

Wrong, D. H. (1997). The oversocialized conception of man in modem sociology. In J. Alexander, R. Boudon, & M. Cherkaoui (Eds.), *The Classical Tradition in Sociology: The American Tradition*, Vol. 3 (pp. 25–39). London: Sage.

Zajak, S. (2017). *Transnational Activism, Global Labor Governance, and China*. Basingstoke: Palgrave Macmillan.

PART 4

What Is the Global in Labor Markets?

Introduction to Part 4

What Is the Global in Labor Markets?

Rebecca Gumbrell-McCormick and Eleonore Kofman

Although globalization only became a buzzword in the 1990s (James & Steger, 2014), it has a long history stretching back to at least the early modern period and, from the sixteenth century, the expansion of capitalism beyond Europe and colonial empires, resulting in the beginning of large-scale population movements, trade and global connectedness (Kofman, 2008). Marx and Engels noted that, "the bourgeoisie has through its exploitation of the world market given a cosmopolitan character to production and consumption in every country" (Marx & Engels, 1977, p. 39). Other terms such as the "universal" were commonly applied once the world had been fully explored and conquered by Western powers, as in Elisée Reclus' (the French anarchist geographer) numerous volumes of *La Nouvelle Géographie Universelle* (1872–1895) where he argued that it was increasingly meaningless to speak of the history of a single country and wrote in detail about the expansion of global capitalism and imperialism.

Globalization has, from its inception, had many aspects, with the labor market only one in a series of interconnected factors. Globalization was described by Held as the "transformation in the spatial organization of social relations and transactions—assessed in terms of their extensity, intensity, velocity and impact" (Held, Goldblatt, McGrew, & Perraton, 1999) and, from the earliest stages, it has proceeded through advances in technology (such as the development of the steam engine), transport (improved sailing ships, followed by railways and steam ships), and communication (the telegraph and the universal postal service), to name a few examples from the nineteenth century (Hirst & Thompson, 1999). The late nineteenth century also saw the emergence on a large scale of multinational corporations (MNCs), although these also date back to the foundation of the East India Company in 1600 (Ietto-Gillies, 2005). These changes have facilitated cross-national and regional movements of people: By the late nineteenth and early twentieth century, a period known as the golden age of globalization, global connectedness was characterized by intense migration, not just transatlantic and intra-European, but also Asia-Pacific, generating transcontinental or inter-regional flows (Held et al., 1999). This period of intense globalization declined from the beginning of World War I but picked up in the post-WWII period. Particularly in the late nineteenth and early twentieth century, and again after World War II, globalization led to the development of international organizations (for example, the labor and women's movements of the late nineteenth century) and the first intergovernmental agreements concerning labor market issues and the first intergovernmental institutions (such as the International Labour Organization, founded in 1919). In the 1940s, a form of global civil society and discourse emerged as a network of public intellectuals broke out of the unit of the state to conceive a new vision of world order for the postwar period or globalism as a political category.

More recently, although Western economies were experiencing a period of economic stability and growth by then, the 1970s saw the relocation of production to cheaper sites in the Global South as part of the shift in capitalist accumulation and expansion, known as the new international division of labor. Together with world systems analysis (Wallerstein, 1979) comprising core, semi-periphery, and periphery, this was a precursor to a geographically inflected global understanding of the capitalist system and division of labor. From the 1970s, a new division of global spaces replaced the previous colonial and imperial spaces which had been fragmenting since World War II and, from the 1980s, neoliberalism took hold and increasingly pushed the boundaries of the global.

It was not until the 1990s that a third wave of globalization followed the demise of the Soviet Union and the emergence of new economic powers such as China and India that had begun to open up their economies and become integrated into a world market. Neoliberal capitalism sought to privilege the rights of capital over labor and to further develop a division of labor encompassing the globe (Jessop, 2018).

Aside from the movement of raw and manufactured commodities, as well as services and people, throughout the world, backed up by improved international communications, transport, and institutions, the concept of globalization as the sense of living in a connected world, that is, globalization as a social imaginary, took a much longer time to emerge (James & Steger, 2014). The development of international organizations in the nineteenth century played a role in this, in particular those related to labor market issues such as international trade unions, at first largely Europe-based, (Gumbrell-McCormick, 2008), and political movements (such as the socialist and anarchist movements). The international exchange of specialists and intellectuals in a number of fields also contributed to the development of global awareness and a global discourse.

The new means of communications speeded up transactions and, most importantly, made it now possible to "work as a unit in real time on a planetary scale. Hence the most recent period generated new ways of connecting workers, producers, and consumers" (Castells, 1996, p. 27). It also created an increasing sense of living in a single connected world, resulting from contemporary shifts in space, time, and social relations. In this increasingly interdependent economy and society, the skilled have tended to benefit the most from the ability to move more freely compared to the less skilled, whose movements have become more regulated and restricted spatially and temporally, contributing to what Czaika and de Haas (2014) note is a channeling and skewing of global migratory flows to a reduced number of cities and states.

In the past decade or so, the nature of work has continued to be rapidly transformed with an increasing modularization of tasks that can be undertaken anywhere in the world connected to the internet. What some have called a planetary labor market (Graham & Anwar, 2018), created through computerization and digitalization, has enabled a mass migration of labor or jobs (platform or gig economy) rather than primarily the migration of people or relocation of production as in the past. It also contributes to the growing diversity of labor contractual arrangements between labor and capital characterized by flexibility and individualization.

Consequently, at present, a global labor market might result from the movement of labor without workers moving as well as the physical movement of people circulating around the globe for different reasons (work, family, study, or asylum) and for different periods of time (regular cross-border, circular, temporary, or permanent migration). These movements may be constrained by states for political reasons although a variety of bilateral, regional, and global agreements have emerged to facilitate the exchange of workers. Over time, state regulations may change in such a way as to privilege domestic, regional, or global scales in the making of labor markets. On the whole, states have intervened less in the formation of labor markets based on the platform economy, although some cities (for instance, Berlin and San Francisco), have regulated and/or restricted their operation in selected sectors, such as travel (Uber). As Graham and Anwar (2018) remind us, although this type of work may be more difficult to organize, the digital economy still takes place in specific jurisdictions and is able to be regulated to some extent, for example, with decisions on whether we interpret particular contractual relationships as employment or self-employment, and the associated rights that derive from this distinction. Legislation on whether zero hours contracts are permitted is also another form of regulation here.

In the current world health crisis, which arose as this book was nearing completion, the domestic or national level has once again come to the fore, as countries seek to assure continuity of production of medications, health-related equipment, and even basic foodstuffs in a situation where the globalized economy has once again been called into question, as it did in the 1930s. There is, consequently, much discussion on deglobalization (Bergeijk, 2020) based on an analysis of trade and finance, which have noticeably decreased. It is, however, a trend which had already emerged prior to the COVID-19 pandemic and following the 2008 financial crisis. The pandemic may well lead to countries in the Global North seeking to produce basic goods that they had previously outsourced globally to cheaper production sites. Yet less attention has been paid to what this shortening of supply and value chains might mean for labor markets.

In this part on global labor markets, the three chapters engage with different dimensions of the global and show how these have evolved over time, how the state continues to play a part in determining the boundaries and interaction between different scales, the discourses underpinning changes in the structure of the global scale, and the different actors that play a part in such developments.

In the first chapter, Eleonore Kofman argues that the global is heterogeneous and stratified and composed of different scales (local, national, or supranational) in the production of goods, services, and the movement of people. Although some argue the state has lost much of its power in the context of a neoliberal capitalist system, others maintain that it continues to play a major part in determining the economic and political relationships in the construction of labor markets through immigration policies. This is illustrated through the recent history of the UK's development of two parallel migrant labor markets, one based on the global scale and the other on the regional scale of the European Union, which it has combined within a single system. As Kofman points out, it has done this through a withdrawal from the European Union (as of 1 January 2021) to create a single global entity based in part on a nostalgic return to an imperial vision of taking back control of its sourcing of labor at a time of a more generalized deglobalization. Whilst this political strategy may recommodify its European-sourced labor, that is, reduce its social protection and rights, it risks disrupting the availability and creating insecurity in the supply of labor.

The next chapter, by Rebecca Gumbrell-McCormick, further explores the nature of the global and how it differs from the national (or domestic), focusing on the powers of global actors and the development of global institutions. She argues that, while there is some overlap in the role of industrial relations actors (employers, trade unions, and government agencies) at the national and international levels, they all have fewer forms of action open to them and much more limited regulatory powers at the international or global level. As Gumbrell-McCormick shows, this is particularly true of the role of governments and quasi-governmental agencies, such as the International Labour

Organization or the rest of the UN system, which are severely constricted in their ability to intervene by the unwillingness of national governments to give up any element of sovereignty. The European Union is a partial exception to this, with significant regulatory powers in financial and economic affairs and, to a more limited extent, in labor market issues. However, the intergovernmental institutions, whether at regional or global level, form the context in which other actors operate within the global system and play an increasing role in shaping and influencing the global labor market.

Finally, Bühler and Werron's chapter focuses on the prerequisites for global markets. While it does not deal directly with the labor market, the chapter shows how historical developments from the late nineteenth century onward created the conditions under which global markets, including labor markets, were able to flourish. Using the concepts of new economic sociology, Bühler and Werron show how the construction of global markets was based on the imagining and addressing of universal market audiences, or global publics, similar to the focus on global civil society in the preceding chapters. Their study focuses on products rather than labor markets, in particular the global market for wheat in the late nineteenth century, which led to public discourses that compared and evaluated products and prices on a continual basis. The authors' key argument is that this established a particular social structure that mediated between producers and their publics. The "globality" of global markets, according to this argument, is a matter, not of networks of local market actors, but of a particular kind of global imagination created in public discourse.

References

Bergeijk, P. A. G. van (2020). *Deglobalisation 2.0*, Cheltenham: Edward Elgar.

Castells, M. (1996). *The Rise of the Network Society,* Vol. 1. Oxford: Blackwell Publishers.

Czaika, M. & De Haas, H. (2014). The globalization of migration: Has the world become more migratory? *International Migration Review, 48*(2), 283–323.

Graham, M., & Anwar, M. (2018). Digital labour. In J. Ash, R. Kitchin, & A. Leszczynski (Eds.), *Digital Geographies* (pp. 177–187). Sage: London.

Gumbrell-McCormick, R. (2008) International actors and international regulation. In P. Blyton, N. Bacon, J. Fiorito, & E. Heery (Eds.), *The Sage Handbook of Industrial Relations* (pp. 325–345). Sage: London.

Held, D., Goldblatt, D., McGrew, A., & Perraton, J. (1999) *Global Transformations*. Cambridge: Polity Press.

Hirst, P & Thompson, G (1999). Globalisation: Frequently asked questions and some surprising answers. In P. Leisink (Ed.), *Globalisation and Labour Relations*, (Chapter 2, pp. 36–56). Cheltenham: Edward Elgar.

Ietto-Gillies, G. (2005). *Transnational Corporations and International Production.* Cheltenham: Edward Elgar.

James, P. & Steger, M. (2014) A genealogy of globalization: The career of a concept. *Globalizations, 11*(4), 417–34.

Jessop, B. (2018). Neoliberalization, uneven development, and Brexit: Further reflections on the organic crisis of the British state and society. *European Planning Studies, 26*(9), 1728–1746.

Kofman, E. (2008) Political geography and globalization in the twenty-first century. In E. Kofman & G. Youngs (Eds.), *Globalization. Theory and Practice.* London: Continuum.

Marx, K. & Engels, F. (1977). *The Communist Manifesto.* Chapter 1.

Wallerstein, I. (1979). *The Capitalist World Economy.* Cambridge: Cambridge University Press.

CHAPTER 12

Scales and Spaces of Global Labor Markets

Eleonore Kofman

1   **Introduction**

The global does not constitute a single undifferentiated set of connected points, either within the capitalist economy or socially and politically. In earlier writings on globalization, there was a tendency for many authors to highlight the deterritorialization of societies, the breaking down of borders, redundancy of geography, and the concomitant weakening of nation states (Castells, 1996; O'Brien, 1995). However, more recent writing has drawn attention to the variegated and stratified nature of the global with its shifting power geometries (Massey, 1993) in the production of goods, services, trade, and the movement of people. Although the global refers to interdependent economies, including labor markets and societies, these are organized around different scales of operation from the local, the regional within states, the nation state, the regional above the state, and the world level (see Bühler & Werron in this volume on the networked dimension of the global). In relation to labor markets, the governance of these different scales has changed in the past few decades in the context of the extension and penetration of neoliberal capitalism, the emergence of significant regional frameworks. and the changing relationship of the state to capitalist processes transcending borders and regional institutions (Jessop, 2016). As noted in the introduction to this part, one of the key aspects in the recent evolution of labor markets has occurred through international migration and changing mobility regimes through regional integration, especially in the case of Europe. States have to varying degrees become reliant on migrant labor beyond their national borders, but this is not necessarily fixed as we shall see in the case of recent shifts between national, regional, and global scales and spaces.

What I want to argue is, first, that other scales, and in particular the regional, have become more significant in the past few decades and that these may be as important as the global for the formation of labor markets and the circulation of capital. Second, states may be dynamic players in the determination of the boundaries of labor markets, not only in response to economic demands but also increasingly due to pressure for greater control, and even sometimes closure, from anti-immigrant populist and nationalist movements. While the state is no longer seen as a container (Taylor, 1994), it nevertheless retains considerable regulatory power within which to generate its sources of labor supply using different scalar arrangements (McGovern, 2012). We see this most clearly in the discourses and practices of the British state in relation to the regional, in this case the EU, and the global, where in the past 20 years it has reconstructed a division of labor within an expanding European spatiality, providing it with flexible sources of labor and skills (Ruhs & Anderson, 2010).

A number of geographers and political economists have elaborated on the spatial-temporal fixes and spatial strategies pursued by states and other political and civil society actors in the course of the collapse of the Fordist mode of production and the restructuring of world capitalism through the embedding and extension of neoliberalism (Jessop, 2008). The analysis of the production of space and its reordering and reimagining drew upon a number of interconnected spatial categories—territories, networks, places, and scales but the latter has probably generated the most discussion. Unlike the Fordist period with the nation state as the key spatial unit, it has been argued that the current period of globalization involves a proliferation of spatial scales, and an increasingly convoluted mix of scale strategies as economic and political forces seek the most favorable conditions for insertion into a changing international order (Jessop, 2002). This may—at a time of a return to organized capitalism—involve a partial return to the national dimension (Nölke, 2017).

Scale as a means for ordering the world—local, regional, national, and global—is not necessarily a preordained hierarchical framework. It is instead a contingent outcome of the tensions that exist between structural forces, of human agents as well as cultural and political imaginaries. The concern has been about how particular scales become constituted and transformed in response to social-spatial dynamics. Their reordering also has implications for the way sovereignty is conceptualized, for example from the classic sovereignty of the state to the integrative sovereignty of regional bodies such as the European Union. These scales are also the object of governance and not just the socio-spatial framework through which socio-economic processes occur. Scales are deployed by different actors as discursive practices to locate problems, causes, and solutions at particular levels. The shift from one scale to another may reflect not only the spatialities through which different factors of production circulate but also cultural and political imaginaries, as we shall see in the analysis of how the British state has strategically combined the national, the regional, and the global over the last 40 years (Jessop, 2016).

In the past few decades, regional organizations have become more significant. Some have developed institutional structures in the same way as states, such as the EU, while others are looser trading blocs, such as NAFTA. The EU, the most developed institutionally, has reoriented the socio-economic boundaries of the nation state, shaping the formation of labor markets by enabling the free movement of labor and the availability and transfer of social protection on equal or almost equal terms with national labor although, for the more precarious, the right to mobility with social protection has been increasingly challenged (Barbulescu and Favell, 2019). However, the EU has developed a highly complex mobility regime which was conceived as desirable mobility for its citizens post-enlargement, enabling the EU to compete with the United States, on the one hand, and controlled immigration of third-country nationals on the other, resulting in a sharp divide between the two.

Freedom of worker mobility had been implemented between the six original members of the European Community in 1968 and from that time onwards it widened the groups of EU citizens who could exercise such rights. In 1992, the Treaty of Maastricht made free movers into European citizens, culminating with the Citizens Directive 38/2004 at the time of its first enlargement eastward. Development of mobility regimes has now become more complex and encompassed a range of categories and temporalities, comprising the free movement of European citizens, including some non-EU, who after a period of five years' residence may be able to move to another EU country, Directive 2003/109/EC concerning the status of third-country nationals who are long-term residents, and the Blue Card granting movement rights to specified non-EU employees, such as researchers or other highly skilled individuals. A further form of mobility is that of posted workers, a Directive passed in 1996 in relation to "an employee who is sent by his employer to carry out a service in another EU Member State on a temporary basis, in the context of a contract of services, an intra-group posting or a hiring out through a temporary agency." Germany, France, Belgium, and Austria are the biggest receivers of posted workers. Unlike mobile citizen workers, they do not acquire social rights but are expected to be paid minimum wages. Following substantial critique, a revised Directive was passed on June 28, 2018 (Official Journal of the European Union (EU) published Directive (EU) 2018/957) to be applied from July 30, 2020.

It should be noted that not all EU states have participated in the full panoply of Directives. Denmark, Ireland, and the (now former EU member state) UK have largely refrained from most of the additional migration Directives and maintained their national systems. In addition, the UK and Ireland did not sign up in 1995 to the Schengen Area enabling mobility without travel documents within the EU. Hence, theirs was a much more hybrid system combining national and EU regimes and scales and retaining a higher level of control and sovereignty. Although visa restrictions had been lifted for those from Eastern Europe in 2001, Ireland, Sweden, and the UK were the only ones to embrace free movement from the outset in 2004. Austria and Germany, on the other hand, applied the full transition period of seven years (2011 and 2014 for Bulgaria and Romania, respectively) for free movement.

Just as significantly, free movement has been contested particularly for those seeking to make use of social assistance and/or not qualifying as workers. Research also showed that two diverging mobility patterns coexist in the EU: more affluent EU-15 migrants are often described as "mobile Europeans," while those coming from the new member states are referred to as "immigrants" and may face discrimination regardless of their EU citizenship status so that these two groups are frequently viewed in somewhat different terms based on the reasons for their migration. The right of mobility for the lower skilled has been questioned most in states receiving large numbers of Eastern European migrants, such as in Austria, Germany, the Netherlands, and the UK whose ministers of the interior wrote a letter in 2013 to the European Commission and Council warning of the need to toughen the conditions regarding free movement, that is, to ensure that the original stipulation of not creating a burden for states was complied with. Political attempts to restrict entry of free movers, especially those seeking work as opposed to having a job lined up, were strongest in the UK. Discourses of welfare tourism and scroungers added pressure for measures to curtail access to welfare, either for those who did not qualify as workers after the first three months of residence in another member state, former workers, job seekers, or those with adequate resources to be self-sufficient, as several court judgments demonstrated in the case of Dano (2014) and Almanovic (2015) in Germany (Babulescu, 2017). In the UK, proposals were made to limit access to noncontributory benefits for the first four years. By 2015, 60% of respondents in a poll thought free movement should be restricted due to pressure on public services and housing and on the benefit system (D'Angelo and Kofman, 2017).

2 Juggling Scales and Spaces

I have argued that the regional is an increasingly important scale in the construction and composition of labor markets and circulation of skills. The UK, as a liberal capitalist and highly deregulated economy, has combined different scales and spaces in its attempt to plug the gaps between demand and supply of skills at both ends of the labor market (high and low) (Afonso & Devitt, 2016). Depending on skills produced beyond the nation state is nothing new but the past 30 years have been particularly interesting as the UK's strategies have varied in combining different scales according to the reorganization of capitalist spatialities as well as political ideologies and pressures.

In this section, I shall examine how the UK's colonial supply of labor, imperial sovereignty, and political imaginaries led to at times tense and conflictual engagements with a supply of external labor based on citizen rights (EU) rather than mobile workers with much less social protection (D'Angelo & Kofman, 2018). It led the country to juggle in different ways the national, the regional, and the global through the development of two parallel and complementary migratory regimes. Now post-Brexit, it is seeking to undo these two regimes and unify them so as to level down social rights, access to welfare, and the right to settlement of privileged EU citizens.

In the first referendum on the UK's membership of the European Economic Community (EEC), held in 1975 not long after the country had joined in 1973, one of the main slogans in the "No to Europe" campaign was "the right to rule ourselves," criticizing submission to laws they had not made (O'Toole, 2018). At that time, the No vote lost. After its entry into the EEC, the UK continued to make its immigration regulations stricter under a Conservative government elected in 1979 against migrant flows from the former Commonwealth and their right to settle and acquire British citizenship. The migration of EU citizens remained low and fairly stable until the second half of the 1990s at a time of higher economic growth. The harmonization of European labor markets through the mutual recognition and accreditation of qualifications facilitated the movement of professionals through the regulation of a regional labor market (Hay, 2000). Even so, in the 2001 census, EU citizens formed less than 15% of the total migrant population in the UK and they were largely from Western Europe. London in particular had grown in popularity as a destination for professionals from Western Europe (Morgan, 2004).

Despite the growing demand for labor, the Conservative Party remained opposed to opening up immigration. It was not until the advent of the New Labour government, espousing a Third Way ideology, that the UK sought to place itself within a globalized and competitive system. Barbara Roche, the Immigration Minister in 2000, initiated the theme of a global world in a speech in which she said that international migration had potentially huge economic benefits for the UK. The theme of mobility and circulation of people as a factor of production echoed those of the European Commission in the early years of the decade.

Acceptance of immigration and the need to adopt a managed migration approach were officially enshrined in the introduction to the White Paper (Home Office, 2001). The rhetoric of managed migration enabled the state to demonstrate it could pull together a multiplicity of statuses and agents involved in the migratory process, the ability to exert control in a context of uncertainty and risk produced by globalizing processes, and the capacity to measure benefits against costs (Kofman, 2008). It was intended as an argument for the expansion of labor migration or a third way between restrictionist and expansive policies at a time when the myth of zero migration was being challenged and the reality of labor migration acknowledged (Spencer, 2003). In the UK, as in other European states, such as Germany, managed migration would serve to resolve labor shortfalls at a time of economic growth and confirm a more modern image of a society attuned to and able to benefit from globalization.

The idea of globalization was coupled with the skilled who were viewed as a mobile population and likely to return to their countries of origin, or at least not seek to settle. Opening to global flows, with competition between a number of states, generally meant restricting migratory routes for the less skilled. There would in any case be no need for non-European racialized labor following the enlargement round, first in 2004 (A8, Cyprus, and Malta) and then in 2007 (Bulgaria and Romania) which provided the UK with a source of young, relatively educated and white labor (McDowell, Batnitzky, & Dyers, 2009). From the British perspective, it served to reorient sources of labor away from its postcolonial sources, which had filled less skilled streams in sector-specific schemes such as hospitality and food processing. Instead, in a Points Based Scheme (PBS) formally implemented in 2008, the route for less skilled workers existed but was not operationalized. And so it was that the UK, together with Ireland and Sweden, opened its borders immediately to Eastern Europeans without a transition period. Though initially estimated to attract 13,000 migrants from Eastern Europe, admittedly on the assumption that Germany would participate immediately in the enlargement, from May 2004 to September 2008, 932,000 workers from Eastern Europe registered. This did not represent the true total since it was estimated that 20–45% of those who should have registered did not and it did not include the self-employed who did not have to (Pollard, Latorre, & Sriskandarajah, 2008).

The full implementation of the two migration regimes—PBS for non-Europeans and free movement for EU citizens—culminated in two complementary but parallel systems. The new Conservative-Liberal Democratic coalition government with its rhetoric of bringing down migration to under 100,000 net migrations, i.e., levels last seen in the 1990s, reinforced the PBS making it an entirely graduate route. Now the PBS was for the global skilled, especially in the IT and health sectors, as well as intra-company transfers. Just as significantly, the changes introduced by the Conservative Coalition government affirmed its commitment to temporariness and the cutting of the link between migration and settlement, as indicated in 2010 by Theresa May, then Home Secretary:

> It is too easy, at the moment, to move from temporary residence to permanent settlement ... Working in Britain for a short period should not give someone the right to settle in Britain ... Settling in Britain should be a cherished right, not an automatic add on to a temporary way in.
>
> cited in CONSTERDINE, 2019

In effect, work-related immigration from outside the EU halved between 2004 and 2010 so there was much need for EU migration which suited a liberal system with little regulation and declining training opportunities, for example through apprenticeships. Eastern Europeans (MAC, 2014) and later young, educated Southern Europeans (D'Angelo & Kofman, 2017), largely filled the need for less skilled and medium skilled labor. Another dimension of EU migration was its distribution into rural and small and medium town localities in the UK which had not experienced postcolonial migrations (Kofman et al., 2009) and which was a contributory factor in pushing immigration to be a major issue of concern, particularly in relation to the less skilled. "Open-door migration has suppressed wages in the unskilled labor market, meant that living standards have failed and that life has become a lot tougher for so many in our country." (Farage, leader of the UKIP party cited in *The Express*, June 21, 2016).

Although there had been considerable discussion about the economic impacts of large-scale EU migration on jobs for British workers and pressure on wages, especially at the bottom end, it was pressure on public services and claims on welfare that came to the fore and would result in freedom of movement becoming by 2015 the most contentious issue for the British public (Nardelli, 2015). Immigration became a major issue in the 2016 referendum whose outcome was a narrow vote (52%) in favor of leaving the EU and withdrawing from regional sovereignty.

3 Post-Brexit Regimes of Migration

In terms of changes to labor markets, Brexit started before the vote in favor of withdrawal. Even before the transition period ended (31 December 2020), labor market sourcing had begun to change substantially. After the June 2016 referendum, there was a sharp decline in long-term EU migration, (Chu 2018; Sumption, 2018). In any case, the EU had not been able to supply the necessary demand in skilled labor, especially for the IT sector dominated by Indians and the health sector, for which in 2018 the government was pushed into designating it a shortage area to be given priority in relation to the quota for Tier 2 and not subject to the resident labor market test. And then well before the end of the transition period, the government radically extended the shortage sectors under Tier 2. From October 1, 2019, the shortage occupation list for Tier 2 skilled workers was significantly expanded to include occupations covering about 2.5 million workers, or about 9% of total employment: up from 180,000 workers, or less than 1% of total employment. Also announced in November 2019 was a special NHS visa for doctors, nurses, and allied health professionals.

The post-Brexit proposal is thus intended to get rid of the two parallel systems. As the Conservative government stated,

> For too long, distorted by European free movement rights, the immigration system has been failing to meet the needs of the British people. Failing to deliver benefits across the UK and failing the highly-skilled migrants from around the world who want to come to the UK and make a contribution to our economy and society ... From 1 January 2021, EU and non-EU citizens will be treated equally.
> Home Office. 2020

Equality in this case means subjecting EU citizens to the same conditional access to welfare, i.e., recommodification of their labor (Consterdine, 2019; McGovern, 2012) as other migrants, including the difficulties of navigating family migration regulations, and turning them into mobile workers once again (D'Angelo & Kofman, 2018). Furthermore, it forces all migrants into a probationary period, thus reinforcing a sense of precarity (Anderson, 2010), even for the skilled, and disrupting the link between temporariness and settlement.

So, what might be the implications for labor in a post-Brexit landscape where the UK withdraws from a regionally integrated space and returns to an earlier period of a largely global space that matches its rhetoric of taking back control (Menon and Wager, 2020), the key Leave slogan in the Brexit campaign? It would supposedly enable it to acquire more power through its position as an unfettered global player and independent sovereign state. The term "Global Britain" was repeated seventeen times by (former) British Prime Minister Theresa May in her acceptance speech. For some, it also represents a reengagement with the Empire and imperial sovereignty, especially a harkening back to the Commonwealth, and a more Anglocentric and Atlanticist outlook (Agnew, 2020). In the leaders debate before the 2015 general election, the UKIP leader Nigel Farage described leaving the EU as a chance to reconnect with the rest of the world, "starting with our friends in the Commonwealth" (cited in Virdee and McGeever, 2018).

In practical terms, how will the government deal with the gap between a demand for labor in an economy with a relatively large low-wage sector and shortages of skills across a range of sectors. Most of the attention and published documents have dealt with skilled migration. The proposed PBS consists of two levels: 1. Exceptional talent with no quotas as is currently the situation. 2. Skilled Worker category which is much more expansive than the current Tier 2 in particular because of a much lower minimum educational qualification, starting from RFQ3 or A Level equivalent, thus covering many medium-level skilled occupations and encompassing the largest range of employment of both British and EU workers (Sumption & Fernandez-Reino, 2018). Its minimum salary level at £25,400, and in certain circumstances even less, is also lower than had been previously suggested at £30,000. The rigid quota or cap on numbers would be replaced by advice from the Migration Advisory Committee (MAC). A special expedited NHS permit (much cheaper visa and options for paying the health surcharge from salary rather than ahead of time for the whole period with the visa) for doctors, nurses, and allied health professionals was proposed in November 2019. With COVID-19, which has shown to what extent the UK depends on migrant health care workers, this is likely to be implemented well before the PBS is fully applied.

There is a complete lack of clarity or pronouncement about how gaps for the less skilled would be filled. The Migration Advisory Committee (MAC, 2018) had forcefully argued against including a route for those working in less skilled jobs on grounds that immigration should not be used to solve issues of low pay and poor working conditions. At present, less skilled jobs, such as care workers (Turpenny and Siddiq, 2018) cleaners, drivers, and waiters, have often been undertaken by Eastern and Southern Europeans, many of whom have at least a medium level of education. A total of 500,000 EU citizens are working in less skilled jobs in the UK though the largest number, as with British workers, are in medium skilled employment. In 2017, 57% of EU-born workers were in middle-skilled jobs, compared to 55% of the non-EU born and 63% of the UK born (Sumption & Fernandez-Reino, 2018).

Two possibilities for plugging the gap have been mentioned. In its July 2018 White Paper (HM Government, 2018), the government said that it hopes to negotiate a UK-EU youth mobility scheme (YMS) modeled on the existing Tier 5 scheme, which permits participants aged 18 to 30 to do any kind of work without requiring a sponsor within the two-year permit (HM Government, 2018). Currently, this is based on bilateral agreements with selected countries with quotas allocated per country. Since there is no sponsor, little is known about the kind of work undertaken although a small-scale study of Australians (Consterdine, 2019), by far the largest group, concludes that the scheme would be no panacea for replacing free movement. Those surveyed in London were largely doing medium and highly skilled jobs; they were from middle class backgrounds and highly educated. The reasons they had come to the UK would probably not be the same for young Europeans. MAC (Migration Advisory Committee) (2020) noted that even in the current absence of a route for lower-skilled migration from outside the EU, there are estimated to be 170,000 recently arrived non-EU citizens in lower-skilled occupations which includes people such as the dependents of skilled migrants, but these are not new workers. We could also add that there are a number of other sources of labor such as international students, family migrants joining permanent residents, and British citizens and asylum seekers, but these categories are already in the UK so would not fill needs post-Brexit.

4   Conclusion

Dismissing the need for external workers to fill jobs in low-skilled sectors would require, as Afonso and Devitt (2018) commented, changing the British model of capitalism to become less dependent on external labor or on developing a hyper-exploitative deployment of labor on temporary contracts. Some scholars do see a return to a more interventionist regime of organized capitalism (Nolke, 2017). One also hears of automation and technology replacing labor, but this would need time and is not suitable for certain sectors, such as social care. Nonetheless, the government reiterated on April 8, 2020, that it was not going to open up routes for those working in less skilled sectors, apart from an expanded entry for agricultural workers. Hence the UK "is engaging in a massive labour market experiment by becoming the first major economic nation to completely close off 'unskilled migration'" (McGovern, 2020). Whether it is able to do so by returning to a more nationally sourced labor regime without creating massive labor shortages is still open to question. What might change the parameters are the effects of COVID-19 on rates of unemployment and more interventionist labor market policies.

COVID-19 has led to much debate and political public reconsideration of the value of those doing work which sustains society but is poorly remunerated (Goodfellow, 2020). The term "key workers" covers all skill levels from the doctors and nurses in the National Health Service to poorly paid carers who today are more likely to be Europeans. While their contribution to maintaining life may result in some re-evaluation of those who fill less skilled sectors, it would require the UK government to reconsider its Points Based System for entry and the rights at work and conditions of residence once in the UK for it to make a difference. When the UK speaks of equalizing all migrants based on global recruitment, it means reducing the economic and social rights of the currently more advantaged EU citizens. The meaning of taking back control is to make all migrants mobile workers who are subject to a probationary period. Another possibility, likely to be hastened by sectoral support is greater intervention in the educational sector to expand vocational training at both degree and sub-degree level. And, of course, high levels of unemployment in certain sectors arising from COVID may push British youth to fill low-skilled sectors (Bell & Slaughter, 2020) and thus reduce the reliance on externally sourced labor and modifying its model of capitalism.

This chapter has shown how the state continues to play a major role in whether to source labor globally from any country in the world and under what conditions. Hence, the global is a potential field that may or may not be utilized. We have seen other countries open up to global migratory spaces to fill gaps in labor markets beyond the regional domain, particularly for skilled migrants. In the case of the UK, the global field of labor migration has a long history going back to its colonial and imperial era of world power. The return to the exclusively global has been strongly embraced for ideological reasons to assert its ability to "take back control," redolent of its glorious past and its ability to select its sources of labor, their rights and degree of commodification, unshackled by regional commitments and sovereignty.

References

Afonso, A., & Devitt, C. (2016). Comparative political economy and international migration. *Socio-Economic Review, 14*(3), 591–613.

Afonso, A. & Devitt, C. (2018). To be less dependent on immigration, Britain must change its model of capitalism. LSE: *British Politics and Policy*. Retrieved August 18, 2021, from https://blogs.lse.ac.uk/politicsandpolicy/to-be-less-dependent-on-immigration-britain-must-change-its-model-of-capitalism/.

Agnew, J. (2020). Taking back control? The myth of territorial sovereignty and the Brexit fiasco. *Territory, Politics, Governance, 8*(2), 259–272.

Anderson, B. (2010). Migration, immigration controls and the fashioning of precarious workers. *Work, Employment and Society, 24*(2), 200–17.

Barbulescu, R. (2017). From international migration to freedom of movement and back? Southern Europeans moving north in the era of retrenchment of freedom of movement rights. In J.-M. Lafleur & M. Stanek (Eds.), *South-North Migration of EU Citizens in Times of Crisis* (pp. 15–32). New York: Springer.

Barbulescu, R. & Favell, A. (2019). Commentary: A citizenship without social rights? EU freedom of movement and changing access to welfare rights. *International Migration, 58*(1), 151–65.

Bell, T. & Slaughter, H. (2020). Crystal balls vs rear-view mirrors. The UK labour market after coronavirus. *The Resolution Foundation*, 7 April. Retrieved August 18, 2021, from https://www.resolutionfoundation.org/publications/crystal-balls-vs-rear-view-mirrors/.

Castells, Manuel (1996). *The Rise of the Network Society,* Blackwell.

Chu, B. (2018). Number of EU migrant workers shows biggest fall on record, official data shows. *The Independent,* 13 November. Retrieved August 18, 2021, from https://www.independent.co.uk/news/business/news/migrant-workers-eu-uk-labour-market-brexit-september-data-ons-a8631366.html.

Consterdine, E. (2019). Youth mobility scheme: the panacea for ending free movement. *National Institute Economic Review, 248*(May).

D'Angelo, A. & Kofman, E. (2017). UK: large-scale European migration and the challenge to EU free movement. In J. M. Lafleur & M. Stanek (Eds.) *Old Routes, New Migrants: Lessons from the South-North Migration of EU Citizens in Times of Crisis,* ch. 10, Springer IMISCOE Series, pp. 175–192.

D'Angelo, A. & E. Kofman (2018). From mobile worker to fellow citizen and back again? The future status of EU citizens in the UK. *Social Policy and Society, 24*(2), 331–43.

Goodfellow, M. (2020). While low skilled migrants are saving us, the government is cracking down on them. *The Guardian,* 11 April. Retrieved August 18, 2021, from https://www.theguardian.com/commentisfree/2020/apr/11/low-skilled-migrants-government-cracking-down.

Hay, C. (2000). Contemporary capitalism, globalisation, regionalisation and the persistence of national variations. *Review of International Studies, 26,* 509–31.

HM Government (2018). *The Future Relationship between the UK and the European Union.* London: HM Government.

Home Office (2001). *Secure Borders, Safe Haven: Integration with Diversity in Modern Britain.* Home Office, CM 5387.

Home Office (2020). The UK's points-based immigration system: Policy statement. Retrieved August 18, 2021, from https://www.gov.uk/government/publications/the-uks-points-based-immigration-system-policy-statement/the-uks-points-based-immigration-system-

Jessop, B. (2002). The Future of the Capitalist State. Polity.

Jessop, B. (2008). Avoiding traps, rescaling the state, governing Europe. In R. Keil & R. Mahon (Eds.), *Leviathan Undone? Political Economy of Scale.* University of British Columbia.

Jessop, B. (2016). Territory, politics, governance and multispatial metagovernance. *Territory, Politics, Governance, 4*(1), 8–32.

Kofman, E. (2008). Managing migration and citizenship in Europe: Towards an overarching framework. In C. Gabriel & H. Pellerin (Eds.), *Governing International Labour Migration. Current Issues, Challenges and Dilemmas* (pp. 13–26). Routledge.

Kofman, E., Lukes, S., D'angelo, A., & Montagna, N. (2009). The Equality Implications of Being a Migrant in Britain. Research Report 19, Equality and Human Rights Commission.

Massey, D. (1993) Power geometries and progressive sense of place. In J. Bird, B. Curtis, P. Putnam, & L. Tickner (Eds.), *Mapping the Futures: Local Cultures, Global Chance* (pp. 59–69). Routledge.

McDowell, L., Batnitzky A., & Dyer, S. (2009). Precarious work and economic migration: Emerging immigrant divisions of labour in Greater London's service sector. *International Journal of Urban and Regional Research, 33,* 3–25.

McGovern, P. (2012). Inequalities in the (de-)commodification of labour: Immigration, the nation-state and labour market stratification. *Sociology Compass, 6*(6), 458–68.

McGovern, P. (2020). Who are you calling unskilled? *LSE Blog,* 6 March. Retrieved August 18, 2021, from https://blogs.lse.ac.uk/brexit/2020/03/06/long-read-who-are-you-calling-unskilled/.

Menon, A., & Wager, A. (2020). Taking back control: Sovereignty as strategy in Brexit politics. *Territory, Politics, Governance, 8*(2), 279–284.

Migration Advisory Committee (2014) *Annual Report of the Migration Advisory Committee for the Year 2013 to 2014.* Retrieved August 26, 2021, from https://www.gov.uk/government/publications/migration-advisory-committee-annual-report-2013-to-2014.

Migration Advisory Committee (2018) *EEA Migration in the UK: Final Report.* Retrieved August 26, 2021, from https://assets.publishing.service.gov.uk/government/uploads/system/uploads/attachment_data/file/741926/Final_EEA_report.PDF.

Migration Advisory Committee (2020). *A Points-Based System and Salary Thresholds for Immigration.* Retrieved August 26, 2021, from https://assets.publishing.service.gov.uk/government/uploads/system/uploads/attachment_data/file/873155/PBS_and_Salary_Thresholds_Report_MAC_word_FINAL.pdf.

Morgan, T. (2004). *The Spanish Migrant Community in the United Kingdom.* Cambridge: Anglia Polytechnic University.

Nardelli, A. (2015). EU referendum: Polling reveals freedom of movement most contentious issue. *The Guardian,* 9 October. Retrieved August 18, 2021, from https://www.theguardian.com/news/datablog/2015/oct/09/eu-referendum-polling-reveals-freedom-of-movement-most-contentious-issue.

Nolke, A. (2017). Brexit: Towards a new global phase of organized capitalism. *Competition and Change, 21*(3), 230–41.

O'Brien, R. (1992). *Global Financial Integration: The End of Geography.* Pinter.

O'Toole, F. (2018) *Heroic Failures: Brexit and the Politics of Pain.* Head of Zeus.

Pollard, N., Latorre, M., & Sriskandarajah, D. (2008). *Floodgates or Turnstiles? Post EU Enlargement Migration Flows to (and from) the UK*. London: Institute for Public Policy Research.

Ruhs, M., & Anderson, B. (Eds.) (2010). *Who Needs Migrant Workers? Labour Shortages, Immigration, and Public Policy*. Oxford: Oxford University Press.

Sumption, M. (2018). *BRIEFING: Work Visas and Migrant Workers in the UK*. Migration Observatory, Oxford University.

Sumption, M., & Fernández-Reino, M. (2018). *REPORT: Exploiting the Opportunity? Low-Skilled Work Migration after Brexit*. Migration Observatory.

Taylor, P. (1994). The state as container: Territoriality in the modern world-system. *Progress in Human Geography, 18*(2), 151–162.

Turnpenny, A. S. H., & Siddiq S. (2018). Migrant care workers and their future in the UK context. *Sustainable Care Policy Perspectives*. Circle.

Virdee, S., & McGeever, B. (2018). Racism, crisis and Brexit. *Ethnic and Racial Studies, 41*(10), 1802–1819.

CHAPTER 13

Global Institutions and Governance

Rebecca Gumbrell-McCormick

1   **Introduction**

This chapter further explores the theme of the global by focusing on the institutions that have emerged to facilitate the cross-border mobility of capital and labor—or, alternatively, to control or block their mobility. I examine the extent to which these actors and institutions resemble or differ from nation-states and other national-level bodies, how they operate, the nature of their governance and regulatory powers, and the degree to which they work together, or separately, to structure, channel, or regulate the labor market at the global level. This presents challenges, both theoretically and empirically. The main theoretical challenge is that until recently, most social science research has been oriented around the nation-state, and the development of theory around the global, one of the major tasks of this research project, is at a less developed stage. Linked to this is the challenge of the nature of governance and its distinction from government, as in the debate over hard versus soft law. The main empirical challenge is that research into global and international labor markets and industrial relations is still limited compared to research on the national level and on the comparison between nations (often confused with "international"). Further, insofar as such research is growing, it remains highly "siloed" with little communication between different academic fields.

One of the many advantages of the research project that gave rise to this book is that it was interdisciplinary as well as international. This chapter is nonetheless rooted in a particular academic tradition, industrial (or employment) relations, although it does seek to include other traditions. At the empirical level, while other chapters focus on specific bodies, such as employment agencies and other intermediaries, or on particular "globalized" occupations or professions, this chapter will look at the broader issues of developing a set of institutions and norms which over the past century have sought to structure and regulate labor markets at the global level. I shall begin by addressing some conceptual and definitional issues, before exploring the similarities and differences between the national and inter-national or global levels, then outlining the structure of the international industrial relations system and some of the main instruments of supranational regulation, again comparing and contrasting with their national analogues and considering to what extent their powers are at all comparable to those of nation-states. The aim is to contribute to our understanding of the structuring, norms, and capacities for regulation of the global labor market.

2   Definitions

As the previous chapter has explored definitions of the "global," this section will focus more on the extent to which the definitions used in industrial relations literature differ. The main difference is probably in the use of the term "global" as opposed to "international." While used interchangeably here, they are not quite the same. The term "international" derives its meaning from the "national" and is still founded on the nation-state and the relations between states. The term "global" is broader, and while it can encompass the term "international," it also refers to interactions that bypass national states or go beyond them. Various grassroots citizens' initiatives, including some "international" non-governmental organizations (NGOs) and some grassroots workers' networks or organizations, fit into this category. The "global" level marks a significant development, not so much in formal governance, perhaps, but in the development of a "global" civil society and set of norms. However, there are probably fewer genuinely "global" networks, organizations, and institutions than "international" ones, as most "global" institutions and organizations are still based on formal structures that rely on the nation-state or at least the national level. And as has been pointed out elsewhere in this book, the labor market itself is not truly "global" in the sense that it does not cover all regions of the world equally (Meardi & Marginson, 2014; Munck, 2018).

Another conceptual distinction applies to the terms "government" and "governance." (Hassel, 2008; Meardi & Marginson, 2014) In his model of industrial relations, discussed below, John Dunlop (1958) identified three groups of actors in industrial relations: trade unions, employers' associations, and "governmental agencies" (Dunlop, 1958). This term is less clear than either "state" or "government" and indeed Dunlop places much less emphasis on this third actor than either of the other two (see Hyman, 2008). Clearly, at the national level we can speak primarily of "government," but this is not true of the global or international level. Bulmer (1998, p. 366) argued, in the context of the EU, that the latter "does not resemble, or have, a government, so governance offers some descriptive purchase on the character of the polity," a point later taken up by Leisink and Hyman (2005). And the global intergovernmental institutions, such as the UN system, bear even less resemblance to "government" than the EU. The practical meaning of "governance" is often unclear, since the concept leaves open questions of power relations, means of enforcement, and implementation. There is also a tension between the descriptive or analytical use of the term "global governance," and the normative or programmatic usage which calls for a regulatory order to compensate for a presumed loss of national capacity (Dingwerth & Pattberg, 2006). We shall return to these concepts later.

As the previous chapter pointed out, the labor market extends from the local, subnational, national, and regional to the international and global levels, but these levels interact with each other imperfectly, so that they do not form a perfect continuum.

3 National and International: Parallels and Differences

According to Herod, "The global and the local each derive meaning from what they are not" (2011, p. 228) and, indeed, it is only by comparing the national and the international that we can appreciate their differences and similarities. We begin with the concept of an industrial relations system, inspired by the ideas of John Dunlop (1958), oriented around the interrelationships of three sets of actors within a regulatory and normative setting. His model was nationally bounded; and while his aim was in part to compare and contrast different national systems, the idea of an international or global system was not addressed. The concept of regional and international industrial relations systems has developed more recently. Writing of developments within the European Union (EU), Jensen, Madsen and Due (1999) argue that we can identify supranational equivalents of Dunlop's three actors—representative organizations of workers and employers, and governmental agencies—and that their interactions are creating a supranational body of rules. Hence, they conclude, a European industrial relations system exists. But can the same be said of an international or global system? How far do the international "actors" match our understanding of trade unions, employers' associations, and governments at national level? And how far do the rules they create match the laws and collective agreements normally seen as typical of national employment regulation and, in the European case, of regional regulation?

As noted above, much analysis of the international level of industrial relations has proceeded by analogy with the national. This is misleading. The state has citizens; despite the occasional rhetoric of "world citizenship," individuals do not possess an analogous set of rights and responsibilities vis-à-vis international institutions. (There are a few very limited exceptions, such as travel documents for stateless persons, under the UN's 1954 Convention relating to the Status of Stateless Persons.) As for the other actors, trade unions have members who directly contribute to union funds and possess corresponding rights and obligations; international union organizations possess members only indirectly, through the affiliation of national bodies (although recently there are a few exceptions, mentioned below). Most national confederations are also removed from individual members, in the sense that their members are usually individual sectoral bodies, but union internationals are one step even further removed from individual members: their internal political dynamics can only to a limited degree be compared with individual nation unions (Cotton & Gumbrell-McCormick, 2012). This distance has been an important area of debate, with some arguing that this has allowed trade union internationals to misrepresent the concerns of individual members (Thompson & Larson, 1978, Waterman, 2001). Likewise, international employers' associations generally affiliate national organizations rather than individual companies. Indeed, with the increased power of individual multinational companies, leading MNCs are now choosing to operate outside of national, let alone international, employers' associations (Traxler, 2000).

Another important distinction between the national and inter-national levels is the basis of legitimacy and nature of decision-making at international level. The intergovernmental organizations are generally expected to operate democratically. Looking at the other actors, while there are no expectations for individual employers to operate democratically (although they are bound by national law to act legally and by their own interests to act in a way that does not alienate their employees (see Budd, 2004)), their associations are expected to do so, much like international trade unions. But for both international employers' associations and international trade unions, the distance from their base makes this difficult; moreover, international bodies must deal not only with the core issues which affect members at national level, but also with world politics and political rivalries between nations. For employers' associations, this is not necessarily a problem; for trade unions it is because the labor movement relies on its members and their capacity to act (Hyman, 2005a; Offe & Wiesental, 1985).

Finally, an essential difference between the national and the international levels of industrial relations institutions is the nature of sovereignty and the ability to enforce decisions and impose sanctions if they are not executed. As "meta-organizations" (Ahrne & Brunsson, 2008, Cotton & Gumbrell-McCormick, 2012; Hyman & Gumbrell-McCormick, 2020), the affiliates of international organizations are not discrete individuals but institutions with their own resources and decision-making procedures, and they are usually reluctant to cede capacities to the umbrella body. This is closely related to the issue of governance, to which we return below. In the next section, we focus in greater detail on the differences between the national and international levels in terms of the nature of governance and regulation.

Precisely because intergovernmental institutions and global organizations rarely possess the ultimate sanction of force to implement their decisions, the distinction between government and governance links to that between "hard" and "soft" law (Abbott & Snidal, 2000; Cammack, 2005). "Soft law" indicates decisions which those to whom they are addressed are expected to observe but which cannot be juridically enforced; their efficacy depends on peer pressure and the possibility of less formalized means of retaliation, and on the extent to which the underlying norms of conduct are "internalized" by decision-makers at national level (Koh, 1999). Much international regulation in the field of industrial relations is precisely of this character. There is considerable disagreement as to whether nonbinding norms can exert hard effects; those who assert the value of such approaches insist that "soft law" may help "frame" the political debate at national as well as international level, providing an important resource for those actors pressing for stronger national regulation (Zeitlin & Pochet, 2005). Indeed, national governments do not always use "hard law" in practice: generally, they rely on voluntary obedience to their regulations, through the "social contract."

4 The Nature of Global Actors and the International Regulatory System

This section will continue our exploration of differences between the national and international levels (and, to some extent, the regional level, in the case of the European Union), by going into more detail on the three sets of actors (governmental agencies, employers, and trade unions) along with an additional set of actors that Dunlop (1958) did not consider, non-governmental organizations, which has grown in importance since the time he wrote, and will then consider the structure and nature of the international regulatory system itself. To some degree, the governmental or quasi-governmental actors overlap with the regulatory system itself—national governments, for example, are actors within intergovernmental institutions such as the International Labour Organization (ILO), and these intergovernmental bodies themselves formulate policies and programs that in turn have an effect on the nature and scope of international regulation, but it is important to maintain a conceptual distinction between their role as actors and as components of the supranational system. While only the quasi-governmental actors (those most similar to nation-states) matter in terms of deciding and implementing regulations at the inter-national or global level, the other actors are nonetheless an essential part of the process, in acting as advocates at the global level and within the intergovernmental bodies for the concerns and demands of global civil society. They also provide legitimacy to the international system as a whole. And, of course, the ILO formally incorporates representation of the two other industrial relations actors, while parts of the broader UN system also include representatives of other non-governmental organizations. Of key significance here are the institutions that have been established to regulate the international economy and polity. These include the International Labour Organization (ILO), the Bretton Woods institutions and the rest of the UN system, the Organisation for Economic Co-operation and Development (OECD) and the WTO (see also Gumbrell-McCormick, 2008).

4.1 *Intergovernmental Institutions*

All intergovernmental institutions suffer from a lack of regulatory powers compared to nation-states. Since the Treaty of Westphalia in 1648, the sovereignty of nation-states has been a fundamental principle of international politics; in normal circumstances, the right of self-determination can only be voluntarily abrogated. In general, nations have been willing to assign only tightly bounded powers to intergovernmental institutions, imposing decision-making rules which restrict the chances that they will be bound by policies to which they object. Prior to the creation of the ILO in 1919, a small number of international legal instruments adopted by the major European nations regulated certain health and safety issues (Shotwell, 1934, pp. 492–496). These set the precedent for international standards in industrial relations matters alongside those governing the actions of states in wartime and other international issues and marked an important step in the development of the intergovernmental system as a whole. From the beginning, government ministers and other industrial relations actors were conscious of the difficulties of assuring the implementation of international law by nation-states without infringing on their sovereignty; for this reason, international law generally requires transposition into national law and enforcement by national governmental agencies. The nature, purpose, and means of enforcement of international legal instruments have been much debated by legal and industrial relations scholars (Hassel, 2008; Langille, 2005; Sengenberger, 2002; Wedderburn, 2002).

International organizations of states and governments were formed in the aftermath of both World Wars. The oldest major organization still in existence is the ILO, founded in 1919 as part of the League of Nations and incorporated in the UN system in 1946 (Alcock, 1971; Hughes, 2005; ILO, 1931; Shotwell, 1934).

Most discussed here are formally intergovernmental, that is, they represent the governments of national states directly, although the forms of representation and selection may vary. (The ILO is distinctive, representing workers and employers as well as states in a tripartite system, which means that it is more complex than a purely intergovernmental body, as discussed below.) As mentioned above, all intergovernmental institutions suffer from a lack of regulatory powers compared to nation-states. This was one of the main areas of debate in the creation of the ILO, that is, the extent to which its decisions would be binding to all member states and that member states would therefore give up some degree of sovereignty (Van Goethem, 2000). It is no surprise that the main drafter of the ILO Constitution, George Barnes, was a British government minister, as even then the British government was very keen to keep full control over its sovereignty. There are parallels here with the EU and the implementation of its directives. But while the ILO has no powers to force member states to transpose and then implement the international legal instruments, on some very specific issues, the EU is competent to do this (see below). For the ILO, the more serious sanction is the expulsion of a member state, which we discuss below. Under the ILO Constitution, instead of giving up any of their sovereignty, the member states are obliged to transpose the legal instruments decided by the organization into national law. Intergovernmental organizations, while acting on behalf of national states, do not enjoy analogous powers or legitimacy.

Nevertheless, the ILO conventions and recommendations are considered to have the force of international law (Valticos, 1998). The most important for this discussion are the group of conventions adopted by the ILO that have won international recognition as essential for protecting the legal and social rights of workers and their representatives (Bellace, 2014a). These "core" conventions were first identified at the World Social Summit in Copenhagen in 1995 and were formally adopted in the ILO's Declaration on Fundamental Principles and Rights at Work (1998). These conventions are significant, not only because they have been recognized as "core" by the ILO itself, but because of the legitimacy they have acquired within world public opinion. They form the basis of most of the voluntary codes of conduct adopted by individual companies or industries and are accepted by governments in north and south alike. The core conventions are given added weight by the 1998 Declaration, which requires states to observe them irrespective of formal ratification. As with other ILO conventions, the means of ensuring implementation are limited, and these rely mostly on the carrot of technical assistance and the stick of "naming and shaming." However, the ILO considers one core convention, that on Freedom of Association (no. 87), so important that it created a Committee on Freedom of Association in 1951 to monitor its implementation, whether or not member states had ratified it, on the basis of complaints raised by recognized representatives of workers or employers as well as by other states. Cases have been taken against governments in every region of the world and have often led to substantial improvements in such areas as union organizing rights (as with public sector workers in Japan in 1973 and the UK in 1988, Gumbrell-McCormick, 2000, p. 434), although many cases have been less successful (as against several Latin American countries in the 1970s and '80s, and more recently against the government of Venezuela in 2018). In some of these cases, member states have been ostracized as a result of condemnation by the Committee and have resigned their membership in order to avoid expulsion, as in the cases of South Africa in 1966 or Vietnam in 1985. The strongest sanctions ever taken by the ILO were against the government of Myanmar following a decision by the Governing Body in 2000 concerning that country's failure to abide by the Forced Labour Convention. This was the first time the ILO invoked Article 33 of its constitution, and the measures included requesting the UN, other intergovernmental organizations (such as the EU) and national governments to "consider" suspending relations with the country. These measures proved effective in leading to reforms, and the measures were lifted 12 years later.

The ILO's role has changed in recent years; in some ways, it has moved from a strictly legal approach (through the setting of legally binding international standards) to one of advocacy and the power of persuasion, toward an emphasis on "soft law" (or governance) as opposed to "hard law" (or government) (Bellace, 2014a). This can be seen in the Decent Work campaign launched under the period in office of Secretary-General Juan Somavia, from 1999 to 2012 (Vosko, 2002). This campaign relied on persuasion and moral argument rather than binding international conventions, although it was inspired by the ILO's core standards (see Standing, 2008 and Munck, 2018 for trenchant critiques of the Decent Work campaign). A related initiative, taken together with the UN, was the UN Global Compact, which has a membership of companies, rather than governments, and is also inspired by ILO labor standards. It provides for annual reporting (which not all member bodies carry out) and has no form of sanction other than "naming and shaming." In Bellace's words (Bellace, 2014a, p. 447), "this non-legalistic, non-mandatory orientation is consistent with the traditional view of CSR" [corporate social responsibility] rather than the traditional legal approach of either the ILO or the UN system.

The ILO is noteworthy in that it is not purely an *intergovernmental* institution, as under its tripartite system it incorporates the representation of employers' and workers' associations (in almost all cases, trade unions). This particular form of tripartism gives a greater weight to representatives of governments than to the other two actors, with half the national delegations to the annual International Labour Conference going to governments, and one-quarter each to employers and workers' representatives. This form of representation applies to almost all parts of the ILO, not only to its annual International Labour Conference, which makes major decisions and adopts international labor standards, but also to the many committees and subcommittees that consider new international instruments at an earlier stage, and also to some elements of the International Labour Office, which has both a Bureau for Workers' Activities and a Bureau for Employers' Activities.

Beyond the ILO, the UN system is recognized by and represents the largest number of nation-states on a permanent basis and is granted the legitimate right to use force under very limited conditions. No other intergovernmental body—at least at the world level—enjoys such powers, but nation-states are rarely willing in practice to grant the UN the freedom to act in emergency situations that is allowed in theory, and the UN system has been rife with interstate and interregional rivalries and has been subject to the veto power of individual states, in particular, the US.

Looking at the remaining global intergovernmental institutions, the OECD also incorporates a form of tripartism, with Advisory Committees representing both employers and trade unions. This dates back to the founding of its predecessor, the Organisation for Economic Co-operation in Europe (OEEC), which was established in 1948 as part of Western Europe's efforts to harness the legitimacy of trade unions and win the support of employers in the postwar Marshall Plan (Carew, 1987; 2000). Today the OECD includes 37 of the world's richest countries, and while it possesses fewer formal powers that the UN institutions, it is often seen as a vehicle of "soft law." Its most important measure in social and labor affairs is probably the 1976 Declaration on International Investment and Multinational Enterprises (Gumbrell-McCormick, 2008). These guidelines, updated in 2000, allow OECD member states, recognized trade unions, and employers' representatives to ask for "clarification" of their implementation by individual MNCs. Here, too, the main form of implementation has been "naming and shaming" or "soft law" and the guidelines have been hampered by applying to OECD member states only. The influence of the Trade Union Advisory Committee (TUAC) has no doubt played a role in the successful use of these guidelines.

At the opposite extreme, the International Financial Institutions (IFIs) which define the rules of the global economic game, have no formal involvement of trade unions but do have a strong informal involvement of employers' associations and individual MNCs. The Bretton Woods agreements of 1944 resulted in the creation of the International Monetary Fund (IMF) and what was to become the World Bank (WB). Their original mission, as integral parts of the new UN system, was to reduce poverty and inequality between nations; but from the 1950s, financial support to developing countries was made conditional on "structural adjustment programs." More recently, they have moved towards closer coordination within the UN system (especially with the ILO) and a return to some extent to their original goals (Panić, 2003; Toye, 2003). Neither body has strong formal regulatory powers, but they do possess very powerful powers of influence through the conditions they impose on loans, as can be seen in their role in the Troika, together with the European Commission. A similarly strong influence is enjoyed by the WTO, the successor to the General Agreement on Tariffs and Trade (GATT), established in 1995. With some 150 members, it has a cumbersome governance structure and positions are often polarized, as is evident from the deadlock in numerous attempts to achieve further trade liberalization. However, while social clauses have proved elusive at the top level, there have been a number of recent bilateral trade agreements that do include such measures (Ebert & Posthuma, 2011, cited in Meardi & Marginson, 2014).

To move to the regional intergovernmental level, the European Union and its predecessors from an early stage also incorporate an element of tripartism. The EU has followed the emergence in postwar Europe of "corporatist" or "political exchange" arrangements whereby the "social partners" were assigned a formal role in social and economic policymaking (Croucher & Wood, 2015; Jahn, 2016). As there is a great deal of literature on this topic (see Hyman, 2001 and Gumbrell-McCormick & Hyman, 2018) we will not dwell on the EU structures here, except to say that of all the international intergovernmental institutions, it has the strongest powers of regulation. The Court of Justice of the European Union (CJEU) has superior authority over national courts, in those areas where the Treaties give the EU institutions regulatory competence. This competence has been enhanced in recent years under the "new economic governance" which gives the European Commission and the Council the power to impose sanctions on countries which breach macroeconomic discipline (Erne et al., 2015). More radically, the Troika of the Commission, the European Central Bank, and the IMF can impose conditions on loans to member states in economic difficulties, as occurred in a number of cases after the crisis of 2008, leading to radical encroachments in industrial relations institutions and collective bargaining processes (Koukiadiki, Távora, & Martinez Lucio, 2016; Lehndorff, 2014; Pernicka & Glassner, 2019). Finally, the EU has close links with the remainder of the intergovernmental system: its directives have often inspired or been inspired by the international regulations and standards of the ILO and UN (Mechi, 2013), while its formal involvement in other bodies, including the ILO and the UN system, means that the EU has influence on international regulation far beyond its boundaries.

To summarize, even those international organizations with relatively strong sets of competences (i.e., the UN system or the EU) lack key defining characteristics of governments. If anything, the international system is moving away from a formal legalistic approach to one of advocacy and "naming and shaming." National states, according to Weber's definition, hold the monopoly of the legitimate use of violence within a given territory. Inter-national and intergovernmental organizations lack this capacity—even if the UN, in exceptional circumstances, may be empowered to intervene forcefully if one state threatens the security of another, or collapses into civil war. The next section continues this theme by looking more in detail at the structure and powers of the remaining actors within the international system.

4.2 Employers' Associations and Trade Unions

International NGOs, particularly those representing employers and workers, are only indirectly part of the regulatory system (except, as noted, in the ILO, and, to some extent, the OECD and EU) but play an important role in developing and advocating the ideas that eventually become accepted policy, in providing legitimacy to the intergovernmental institutions, and in acting as a voice for their constituents. They have even fewer powers to implement and enforce decisions than the international intergovernmental bodies, both externally and internally. Externally, employers' organizations and trade unions have a formal role within the ILO, EU, and some parts of the UN, as mentioned above. Internally, these international organizations face some of the same difficulties as the major intergovernmental bodies: their national affiliates are no keener to give up their sovereignty to a regional or international body than are governments. The subsidiarity principle applies here even more than with intergovernmental bodies.

Turning first to employers' associations, the International Organisation of Employers (IOE), formed in 1920 after the ILO was established (Birk & Maack, 2009; Rojot, 2006), represents employers' interests within the ILO and the UN system. It comprises national associations in some 140 countries and cooperates with a variety of regional employers' organizations, and also with the Business and Industry Advisory Committee to the OECD (BIAC). Another influential body is the International Chamber of Commerce (ICC), established in 1919. This is a strong advocate of neoliberalism. While it lacks the legitimacy as a "social partner" enjoyed by the IOE, it has nevertheless been allowed a significant role within the UN system (Kelly, 2005). Numerous organizations also represent employer interests in individual industries and sectors.

Employers' associations have traditionally maintained a low profile within the ILO and other intergovernmental institutions, partly because they do not seek the same level of intervention in international labor standards as do the trade unions, and indeed act as a "brake" on their initiatives, as memorably phrased by Albert Thomas, the first Secretary-General of the ILO: "the Director was the train driver, the Employers were the brakesmen wanting to slow down the train and the Workers were the firemen wanting the train to go faster" (Bellace, 2014b, p. 66). Partly for this reason, employers' associations have received less academic attention than have trade unions, except at the European level (see Traxler, 2004), but this has changed very recently as a result of conflicts within the ILO over the definition of the right to strike. This conflict, which arose at the International Labour Conference in 2012 (Bellace, 2014b; Vogt, 2014) marked an unanticipated shift in the employers' position on the topic at hand, but also highlighted a more gradual decline in their willingness to cooperate with trade unions within the ILO machinery in the spirit of cooperation that is essential to tripartism. While this particular dispute has been resolved (although it was a major bone of contention at the 2018 congress of the International Trade Union Confederation (ITUC)), the more assertive role of the employers' associations within the ILO has remained, reinforcing its general shift away from a reliance on formal legal international instruments.

There is much more literature on *international and global trade union bodies* than on employers' associations, so we will cover them more briefly here (Croucher & Cotton, 2009; Fairbrother & Hammer, 2000; Gumbrell-McCormick, 2000, 2013). As with intergovernmental institutions, their international confederations are almost all based on national-level trade union centers, but recent years have seen the development of regional or industry-based networks that bypass the inter-national bodies, such as the international shop stewards network that was formed in response to the Liverpool dock strike (Bradley & Knight, 2004; Bronfenbrenner, 2007; Marren, 2016; Munck, 2018; Waterman & Wills, 2012; Waterman, 1998). While it is true that trade unions officially represent only a small percentage of the global workforce, they remain the only internationally recognized actors that represent all workers and cannot easily be replaced.

International trade union bodies are based either on industrial sectors or on national centers. The earliest trade union internationals, founded at the end of the nineteenth century, were *industry-based*, becoming known as International Trade Secretariats (ITSs), now known as the Global Union Federations (GUFs). There developed a division of labor, with the ITSs/GUFs concentrating on practical organizing and solidarity work within their sectors, and the confederations of national centers addressing broader political issues (Croucher &

Cotton, 2009; Gumbrell-McCormick, 2013). While the ITS/GUFs are keen to maintain their independence from the ITUC (today's leading international trade union body), and while their main activities are to some extent very different, the two types of bodies are otherwise very similar in terms of their internal organization, powers, and governance. Trade unions, unlike employers' associations, have internal democracy as one of their guiding principles (although this is not always practiced, see Hyman & Gumbrell-McCormick, 2020) and depend on internal democracy in order to formulate policy, to endow legitimacy, and to provide a capacity to act (Offe & Wiesenthal, 1985). To be effective, unions must be regarded as representative by outside bodies, such as employers and governments.

International trade unions, however, as stated above, are one step further from individual workers than are national unions and are less transparent in their decision-making and more lacking in the other trappings of internal democracy than trade unions at the national level. This is partly because national unions have traditionally prioritized national issues, especially now that labor movements are in decline in most major industrialized countries and have largely left the international trade union bodies to run themselves. International trade unionism has tended to be a niche area, partly because of the requirement to have knowledge of foreign languages and the complex workings of international systems and law (Hyman, 2005a).

The *regional level of trade unions* is little different in this respect, although as they are slightly closer to the affiliates and individual members, there are greater possibilities for internal scrutiny and democracy. The first international organizations were almost exclusively European in coverage, and the weight of membership and financial resources has always ensured strong European influence in global unionism. As with the European Union at the intergovernmental level, the European Trade Union Confederation is the largest and most influential regional trade union body, with both formal and informal forms of influence within the European Commission and Union. Among its strongest forms of influence is the power to negotiate agreements with the European organizations of employers to reach agreements which, under the terms of the 1992 Maastricht Treaty, are then enacted as directives and agreements on parental leave and part-time work were given legal effect. But hereafter, the employers' organizations were unwilling to reach agreements that could become "hard" law. At sectoral level, such agreements still occurred, but the Commission refused to initiate legislation on the basis of a 2012 agreement on health and safety in hairdressing and in the case of a 2015 agreement on central government (Tricart, 2019). The ETUC is also handicapped by the limited powers granted to it by its member affiliates, with differing views on the importance of pursuing a common policy or take common action at EU level, as can be seen in the recent wrangling over the proposal for a European minimum wage, which has been backed primarily by the poorer member states and opposed by the richer, in particular the Nordic countries and Italy (Seeliger, 2019).

The international and European trade unions have, however, a further form of influence on the international regulatory system in two important areas: at the European level, through European Works Councils; and at the global level. through International or Global or Transnational Framework Agreements (IFAS, GFAS, or TFAS) (Gumbrell-McCormick & Hyman, 2018) There is a great deal of literature on European Works Councils (EWCs) (Hann, Hauptmeier & Waddington, 2017; Hertwig, Pries, & Rampeltshammer, 2009) so we will focus here on IFAs, although it is worth noting that they have much in common (and indeed most IFAs are European based, see Telljohan, da Costa, Müller, Rehfeld, and Zimmer 2009). Neither IFAs nor EWC agreements are legally binding (except insofar as such agreements may be binding in individual national law) but they provide one avenue for applying international instruments or national legislation in the home countries to a European or global setting, nor is either really an example of international collective bargaining (Gumbrell-McCormick, 2008) although these agreements have nonetheless encouraged the development of collective bargaining in the countries whose affiliated unions are parties to the agreement. Both EWCs and IFAs are recent inventions. In the case of EWCs, they were adopted after years of discussion by the EU in 1994 and are therefore officially promoted by the European institutions, although they are not mandatory (Pries, 2019).

The case of the IFAs is rather different, in that they arose through individual initiatives by individual Global Unions with their interlocutors in major MNCs. What are now called IFAs started in 1988 with the agreement between Danone/BSN and the International Union of Food and Allied Associations (IUF) (see Koch-Baumgarten & Rütters, 1991) but most have been signed since 2000. Such framework agreements are usually based on the ILO core conventions, especially conventions 87 and 98, on freedom of association and collective bargaining (Telljohan et al., 2009). They also tend to provide for independent monitoring by NGOs or by the trade unions themselves. International framework agreements are a potentially important form of regulation combining the best features of international labor standards and voluntary codes of conduct. There are still too few of them in operation and most are too recent to be able to judge their effectiveness, though numbers are increasing (Miller, 2004; Telljohan et al., 2009; Wills, 2002).

4.3 (Other) Non-governmental Organizations

There is now considerable literature on the role of civil society, social movements, and non-governmental organizations (NGOs) as a fourth category of industrial relations actors (Heery & Frege, 2006). These bodies are particularly important at the global level of industrial relations, where some scholars have claimed that some NGOs have acquired a greater impact than trade unions or employers' organizations (Elliot & Freeman, 2003). NGOs often campaign forcefully and effectively against the adverse impact of neoliberal globalization on work and employment (Munck, 2002). Most of the older democracies have seen a decline in membership and activism within trade unions and political parties, and an increased role of "single-issue" or "pressure" groups (Koenig-Archibugi, 2003). Many of the latter have a direct or indirect concern with industrial relations issues. We can observe a growing rapprochement between international trade unionism and international NGOs as actors in a "global civil society" (Hyman & Gumbrell-McCormick, 2017; Waterman & Timms, 2005). This can be seen, for example, in the experience of the annual World Social Forum (WSF), first convened, mainly by Third World NGOs, in Porto Alegre, Brazil in 2001 as a movement for "globalization from below" (Sen et al., 2004). Initially, the official trade union organizations largely remained aloof but have become increasingly active participants; the same is true of the European Social Forum (ESF), first held in Florence in 2002 (della Porta, 2005).

To conclude this section, the major international actors form a network of relationships, norms, rules, and regulations that provide the basis for the international industrial relations system. But as I have shown, the international actors are not endowed with the same powers or sense of legitimacy as national actors; international law is not enforceable in the same way as national law; and the main instruments of action are not always directly comparable. However, an international industrial relations system with at least some instruments of action and some rules can be said to exist.

5 Conclusion and Future Directions

The preceding pages have introduced the reader to international industrial relations actors—governments and intergovernmental bodies, trade unions, NGOs, and employers' associations. Certainly, these actors operate primarily at the national level, but they have by now built up a set of institutions at the regional and global levels that has remained intact throughout most of the past century. To a degree, these actors possess a common set of norms based on the ILO core conventions, and these appear to be shared by wide sectors of public opinion. Further, there are intergovernmental institutions involved in regulating industrial relations matters: the ILO and the rest of the UN system, the WTO and OECD. These, too, have proved stable over the past 75 years, and, in the case of the ILO, over a century. But these international institutions lack key characteristics of states—democratic accountability (if not legitimacy), the ability to monitor compliance, and the power to impose sanctions on those who breach the requirements. Furthermore, in some respects, they seem to be moving away from a legal regulatory system rather than further toward it.

If an international industrial relations system simply means a larger version of national systems, we would have to conclude that it does not (yet) exist. But as I have argued, the two are not analogous. Trade unions at the international level rarely carry out collective bargaining or strikes, but they pursue much the same ends through other means: international campaigns, coordination of national or sectoral demands, coordinated approaches to corporate head offices. International employers' associations are weak, but individual employers operate on a global scale, with more flexibility, greater means, and a higher degree of coordination than trade unions. The most problematic element here is the governmental bodies: the ILO cannot simply send in international inspectors any more than the UN can send in peacekeeping forces, without the consent of member states. But, as Langille argues (2005, pp. 20–22), international law does not have to be enforceable in the same way as national law—the implementation of ILO conventions, for example, depends on member states and employers understanding that this is in their best interests. And as Meardi and Marginson point out (2014; see also Werron's chapter in this volume) the development of a global discourse is crucial to the development of a truly global labor governance. This is essentially the approach of "soft law" or "governance" (as opposed to "government" applied on a global scale).

Academic analysis of global issues and of the global labor market has been weakened by the demarcation into separate fields, or "silos," which this research project has sought to overcome. While this chapter draws primarily on the field of industrial relations, it has sought to show awareness of the fields of international relations, international and labor law, sociology and labor economics; and, of course, this book in its entirety contributes to a richer appreciation of the global labor market in its entirety.

Is there a global labor market? As other chapters have suggested, there are numerous layers and scales that together make an imperfect web. In the case of global regulation, the intergovernmental institutions have a global reach, but their capacity to regulate is severely limited. However, when we look at the various institutions and organizations as an ensemble, the web appears to be denser than ever before, and there is at least the beginning of a common discourse, or set of norms, that forms the nucleus of a global system.

References

Abbott, K. W. & Snidal, D. (2000). Hard and soft law in international governance. *International Organization, 54*(3), 421–56.
Ahrne G. & Brunsson N. (2008). *Meta-organizations*. Cheltenham: Edward Elgar.
Alcock, A. (1971). *History of the International Labour Organisation*. London: Macmillan.
Bellace, J (2014a). Hoisted on their own petard? Business and human rights. *Journal of Industrial Relations, 56*(3), 442–457.
Bellace, J. (2014b). The ILO and the right to strike. *International Labour Review, 153*(1).
Birk, R., & Maack, N. (2009). The International Organisation of Employers. In C. Tietje (Ed.), *Handbook of Transnational Economic Governance Regimes*. Leiden: Brill.
Bradley, P., & Knight, C. (Eds.) (2004). *Another World is Possible: How the Liverpool Dockers Launched a Global Movement*. London: Radical Anthropology Group.
Bronfenbrenner, K. (Ed.) (2007). *Global Unions: Challenging Transnational Capital through Cross-Border Campaigns*. Ithaca: Cornell.
Budd, J. (2014). *Employment with a Human Face: Balancing Efficiency, Equity, and Voice*. Ithaca: Cornell University Press.
Bulmer, S. J. (1998). *New Institutionalism and the Governance of the Single European Market*. Manchester University Press.
Cammack, P. (2005). The governance of global capitalism: A new materialist perspective. In R. Wilkinson, (Ed.), *The Global Governance Reader* (pp. 156–73). London: Routledge.
Carew, A (2000). Towards a free trade union centre: The International Confederation of Free Trade Unions (1949–1972). In A. Carew, M. Dreyfus, G. Van Goethem, R. Gumbrell-McCormick, & M. van der Linden, *The International Confederation of Free Trade Unions* (pp. 187–337). Bern: Peter Lang.
Carew, A. (1987). *Labour under the Marshall Plan*. Manchester: Manchester UP.
Cotton, E. & Gumbrell-McCormick, R. (2012). Global unions as imperfect multilateral organizations. *Economic and Industrial Democracy, 33*(4), 707–728.
Cox, R. (1971). Labor and transnational relations. *International Organization, 25*(3), 554–84.
Croucher, R. & Cotton, E. (2009). *Global Unions Global Business: Global Union Federations and International Business*. London: Middlesex University Press.
Croucher, R. & Wood, G. (2015). Tripartism in comparative and historical perspective. *Business History, 57*(3), 347–357.

della Porta, D. (2005). *The Social Bases of the Global Justice Movement: Some Theoretical Reflections and Empirical Evidence from the First European Social Forum*. Geneva: UNRISD Programme Paper 21.

Dingwerth, K. & Pattberg, P. (2006). Global governance as a perspective on world politics. *Global Governance, 12*, 185–203.

Dunlop, J. T. (1958). *Industrial Relations Systems*. New York: Holt.

Ebert, F & Posthuma, A. (2011). Labour provisions in trade agreements. *Discussion Paper 205*, International Institute for Labour Studies, International Labour Office, Geneva.

Erne, R., Bieler, A., Golden, D., Helle, I., Kjeldstadli, K., Matos, T. & Stan, S. (2015). Introduction. Politicizing the transnational. *Labor History, 56*(3), 237–245.

Fairbrother, P., & Hammer, N. (2005). Global unions: Past efforts and future prospects. *Relations industrielles, 60*(3), 405–31.

Gumbrell-McCormick, R. (2000). Facing new challenges: The International Confederation of Free Trade Unions (1972–1990s). In A. Carew, M. Dreyfus, G. Van Goethem, R, Gumbrell-McCormick, & M. van der Linden, *The International Confederation of Free Trade Unions*. Bern: Peter Lang.

Gumbrell-McCormick, R. (2004). The ICFTU and the world economy: A historical perspective. In R. Munck, (Ed.), *Labour and Globalisation* (pp. 34–51). Liverpool: Liverpool University Press.

Gumbrell-McCormick, R. (2008). International actors and international regulation. In P. Blyton, N. Bacon, J. Fiorito, & E. Heery. (Eds.), *The Sage Handbook of Industrial Relations* (pp. 325–345). Sage: London.

Gumbrell-McCormick, R. (2013). The International labour movement: Structures and dynamics. In P. Fairbrother, M.-A. Hennebert, & C. Lévesque (Eds.), *Transnational Trade Unionism: Building Union Power*. London: Routledge.

Hann, D., Hauptmeier, M., & Waddington, J. (2017). European Works Councils after two decades. *European Journal of Industrial Relations, 23*(3), 209–224.

Hassel, A. (2008). The evolution of a global governance regime. In *Governance: An International Journal of Policy, Administration and Institutions, 21*(2), 231–251.

Heery, E., & Frege, C. (2006). New actors in industrial relations. *British Journal of Industrial Relations, 44*(4), 601–4.

Herod, A. (2011). *Scale*. Abingdon: Routledge.

Hertwig, M., Pries, L., & Rampeltshammer, L., (Eds.) (2009). *European Works Councils in Complementary Perspectives*. Brussels: ETUI.

Hughes, S. (2005). The International Labour Organisation. *New Political Economy, 10*(3), 413–25.

Hyman, R. (2001). *Understanding European Trade Unionism: Between Market, Class and Society*. London: Sage.

Hyman, R. (2005a). Shifting dynamics in international trade unionism: Agitation, organisation, diplomacy, bureaucracy. *Labor History, 46*(2), 137–54.

Hyman, R. (2005b). Trade unions and the politics of European integration. *Economic and Industrial Democracy, 26*(1), 9–40.

Hyman, R. (2008). The state in industrial relations. In P. Blyton, N. Bacon, J. Fiorito, & E. Heery. (Eds.), *The Sage Handbook of Industrial Relations* (pp. 258–283). Sage: London.

Hyman, R. (2018). What future for industrial relations in Europe?. *Employee Relations, 40*(4), 569–579.

Hyman, R., & Gumbrell-McCormick, R. (2017). Resisting labour market insecurities: Old and new actors, rivals or allies? *Journal of Industrial Relations, 59*(4), 538–561.

Hyman, R. & Gumbrell-McCormick, R. (2020). (How) can international trade union organisations be democratic? *Transfer, 26*(3), 253–272.

ILO (1931). *Dix ans de l'Organisation Internationale du Travail.* Geneva: ILO.

ILO (1998). *Declaration on Fundamental Principles and Rights at Work.* Retrieved August 18, 2021, from https://www.ilo.org/declaration/lang--en/index.htm.

ILO (2004) *A Fair Globalization: The Role of the ILO*. Report of the Director-General on the World Commission on the Social Dimension of Globalization. Retrieved August 18, 2021, from https://www.ilo.org/public/libdoc/ilo/2004/104B09_112_engl.pdf.

ILO (2006). *The End of Child Labour: Within Reach.* Geneva: ILO.

Jahn, D (2016). Changing of the guard: Trends in corporatist arrangements in 42 highly industrialized societies from 1960 to 2010. *Socio-Economic Review, 14*(1), 47–71.

Jensen, C. S., Madsen, J. S., & Due, J. (1999). Phases and dynamics in the development of EU industrial relations regulation. *Industrial Relations Journal, 30*(2), 118–34.

Kelly, D. (2005). The International Chamber of Commerce. *New Political Economy, 10*(2): 259–71.

Koch-Baumgarten, S., & Rütters, P. (Eds.) (1991). *Zwischen Integration und Autonomie.* Cologne: Bund.

Koenig-Archibugi, M. (2003). Global governance. In J. Michie, (Ed.), *The Handbook of Globalisation* (pp. 318–30). Cheltenham: Edward Elgar.

Koh, H. H. (1999). How is international human rights law enforced? *Indiana Law Journal, 74,* 1397–1417.

Koukiadaki, V. A., Távora, I., & Martínez Lucio, M. (Ed.) (2016) *Joint Regulation and Labour Market Policy in Europe during the Crisis.* Brussels: ETUI.

Langille, B. (2005). *What Is International Labour Law For?* Geneva: IILS.

Lehndorff, S. (Ed.) (2015). *Divisive Integration: The Triumph of Failed Ideas in Europe—Revisited.* Brussels: ETUI.

Leisink, P., & Hyman, R. (2005). Introduction: The dual evolution of Europeanization and varieties of governance. *European Journal of Industrial Relations, 11*(3), 277–86.

Marren, B. (2016). The Liverpool Dock Strike, 1995–98: A resurgence of solidarity in the age of globalization. *Labour History, 57*(4), 463–481.

Meardi, G., & Marginson, P. (2014). Global labour governance: Potential and limits of an emerging perspective. *Work, Employment, and Society, 28*(4), 651–662.

Mechi, L. (2013). Du BIT à la politique sociale européenne: les origines d'un modèle. *Le Mouvement Social, 244*(3), 17–30.

Munck, R. (2002). *Globalisation and Labour: The New 'Great Transformation'*. London: Zed.

Munck, R. (2018). *Rethinking Global Labour*. Newcastle: Agenda.

Offe, C. & Wiesenthal, H. (1985). Two logics of collective action. In C. Offe, *Disorganized Capitalism* (pp. 170–220). Cambridge: Polity.

Panić, M. (2003). A new Bretton Woods? In J. Michie (Ed.), *The Handbook of Globalisation* (pp. 370–382). Cheltenham: Edward Elgar.

Pernicka, S., & Glassner, V. (2019). The Europeanisation of wage bargaining coordination. In J. M. Kiess & M. Seeliger (Eds.), *Trade Unions and European Integration* (pp. 70–93). London: Routledge.

Pries, L. (2019). EWC: Ineffective bureaucratic body or institutionalising labour regulation at European company level? In J.M. Kiess & M. Seeliger (Eds.), *Trade Unions and European Integration*. London: Routledge.

Rojot, J. (2006). International collective bargaining. In M. J. Morley, P. Gunnigle, & D. G. Collings (Eds.), *Global Industrial Relations*, (pp. 254–72). London: Routledge.

Seeliger, M. (2019). *Trade Unions in the Course of European Integration*. London: Routledge.

Sengenberger, W. (2002). *Globalization and Social Progress: The Role and Impact of International Labour Standards*. Bonn: Friedrich Ebert Stiftung.

Shotwell, J. T. (Ed.) (1934). *The Origins of the International Labor Organization*. New York: Columbia UP.

Standing G. (2008). The ILO: An agency for globalization?. *Development and Change, 39*, 355–384.

Telljohan, V., da Costa, I., Müller, T., Rehfeld, U., & Zimmer, R. (2009). *European and International Framework Agreements*. Dublin: Eurofound.

Toye, J. (2003). The International Monetary Fund and the World Bank. In J. Michie, (Ed.), *The Handbook of Globalisation* (pp. 358–69). Cheltenham: Edward Elgar.

Traxler, F. (2000). Employers and employer organisations in Europe: Membership strength, density and representativeness. *Industrial Relations Journal, 31*, 308–316.

Tricart, J-P (2019). Legislative implementation of European social partner agreements: Challenges and debates. Brussels: ETUI *Working Paper, 09*.

Valticos, N. (1998). International labour standards and human rights: Approaching the year 2000. *International Labour Review, 137*(2), 135–147.

Van Goethem, G. (2000). Conflicting interests: The International Federation of Trade Unions (1919–1945). In A. Carew, M. Dreyfus, G. Van Goethem, R. Gumbrell-McCormick, & M. van der Linden, *The International Confederation of Free Trade Unions*. Bern: Peter Lang.

Waterman, P. (1998). *Globalization, Social Movements and the New Internationalisms*. London: Mansell.

Waterman, P. (2001). The problematic past and uncertain future of the International Confederation of Free Trade Unions. *International Labour and Working Class History, 59*, 125–132.

Waterman, P. (2001). Trade union internationalism in the age of Seattle. In P. Waterman & J. Wills (Eds.) (2012), *Place, Space and the New Labour Internationalisms*. Oxford: Blackwell.

Wedderburn, K. W. (2002) Common law, labour law, global law. In B. Hepple (Ed.), *Social and Labour Rights in a Global Context* (pp. 19–54). Cambridge: CUP.

Zeitlin, J., & Pochet, P., (Eds.) (2005). *The Open Method of Co-ordination in Action: The European Employment and Social Inclusion Strategies*. Brussels: P.I.E.-Peter Lang.

CHAPTER 14

What Is Global about Global Markets?
A Historical Sociological Approach

Martin Bühler and Tobias Werron

1   Introduction

Goods and people have always traveled far and wide for new economic opportunities. No wonder that social scientists have been interested in global markets for a long time now. This interest became particularly evident in the mid-nineteenth century: "The bourgeoisie," Karl Marx and Friedrich Engels argued in the Communist Manifesto, "has through its exploitation of the world market given a cosmopolitan character to production and consumption in every country" (Marx & Engels, 1977, p. 39). The rhetoric of world market from the nineteenth century foreboded the current debate on globalization. Chains of production stretch around the globe and jobs are being increasingly shifted globally or on a global scale. Global markets are used to explain local job cuts or to legitimize looming trade wars, and economic text books are brimming with evidence of their existence (e.g., Krugman & Obstfeld, 2005). Nowadays, therefore, global markets appear to be self-evident, leading some to the conclusion that we live in an increasingly "flat" world where everyone is affected by global market forces (Friedman, 2005). But what exactly are the prerequisites of global markets, and how can a conceptualization of global markets improve our understanding of global labor markets?

Remarkably, sociologists rarely raise these questions: "While there is wide acceptance that the globalization of economic relations is an important feature of contemporary capitalism, the study of 'global' markets has so far received relatively little systematic attention from economic sociologists" (Quack, 2009, p. 125; Aspers, 2010, p. 194). It seems that this assessment is still valid to this day: There is a strong discrepancy between the rhetoric about global markets, on the one hand, and sociological thinking about them, on the other hand.

Against this background, the present chapter aims to establish a new sociological understanding of what is global about global markets.[1] We start with the

---

1   This chapter is a translated, abridged, and revised version of Bühler and Werron (2013).

suggestion that the "globality" of markets should not be taken for granted but treated as a challenging conceptual and historical problem.[2] This means taking a closer look at the social processes that go into the construction of global markets and at the historical prerequisites for the emergence of these markets since the mid- to late nineteenth century. For this purpose, our analysis combines insights from two strands of sociological research: from the discussion on markets in the new economic sociology and from studies on globalizing dynamics and global forms of competition since the mid- to late nineteenth century. It is the latter strand of research which, we believe, also makes our reasoning relevant for the study of labor markets. While we draw mainly on the literature on product markets and (to some extent) financial markets, we also use insights from the globalization and world society literature to argue that all global markets share a similar logic of social construction, irrespective of whether the "goods" on offer are products, real estate, stocks/bonds, or jobs. Thus, we hope to inspire and inform a comparative discussion about the prerequisites and historical trajectories of different types of global markets, including global labor markets.

The argument proceeds in four steps. The first section discusses modes of thinking about the "globality" of markets in new economic sociology, arguing that existing approaches tend to ignore the phenomenological or "awareness" dimension of the global. In the second section, we review existing approaches to the analysis of markets in new economic sociology and develop a complementary perspective to the social construction of markets. The third and main section combines ideas from the preceding sections and presents a new concept of global markets. Our main point is that the construction of global markets is based on the imagining and addressing of universal market audiences, or global publics. These publics emerge as products of public discourses which compare and evaluate products and prices on a continual basis, establishing a particular kind of social structure that mediates between the producers and their publics. The "globality" of global markets, according to this argument, is a matter not of networks of local market actors but of a particular kind of global imagination created in public discourse. We illustrate these hypotheses using a case study of the emerging global market for wheat in the late nineteenth century. While we base our model mainly on product markets, we also aim at inspiring comparative research on global markets. The conclusion, therefore, raises a number of questions derived from our model for the analysis of

---

2   For the opposite view, see Neil Fligstein (2001, p. 94), who assumes that "the only difference between a global market and a local one is geographic spread. The definition of a market ... can be applied to globalization in a straightforward way."

global labor markets and for the comparative study of different types of global markets.

2 New Economic Sociology on Global Markets: Heuristic Considerations

Contrary to common discourse, leading scholars of new economic sociology are skeptical about the existence and relevance of global markets. For instance, on the basis that there will always be people or locales which are not included in a market, Sigrid Quack concludes "that there is no such thing as a global market" (Quack, 2009, p. 126). What we find instead, Quack argues, are historical contingent forms of "transnational" markets emerging from culturally institutionalized trade networks (see also Quack in this volume). While Neil Fligstein (2001, p. 94) does not categorically exclude the possibility of global markets, he is skeptical about their number and relevance, arguing that the overwhelming majority of economic activity takes place on the national level.

There are, however, also sociological studies that accept the existence and significance of global markets, analyzing them from different perspectives. Prominent examples are (a) studies on global commodity/value chains that trace goods, such as coffee, from their place of origin and then around the globe to their place of consumption, observing changes in value/prices along the trade chain (for an overview, see Gereffi, 2005), (b) studies on global foreign exchange markets by Karin Knorr Cetina and Urs Bruegger (2005; 2002), and (c) Patrik Aspers' (2011) analysis of global garment markets. These views presuppose or imply three distinct understandings of what it means for a market to be global:

(1) *"Globality" as global chains of trade and manufacturing.* This notion of the global is accompanied by an interest in economic networks and a transgression of heterogeneous regulations (Quack, 2009) or by an interest in price developments and social inequalities due to global sourcing of goods (for example, the "coffee paradox," see Daviron & Ponte, 2005). In this perspective, global markets are mainly phenomena of interconnectedness: Actors either bridge heterogeneous regimes and geographical spaces, or sociocultural inventions such as product standards and conventions facilitate transactions between globally dispersed actors. In both cases, the "globality" of the market is viewed as the global extension of trade networks.

(2) *"Globality" as the extension of common conceptions of controlling* globally dispersed producers within a shared institutional framework

(Fligstein, 2001, pp. 94–97). The second notion of "globality" is linked to an interest, first raised by Harrison White, in the (surprising) stability of markets as "tangible cliques of producers" (White, 1981/82, p. 543). Neil Fligstein adds a political-institutional dimension to White's view, highlighting that the stabilization of markets requires a shared institutional framework and, in the case of global markets, a *global* institutional framework, including, most notably, international regulation. As market regulations are still mostly based on national law, Fligstein (2001, pp. 94–97, pp. 221–222) is skeptical when it comes to the existence and relevance of global markets—and rightly so, given his conceptualization of global markets as dependent on global political institutions (see also Gumbrell-McGormick in this volume).

(3) *"Globality" as geographical distance between (numerous) local market participants.* The final distinct notion of the global in current market literature reflects an interest in *problems of coordination* (Beckert, 2009). Sometimes the focus is on global interaction and coordination through product categories or standards which allow producers to recognize each other as competitors (Aspers, 2010, p. 146). In other cases, the focus lies on technologies that integrate traders into transnational communication networks by allowing market participants to react simultaneously to the same information presented on screens ("scoping" mechanism; Knorr Cetina, 2003). In these perspectives, "globality" serves as the antonym of locality: By bridging distances between local market participants, product standards and technologies integrate these actors into one and the same trade and/or communication network.

These fields of research highlight important aspects of the creation, development, and limitations of global markets. However, they also share a common notion of the global which, in our view, restricts their ability to explain the prerequisites of global markets. They see the global market as an outcome of interaction between dispersed local actors and of social and technical innovations that enable trade, interaction, and cooperation between these actors. This notion of the global raises the question at what point the degree of dispersion of actors is deemed to be large enough to refer to as a global phenomenon. Are two actors located on either side of an international border sufficient to define a market as global? Does a global market require market actors on every continent or even in every nation state? Do market regulations or control have to encompass each and every nation state for a market to be considered to be global?

Considering these questions, it would be easy, and indeed plausible, to conclude that there is no such thing as a global market. However, we think there is an alternative way of thinking about global markets that requires a different understanding of the global. Global markets are not just about global connections between local actors; they are also about the establishment of *global horizons of comparison* which enable global market structures and competitive relationships to exist largely independently of the direct interaction between actors (Werron, 2015b; Heintz & Werron, 2011). This phenomenological take on globalization reflects Roland Robertson's insight that globalization is based not only on increasing interconnectedness but also on increasing global awareness (Robertson, 1992, p. 8). Moreover, it also aims to *explain the social processes that make global awareness possible*—on markets as well as in politics, science, sports, the arts, and other fields of society.

Thus, the foreign exchange market as described by Karin Knorr Cetina, for instance, can be seen as a global market, although the trading floors are located in a small number of global cities, and exclusively in OECD countries. They are "global," however, not because the traders work on all continents or operate from every single nation state in the world but because all kinds of events that might affect currencies are presented simultaneously on the traders' screens, allowing a certain awareness of "the world" to shape the market. The "globality" of these markets is a product of simultaneous inclusion in a common concept of the world; it is based on a shared sense of economic opportunities in terms of currencies and current and future exchange rates (Werron, 2015a). To understand global markets, then, we need to study how this global sense of opportunities is socially constructed and has developed historically. In order to do so, however, we first have to be clear about precisely what we mean when referring to markets.

3 Analyzing Markets: Three Heuristic Moves

There are various epistemic angles on markets that serve different, and equally legitimate, purposes. We suspect that a historical sociological approach to global markets also requires a distinct method of analyzing the markets. For this purpose, this section discusses a number of distinctions that guide much of the sociological market literature in explicit and implicit ways, arguing that the analysis of global markets requires an emphasis on the second variable of each distinction. Rather than asking how markets can be stable, we ask how they can exist in the first place; rather than thinking about markets in terms of dyadic trade, we propose thinking about them in terms of triadic competition; and rather than focusing on the perspective of producers, we propose taking the perspective of third parties, particularly the public, into account.

3.1 *From the Stability of Markets to the Possibility of Markets*

Harrisons White's (1981/82) market model was one of the starting points of the resurgence of market sociology (Fligstein & Dauter, 2007). White's model is based on an analysis of what he calls "producer markets," and on an interest in what he saw as the surprising stability of these markets. At the core of his reasoning is the observation that producers cannot determine the type, volume, or prices of their products by simply observing or surveying consumers because consumer preferences are notoriously difficult to detect. He concludes that consumers are anonymous and their preferences fundamentally unknown. Producers, therefore, tend to observe each other rather than consumers, which, according to White, explains why markets are prone to becoming relatively stable "self-reproducing cliques of producers" (1981/82, p. 518). On the basis of this model, markets can be described as survival networks of producers which emerge from efforts to deal with the uncertainty introduced from the buyer side. In other words, it is not a question of efficiency but of reproducibility in a largely unpredictable environment (Leifer & White, 1987, p. 86).

This line of thought has found broad support in economic sociology, as it highlights *social* aspects of markets that tend to be ignored in neoclassical economics. However, there is an implication of White's model that has not yet found the attention it deserves: The model points to an asymmetry between producers and consumers based on the uncertainty introduced from the consumer side *without* asking where this uncertainty comes from. It treats this uncertainty as a given and so fails to discuss the social processes that include the audience in the structure of the market. In order to address this limitation, it may be useful to focus on problems of *possibility* rather than just stability, of markets. For this purpose, more attention needs to be paid to the buyer-seller interface and to the meaning of entities such as "the consumer": How are consumers imagined as a source of uncertainty that affects the social construction of markets?

3.2 *From Dyadic Trade to Triadic Competition*

Our discussion of Harrison White's take on markets as "cliques of producers" also draws attention to another guiding distinction in the sociological analysis of markets: A market emerges and stabilizes if producers vie for the same set of potential buyers. The market, therefore, does not equal the sum of transactions or price movements. Rather, it is based on *relationships of observation and competition* among producers in view of a shared market public. This observation points to a distinction that is currently being discussed in both sociological theory and market sociology: between *dyadic trade* or *exchange*,

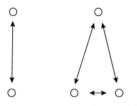

FIGURE 14.1   Trade vs. market
SOURCE: ASPERS, 2011, P. 8

on the one hand, and *triadic competition*, on the other. It goes back to classical sociologist Georg Simmel's "sociology of competition" (Simmel, 2008), where he defines the "pure" form of competition as the struggle for the scarce favor of third parties (Werron, 2010, 2015c). In market sociology, Patrik Aspers (2011, pp. 7–8) refers to this concept to explain his distinction between trade and market (see Figure 14.1). While trade emerges from dyadic exchange between two parties, markets are triadic structures, where (at least) two sellers compete for the favor of (at least) one buyer (Bühler, 2019, pp. 19–22).

Seeing markets as triadic social structures involves taking an interest in the roles and expectations of third parties and asking the following questions: How do third parties contribute to the social construction of the market? And how are the social roles of these third parties related to the uncertainty and influence of the market public?

3.3   *From Producers to Audiences and Intermediaries*

These questions lead us to the final distinction we would like to discuss here: the distinction between conceptualizations of markets that focus on the perspective of producers and those that take the perspective of the market public (buyers and consumers) into account. Again, a discussion of Harrison White's market model is useful for understanding the significance of this distinction. A closer analysis shows that the consumer public plays a dual role in White's model: it is central yet obscure. On the one hand, it is at the center of the model, acting as the source of uncertainty that pushes producers to stabilize the market by observing each other (see also Aspers, 2010, p. 34, pp. 40–45). On the other hand, and precisely because it is seen as fundamentally an unknown entity, as the "mysterious consumer" (Leifer & White, 1987, p. 92),[3] it is largely excluded from sociological analysis.

---

3   In her analysis of foreign exchange traders, Karin Knorr-Cetina (2003, p. 12) expresses the same kind of notion: "(The market on screen) is probably like 99.99999% anonymous."

Viewing potential buyers as mysterious to producers or sellers, however, does not and should not preclude us from studying the role of audiences in the social construction of markets. Ezra Zuckerman (1999) demonstrates the virtues of such an approach in his seminal study of how business analysts can affect the price of shares: by introducing fixed sets of categories to classify companies according to industry, analysts cause companies that do not fit these categories to risk being overlooked and significantly undervalued ("categorical imperative"). This analysis leads Zuckerman to criticize the new economic sociology for losing sight of the consumer public. Rather than ignoring the audience, he argues, market sociologists should account for the fact that markets are often "mediated markets" (1999, p. 1400) where third parties such as journalists and other "market critics" (1999, p. 1402) influence the audience while also creating a public market sphere that all market actors can use to observe each other indirectly.

Zuckerman's analysis of mediated markets has important implications for the sociological analysis of markets beyond this particular case. In mediated markets, producers are constantly observed by third parties addressing and articulating the expectations of the market audience. In these markets, producers can not only observe each other but they can also observe these third parties in order to detect the expectations of potential buyers as well as the intentions of their competitors, implying that it is possible that "producers watch each other in the media more than through direct observation" (Kennedy, 2005, p. 205). These insights suggest that the sociological study of global markets should include an interest (1) in the *social construction of audience expectations* and (2) in *intermediary processes* between producers and the public that allow producers and audiences to observe each other. They also raise important questions regarding the historical emergence of such markets: Since when are producers constantly observed by third parties that mediate between them and their audiences? How has this affected the characteristics of markets? And how does "mediation" play into the construction of global markets?

4   The Social Construction of Global Markets

Global markets cannot exist on the basis of personal interaction alone and are, therefore, by necessity mediated markets. They are based on mediated communication (letters, telegraph, mass media, internet, etc.) and on mediating third parties (e.g., business analysts, critics, information providers, and journalists) that help market participants make sense of the social sphere in which they operate. With regard to global markets, therefore, all of the questions discussed above prove to be relevant: How is the public introduced into these markets as a source of uncertainty? What roles do third parties play in the social construction of global markets? How do they mediate between the producers and their publics? With these questions in mind, let us now attempt to establish our approach to the analysis of global markets.

4.1   Modern Markets as Products of Public Discourse

The literature sometimes alludes to the publicness of markets but, to date, this has not received the attention it deserves. Eric Leifer and Harrison White (1987, p. 105) mention in passing that their "argument largely rests on the 'publicness' of information and not its presence or absence." Similarly, Patrik Aspers (2011, pp. 7–8) states that "the difference between trade and market, both of which are instances of economic exchange, suggests that the connotation … of the market as something 'public', or transparent, is important." But how can we approach the "publicness" of markets in a way that actually explains its role in the reproduction of markets?

One way of addressing this question is to take a closer look at the meaning and history of terms such as "public communication" and "public." Analytically, these terms are meaningful only in relation to some idea of *public discourse* which, as historians have shown, is a modern idea that originated in the seventeenth to eighteenth century. The concept of public discourse has been specified, both historically and conceptually, by literary historian Michael Warner (2002), who explains that public communication emerges in a circular relationship between a manner of speaking, or discourse, on the one hand, and a particular kind of addressee, "a public," on the other: "A public is a space of discourse organized by nothing other than discourse itself. … it exists only as the end for which books are published, shows broadcast, Web sites posted, speeches delivered, opinions produced. *It exists by virtue of being addressed.*" (Warner, 2002, p. 50). In other words, there is no public discourse without a public, and no public without public discourse.

These insights are important, not only for analyzing political institutions like the "public sphere" but also for understanding the "publicness" of markets. Modern markets, like modern politics, are largely based on public discourse mediating between buyers and sellers, with the equivalent to the political public on markets often described in terms of "consumers" or "investors" (Heintz & Werron, 2011; Bühler, 2019; Werron, 2014). This is of particular relevance to *global* markets: Here, the idea of a public consisting of potential consumers or investors is at the core of the public communication of (and on) offers made by producers of goods and services, the value of stocks and bonds, etc. This

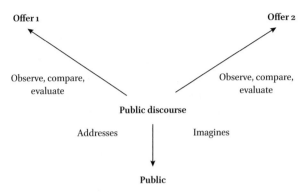

FIGURE 14.2   Model of market
SOURCE: OWN FIGURE

perspective helps unravel the paradox of the influential but fundamentally unknowable market public that we discovered in White's model of producer markets: The public is unknowable precisely because it is, first and foremost, the addressee of a discourse that connects public communication and the public in a circular relationship. As the addressee of public communication, it is, by definition, anonymous, and this is what in turn makes it a public. At the same time, it is at the heart of the social process that makes modern and global markets possible. It influences the market from behind the scenes. Overall, these concepts of the public explain why the public character of the market is so important: It is the anonymous public as addressed in public discourse that is at the center of the triadic structure of modern markets. On this basis, we can expand and further elaborate the analysis of the market by splitting the "third party" into two elements: the public discourse and an imagined buyer or consumer public (see Figure 14.2):

Our proposal makes it possible to integrate various technological and sociocultural prerequisites of markets that have been studied in separate areas of research into a single comprehensive model: the actor-network theoretical concept of the performativity of markets (e.g., Callon, 2007), the micro-sociological analysis of computer-assisted foreign exchange markets (Knorr-Cetina & Brügger, 2002), and research into the role of market categories and product standards. In our model, public discourse and comparison play a similar role to Bruno Latour's (1988, pp. 59–60) "centres of calculation" or Karin Knorr-Cetina's (2003, 2007) "scoping systems" or "global reflex systems." Both "centralize" (in Latour's sense) or "reflect" (in Knorr-Cetina's sense) a wealth of relevant market data. They collect, chart, analyze, and evaluate transactions and bring them to the attention of potential market participants.[4] Our focus on public *comparison* points to the role of product standards, which forms a basis for comparison. This, in turn, allows us to incorporate research on product categories and the evaluation of economic goods (see, paradigmatically, Hsu, Negro, & Koçak, 2010; Rosa, Porac, Runser-Spanjo, & Saxon, 1999). In addition to bringing these fields of research together, our model highlights a characteristic of mediated markets that has not yet received the attention it deserves: the fact that "the public," this central institution of the market, is introduced into the market through public discourse.

4.2 Global Markets as Universalized Public Communication

How does this model contribute to the analysis and empirical study of global markets? It suggests that global markets emerge when public discourse mediates between suppliers and potential buyers, with the latter imagined as a potentially worldwide public (see Figure 14.3).[5] In this perspective, the global market is a historical version of the modern market as described above. Therefore, we define the "global" not in terms of interaction between local actors but in terms of the concept of the public as imagined in public discourse. *The market is global if the public of the market is imagined as being global*: as a universal and spatially unlimited audience of consumers, buyers, or investors.

Empirically, this conceptualization highlights three prerequisites of global markets which are largely taken for granted in the literature and have not yet been integrated into a comprehensive analytical framework: (1) *Universal categories of comparison*: Patterns to observe and evaluate economic offers regardless of spatial or social differences, particularly by defining product standards and currencies; (2) *Intermediary public discourse and "universalized" third parties*: Forms of publication and experts or specialist observers centralizing data and publishing comparisons and evaluations of products; (3) *Universal concepts of market publics* which enable competition for the attention and favor of a global audience of potential buyers.

---

[4] Similar in some ways to the concept of "market devices" (Callon, Millo, & Muniesa, 2007), which, however, places a stronger emphasis on materiality and technicality.

[5] A related topic, which we cannot discuss in detail here, is the rise of market and public opinion research since the end of the nineteenth century and the question of how statistical information has formed and changed our views of the public (see Brückweh, 2011). Equally interesting, however, is that this and other knowledge about publics has not changed the fact that publics are a source of uncertainty, as actors from various social fields are still "desperately seeking the audience" (Ang, 1991). On markets, this seems to result in the desperate and fragile strategies that Franck Cochoy describes as "captation" (Cochoy, 2007).

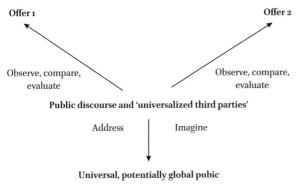

FIGURE 14.3 Model of global markets
SOURCE: OWN FIGURE

4.2.1   Universal Categories of Comparison

According to our model, global markets rely on *universal categories of comparison* which allow us to compare economic offers in a spatially and socially inclusive way and to establish universal horizons of comparison. Normally, comparisons consist of two interwoven operations (on this in general terms, see Heintz, 2010; Heintz, 2016; regarding economic phenomena, see Bühler & Heintz, 2017): On the one hand, *commensuration*: Different objects, things, acts, and actors are seen as sufficiently similar to define them as comparable (assumption of comparability). On the other hand, *detection of further similarities and differences*: Comparable entities are differentiated on the basis of further criteria that make it possible to detect further similarities and differences between them. Apples and oranges are both fruits, and thus comparable *as fruits* (comparability), but you might argue that apples taste better than oranges (detection of differences) or that they both taste equally good (similarity). Similarly, comparisons that constitute global markets are based on two types of criteria: first, categories that establish comparability between products or offers (for instance, product category and currency), and second, criteria to differentiate and evaluate the comparable entities (for example, product quality and price) (see Table 14.1):

Regarding the first dimension, the commensuration of products on offer, our analysis is able to build on ideas from proliferating research on product categories (Hannan, 2010). This research shows that product categories are a prerequisite for the emergence of markets; product categories focus the attention of the market participants on some products on offer and deflect from others; they structure cognition and serve as points of reference for trade and price formation (Hsu, Negro & Koçak, 2010; Rosa, Porac, Runser-Spanjo, &

TABLE 14.1   Practices of comparison in general and on markets

Comparison as a social practice	Categories of comparison (= commensuration, assumption of comparability)	Criteria of comparison (= differentiation of the comparable)
Comparisons constituting markets	Market genres and subtypes (e.g., products, currencies, labor?)	Product qualities (e.g., color, weight, price, labor costs and benefits? Individual features?)

SOURCE: OWN TABLE

Saxon, 1999; Zuckerman, 1999). This is reflected in the fact that, in most cases, the product categories (or subcategories thereof) label the respective market (e.g., car market: market for minivans; foreign exchange market: market for US dollars). To these insights we can now add the concept of *global* markets: The emergence of global markets depends on the establishment of *universal* product categories, which allow for comparisons of various offers regardless of spatial or social differences. A case in point is the standardization of categories of wheat in the late nineteenth century (Cronon, 1991, pp. 97–147; Bühler, 2019). Through fixing certain properties of wheat, irrespective of specific local harvests, traders from around the globe were able to use these properties not only to submit offers but also to compare the quality and prices of wheat with different local origins (comparability).

In order to differentiate between and evaluate what is on offer within the same product category, however, further criteria were needed (differentiation of the comparable). This insight allows us to integrate insights from another burgeoning branch of research in economic sociology: evaluation studies (Beckert & Musselin, 2013; Beckert & Aspers, 2011). This research assumes that the quality of things is not inherently given but rather a social construction. However, it has not yet addressed the question of how *global* qualities are constructed. This, we argue, requires *universal criteria of comparison* which make it possible to evaluate various offers irrespective of their origin or social and cultural differences. For global markets to develop, these criteria are presented as objectively given and their inventors and users as devoid of vested interest and only concerned with product quality and price (Bühler & Heintz, 2017; Bühler, 2019, pp. 107–118). We can think of a plethora of different criteria, e.g., color, size, configuration, quality of material, accuracy of production as well as temporal criteria such as delivery time (Aspers, 2010, pp. 119–122) or social criteria such as the status ascribed to goods and their producers (Aspers, 2010, pp. 50–54; Podolny, 1993).

Against the backdrop of an emerging global market, spatial criteria can gain particular importance: Origin might be used as a status signal and entrenched brand promising reliable consumer experiences or prestige (e.g., Scotch whisky, Swiss watches) often shaped by local factors of production (terroir, labor, education, or resources), sometimes secured through appellations (e.g., Champagne, Harris Tweed, or strawberries from the Loire region), or because transport is time-sensitive (fashion, emergency services, or high-frequency trade in financial markets). Again, the market for wheat is a prime example (Bühler, 2019, pp. 52–65, pp. 107–118). Up until the nineteenth century, the criteria were diffuse and mainly depended on the sensual faculties and individual experiences of discerning buyers (e.g., the "translucidness" of the grain or the ear-pleasing sound of a handful of spilled corn, see Kaplan, 1984). In the latter half of the nineteenth century, these indicators were increasingly replaced by objectified criteria and technical instruments (e.g., the percentage of damaged kernels per volume indicated, a fixed weight/volume relation automatically weighed). If individual measurements were required, certified grain inspectors with a standard education, acting as apparently impartial experts, used objective techniques (scales, probes, and technical devices) to evaluate the wheat (Bühler, 2019, pp. 114–117). These universalized criteria allowed comparisons and evaluation of product qualities that were no longer embedded in local particularities and individual knowledge but were seen as objective and independent of a certain locality.

4.2.2   Public Discourse and Universalized Third Parties

For a global market to emerge, universal product categories and universal quality criteria need to be institutionalized within the triadic structure of the market. This requires a public discourse that creates the triadic structure of modern markets by mediating between (potential) sellers and buyers. This insight highlights two issues. First, it draws attention to the modes of publication market actors use to stay informed about qualities and prices (trade journals, daily or specialized press, consumer magazines, advertisements, etc.). Second, it emphasizes the roles of what might be called universalized third parties: experts who act as "impartial" intermediaries or "market critics" (Zuckerman, 1999, 2000) and constantly compare and evaluate products and market trends (e.g., economic journalists, business analysts, financial and data services, news agencies, trade boards). These third parties define product categories, compare offers and suggest criteria for comparing offers, effectively "making" the market.[6] In their publications, quality and price are made visible, comparisons are performed, product recommendations are made, consumer expectations created, etc. We refer to them as "universalized" third parties to emphasize that by acting as "impartial" observers, they contribute to the legitimation and institutionalization of universal criteria of comparison and, by implication, global markets.[7]

Again, the global market for wheat is a case in point. The growing telegraph network of the mid- to late nineteenth century allowed offers from any location to be communicated instantly, enabling comparisons of up-to-date offers from all around the world (Wenzlhuemer, 2013; Wobring, 2005). Market news was able to travel fast, too. In the late nineteenth century, new kinds of publications emerged that brought together market information from different parts of the world and made them almost instantly accessible to readers. Given this situation, prices from North American grain exchanges were used as global points of reference (Bühler, 2019, pp. 141–146). The immediate local effects are evident in contemporary sources: An American counsellor, reporting from the Russian Empire in 1903, was surprised "to observe a fact which a short time ago would have been altogether incredible. The peasants on arrival at the market [in Nikolaiev] with their grain were asking 'What is the price in America according to the latest telegram?'" (cited in Goodwin & Grennes, 1998, p. 408). These prices were put in tables and published globally in newspapers and trade journals. The *Corn Trade News*, established in 1888 and one of the leading journals of its time, has been described as follows: "The theory on which Mr. Broomhall has worked is this—that a corn trade daily journal to be worth its salt, should provide its readers with the most exact knowledge, provided by cable, from all parts of the world of all events that can have any bearing on what is generally known as the statistical position of wheat" (Barker, 1920, p. 85). As we are used to this type of discourse today, it is easy to overlook its contribution to the emergence and institutionalization of global markets.

4.2.3 Imagining of Universal Market Publics

The imagining and addressing of universal publics, the third prerequisite of global markets, implies two connected issues. First, how are universal, as opposed to local (or national or regional), publics constructed? Second, how

---

6 On a similar note, but without reference to global markets, see the "judgment devices" in Karpik (2010, pp. 44–54), Beckert and Aspers (2011, pp. 19–23).
7 For a more detailed description of the concept of the "universalized third party," see Koloma Beck and Werron (2018).

is the favor (attention or appreciation) of the global public constructed as a scarce good to be competed for? Again, we can shed light on both of these points by using the example of the emerging global market for wheat:

(1) The *Corn Trade News* was read around the world. Although the journal explicitly addressed a British audience, it had a readership that was imagined as global. In the words of its founder, it gathered information globally and disseminated it on a large scale until there were "no worlds left to conquer" (Broomhall & Hubback, 1930, pp. 71–72). Similarly, the latest prices from the American grain exchanges were globally distributed in newspapers and trade publications with a local readership. Although these newspapers only served a local (or national) public, they contained information that was imagined as being relevant for a global public of market participants. On the basis of these publications, grain traders around the world had to take American prices into account, assuming that everyone else could be using these prices as points of reference, too (although in reality, it is likely that not everyone did). The imagining of global market publics thus contributed to the emergence of a global market held together by the expectation of a shared level of information. In light of this, the global convergence of wheat prices should be seen not only as a consequence of cheaper transport (prominently O'Rourke & Williamson, 2002) but also of the institutionalized assumption, based on these publications, that all potential participants on the global market observe the same products and react to the same prices.

(2) These publications also shaped the idea that resources, time, attention, and ultimately opportunities for transactions were something scarce, creating a competitive space without spatial or social limits. To a large extent, this was based on statistical information guiding market prognosis: *Beerbohm's Evening Corn Trade List* or *Dornbusch's Floating Cargoes List* registered shipments of grain en route to their destinations. The US Department of Agriculture was at the time—and still is—seen as "the final word on demand and supply conditions for agricultural commodities ... throughout the world" (Stasko, 2003, p. 225). And textbooks for prospective traders did not fail to mention that this data represented a global state of affairs (Jöhlinger, 1910, pp 321–333). Then, as now, one of the goals of these kinds of publications was to ease the uncertainty about the behavior and preferences of the global market public while, paradoxically, also contributing to the (re-)production of this very same uncertainty.

5   Conclusion

In this chapter, we have developed a model of global markets that aims to identify the social prerequisites of global markets and guide historical research on the emergence of global markets. We have argued that this requires a perspective on markets that focuses on how markets are *possible* (rather than stable), that views markets as *triadic* structures of competition (rather than dyadic trade relations), and that takes an interest in the roles of *third parties*, particularly *publics*, in the creation of markets (rather than producers). On the basis of this, we have proposed viewing global markets as a type of mediated markets: markets made possible by public discourses that address global publics while using universal product categories and applying universal criteria of comparison. The "globality" of such markets is not a matter of connections between globally dispersed market actors and trade networks. Rather, it is based on the *institutionalized imagining of universal publics* of potential buyers and is thus "global" irrespective of where and how many people actually buy and sell on these markets. The market is global if the public targeted by the market is imagined as global. We have modeled our study on product markets, particularly wheat markets, to show how such global markets first emerged in the mid- to late nineteenth century. However, we also intend the model to inspire comparative research on different types of markets, including labor markets.

What are the possible implications of our insights for the analysis of labor markets? First and foremost, our model proposes viewing global labor markets not just as global chains of production, transnational migration flows, outsourcing of labor or headhunting of specialists, but as triadic structures created in public discourse. The model therefore draws attention to specific prerequisites of global labor markets such as universal categories (of jobs or positions) and criteria (of qualifications or skills) that allow for the global comparison of jobs, but also to third parties and universal notions of publics that allow for the global comparison of job offers. This implies a number of questions regarding the social construction of global labor markets.

Do labor markets operate differently if they operate on the basis of universally standardized categories of professions (e.g., professor for economic theory; violinist)? Are some categories of jobs and criteria of quality more universalized than others (e.g., CVs demonstrating certain achievements—foreign postings, publications, etc.—for positions in international development or academia; standardized language tests)? Are there media outlets, social networks (e.g., Xing, LinkedIn, and Academia) or recruiting professionals, HR departments, or job fairs that act as market intermediaries and "universalized third parties," and how do these publications and third parties influence the formation and dynamics of global labor markets? How is the history of global labor markets related to the history of telecommunication technologies? How does it compare, in this regard, to the trajectories of global product markets? Does the emergence of universal labor market publics also date back to the mid- to late nineteenth century? Do terms such as "employer" and "employee" convey a similar universal meaning to terms such as "producer" and "consumer"? Is the role of the anonymous market public in labor markets associated with job seekers and, consequently, unknown "suppliers," rather than the mysterious consumers? If so, how are local labor markets affected by, and embedded in, the imagination of global publics of potential job applicants?

These questions indicate that research on global labor markets might benefit from comparing global labor markets with other types of global markets, using our model as a heuristic device. Comparative research on these questions might help to establish a new sociological view of global markets, one which, rather than rejecting the "globality" of markets or taking it for granted, takes it seriously as a major conceptual and empirical challenge.

References

Ang, I. (1991). *Desperately Seeking the Audience*. London; New York: Routledge.
Aspers, P. (2010). *Orderly Fashion. A Sociology of Markets*. Princeton: Princeton University Press.
Aspers, P. (2011). *Markets*. Cambridge: Polity.
Barker, A. (1920). *The British Corn Trade: From the Earliest Times to the Present Day*. London, Bath, Melbourne, New York: Isaac Pitman & Sons.
Beckert, J. (2009). The social order of markets. *Theory and Society, 38,* 245–269.
Beckert, J., & Aspers, P. (Eds.). (2011). *The Worth of Goods: Valuation and Pricing in Economy*. Oxford: Oxford University Press.
Beckert, J., & Musselin, C. (Eds.) (2013). *Constructing Quality: The Classification of Goods in the Market*. Oxford: Oxford University Press.
Broomhall, G. J., & Hubback, J. H. (1930). *Corn Trade Memories: Recent and Remote*. Liverpool: Northern Pub. Co.
Brückweh, K. (Ed.) (2011). *The Voice of the Citizen Consumer. A History of Market Research, Consumer Movements and the Political Public Sphere*. Oxford: Oxford Univ. Pr.
Bühler, M. (2019). *Von Netzwerken zu Märkten: Die Entstehung eines globalen Getreidemarktes*. Frankfurt a.M.: Campus.
Bühler, M., & Heintz, B. (2017). Seen but not noticed: The role of comparisons in economic sociology. *Economic Sociology. The European Electronic Newsletter, 18*(3), 9–18.

Bühler, M., & Werron, T. (2013). Zur sozialen Konstruktion globaler Märkte: Ein kommunikationstheoretisches Modell. In A. Langenohl & D. J. Wetzel (Eds.), *Finanzmarktpublika* (pp. 271–299). Wiesbaden: VS Verlag für Sozialwissenschaften.

Callon, M. (2007). What does it mean to say that economics is performative? In D. MacKenzie, F. Muniesa, & L. Siu (Eds.), *Do Economists Make Markets? On the Performativity of Economics* (pp. 311–357). Princeton: Princeton University Press.

Callon, M., Millo, Y., & Muniesa, F. (Eds.). (2007). *Market Devices*. Oxford: Blackwell Publishing.

Cochoy, F. (2007). A brief theory of the 'captation' of publics. Understanding the market with Little Red Riding Hood. *Theory, Culture & Society, 24*(7–8), 203–223.

Cronon, W. (1991). *Nature's Metropolis: Chicago and the Great West*. New York: W. W. Norton.

Daviron, B., & Ponte, S. (2005). *The Coffee Paradox: Global Markets, Commodity Trade and the Elusive Promise of Development*. London: Zed Books.

Fligstein, N. (2001). *The Architecture of Markets*. Princeton: Princeton University Press.

Fligstein, N., & Dauter, L. (2007). The sociology of markets. *Annual Review of Sociology, 33*, 105–128.

Friedman, T. L. (2005). *The World Is Flat*. New York: Farrar, Straus and Giroux.

Gereffi, G. (2005). The global economy. organization, governance, and development. In N J. Smelser & R. Swedberg (Eds.), *The Handbook of Economic Sociology* (pp. 160–182). Princeton, NJ, New York: Princeton University Press.

Goodwin, B. K., & Grennes, T. J. (1998). Tsarist Russia and the world wheat market. explorations in economic history. *Explorations in Economic History, 35*(4), 405–430.

Hannan, M. T. (2010). Partiality of memberships in categories and audiences. *Annual Review of Sociology, 36*, 159–181.

Heintz, B. (2010). Numerische Differenz. Überlegungen zu einer Soziologie des (quantitativen) Vergleichs. *Zeitschrift für Soziologie, 39*(3), 162–181.

Heintz, B. (2016). „Wir leben im Zeitalter der Vergleichung." Perspektiven einer Soziologie des Vergleichs. *Zeitschrift für Soziologie, 45*(5), 305–323.

Heintz, B., & Werron, T. (2011). Wie ist Globalisierung möglich? Zur Entstehung globaler Vergleichshorizonte am Beispiel von Wissenschaft und Sport. *Kölner Zeitschrift für Soziologie und Sozialpsychologie, 63*, 359–394.

Hsu, G., Negro, G., & Koçak, Ö. (Eds.) (2010). *Categories in Markets: Origins and Evolution*. Bingley: Emerald.

Jöhlinger, O. (1910). *Die Praxis des Getreidegeschäftes an der Berliner Börse: Ein Hand- und Lehrbuch für den Getreidehandel*. Berlin: Julius Springer.

Kaplan, S. (1984). *Provisioning Paris: Merchants and Millers in the Grain and Flour Trade during the Eighteenth Century*. Ithaca, London: Cornell University Press.

Karpik, L. (2010). *Valuing the Unique: The Economics of Singularities*. Princeton: Princeton University Press.

Kennedy, M. T. (2005). Behind the one-way mirror: Refraction in the construction of product market categories. *Poetics 33*(3–4), 201–226.

Knorr-Cetina, K., & Brügger, U. (2002). Global microstructures: The virtual societies of financial markets. *American Journal of Sociology, 107*, 905–950.

Knorr-Cetina, K. (2003). From pipes to scopes: The flow architecture of financial markets. *Distinktion, 7*, 7–23.

Knorr-Cetina, K. (2007). Global markets as global conversations. *Text & Talk, 27*, 705–734.

Knorr-Cetina, K., & Preda, A. (Eds.). (2005). *The Sociology of Financial Markets*. Oxford: Oxford University Press.

Koloma Beck, T., & Werron, T. (2018). Violent conflictition. Armed conflicts and global competition for attention and legitimacy. *International Journal of Politics, Culture, and Society, 31*(3), 275–296.

Krugman, P. R., & Obstfeld, M. (Eds.). (2005). *International Economics: Theory & Policy* (8 ed.). Boston: Pearson Addison Wesley.

Latour, B. (1988). Visualisation and cognition. Drawing things together. In M. Lynch & S. Woolgar (Eds.), *Representation in Scientific Practice* (pp. 19–68). Cambridge, Mass.: MIT Press.

Leifer, E. M., & White, H. C. (1987). A structural approach to markets. In M. S. Mizruchi & M. Schwartz (Eds.), *Intercorporate Relations* (pp. 85–108). Cambridge: Cambridge University Press.

Marx, K., & Engels, F. (1977). *Manifesto of the Communist Party* (2 ed.). Moscow: Progress Publishers.

O'Rourke, K. H., & Williamson, J. G. (2002). When did globalisation begin? *European Review of Economic History, 6*(1), 23–50.

Podolny, J. M. (1993). A status-based model of market competition. *American Journal of Sociology, 98*(4), 829–872.

Quack, S. (2009). "Global" markets in theory and history. Towards a comparative analysis. In J. Beckert & C. Deutschmann (Eds.), *Wirtschaftssoziologie. Sonderheft der Kölner Zeitschrift für Soziologie und Sozialpsychologie* (Vol. 49, pp. 125–142). Wiesbaden: VS Verlag für Sozialwissenschaften.

Robertson, R. (1992). Globalization as a problem *Globalization* (pp. 8–31). London: Sage.

Rosa, J. A., Porac, J. F., Runser-Spanjo, J., & Saxon, M. S. (1999). Sociocognitive dynamics in a product market. *Journal of Marketing, 63*, 64–77.

Simmel, G. (2008). Sociology of competition. *Canadian Journal of Sociology, 33*, 957–978.

Stasko, G. F. (2003). *Marketing Grain and Livestock*. Ames, Iowa: Iowa State Press.

Warner, M. (2002). Publics and counterpublics. *Public Culture, 14*(1), 49–90.

Wenzlhuemer, R. (2013). *Connecting the Nineteenth-Century World: The Telegraph and Globalization*. Cambridge: Cambridge University Press.

Werron, T. (2010). Direkte Konflikte, indirekte Konkurrenzen: Unterscheidung und Vergleich zweier Formen des Kampfes. *Zeitschrift für Soziologie, 39*, 302–318.

Werron, T. (2014). On public forms of competition. *Cultural Studies <=> Critical Methodologies, 14*(1), 62–76.

Werron, T. (2015a). Gleichzeitigkeit unter Abwesenden. Zu Globalisierungseffekten elektrischer Telekommunikationstechnologien [Special issue] *Zeitschrift für Soziologie,* (2), 251–270.

Werron, T. (2015b). What do nation-states compete for? A World-societal perspective on competition for 'soft' global goods. In B. Holzer, F. Kastner, & T. Werron (Eds.), *From Globalization to World Society. Neo-institutional and Systems-theoretical Perspectives* (pp. 85–106). London: Routledge.

Werron, T. (2015c). Why do we believe in competition? A historical-sociological view of competition as an institutionalized modern imaginary. *Distinktion: Scandinavian Jounal of Social Theory, 16*, 186–210.

White, H. C. (1981/82). Where do markets come from. *American Journal of Sociology, 87*, 517–547.

Wobring, M. (2005). *Die Globalisierung der Telekommunikation im 19. Jahrhundert: Pläne, Projekte und Kapazitätsausbauten zwischen Wirtschaft und Politik.* Frankfurt a. M.: Lang.

Zuckerman, E. W. (1999). The categorical imperative: Securities analysts and the illegitimacy discount. *American Journal of Sociology, 104*, 1398–1438.

Zuckerman, E. W. (2000). Focusing the corporate product: Securities analysts and dediversification. *Administrative Science Quarterly, 45*(3), 591–619.

Concluding Remarks and Avenues for Future Research

Ursula Mense-Petermann, Thomas Welskopp and Anna Zaharieva

With this collective volume, the ZiF Research Group has sought to put global labor markets as a phenomenon sui generis center stage. The contributions to this volume shed light on and discuss core conceptual issues that arise when it comes to conceiving of and analyzing cross-border labor markets. Overall, they provide important new theoretical and empirical insights and lay the ground for more in-depth future research on a hitherto largely neglected phenomenon.

1 Cross-Border, Transnational, or Global? How Should We Understand Labor Markets That Transgress National Borders?

As elaborated in the introductory chapter, one central issue is the question of how to conceptualize the cross-border property of labor markets that transgress national borders. Whereas references to "global" labor markets might be immediately rejected for not fitting the shape and geographical reach of most empirical cross-border labor markets, historians point to the fact that simply speaking of cross-border relations could not replace the wider notion of the "global"—not least because historically "cross-border" presupposes the existence of nation-states, a phenomenon not much older than the nineteenth century.

The contributions to the present volume, particularly those in Part 4, examine the term "global" closely and draw a detailed picture of what the "global" in "global labor markets" may refer to. All members of the ZiF Research Group agree that truly global labor markets, in the sense that workers compete for jobs and employers compete for workers, rarely exist on a planetary basis. In this narrow sense, only a handful of empirical global labor markets could be identified. Some of the contributors, therefore, prefer the terms "cross-border" or "transnational" labor markets to refer to more regionally bounded exchanges of labor power involving a limited number of nation-states. Yet, given the understanding of "the global" as developed by Eleonore Kofman, i.e., the global as one of several scales of embeddedness, and by Rebecca Gumbrell-McCormick, i.e., embeddedness of labor markets in rules and regulations set by global actors, for instance, industrial relations actors, these transnational labor markets may also be said to be globally embedded.

Whereas this volume underpins the importance of nation-states for cross-border labor markets to emerge and to be shaped that has already been emphasized in previous literature (Fligstein, 2001), to leave it at this would provide a rather narrow and one-sided picture. Considering the role and impact also of other scales beyond the national, i.e., the multilayered embeddedness (Quack in this volume) of cross-border labor markets represents a pending research gap. This volume takes the first conceptual steps toward exploring the different layers and scales of embeddedness. Yet, in particular the question of how the different scales interact in enacting, shaping, and governing cross-border labor exchanges has still to be studied in detail.

Another understanding of the "global" developed by Martin Bühler and Tobias Werron, i.e., the "global" as an imagination created in public discourses, has also rarely resonated in labor market or migration research to date. According to this viewpoint, the "globality" of labor markets is not a matter of specific networks or exchanges, but of a global horizon orienting market actors' observations, comparisons, and evaluations. Push and pull factors, i.e., the reasons for migration such as differences in earnings, better job prospects and educational opportunities as well as stronger social protection in the receiving countries or preexisting social networks, have been extensively examined in migration studies from different disciplinary angles to date. Conversely, the cognitive orientations of migrant workers and of employers as market actors—orientations that shape their agency—represent a major research gap and urgently require empirical analysis.

2 Is There a Market? Benefits and Problems of a Market Lens on Labor Migration

Any market necessitates exchange objects. For labor markets, this is no trivial requirement, considering Karl Polanyi's characterization of labor as a "fictitious commodity," and his discussion of the social tensions that result from treating labor as an exchange object to be traded on markets.

Another key contribution that helps lay the grounds for future research on global labor markets—in the sense established above—lies in the in-depth debate on the question of what the commodity exchanged in labor markets actually is. The detailed discussion from different perspectives, particularly in Part 1 of this volume, urges us to step back from established ideas about the employment relationships that many of us (in the Global North) have become accustomed to. A "global" and historicizing perspective on labor markets makes it clear that the standard employment contract is only part of the picture, and that many other patterns of allocation of labor have existed and still exist to this day in parallel and come to the fore in particular when we analyze cross-border labor exchanges.

One of the most important departure points for future research on global labor markets is the question of for which of these manifold labor regimes the term "labor market" should be reserved. The relevant debates in this volume, however, not only serve as an eye-opener for the great variety of employment and labor regimes, but also prompt the questions of why and under what conditions "unfree" forms of labor prevail in parallel to "free" wage labor in contemporary capitalism and the questions of why and how "free" wage labor employment contracts often tend to shift toward bonded forms of labor after the conclusion of the contract in cross-border labor markets (Welskopp, in this volume; see also the empirical example of the meat industry: Mense-Petermann in this volume).

Considering these debates, one might ask whether the market concept is in fact an appropriate analytical tool for examining cross-border exchanges of labor power. The detailed response—in Part 2 of this volume—as to what extent a labor market is a genuine market and what the merits of the term "market" are for analyzing the cross-border exchange of labor power underscores the benefits of the market concept, yet it also emphasizes the peculiarity of labor markets compared with other commodity or service markets. The latter calls for additional theoretical tools catering to the specifics of labor power. A market lens allows us to differentiate the market exchange of labor power (as a voluntary exchange) from other types of "labor exchange" such as trafficking or modern forms of slavery, and therefore gives us a much more detailed picture of cross-border labor migration. Moreover, processes of (self-) commodification and decommodification only come to the fore in a market perspective.

3   Enablers of Global Labor Markets: Market Makers, Infrastructure, Rules and Regulations

When it comes to the question of what enables labor to cross borders, as discussed in Part 3 of this volume, three main enablers come to mind.

As shown by Mense-Petermann (in Part 3 of this volume), enterprises, the large meatpackers in her case study, can be considered to be important market organizers. Put more generally, huge organizations in the different functional systems of society: universities (for academics), business schools and MNCs (for managers), FIFA and the large football clubs (for soccer players), the Catholic Church (for priests), to give but a few examples, are all organizations that— either as employers or as standard setting agencies—contribute to the social constitution of transnational labor markets.

These enterprises function as important *market makers* (Abolafia, 1998; Fligstein, 2001). Yet there are also other types of market actors who may play key roles in enacting, shaping, or even organizing cross-border labor markets. Markets do not emerge from scratch, but they are "fashioned" (Aspers, Bengtsson, & Dobeson, 2020) by (different types of) actors, or even "organized" (Ahrne, Aspers, & Brunsson, 2015). Most markets depend on intensive "investments in forms" (Thevenot, 1984), or organization in order to emerge and be stabilized (Engels, 2009; Fligstein, 2001). Consequently, a promising avenue for future research is to explore the social process of market making and identify the (collective) actors who as *market makers* contribute—intentionally or unintentionally—to the social constitution of cross-border labor markets.

Furthermore, nation-states can be considered even more important market makers (Ahrne et al., 2015; Beckert, 2006; Fligstein, 2001), as also stressed in this volume. In general, states contribute to the making of cross-border labor markets through their more or less restrictive and selectively permeable border and visa regimes. Studying the impact of different border regimes (e.g., the EU freedoms versus restrictive regimes that instigate illegal trafficking, and in-between border regimes such as contingent agreements, recruiting programs, etc.) and resulting employment regimes is another underexplored direction for future research.

Moreover, states play a key role in evaluating, certifying, and classifying the skills and qualifications of workers, which is a relevant stepping-stone for the functioning of cross-border labor markets, particularly in highly skilled professions and occupations. Skill certification reduces uncertainty and informational frictions inherent in employment relationships, especially in cross-border matching. Although some of these functions are delegated to private labor market intermediaries (e.g., language testing), states keep their dominant role in defining international qualification standards.

The role and importance of intermediaries in cross-border labor markets has been established in existing research from across different disciplines (Shire et al., 2018; Mense-Petermann, 2020; Lindquist, Xiang, & Yeoh, 2012). The collaborative work of the ZiF Research Group underscores this research, but it also emphasizes even stronger intermediaries as a sine qua non prerequisite of cross-border labor markets. In the absence of intermediaries, cross-border labor markets could hardly emerge. Given the lack of—or only very weakly institutionalized—rules and regulations at a transnational, or even global scale, intermediaries create private law to enact and govern transnational labor markets. They thus compensate for a lack of formal rules and regulations.

These intermediaries may be state agencies (such as the Philippines Overseas Employment Administration (POEA); see Aspers & Sandberg, 2020), temporary agencies (Shire et al., 2018, Shire, 2020), nonprofit (informal) or for-profit recruiters (Bludau, 2015), subcontractors (Mense-Petermann in this volume), talent scouts for soccer players, or illegal traffickers as well as transnational jobs or crowdsourcing platforms such as Amazon Mechanical Turk or Upwork (Vogl, 2018). There is scope for future research on the role and impact of different types of intermediaries for the enactment, shaping, and governance of cross-border labor markets, and how these matter.

Finally, (collective) actors who are not part of the market themselves but who act in the interest of participants negatively affected by the market (called "others" by Ahrne et al., 2015), namely NGOs or regulators such as the ILO or the International Organization for Migration (IOM), or journalists and other "market critics" (Zuckerman, 1999) who report and comment on markets from the point of view of an external observer (Bühler and Werron in this volume) have an important contribution to make to the organization of cross-border labor markets.

A second enabling feature for cross-border labor markets to emerge are social and physical *infrastructures*. As Lindquist et al. (2012, p. 7) emphasize, "[a]lthough much is known about why migrants leave home and what happens to them upon arrival, considerably less is known about the forms of infrastructure that condition their mobility." Transnational labor markets depend on the cross-border mobility of labor, capital, or tasks. This mobility first depends on physical infrastructures, such as information systems or platforms that aid people to become informed and apply for jobs or hire workers abroad, and/or transportation and accommodation facilities that enable relocation, or that allow and facilitate cross-border capital transfers and the relocation of tasks. Second, it depends on social infrastructures such as (informal) networks or family support (Portes, 1995) that help finance the migration and access jobs, or labor forces, respectively.

In this volume, Anna Zaharieva addresses one important type of social infrastructures, namely social networks. She shows that social networks are often used as a job search channel in situations of high uncertainty and asymmetric information between workers and potential employers. The reason for this is that networks transmit information and reduce search frictions; for instance, workers can use their social ties abroad to learn about the hiring standards and working conditions of potential employers across the border, while firms can learn more about the qualities of the prospective foreign worker. Although professional recommendations are common among highly skilled workers (see Nohl, Schittenhelm, Schmidtke, & Weiß, 2006), empirical data show that informal referrals are even more widespread in low-skilled occupations. Moreover, they are particularly relevant for immigrant workers. Multiple migration studies have pointed to the importance of informal, ethnicity-based networks for the transnational mobility of—mostly unskilled—migrants (Bommes, 2011; Kritz & Zlotnik, 1992; Massey & Zenteno, 1999). Networks play an important part in engendering the willingness to migrate and shaping decisions on destinations (Portes, 1995). At the same time, there is a shadow side of network search and informal matching, since referral hiring is often associated with low-quality jobs, for example, occupational mismatch and skill downgrading (Alaverdyan & Zaharieva, 2019; Bentolila et. al., 2010, Horvath, 2014). But if informal matching is more relevant for cross-border matching, then should we expect more skill mismatch and/or precarious working arrangements across borders? This dual feature of informal matching and other types of social infrastructures that enable and shape cross-border labor markets beyond networks still needs to be explored in future research.

Going beyond what is discussed in the present volume, physical infrastructures also represent important enablers of cross-border labor markets. As far as physical infrastructures are concerned, crowdsourcing platforms have recently attracted increasing scholarly attention (Bergvall-Kåreborn & Howcroft, 2014; Srnicek, 2017; Vogl, 2018). Yet whether and how such platforms, including cross-border job platforms, work across borders in practice remains underexplored.

Research on the "migration industry" (Gammeltoft-Hansen & Sørensen, 2013) has examined other physical infrastructures such as shuttle bus companies and other means of transportation, barracks and dormitories for unskilled migrant workers or luxurious gated compounds for expatriate managers, movers, childcare and schools that cater for migrant workers' children, interpreter services, and the like.

Finally, media infrastructures play a crucial role in providing public and private communication networks which market participants can—and often have to—use to identify market opportunities, to inform themselves about jobs and wages, and to observe possible competitors. This includes the job sections in newspapers as well as online job platforms and informal information channels such as, for instance, internet forums used by migrant communities. Analyzing these forms of physical infrastructures is an avenue for future research that promises important new insights on how cross-border labor markets are able to emerge, and how their geographical reach and structures are shaped.

Lastly, the *rules and regulations* that help enact, shape, and govern cross-border labor markets, i.e., transnational institution building (Quack in this volume), constitute a third type of enablers for cross-border labor markets. For Abolafia (1998), rules are constitutive of all markets (see also Beckert, 2009). Rules can be either formal or informal. They may evolve from the repeated interaction of buyers and sellers (Abolafia, 1998) or from market organizers such as states, enterprises, or intermediaries (Ahrne et al., 2015; Fligstein, 2001). Questions that arise here are: What types of formal and informal rules and regulations emerge to fashion cross-border labor markets? At what scales (global, national, international, or world regional) can such institution building be observed?

One type of (formal or informal) rules and regulations are those that help commodify labor power transnationally, i.e., equalize and commensurate locally and nationally different categories of qualifications. On the other hand, rules and regulations that contribute to decommodifying labor power in cross-border labor markets are another relevant issue. This connects back to the above-mentioned question regarding global industrial relations actors. As Rebecca Gumbrell-McCormick shows, these actors only possess weak powers and rules and regulations do not exert much regulatory power at the scales beyond the nation-state (with the EU as an exception here). Hence, decommodification and worker protection are urgent issues in cross-border labor markets (see also Gumbrell-McCormick & Hyman, 2020; McGovern, 2007; Mense-Petermann, 2020) which are, however, underexplored to date.

To sum up, applying a labor market lens to the cross-border mobility of workers, jobs, and/or tasks has proven particularly fruitful and offers new insights into the preconditions for these phenomena to emerge and the—more or less—problematic outcomes of this.

References

Abolafia, M. Y. (1998). Markets as cultures: An ethnographic approach. *The Sociological Review, 46*(S1), 69–85.

Ahrne, G., Aspers, P., & Brunsson, N. (2015). The organization of markets. *Organization Studies, 36*(1), 7–27. doi:10.1177/0170840614544557.

Alaverdyan S., & Zaharieva, A. (2019), Immigration, social networks and occupational mismatch, *Bielefeld Working Papers in Economics and Management, 4*.

Aspers, P., & Sandberg, C. (2020). Sailing together from different shores: labour markets and inequality on board merchant ships. *Global Networks, 20*(3), 454–471. doi:10.1111/glob.12252.

Aspers, P., Bengtsson, P., & Dobeson, A. (2020). Market fashioning. *Theory and Society, 49*(3), 417–438.

Beckert, J. (2006). Wer zähmt den Kapitalismus. In J. Beckert & W. Streeck (Eds.), *Transformationen des Kapitalismus. Festschrift für Wolfgang Streeck zum sechzigsten Geburtstag* (pp. 425–442). Frankfurt am Main: Campus.

Beckert, J. (2009). The social order of markets. *Theory and Society, 38*(3), 245–269.

Bentolila, S., Michelacci, C., & Suarez, J. (2010). Social contacts and occupational choice. *Economica 707* (305), 20–45.

Bergvall-Kåreborn, B., & Howcroft, D. (2014). Amazon Mechanical Turk and the commodification of labour. *New Technology, Work and Employment, 29*(3), 213–223.

Bludau, H. (2015). Creating a transnational labor chain between Eastern Europe and the Middle East: A case study in healthcare. *InterDisciplines. Journal of History and Sociology, 6*(1).

Bommes, M. (2011). Migrantennetzwerke in der funktional differenzierten Gesellschaft. In M. Bommes & V. Tacke (Eds.), *Netzwerke in der funktional differenzierten Gesellschaft* (1st ed., pp. 241–259). Wiesbaden: vs Verlag für Sozialwissenschaften.

Engels, A. (2009). Die soziale Konstitution von Märkten. [Special issue]. *Kölner Zeitschrift für Soziologie und Sozialpsychologie, 49*, 67–86.

Fligstein, N. (2001). *The Architecture of Markets: An Economic Sociology of Twenty-First Century Capitalist Societies.* Princeton, NJ: Princeton Univ. Press.

Gammeltoft-Hansen, T., & Sørensen, N. N. (Eds.) (2013). *Routledge Global Institutions Series: The Migration Industry and the Commercialization of International Migration.* Vol. 69. London, New York: Routledge.

Gumbrell-McCormick, R., & Hyman, R. (Eds.) (2020). In search of global labour markets. [Special issue]. *Journal of Industrial Relations, 62*(2), 167–184.

Horvath, G. (2014). Occupational mismatch and social networks. *Journal of Economic Behavior and Organization, 106*(3), 442–468.

Kritz, M. M., & Zlotnik, H. (1992). Global interactions: Migration systems, processes, and politics. In M. M. Kritz (Ed.) *International Migration Systems.* (pp. 1–16). Oxford: Clarendon Press.

Lindquist, J., Xiang, B., & Yeoh, B. S. A. (2012). Introduction: Opening the black box of migration: Brokers, the organization of transnational mobility and the changing political economy in Asia. *Pacific Affairs, 85*(1), 7–19.

Massey, D. S., & Zenteno, R. M. (1999). The dynamics of mass migration. *Proceedings of the National Academy of Sciences, 96*(9), 5328–5335.

McGovern, P. (2007). Immigration, labour markets and employment relations: Problems and prospects. *British Journal of Industrial Relations, 45*(2), 217–235.

Mense-Petermann, U. (2020). Theorizing transnational labour markets: A research heuristic based on the new economic sociology. *Global Networks, 20*(3), 410–433.

Nohl, A.-M., Schittenhelm, K., Schmidtke, O., & Weiß, A. (2006). Cultural capital during migration—A multi-level approach to the empirical analysis of labor market integration amongst highly skilled migrants. *Forum: Qualitative Social Research, 7*(3).

Portes, A. (1995). Economic sociology and the sociology of immigration: A conceptual overview. In A. Portes (Ed.), *The Economic Sociology of Immigration. Essays on Networks, Ethnicity and Entrepreneurship* (pp. 1–40). New York.

Shire, K. (2020). The social order of transnational migration markets. *Global Networks, 20*(3), 434–453.

Shire, K., Heinrich, S., Imai, J., Mottweiler, H., Tünte, M., & Wang, C. C. (2018). Private labour market intermediaries in cross-border labour markets in Europe and Asia: International norms, regional actors and patterns of cross-border labour mobility. In S. Quack, I. Schulz-Schaeffer, K. Shire, & A. Weiß (Eds.), *Transnationalisierung der Arbeit* (pp. 155–183). Wiesbaden: Springer Fachmedien Wiesbaden.

Srnicek, N. (2017). *Platform Capitalism*. Cambridge, UK, Malden, MA: Polity.

Thevenot, L. (1984). Rules and implements: Investment in forms. *Social Science Information, 23*(1), 1–45.

Vogl, E. (2018). *Crowdsourcing-Plattformen als neue Marktplätze für Arbeit. Die Neuorganisation von Arbeit im Informationsraum und ihre Implikationen*. Baden-Baden: Hampp.

Zuckerman, E. W. (1999). The categorical imperative: Securities analysts and the illegitimacy discount. *American Journal of Sociology, 104*, 1398–1438.

Index

abolition of slavery 30
academics 6–7, 284
accumulation 91–2
  capital's 90
  primary 91
  primitive 69
action
  coordinating 203–4
  industrial 128
  political 59
action repertoires 154–55
actor-centered perspective on transnational labor markets 195
actor constitution in markets 155
actors 78–79, 107–15, 129, 148–50, 153–55, 191–93, 195, 201–5, 210–12, 222–23, 241–44, 253, 262–64, 270–71, 284–85
administration 176, 256
advocacy 246, 249
Africa 22, 30, 40, 66, 76
agencies 4, 121, 179–80, 183, 196, 282, 284
  governmental 222, 240–41, 243
  personnel 169
  recruitment 148
  temporary 149, 156, 196, 227, 285
agency work 74, 209
agreements 78, 140, 166, 251–52
  collective 71, 154, 190, 193, 241
allocating labor 15–16, 50, 56, 58, 60–62
allocation modes 133, 140
Amazon Mechanical Turk 110, 285
associations 26, 56, 66, 193, 240–42, 245–47, 249–54
asylum seekers 234
asymmetries 126–27, 165–67, 265
audiences 203, 265–67
austerity packages 74
authority 29, 81, 123, 126, 209
  centralized 167, 212
  colonial 65
  private 122, 128–29
  sectoral 211
automation 192, 234

bargaining 58, 71, 135, 140, 151
battle for talents 5

Bentham 68
Bielefeld approach 88, 90–91
blaming 128–29, 190, 193–94
bondage 45–47, 138–39
bonded
  forms of labor 283
  labor regimes 51
  servitude 61
border regimes 155–56, 184, 195, 284
borders 2–3, 150–51, 165, 169, 176, 180, 225, 230, 283, 285–86
boundaries 35, 199, 208–9, 211–12, 220, 222, 225, 249
  institutional 210
  national state 199
  sectorial 211
  socio-economic 227
  spatial 213
  territorial 209
bourgeois classes 92
  nineteenth-century 137, 139
bourgeoisie 219
brain drain 3, 94
Bretton Woods 244, 247
Brexit 231–32
Britain 44, 69, 160, 231, 235
business model 64, 75, 80
buyers 53–54, 104, 107, 109–12, 121–22, 125–26, 138, 140, 149, 152–53, 266, 268, 270, 273
  of labor 126

capital 42, 45–46, 50, 52, 68–69, 89, 91, 95, 220–21
capital and labor 50, 91, 239
capitalism 7, 15–19, 34–36, 46–48, 50–52, 54, 56, 58–62, 66, 82, 85, 90, 97–98, 106, 234–35, 260, 283
  financialized 16
  industrial 51, 58, 70, 89, 119
  neoliberalist 88
  organized 226, 234, 238
  shareholder value 74
  social 42
  state-organized 88
capitalist
  class relations 51, 59

capitalist (cont.)
    countries   37, 41
    economy   7, 88–90, 95–96, 225
    production   61, 89, 90–92, 96
    system   55, 220
care   54, 88–94, 96–99, 124, 148, 151
    regimes   88, 93–94
    sector   88
    work   17, 88–91, 93, 96
    workers   4, 94–95, 233
categories of comparison   272
categories of jobs   276
chains   4, 145, 148–49, 192
    care   88, 94–95
    global commodity/value   262
    subcontractor   190
channels   77, 148–49, 151, 171, 173–75, 177, 179–80, 239
    informal hiring   172
    informal information   286
childcare   93, 286
child laborer   22
China   4, 25–26, 28, 30–31, 35, 38, 220
circular migration   95, 120
    corridors   124
citizenship rights   72, 96, 202
classes   139, 154
    laboring   140
    middle   147
click working   61
coercion   24, 27, 67, 139–40
    physical   20, 31, 62
cognitive orientations   146, 155, 157, 282
collective bargaining   50, 115, 190, 201, 252, 254
    organized   22
colonial
    empires   219
    powers   16, 65
    rulers   28, 32, 92
colonialism   28–29, 36–37, 69, 92, 210
commodification   70, 73, 146, 154, 156, 211–13, 283
    of labor   15, 135, 138–39, 141, 154
commodities   20–22, 52–54, 56, 68, 70, 73, 120–25, 128, 154, 282–83
commodity markets   7, 22, 52, 135
Commonwealth   229, 232
Communist Manifesto   260

commuting   172, 174–76, 179, 180
companies   64, 66, 109–10, 113, 169, 171, 173–74, 176, 178, 180, 201, 203, 207, 209–10, 267
competition   21, 35, 41–42, 59, 107–8, 110–11, 113, 121–24, 134, 139–41, 143, 154–55, 200, 207, 211–13, 265–66
competitiveness   73–74, 93
competitors   155, 263, 267, 286
conflicts   50, 55, 91, 202–3, 207, 250
connections   42, 60–61, 152, 173, 177, 192, 276
    economic   40
    long-distance   33
consumerism   137–38
consumers   78, 186, 220, 265–70, 277
consumption   3, 54–5, 92, 137, 219, 260, 262
contingent agreements   188, 284
contracts   29, 31, 53, 55, 68–72, 77, 79–80, 107, 109–12, 114, 125, 150–51, 188
    free market   58
    limited-term   123
    short-term   74
    social   41, 243
    temporary   128, 234
    zero hours   74, 221
contract workers   185
control   82, 114, 200, 202, 211–13, 222, 225, 227, 230, 232, 235, 239
conventions   65–66, 207, 213, 242, 245, 252, 262
cooperation   127, 200, 250, 263
    in markets   200
coordination   106, 200, 202, 204, 210, 248, 254, 263
    in labor markets   2
    problems   8, 125, 153
Corona/covid-19   95–96, 166, 194, 222, 233–34
corporations   40, 73
    multinational   73, 219
costs   29, 34, 73, 80, 82, 91, 126–27, 170, 230
countries   3–4, 36–39, 41–42, 70–74, 76, 87, 90, 94–95, 147–49, 155, 169–70, 172–74, 177–78, 183–84, 188, 221–22, 229, 235, 248–49
    developed   77, 81, 178
    developing   75, 248
    foreign   151, 169, 187

home 87, 151, 155, 173, 176, 188, 193, 206–7, 252
low-wage 41
nonindustrialized 66
OECD 41, 264
sending 3, 34, 124, 127
country of origin 95, 123–24, 146, 151, 170, 230
crafts 166, 186
crisis 74, 82, 90, 92, 248
current world health 221
financial 96, 173, 222
global care 87
refugee 173
reproductive 88, 93
cross-border
capital transfers 285
commuters 170, 176
exchanges of labor 165–66
job platforms 286
labor exchanges 120, 283
labor markets 119–20, 124, 126, 128, 146–47, 149, 152–57, 166–67, 184, 282–87
labor mobility 4, 7, 200–201, 203, 207, 239, 285
matching 7, 145, 149, 169, 171, 177–78, 180, 284, 286
subcontracting 120, 166

debt bondage 7, 78, 127
Decent Work campaign 246
Declaration on International Investment and Multinational Enterprises 247
decommodification 7, 15, 64, 70–73, 82, 141, 146, 154, 157, 283, 287
deglobalization 222
deinstitutionalization 199–211, 213
denationalization of labor markets 141
deportation 67, 77, 81, 126, 128
deregulation 93, 208, 211
destination country 77, 124, 126, 146, 170–71, 173, 177–78, 180
development economics 156
digitalization 221
discourses 7, 67, 149, 220, 226, 228, 268–69, 274
hegemonic 132
on labor markets 7

discrimination 35, 177, 228
division of labor 89, 96, 186, 220, 226, 250
domestic
economy 137–38, 140
services 61
servitude 61
work 89, 92
workers 124, 213–14
work sector 148

earnings 3, 122, 282
Eastern European service providers 155
Eastern European Workers 185
economic globalization 5, 64, 205–6
economics 6–7, 132, 134–35, 138–39, 142–43, 152–53, 265
economic sociology 7, 103–4, 119–21, 153, 157, 265, 272
of labor markets 119
economy 2–3, 90, 109, 120, 139, 232–33
education 88, 91, 119, 152–53, 175, 179, 233, 273
elite 57
higher 175
embeddedness 7, 57, 103, 146, 149, 153, 281–82
multilayered 157, 282
emigration 3, 146–47
employees 5, 37–40, 50, 56, 71, 174–75, 179–80, 185, 187, 195, 200
employer-employee relationship 70
employer functions 195
employer interests 249
employers 21–22, 27–30, 36–38, 41–42, 54–55, 71–73, 76, 80–81, 110, 126, 128, 148–49, 173–74, 189–95, 210, 240–43, 245–47, 249–51, 253, 281–82
employers' associations 250
and trade unions 249
employment 35, 38, 64, 71, 126–27, 151–53, 177–78, 186–88, 233, 253
atypical 74
capitalist 70
decent 127
female 59, 87–88, 96
irregular 88
long-term 32, 42
regular 67
skilled 233

employment
  agencies   169, 174–75, 209, 239
  contracts   71, 80, 120–22, 125–29, 150, 187, 189, 283
  opportunities   74, 88, 95, 123, 169
  regimes   70, 184, 187, 189, 193–94, 284
  regulations   72, 166
  relations   51–52, 106, 119, 123, 126–27, 129, 187–89
  relationships   41, 51, 74, 93, 95, 176, 189, 282, 284
ethnic niching   4, 145
Europe   15, 33, 35–36, 38, 40, 72–73, 88–89, 91, 93
  postwar   64, 70, 248
  preindustrial   18, 27
  southern   174
European
  Commission   228–29, 248, 251
  Community   227
  Convention on Human Rights   66
  employment policies   4, 12
  free movement rights   232
  industrial relations system   241
  labor markets   229
  organizations of employers   251
  Posted Workers Directive   210, 213
  Trade Union Confederation   251
  trade unions   252
  Union   38, 41, 166, 222–23, 226–27, 241, 243, 248, 251
  Works Councils   252
exchange of labor power   120, 122, 125, 129, 195, 201
exploitation   41–42, 51, 65, 75, 77–79, 83, 90–92, 121, 129, 141, 166, 189

factor markets   46–47, 140
Fair Labor Association   209
family networks   200
feminization
  of labor   87
  of migration   87
fictitious commodities   64, 68, 70, 154, 282
financialization   64, 72
financial markets   43, 73, 112, 261, 273, 279
flows   57, 148
  cross-border   198
  global migratory   221
  inter-regional   219
  migrant   229
  of labor   148
  remittance   95
forced labor   16, 59, 61, 64–66, 75, 78–83, 109, 150, 210, 213
Forced Labour Convention   65, 210, 246
foreign
  direct investment   95
  postings   276
  subcontractors   190
for-profit recruiters   149, 151, 154, 156, 195, 285
freedom   51–56, 58, 67–68, 71, 75, 83–85, 140–41, 166, 188, 245, 247, 252
  individual   52
  legal   53
  personal   55
  of association and collective bargaining   252
  of contract   64
  of domicile   140
  of mobility   166
  of movement   58, 95, 141, 231
  of services   166
  of trade   140
free labor   24, 52, 56, 62, 64, 68
free movement   51, 190, 227–28, 230, 236
free wage labor   16, 19, 26–27, 31–32, 35, 50–63

garment workers   213
Gastarbeiter ('guest workers')   187–88
gated compounds   286
gender   42, 87–99, 138, 152
  equality   93, 95
  inequalities   92
  regimes   93, 124, 153
  studies   90, 152
gendered division of labor   17, 88–90, 92, 96, 123
General Agreement on Tariffs and Trade   248
geographical distance   263
geographical proximity   172
German
  economy   187
  employers   190
  employment and social security laws   190
  Federal Employment Agency   176

INDEX 295

government 187–89, 194
labor and wage standards 194
labor law 166, 187, 190, 193
labor market 173
Posting Law 190, 194
Reich 141
social history 16
social security provisions 187, 190
Trade Union Confederation 189, 193
Global Compact 246
global
capitalism 42, 64, 82, 219
care chains 88, 94–95
chains of production 276
chains of trade and manufacturing 262
cities 264
class 142
economy 77
exchange of goods and services 87
governance 142, 241, 256–57
industrial relations 258, 287
inequalities 147
labor force 5, 39
labor governance 254
labor history 51
labor markets 2, 4–8, 15, 88–89, 93–97, 166, 183–84, 198, 214, 221–23, 225–37, 254, 260–62, 276–77, 281–83
market publics 275
markets 31, 96, 223, 260–65, 267–79
migrant streams 40
North 40, 87, 92, 94, 222, 282
political institutions 263
production 39, 75, 77, 87, 92, 129, 165
regulation 201, 254
reserve army 147
scale 17, 26, 28, 157, 199, 221–22, 225, 254, 260, 285
South 36, 39–41, 87, 90, 92, 94, 220
spaces 220, 232
supply chains 39, 209
system 223, 241, 255
unionism 251
value chains 78
workforce 110, 250
globality 223, 261–64, 276–77, 282
globalization 2–3, 5–6, 72–73, 78, 87, 215, 219–20, 223–26, 230, 236, 257–61, 264, 279–80

from below 253
of labor markets 5–6
of migration 223
Global Union Federations 250
globe 7, 37, 94, 214, 220–21, 260, 262, 272
governance 165, 167, 203–4, 225–26, 285
of cross-border labor markets 285
governments 69, 72–73, 190, 193, 232–34, 239–41, 243–47, 249, 251, 253–54
national 223, 243, 246
guilds 57, 59, 109, 143, 200

health
care 87, 124, 149, 195
professionals 151, 232–33
sectors 230, 232
hiring 19, 21, 31–32, 34, 109, 126, 139, 227
history 6, 16–49, 59–60, 62, 77, 87, 123, 141–42, 219, 222, 235, 277
home communities 127
home country regulations 188
host countries 51, 155–56, 169, 187, 189, 207
households 27, 38, 88–89, 92–95
housewifization 91
human rights 66, 81, 128, 189
human trafficking 65, 150, 213

identities 111, 114–15, 155, 157, 212
ideology 57, 69, 103, 136, 229
ILO 15–16, 39, 65–66, 70, 200–201, 207, 210, 213, 243–50, 254–55
Constitution 245
conventions 67, 128, 209, 213–14, 245, 254
core conventions 252–53
definition of labor migration 151
labor standards 246
immigrants 24, 148, 165, 170–71, 173, 178, 228
immigrant workers 170–73, 177–78, 286
immigration 3, 41, 147, 229, 231, 233
controlled 227
illegal 80
impact of 3, 147
work-related 231
imprisonment 77, 79–80
income 20, 23, 27, 65, 82, 121, 151
indebtedness 77

industrialization 59, 89, 123
industrialization policies 142
industrial relations 6, 128, 153–54, 201, 207, 239–41, 243, 253–57
   actors 222, 244, 253, 282
   institutions 242, 248
   systems 70, 153, 241
inequalities 71, 89, 248, 262
   economic 36
   growing income 74
informal institutions 121, 199
informal labor brokers 148
infrastructures 149, 165, 283, 285
   material 148
   media 286
   migration 148, 157
   physical 285–86
insecurity 73–74, 222
institutional
   assemblages 198–200, 211, 214
   change 167, 199, 202, 205–7, 209, 213
   order 204
   repertoires 206
   rules 203–5, 208–11, 214
institutionalization 72, 139, 167, 199–203, 205, 207–8, 211–13, 274
institution building 165, 167, 206, 208–9, 287
institutions 108–11, 119, 146, 148, 151, 153–56, 195, 198–200, 202–3, 205–8, 239–40, 242, 246–48, 253–54
   decommodifying 157
   international 241
   regional 225
   subnational 206–7
   supranational 206–7
   wage-setting 201
   work-related 138
interactions 56, 58, 149, 201, 222, 240–41, 263–64, 270, 287
interests 27–28, 74, 77, 107, 121, 124, 127, 129, 149–50, 258, 260, 262–63, 265–67
   class 72
   powerful 78
   private 68
   public 139
   vested 272
intergovernmental institutions 220, 223, 243–45, 247, 249–50, 254

intermediaries 16, 29, 37, 126–27, 148–50, 152–55, 174–75, 177, 180, 284–85, 287
   private 126, 201
international
   bodies 242, 249
   border regime 187
   financial institutions 247
   framework agreements 252
   industrial relations actors 253
   industrial relations system 239, 241, 253–54
International
   Labour Organization (ILO), 15, 65, 85, 200, 215, 220, 243–44, 255–56
   Labour Conference 247, 250
   Labour Office 160, 247, 256
   Monetary Fund 247
   Organization for Migration (IOM) 285
   Trade Secretariats 250
   Trade Union Confederation 39, 250
international trade unionism 251, 253

job candidates 173, 178
jobs 34–35, 39, 81–82, 110, 112–14, 126–27, 149–52, 155, 165–66, 169–73, 175–78, 180–82, 184–85, 187, 191, 194, 200, 276, 285–87
   decent 82
   full-time 177
   low-skilled 166
   middle-skilled 233
   part-time 166, 177–78
   precarious 16
   skilled 29, 192, 233–34
   temporary 136
job search 11–2, 155, 169–82
   channel 169, 285
   methods 176, 181
job seekers 135, 228, 277
jurisdictions 79, 123, 189, 199, 207, 211, 214–15, 221
   non-territorial 212
   territorial 120, 213

kafala 151
knowledge exchange 134

labor 4–7, 15–18, 21, 61, 70–71, 79, 87–93, 96–97, 103–4, 108–10, 119–28, 132–42,

INDEX   297

165–67, 199–200, 210–12, 220–22, 232–35, 282–83
  cross-border   3, 104, 119, 146, 165
  global   87, 128–29
  low-skilled   4, 166
  skilled   139, 231
labor
  activists   201, 210
  allocation   16, 135–36, 138–39, 142–43, 200, 283
  contract   16–17, 79, 109, 113, 139
  costs   192, 272
  economics   19, 43, 254
  exchanges   5, 34, 104, 119–20, 122, 127–28, 149, 165, 283
  intermediaries   34
  law   128, 194, 200, 202, 254
  legislation   201
  migrants   148, 151, 170
  migration   2, 4, 95–96, 104, 145, 147, 149–52, 230, 235, 282
    cross-border   4, 104, 146–47, 152–53, 156–57, 283
    female   88
  mobility   120, 166
  movements   59, 72, 124, 221, 242, 251
  process   37, 90, 125, 127
  recruitment   34, 42
  regimes   15, 59–60, 62, 283
  regulations   167, 199, 208, 211–13
  relations   27–28, 35, 41, 50–51, 56, 75, 165, 201, 207, 211
  rights   95, 189
  sociology   43, 104, 120, 127
  standards   73, 127–8, 209
  supply   222, 226
labor markets   2–8, 15–16, 18–22, 24–26, 41–42, 70–71, 103–4, 106–36, 138–43, 145–47, 150–54, 156–58, 191–92, 198–200, 221–23, 225, 227–28, 239–41, 276–77, 281–83
  construction of   222
  cross-border   126, 128–9, 146, 149, 156, 184, 281
  history of   123, 133
  migrant   127, 129
  operation of   71, 119, 122, 129
  professional   187
  regional   229

  regulated   123
  unskilled   231
labor power   19, 21–22, 43, 53–54, 68, 70, 76, 103, 109–10, 112–13, 120–22, 124–29, 146–47, 154–57, 191–92, 199–201, 281, 283
  commodify   287
  cross-border exchange of   149–50, 283
  decommodifying   287
  market exchange of   125, 157, 283
  migrant   127
  reproduction of   90, 93
  sellers of   111, 124
  use of   121–22, 125, 200
laborers   27, 29–31, 34–35, 54, 56, 69, 91, 121–22, 125–26, 129, 139–41
laborforce   4, 27, 38, 42, 91–92, 139, 165, 183–84, 285
  cheap   4, 183
  foreign   186–87, 191, 195
  indigenous   36
  world's   23
language barriers   165
language proficiency/skills   169, 171, 173, 177, 180
Latin America   40, 94
legal limbos   154, 157, 194
limitations of global markets   263
livelihoods   55, 62, 89, 122–23
logistics   39, 43, 149, 207
low-wage work   12

Maastricht Treaty   251
macrostructures   121, 153
  cognitive   146
  cultural   103
  institutional   153
manufacturing   26, 33, 174–75, 179, 262
marketability   154
marketable objects   154–55
market
  actors   53, 68, 113, 121, 124, 153–55, 263, 267, 282, 284
  audience   267
  categories   109, 269
  categorization   106
  competition   69
  concept   7, 101, 103–4, 132–33, 146–61, 283
    economic-sociological   156–57
    neoclassical   156

market (*cont.*)
  critics   267, 273, 285
  culture   121
  definitions   195
  economy   89
  ethics   121
  exchange   103, 121, 128, 149, 156
  failures   121
  forces   70, 73, 157
  genres and subtypes   272
  identities   114
  institutions   138, 200
    emerging cross-border labor   198
    national labor   201, 205, 208
  intermediaries   276, 284
  lens   152, 156, 282–83
  makers   7, 148, 152–54, 183–97, 283–84
  model   151, 265, 269
  organizers   149, 152–54, 156, 287
  participants   103, 135, 142, 155, 263, 267, 271, 275, 286
  perspective   104, 145, 156, 283
  prerequisites   108
  publics   270, 277
  regulations   129, 138, 263
  societies   56, 119, 123, 140
  sociology   104, 106, 129, 143, 153, 265–66
  theory   103, 113, 115, 119–31, 138
marketization   103, 137, 139, 141–42
marketplace   122, 132, 135, 137–39
  crowdsourcing   110
markets   4, 15, 18–22, 35–36, 43, 53, 103–18, 120–24, 126–36, 138–43, 145–46, 149–55, 157–59, 195–96, 199–201, 261–74, 276–80, 282–85, 287–88
  domestic   137, 140
  fixed-role   112
  for migrant labor   128
  for wage labor   18, 31
  national   36
  international   73
  slave   22, 24–25
  switch-role   112
markets in new economic sociology   261
Marxist   147
  feminist   88, 90
  critique of capitalism   90
matching   150–51, 165–66, 187–88, 191

  informal   286
  mechanisms   169
matching of migrant workers to jobs   151
matching theory   191
media   4, 183, 189–90, 267
Medieval Europe   21, 200
mercantilism   140
merchants   25, 28
methodological nationalism   166, 213
migrant labor   123–24, 126, 128–29, 166, 225
  low-wage   128
  protecting   129
migrants   40, 123–24, 126–28, 147–48, 150–52, 165–66, 178, 180, 230, 232, 234, 285–86
  documented   171
  family   234
  female   88
  highly-skilled   232
  international   40, 87
  long-term   170
  self-employed   148
  short-term   170
  undocumented   171
migrants and refugees   81
migrants in precarious jobs   16
migrant workers   76, 124, 126, 151, 154, 157, 165–66, 169, 173, 282, 286
migration   3, 87–88, 126, 145–46, 149–52, 156–58, 170, 178, 228–31, 285
  channels   151, 155
  cross-border   148
  economics   148, 152
  female   88, 95–96
  flows   30, 75, 146–47, 152, 156–57
  forced   87
  industry   153, 184, 286
  large-scale   26
  logistification of   148
  long range   2
  lower-skilled   234
  managed   229–30
  pattern   95
  permanent   221
  policies   88
  regimes   80, 96, 132, 146, 160, 230
  research   4, 129, 282
  return   127
  skilled   233

INDEX

studies   3–4, 6, 104, 145–46, 148–50, 157, 282
systems   31, 147, 157
theories   147, 151–52
transnational   148
unskilled   234
Migration Advisory Committee   233–34
minimum wages   71, 78, 189–90, 227
　European   252
　negotiated   189, 193
　statutory   189–90, 193
mobility   148–49, 165–66, 227–29, 239, 285
　cross-border   151, 169, 172, 184, 239, 285, 287
　patterns   228
　regimes   227
　studies   165
modern markets   268–70, 273
modern (forms of) slavery   64, 66, 75–76, 78–79, 83–85, 157, 283
movement rights   227
multi-scalar processes of institutionalization and deinstitutionalization   199

NAFTA   207, 226
naming and shaming   245–47, 249
national
　borders   2, 5, 7–8, 36, 120, 123, 155–56, 201, 214, 225, 281
　employment regimes   78
　employment regulation   241
　industrial relations systems   189
　institutions   120, 123, 142, 198
　labor markets   3, 74, 145–46, 152, 165–67, 183, 185, 208
　labor movements   72
　labor regimes   72
nations   94, 137, 140, 166, 239, 242, 244, 248
　developing   39, 78
　industrialized Western   210
　European   244
　state socialist   19
nation state/s   7, 16, 74, 104, 132–33, 136–38, 140–43, 194, 198–200, 208, 225–28, 239–40, 244–45, 247, 263, 284, 287
neoliberal
　capitalism   220, 225
　globalization   41, 73, 81, 253

　ideologies   103
　policies   81
neoliberalism   80, 82, 220, 226, 249
network hiring   180
network referral   171
networks   7, 33, 113, 145–46, 148–49, 165, 170, 172–73, 282, 285–86
　economic   262
　ethnicity-based   286
　industry-based   250
　migrant   165
　personal   155, 172
　private communication   286
　professional   176–77
non-governmental organizations   243–44, 253
nonmarket prerequisites of markets   103, 153
nurses   232–34

object of exchange   15, 104, 112, 282
object of trade   6, 106–7, 112–13, 124
occupational mismatch   166, 177, 180–81, 286–87
occupations   35, 80–81, 156, 166, 176, 214, 232, 284
　female   88
　globalized   239
　low-skilled   234, 286
　skilled   233
OECD   38, 244, 247, 249, 254
offshoring   4, 183
order in markets   110, 121
organization of markets   149, 287
organization of reproduction work   59
organization of work   127–28
organizations   59, 62, 106–8, 111, 116, 127–28, 149, 184, 240, 249, 251, 253–54, 283–85
　global labor   165
　intergovernmental   242, 245–46
　intermediary   169, 174
　professional   176
outmigration   129
outsourcing of labor   276
ownership   20, 72, 120, 122, 125

pandemic   222
patterns   42, 58, 60, 145, 202–3, 270, 283
　changing recruitment   37
　complex migration   148

patterns (*cont.*)
    migratory 152
    new career 5
people smugglers 77, 81
performativity of markets 269
period
    early modern 26, 219
    interwar 200
    postwar 220
    post-wwii 219
peripheries 7, 211, 220
person 53–54, 57, 59, 62, 65–66, 75, 77, 109, 111, 114, 120, 148, 150–51
    enslaved 22
    free 52, 68
    self-employed 38
perspective 5–6, 103–4, 112–13, 122, 146–48, 150, 199, 201, 262–64, 266, 269–70
    actor-centered 195
    economic-sociological 157
    gendered 59
    historical 42, 60
    historicizing 283
    interdisciplinary 145
    market-sociological 104
    micro-sociological 202
    post-structuralist 138
Philadelphia Declaration 15, 70
place 20–21, 24, 29, 32, 91, 108, 150, 187–89, 193–94, 201, 262
plantations 26
    sugar 30
    tea 30–31, 43
planters 29–30
    coffee 24
platforms 110, 221, 285–86
    crowdsourcing 285–86
    online trading 134
policies 132, 243–44, 249, 251
    anti-social 73
    austerity 142
    colonial 76
    economic 72
    expansive 230
    institutional 202
    interventionist labor market 234
political economists 57, 226
political economy 90, 120–21

politico-economic approaches 3
population 16, 25–26, 35, 66, 86, 121, 124
    male 18
    relative surplus 147
    rural 27
    total migrant 229
post-Brexit regimes of migration 231
postcolonial migrations 231
posting 7, 188–90, 227
    regime 188, 191, 193
powers 33, 70–72, 76, 79, 106, 109, 125, 128, 192–93, 222, 245–49, 251, 253–54
    bargaining 71
    bounded 244
    veto 247
    weak 287
power structures 42
practices of comparison 272
precarity/precarization 41–42, 93, 232
prerequisites 108, 157, 223, 261, 276
    nonmarket 153
    sociocultural 269
prerequisites
    for cross-border labor markets 157
    for global markets 223
    of global labor markets 276
    of global markets 260, 263, 270
prices 20–21, 80, 108, 110, 121, 125, 139, 150, 154, 261, 265, 267, 271–75
pricing in labor markets 110
private property 57, 69, 71
privilege 32, 220–21
    bourgeois 58
    male 41
producer markets 265, 269
producers 58, 185, 190, 192, 194, 220, 223, 261, 263–68, 273, 276–77
    and audiences 267
    and consumers 265
production 50, 53, 56, 87, 89–90, 121–22, 126–29, 137, 186, 200–201, 219–21, 226, 272–73, 275–76
    and reproduction 89
    factors 142, 226
    models 185–87, 191–92
    regimes 50
    sites, cheaper 222
    system 153

INDEX 301

product
    categories 263, 270–73
    qualities 271–73
    standards 262–63, 269–70
professionals 5, 229, 275
professions 17, 52, 138, 151, 156, 214, 239, 276, 284
profit 42, 56, 70, 127, 147, 153, 186, 192
profiteers 153, 192
prohibition 79–80
proletarian concept of labor 136
proletarianization 69, 92
proletarians/proletariat 27, 69, 92
property 19–20, 22, 52, 54, 68, 125–26, 272
    relations 126
    rights 20–21, 107
proprietor 20, 22, 24, 53
    private 53
prostitution 41, 75, 81
protected segments of labor 123
public discourse 223, 261, 268–71, 273, 276, 282
publics 223, 261, 268–70, 274, 276
push and pull factors for migration 3

qualifications 54, 138, 153–54, 169, 177, 200, 229, 233, 177, 276, 284, 287

race 43, 110, 119, 152, 160
rationality 204
    formal 54
recommodification 74, 80, 232
recruiters, specialized 195
recruiting programs 284
recruitment 33, 127, 129, 145, 152, 165–66, 187, 235
    channels 172
referral hiring 169, 171, 174–78, 180–81, 286
referrals 165–66, 169–72, 174, 176–80
    informal 286
regimes 23, 51, 61, 93, 148, 188, 227, 229
    absolutist 28
    colonial 65
    global visa 149
regimes of exploitation 51
regional level 142, 243, 251
regions 31–32, 40, 66, 151, 155, 194, 198, 212, 240, 246

regulation
    of labor markets 123, 139
    of migration 157
regulations 95–96, 119–21, 123, 156–57, 165, 167–68, 187–88, 199, 201, 210, 212–13, 243, 252–53, 285, 287
    international 201, 243, 248–49, 263
    national 166, 243
    regional 241
    supranational 239
regulators 201, 285
regulatory
    frameworks 193, 210
    powers 223, 226, 239, 244–45, 287
    regimes 72, 80
    systems 189, 243, 249, 254
reinstitutionalization 205
relations of production 127
relocation of production 220–21
remittances 3, 150–51
    migrant 95
remuneration 53, 153
representation 124, 128, 193, 244–47
    trade union 124
reproduction 7, 54, 89, 93, 119, 122, 129, 200, 212, 268
reproductive labor 40, 89–90, 94, 96
research
    in economic sociology 272
    on global labor markets 277, 282–83
    on labor migration 104
reserve army 41, 142, 147
residence 76, 227–28, 234
    temporary 231
resistance 64, 79, 82, 190
    union-based 15
resources 59–60, 71, 90, 92, 103, 106, 212, 228, 273, 275
responsibility 56–57, 69, 123–24, 127, 129, 241
    corporate social 246
restriction of labor migration 96
rights 20, 22, 69–70, 72, 103–4, 107, 110, 189, 191, 194, 220, 222, 234–35, 245–46
    citizen 229
    political 92, 141
    social 70, 227, 229, 245
risks 55, 59, 121–22, 124, 128–29, 151, 222, 230
    employer's 34

robots   109, 192
rules   121, 123, 165, 167, 199–200, 202–6, 208–9, 211–15, 241, 253, 281, 283, 285, 287
   host country   210
   informal   199, 287
   of exchange   108, 134
Russian Empire   274

sailors   2, 33
sale   16, 20–22, 68, 70, 108, 120–22, 124–25, 128, 200
   of labor power   127, 200
scales   5, 165, 167, 192–93, 198, 201, 205, 211–12, 222, 225–29, 254, 281–82, 287
   institutional   210
   jurisdictional   201, 205
   multiple   165, 167
   planetary   220
   regional   222
   regulatory   200
   spatial   226
Schengen Area   227
seafarers   214
search
   channels   169, 175, 177
   frictions   285
   strategies   155
sectors   123–24, 147, 186, 189–91, 194, 207, 209, 231, 233–35, 249–50, 253
   industrial   250
   low-skilled   234–35
   low-wage   36, 233
   skilled   234
self-employment   61, 221
   bogus   74
self-selection   9
sellers   21–22, 53–54, 104, 107, 109, 111–12, 121–22, 124–26, 138, 140, 149, 152–53, 266–68
sending states   127, 129
serfdom   6, 26
   hereditary   61
   industrial   28
serfs   23, 59
servants   29, 32, 58, 76, 80, 140
   domestic   40
   farm   32
   importing   29
service
   contracts   188, 190, 192, 210, 227
   contract workers   183
   providers   184–85, 187–90, 192–94
   services   18, 20, 62, 65–66, 76–77, 87, 94–95, 108–9, 127, 188, 220, 222, 225, 227
   free movement of   155
   professional   109
   public   228, 231
servitude   32, 61–62
   domestic   61
   indentured   29, 61
   involuntary   79–80
   penal   61
settlement   33, 229, 231–32
   permanent   231
sex discrimination   92
sex workers   40, 44, 97–98
shaming   128–29, 190, 193–94
skill
   certification   284
   downgrading   286
   levels   151, 234
   requirements   58
skilled migrants   234–35
skills   23, 110, 119, 149, 152–53, 191, 226, 228, 233, 276, 284
   mismatch   4, 145, 152, 286
slavery   19, 23–24, 26, 29–30, 39, 42–43, 60–63, 65–66, 75–76, 78
   chattel   7, 20, 29, 60–61
   domestic   26
   precolonial   76
slaves   22–26, 29–33, 35, 54, 73, 109–10, 140–41
social construction   154–55, 261, 266–68, 272, 276
   of competition   154–55
   of global labor markets   276
   of global markets   267–68
   of labor markets   154
   of marketable objects   154
   of markets   154–55, 261, 265, 267
social infrastructures   96, 285–86
socialism   38, 82
social networks   3, 165–66, 169–73, 175–81, 276, 282, 285, 287–88
social protections   3, 81, 123, 222, 227, 229, 282
social reproduction   56, 89, 92–93, 96, 123–24

social safety nets   59, 71, 80
social security   37, 71, 190
society   16–17, 57–58, 83–86, 88–91, 93, 120–21, 234–37
   bourgeois   57, 82
   capitalist   103, 132
   civil   57, 193, 253
   consumer   137
   host   189
   liberal   57
   modern   16, 56–58, 205
   traditional   109
sociocultural prerequisites of markets   269
sociological
   analysis of markets   265, 267
   approaches to labor markets   153
   research on labor markets   106
South Africa   246
South Asia   27, 29
South China   23
Southeast Asia   31–32, 45
   early modern   43
   nineteenth-century   26
Southeast Europe   25
Soviet Union   220
stability of (labor) markets   121–22, 129, 263, 265
standards   41, 71, 129, 154, 156, 176, 207, 248, 263
   ILO's core   246
   skill   187
states   34, 36, 64–65, 79, 93, 95–96, 148, 154, 156–57, 220–22, 225–30, 237–38, 240–41, 244–46, 284
   federal   140, 193
   independent sovereign   232
   liberal-conservative   141
   national   167, 240, 245, 249
status markets   111
status of migrant workers   76
stock exchanges   134, 140, 153
subcontracting   61, 185, 187
subcontractors   18, 149, 155, 166, 184–85, 190, 192, 195, 285
subjectification   50, 57–58
subnational   199, 201, 205–6, 241
subordination   89, 126–27, 129
   of migrant labor   126
subsidiaries   190, 193
   foreign   207

subsistence   68
   labor   23
supermaid program   148
suppliers   21, 126, 186, 192, 209, 270, 277
   of labor   126
supply chains   39, 78–79, 213
supranational   153, 167, 222
   body of rules   241
system   19, 23, 31, 62, 67–68, 70–72, 76, 81, 188–89, 240, 244, 246–49, 254
   human resource management   207
   indenture   45
   intergovernmental   244, 248
   international   154, 244, 249, 251
   kafala   61, 76, 81
   long-distance trading   200
   social security   80, 153, 188, 193
   supranational   243
   tripartite   245–46

tasks   50, 89, 106, 110–13, 200–201, 203, 207, 221, 285, 287
tax havens   82
Taylorist mass production model   186–87
Taylorist mode of production   166
Taylorist work regime   191
technologies   74, 79, 192, 219, 234, 263
   telecommunication   277
territories   37, 79, 138, 140, 210, 226, 249
   colonial   28
   overseas   210
theory   56–58, 103–4, 106–7, 134, 136, 140–41, 205, 208, 274
   economic-sociological   157
   institutional   199
   macro   19
   neoclassical   147
   sociological labor market   183
   of labor markets   107, 120, 122, 129, 166
third-country nationals   227
town markets   135, 139
trade   6, 31, 34, 36, 103, 106–9, 112–13, 140, 142, 174–75, 219, 222, 225, 262–63, 266, 268
   international   2, 25, 32–33, 39
   in labor power   103
   in slaves   31
   liberalization   3, 248
   networks   262, 276

traders   263–64, 272
    foreign exchange   266
trade unionism   80
trade unions   34, 73, 222, 240–43, 246–47, 249–54
    international   220, 242, 251
traffickers/trafficking   81, 61, 75, 77, 87, 157, 283–85
transactions   21–22, 42, 108, 111, 122, 127, 219–20, 262, 265, 269, 275
    commercial   21
transformation of labor power   120, 127, 129
transformation problem   127
transnational   166, 169, 195, 198–200, 205–6, 209, 211, 281, 285
    arenas of industrial relations   154
    assemblage   213
    communities   206–7
    institution building   167, 199, 201, 206–7, 214, 287
    institutions   201, 206–8
    jobs   285
    labor allocation   142
    labor governance   202
    labor laws   154
    labor markets   167, 169, 189–91, 193–99, 201, 211–14, 281–82, 284–85
    labor regulations   165, 167, 199, 208, 210, 212–14
    labor standards   209
    markets   211, 262
    migration flows   276
    mobility   5, 286
    regulation   167, 199, 205, 211, 213
        of labor   199, 211–12
transnationalization   37, 39
transport   33, 39, 77–78, 165, 175, 179, 219–20, 273, 285–86
triadic competition   264–66
tripartism   246–48, 250

UK-EU youth mobility scheme   233
UK's colonial supply of labor   229
underemployment   166
undocumented migrant workers   77
unemployment   19, 40, 55, 71, 74, 135, 138, 173, 234–35
    duration   177
    insurance   201

unfree labor   6–7, 51, 54, 56, 60, 62, 67, 75, 77–79, 80, 82, 92
    regimes   16
    relations   77
    wage laborers   27, 35
union representatives   210
unions   41, 59, 106, 114–15, 124, 184, 191, 193, 201, 246, 251
universal market audiences/publics   223, 261, 274
unskilled workers   171, 186, 191

vacancies   172, 174, 178
value chains   191–92, 222
    extending global   62
violence   16, 64–85, 249
    cultural   67, 69
    personal   67, 69
    physical   67, 81
    psychological   67
    soft   67
    structural   67, 69, 74, 79
    symbolic   67–68
visa   126, 233
    temporary   123
visa regimes   284
visa restrictions   227
vocational training   88, 235

wage differentials   42, 147
    cross-country   123
wage labor   16, 18, 20, 22–23, 26–27, 29, 32–33, 35, 50, 56, 77, 153
    capitalist   80
    dependent   69
wage laborers   23–25, 33, 35, 37, 69
wages   26–27, 32, 36–37, 65, 68, 77, 79, 125–26, 146–47, 172, 177, 190–93
    low   92, 96, 110, 123
wealth   2, 28, 269
    growing   186
welfare   88, 93, 141, 200, 212, 228–29, 231–32
    institutions   136, 141
    organizations   193
    regimes   73, 93
    states   93, 141, 190, 200
    systems   92
Western Europe   25, 72, 170, 229
women   35, 39–40, 87–96, 123, 176

INDEX

matching 166
migrant 94
proletarian 91
skilled 40
unpaid work 91
work 21–25, 42–43, 45–46, 50–51, 53–55, 58–59, 61–62, 64–68, 76–79, 95–96, 108–13, 115, 125–28, 136–39, 150–51, 154–55, 212–13, 220–21, 233–35
  commodified 93
  exploitative 75, 123
  indecent 68, 74, 81
  informal 39, 213
  low-paid 91
  low-skilled 91
  part-time 251
  precarious 174
  reproduction 59
  seasonal 23
  service 110
  sex 66, 81–83
  skilled 23
  subsistence 17
  unfree 77
  unpaid 94, 96
  unskilled 156, 187
  women's 87, 89, 95
work contracts 95
worker protection 287
workers 27, 29, 34–42, 52–56, 58–59, 68, 70–73, 75–81, 137, 149–50, 154–55, 169, 171–78, 184, 186–94, 209–10, 228, 232–33, 245–47, 284–85
  bonded 76

construction 4, 18
contracted 188, 190–91, 193
cross-border 167
educated 175, 178
enslaved 32
foreign 37, 81, 169–70, 178, 184
free 21, 24, 27, 52
garment 213
high-skill 173
low-skill 173, 180
male 174, 176
mobile 154, 229, 232
posted 12, 154, 166, 189, 197, 227
precarious 41
skilled 147, 230, 232, 286
work ethics 45–46
workfare 67, 80–81
workforce 58, 74, 94–95, 124
  factory 136
  female 92
  migrant 51
  worldwide 40
working
  classes 33–34, 37, 39, 42, 92
  conditions 37, 62, 112, 127, 140, 151, 187, 189–95, 209, 233
  hours 54, 71, 92, 95
workplace 58, 113, 122, 195
  power relations 92
  representation 71
World Bank 38–40, 95, 248
world market 39, 219–20, 260
World Works Councils 201